Vulnerabilities Position Perspective Opportunities Probability Rewards Mistakes Situations Momentum

孫子兵法

Sun Tzu's
Art of War
Playbook

Book Two
Volumes 4 to 9

Gary
Gagliardi

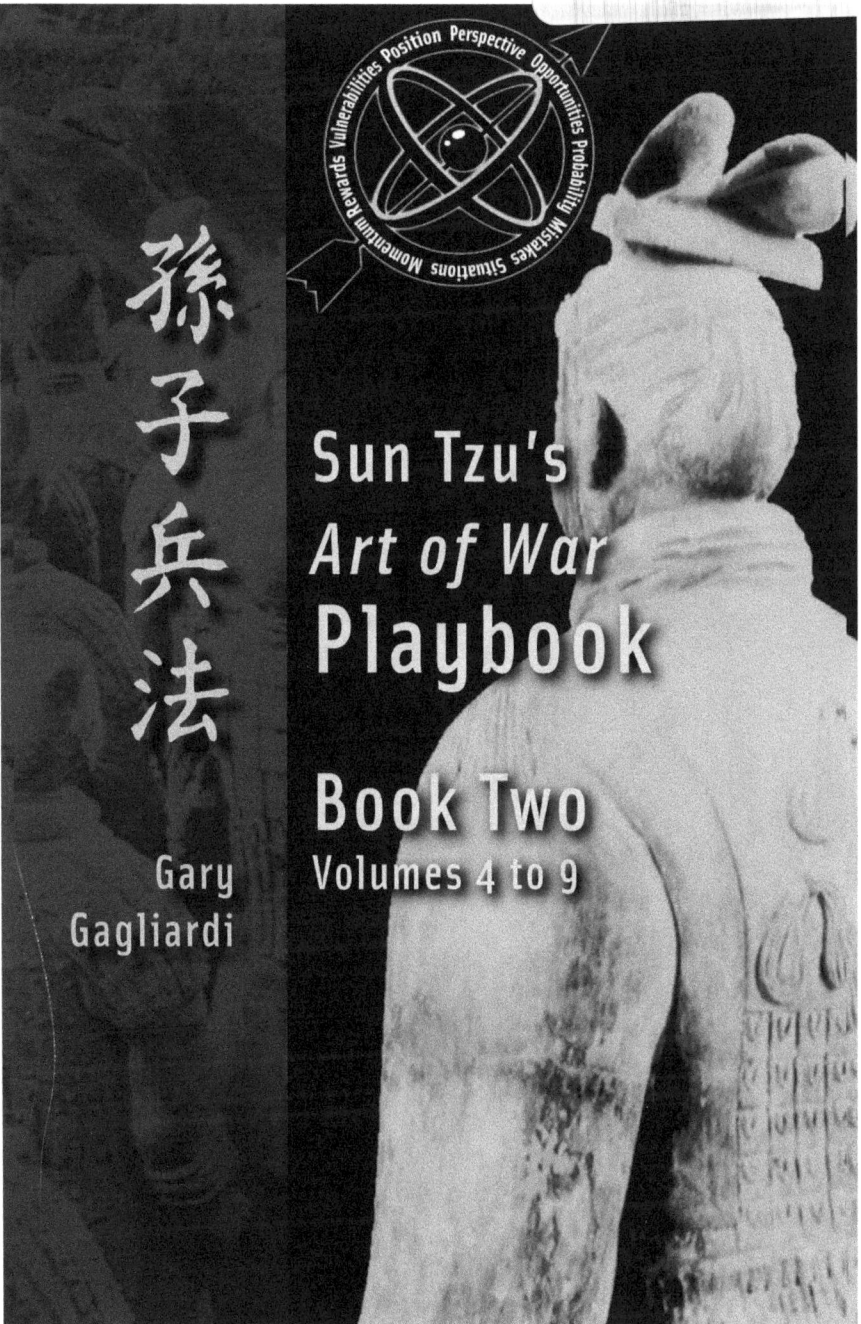

Sun Tzu's Art of War

Playbook

Book Two
Volumes 5-9

by Gary Gagliardi
The Science of Strategy Institute
Clearbridge Publishing

Published by
Science of Strategy Institute, Clearbridge Publishing
    suntzus.com   scienceofstrategy.org

Sun Tzu's PlayBook - Book Two Volumes 5-9
Library of Congress Control Number: 2014909969
First Print Edition
Also sold as Sun Tzu's Warrior Rule Book
Copyright 2010, 2011, 2012, 2013, 2014 Gary Gagliardi
ISBN 978-1-929194-86-5 (13-digit) 1-929194-86-2 (10-digit)

Registered with Department of Copyrights, Library of Congress.

Originally published as a series of articles on the Science of Strategy Website, scienceofstratregy.org. and
later as an ebook on various sites. Ebook ISBN 978-1-929194-63-6

PO Box 33772, Seattle, WA 98133
Phone: (206)542-8947 Fax: (206)546-9756
beckyw@clearbridge.com
garyg@scienceofstrategy.org

Manufactured in the United States of America.
Interior and cover graphic design by Dana and Jeff Wincapaw.
Original Chinese calligraphy by Tsai Yung, Green Dragon Arts, www.greendragonarts.com.

Publisher's Cataloging-in-Publication Data
Sun-tzu, 6th cent. B.C.
Strategy , positioning
        [Sun-tzu ping fa, English]
        Volume One: Art of War Playbook / Sun Tzu and Gary Gagliardi.
        p.197 cm. 23
        Includes introduction to basic competitive philosophy of Sun Tzu

Clearbridge Publishing's books may be purchased for business, for any promotional use,
or for special sales.

Contents

Playbook Overview

Note: This overview is provided for those who have not read the previous volume of Sun Tzu's Art of War Playbook. *It provides an brief overview of the work in general and the general concepts framing the first volume.*

Sun Tzu's **The Art of War** is less a "book" in the modern Western sense than it is an outline for a course of study. Like Euclid's Geometry, simply reading the work teaches us very little. Sun Tzu wrote in in a tradition that expected each line and stanza to be studied in the context of previous statements to build up the foundation for understanding later statements.

To make this work easier for today's readers to understand, we developed the **Strategy Playbook**, the Science of Strategy Institute (SOSI) guidebook to explaining Sun Tzu's strategy in the more familiar format of a series of explanations with examples. These lessons are framed in the context of modern competition rather than ancient military warfare.

This Playbook is the culmination of over a decade of work breaking down Sun Tzu's principles into a series of step-by-step practical articles by the Institute's multiple award-winning author and founder, Gary Gagliardi. The original **Art of War** was written for military generals who understood the philosophical concepts of ancient China, which in itself is a practical hurdle that most modern readers cannot clear. Our **Art of War Playbook** is written for today's reader. It puts Sun Tzu's ideas into everyday, practical language.

The Playbook defines a new science of strategic competition aimed at today's challenges. This science of competition is designed as the complementary opposite of the management science that is taught in most business schools. This science starts, as Sun Tzu did himself, by defining a better, more complete vocabulary for discussing competitive situations. It connects the timeless ideas of Sun Tzu to today's latest thinking in business, mathematics, and psychology.

The entire Playbook consists of two hundred and thirty articles describing over two-thousand interconnected key methods. These articles are organized into nine different areas of strategic skill from understanding positioning to defending vulnerabilities. All together this makes up over a thousand pages of material.

Playbook Access

The Playbook's most up-to-date version is available as separate articles on our website. Live links make it easy to access the connections between various articles and concepts. If you become a SOSI Member, you can access any Playbook article at any time and access their links.

However, at the request of our customers, we also offer these articles as a series of nine eBooks. Each of the nine sections of the entire Playbook makes up a separate eBook, Playbook Parts One Through Nine. These parts flow logically through the Progress Cycle of listen-aim-move-claim (see illustration). Because of the dynamic nature of the on-line version, these eBooks are not going to be as current as the on-line version. You can see a outline of current Playbook articles here and, generally, the eBook version will contain most of the same material in the same order.

6.0 Situation Response   5.0 Minimizing Mistakes

Move   Aim

7.0 Creating Momentum   4.0 Leveraging Probability

1.0 Positioning

8.0 Winning Rewards   3.0 Identifying Opportunities

Claim   Listen

9.0 Using Vulnerability   2.0 Developing Perspective

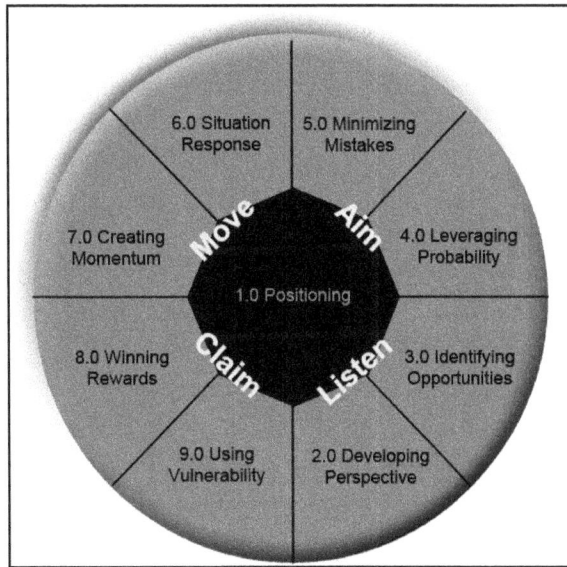

Nine categories of strategic skills define cycle that advances our positions:

1. Comparing Positions,

2. Developing Perspective,

3. Identifying Opportunities,

4. Leveraging Probability,

5. Minimizing Mistakes,

6. Responding To Situations,

7. Creating Momentum,

8. Winning Rewards, And

9. Defending Vulnerabilities.

These are the topic covered in the nine volumes of Sun Tzu's Playbook. Each book focuses on a single skill area.

Playbook Structure and Design

These articles are written in standard format including 1) the general principle, 2) the situation, 3) the opportunity, 4) the list of specific Art of War key methods breaking down the general principle into a series of actions, and 5) an illustration of the application of each of those key methods to a specific competitive situation. Key methods are written generically to apply to every competitive arena (business, personal life, career, sports, relationships, etc.) with each specific illustrations drawn from one of these areas.

A number identifies where each article appears in Playbook Structure. For example, the article <u>2.1.3 Strategic Deception</u> is the third article in the first section of the second book in the nine volumes of the Strategy Playbook. In our on-line version, these links are live, clicking on them brings you to the article itself. We provide them because the interconnection of concepts is important in learning Sun Tzu's system.

Playbook Training

Training in Sun Tzu's warrior skills does not entail memorizing all these principles. Instead, these concepts are used to develop exercises and tools that allow trainees to put this ideas in practice. While each rule is useful, the heart of Sun Tzu system is the methods that connect all the principles together. Training in these principles is designed to develop a gut instinct for how Sun Tzu's strategy is used in different situations to produce success. Principles are interlinked because they describe a comprehensive conceptual mental model. Warrior Class training puts trainees in a situation where they must constantly make decisions, rewarding them for making decisions consist with winning productively instead of destructively.

About Positions

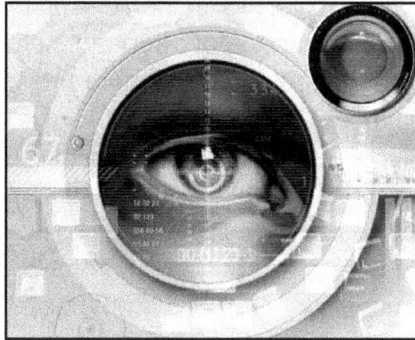

This first volume of Sun Tzu's Playbook focuses on teaching us the nature of strategic positions. "Position awareness" gives you a framework for understanding your strategic situation relative to the conditions around you. It enables you to see your position as part of a larger environment constructed of other positions and the raw elements that create positions. Master Sun Tzu's system of comparing positions, you can understand which aspect of your position are secure and which are the most dynamic and likely to change.

Traditional strategy defines a "position" as a comparison of situations. Game theory defines is as the current decision point that is arrive at as the sum or result of all previous decisions, both yours and those of others. Sun Tzu's methods of positioning awareness are different. They force you to see yourself in the eyes of others. Using these techniques, you broaden your perspective by gathering a range of viewpoints. In a limited sense, the scope of your position defines your area of control within your larger environment. In traditional strategy, five elements--mission, climate, ground, command, and methods--define the dimensions in which competitors can be compared.

Competition as Comparison

Sun Tzu saw that success is based on comparisons. This comparison must take place whenever a choice is made. For Sun Tzu, competition means a comparison of alternative choices or "positions". Battles are won by positioning before they are fought. These positions provide choices for everyone involved. Good positions discourage others from attacking you and invite them to support you. Sun Tzu's system teaches us how to systematically build up our positions to win success in the easiest way possible.

Competing positions are compared on the basis many elements, both objective and subjective. Sun Tzu's strategy is to identify these points of comparison and to understand how to leverage them. Learning Sun Tzu's strategy requires learning the details of how positions are compared and advanced. Sun Tzu taught that fighting to "sort things out" is a foolish way to find learn the strengths and weaknesses of a position. Conflict to tear down opposing positions is the most costly way to win competitive comparisons.

Today's More Competitive World

In the complex, chaotic world of today, we can easily get trapped into destructive rather than productive situations. Even our smallest decisions can have huge impact on our future. The problem is that we are trained for yesterday's world of workers, not today's world of warriors. We are trained in the linear thinking of planning in predictable, hierarchical world. This thinking applies less and less to today's networked, more competitive world.

Following a plan is the worker's skill of working in pre-defined functions in an internal, stable, controlled environment. The competitive strategy of Sun Tzu is the warrior's skill of making good decisions about conditions in complex, fast-changing, competitive environments. Sun Tzu's strategic system teaches us to adapt to the unexpected events that are becoming more and more common in our lives. We live in a world where fewer and fewer key events are planned. Navigating our new world of external challenges requires a different set of skills.

Most of us make our decisions without any understanding of competition. The result is that most of us lose as many battles as we win, never making consistent progress. Events buffet us, turning us in one direction and then the other. Too often, we end up repeating our past patterns of mistakes.

The Science of Strategy Institute teaches you the warrior's skills of adaptive response. There are many organizations that teach planning and organization. The Institute is one of the few places in the world you can get learn competitive thinking, and the only place in the world, with a comprehensive Playbook.

Seeing Situations Differently

Sun Tzu taught that a warrior's decision-making was a matter of reflex. As we develop our strategic decision-making skills, the critical conditions in situations simply "pop" out at us. This isn't magic. The latest research on how decisions are made tells us a lot about why Sun Tzu's principles work. It comes from using patterns to retrain our mind to see conditions differently. The study of successful response arose from military confrontations, where every battle clearly demonstrated how hard it is to predict events in the real world. Sun Tzu saw that winners were always those who knew how to respond appropriately to the dynamic nature of their situation.

Sun Tzu's principles provides a complete model for the key knowledge for understanding conditions in complex dynamic environments. This model "files" each piece of data into the appropriate place in the big picture. As the picture of your situation fills in, you can identify the opportunities hidden within your situation.

Making Decisions about Conditions

Instead of focusing on a series of planned steps, Sun Tzu's principles are about making decisions regarding conditions. It concerns itself with: 1) identifying the relative strengths and weaknesses of competitive positions, 2) advancing positions leveraging opportunities, and 3) the types of responses to specific challenges that work the most frequently. Using Sun Tzu's principles, we call these three areas position awareness , opportunity development , and situation response . Each area that we master broadens your capabilities.

- Position awareness trains us to recognize that competitive situations are defined by the relationship among alternative positions. Developing this perspective never ends. It deepens throughout our lives.
- Opportunity development explores the ground, testing our perceptions. Only testing the edges of perspective through action can we know what is true.
- S ituation response trains us to recognize the key characteristics of the immediate situation and to respond appropriately. Only by practice, can we learn to trust the viewpoint we have developed.

Success in competitive environments comes from making better decisions every day. Sharp strategic reflexes flow from a clear understanding of where and when you use which competitive tools methods.

The Key Viewpoints

As an individual, you have a unique and valuable viewpoint, but every viewpoint is inherently limited by its own position. The result is that people cannot get a useful perspective on their own situations and surrounding opportunities. The first formula of positioning awareness involve learning what information is relevant. The most advanced techniques teach how to gather that information and put it into a bigger picture.

Most people see their current situations as the sum of their past successes and failures. Too often people dwell on their mistakes while simultaneously sitting on their laurels. Sun Tzu's strategy forces you to see your position differently. How you arrived at your current position doesn't matter. Your position is what it is. It is shaped by history but history is not destiny.

In this framework, the only thing that matters is where you are going and how you are going to get there. As you begin to develop your strategic reflexes, you start to think more and more about how to secure your current position and advance it.

Seeing the Big Picture

Most people see all the details of their lives, but they cannot see what those detail mean in terms of the big picture. As you master position awareness, you don't see your life as a point but as a path. You see your position in terms of what is changing and what resources are available. You are more aware of your ability to make decisions and your skills in working with others.

Most importantly, this strategic system forces you to get in touch with your core set of goals and values.

Untrained people usually see their life in terms of absolutes: successes and failures, good luck and bad, weakness and strength. As you begin to master position awareness, you begin to see all comparisons of strength and weakness are temporary and relative. A position is not strong or weak in itself. Its strength or weakness depends on how it compares or "fits" with surrounding positions. Weakness and strength are not what a position is, but how you use it.

The Power of Perspective

Positional awareness gives you the specialized vocabulary you need to understanding how situations develop. Mastering this vocabulary, you begin to see the leverage points connecting past and future. You replace vague conceptions of "strength," "momentum," and "innovation" with much more pragmatic definitions that you can actually use on a day to day basis.

Mastering position awareness also changes your relationships with other people. It teaches you a different way of judging truth and character. This methods allow you to spot self-deception and dishonest in others. It also allows you to understand how you can best work with others to compensate for your different weaknesses.

Once you develop a good perspective of position, it naturally leads you to want to learn more about how you can improve you position through the various aspects of opportunity development covered in the subsequent parts of the Strategy Playbook.

Seeing the Invisible

The "Nazca lines" are giant drawings etched across thirty miles of desert on Peru's southern coast. The patterns are only visible at a distance of hundreds of feet in the air. Below that, they look like strange paths or roads to nowhere. Just as we cannot see these lines without the proper perspective, people who master Sun Tzu's methods can <u>suddenly recognize situations</u> that were invisible to them before. Unless we have the right perspective, we cannot compare situations and positions successfully. The most recent scientific research explains why people cannot see these patterns for comparison without developing the network framework of adaptive thinking.[1]

Seeing Patterns

We can imagine patterns in chaotic situations, but seeing real pattern is the difference between success and failure. In our seminars, we demonstrate the power of seeing patterns in a number of exercises.

The <u>mental models</u> used by warrior give them "situation awareness." This situation awareness isn't just vague theory. Recent research shows that it can be measured in a variety of ways.[2] We now know that untrained people fall victim to a flow of confusing information because they don't know where its pieces fit. Those trained in Sun Tzu's mental models plug this stream of information quickly and easily into a bigger picture, transforming the skeleton's provided by Sun Tzu's system into a functioning awareness of your strategic position and its relation to other positions. Each piece of information has a place in that picture. As the information comes in, it fills in the picture, like pieces of a puzzle.

The ability to see the patterns in this bigger picture allows experts in strategy to see what is invisible to most people in a number of ways. They include:

- People trained in Art of War principles--<u>recognition-primed decision-making</u> --see patterns that others do not.
- Trained people can spot anomalies, things that should happen in the network of interactions but don't.
- Trained people are in touch with changes in the environment within appropriate time horizons.
- Trained people recognize complete patterns of interconnected elements under extreme time pressure.

Procedures Make Seeing Difficult

One of the most surprising discoveries from this research is that those who know procedures, that is, a linear view of events, alone have a ***more*** difficult time recognizing patterns than novices. An interesting study[3] examined the different recognition skills of three groups of people 1) experts, 2) novices, and 3) trainers who taught the standard procedures. The three groups were asked to pick out an expert from a group novices in a series of videos showing them performing a decision-making task, in this case, CPR. Experts were able to recognize the expert 90% of the time. Novices recognized the expert 50% of the time. The shocking fact was that trainers performed much worse that the novices, recognizing the expert only 30% of the time.

Why do those who know procedures fail to see what the experts usually see and even novices often see? Because, as research into <u>mental simulations</u> has shown, those with only a procedural model fit everything into that model and ignore elements that don't fit. In the above experiment, interviews with the trainers indicated that they assumed that the experts would always follow the procedural model. In real life, experts adapt to situations where unique conditions often trump procedure. Adapting to the situation rather than following set procedures is a central focus the form of strategy that the Institute teaches.

Missing Expected Elements

People trained to recognize the bigger picture beyond procedures also recognize when expected elements are missing from the picture. These anomalies or, what the cognition experts [4] describe as "negative cues" are invisible to novices *and* to those trained only in procedure. Without sense of the bigger pattern, people are focused too narrowly on the problem at hand. The "dog that didn't bark" from the Sherlock Holmes story, "Silver Blaze," is the most famous example of a negative cue. Only those working from a larger nonprocedural framework can expect certain things to happen and notice when they don't.

The ability to see what is missing also comes from the expectations generated by the mental model. Process-oriented models have the expectation of one step following another, but situation-recognition models create their expectations from signals in the environment. Research [5] into the time horizons of decision-makers shows that different time scales are at work. People at the highest level of organizations must look a year or two down the road, using strategic models that work in that timeframe, doing strategic planning. Decision-makers on the front-lines, however, have to react within minutes or even seconds to changes in their situation, working from their strategic reflexes. The biggest danger is that people get so wrapped up in a process that they lose contact with their environment.

Decisions Under Pressure

Extreme time pressure is what distinguishes front-line decision-making from strategic planners. One of the biggest discoveries in cognitive research [6] is that trained people do much better in seeing their situation instantly and making the correct decisions under time pressure. Researchers found virtually no difference between the decisions that experts made under time pressure when comparing them to decisions made without time pressure. That research also finds that those with less experience and training made dramatically worse decisions when they were put under time pressure.

The central argument for training our strategic reflexes is that our situation results, not from chance or luck, but from <u>the instant decisions</u> that that we all make every day. Our position is the sum of these decisions. If we cannot make the right decisions on the spot, when they are needed, our plans usually come to nothing. This is why we describe training people's strategic reflexes as helping them "do at first what most people only do at last."

The success people experience seeing what is invisible to others is dramatic. To learn more about how the strategic reflexes we teach differ from what can be planned, read about <u>the contrast between planning and reflexes here</u> . As <u>our many members report</u>, the success Sun Tzu's system makes possible is remarkable.

1 Chi, Glaser, & Farr, 1988, The Nature of Expertise, Erlbaum
2 Endsley & Garland, Analysis and Measurement of Situation Awareness
3 Klein & Klein, 1981, "Perceptual/Cognitive Analysis of proficient CPR Performance", Midwestern Psychological Association Meeting, Chicago.
4 Dr. David Noble, Evidence Based Research, Inc.In Gary Klein, Sources of Power, 1999
5 Jacobs & Jaques, 1991, "Executive Leadership".In Gal & Mangelsdofs (eds.), Handbook of Military Psychology, Wiley
6 Calder, Klein, Crandall,1988, "Time Pressure, Skill, and Move Quality in Chess". American Journal of Psychology, 101:481-493

Sun Tzu's Playbook

Volume 5:
Mistakes

About Minimizing Mistakes

In Volume Five, Sun Tzu's Plabooks explains the safest way to explore an opening as an opportunity for advancing a position. Though we learn more from our mistakes than our successes, we must design new ventures so any mistakes don't damage our current position.

All new ventures fail if we pursue them with half measures. However, even if we pursue new ventures wholeheartedly, many will still fail. How do we make sure that those failures don't damage our position? We need the principles for minimizing mistakes to test our ideas. They minimize our risk and the impact of our failures. They also dramatically increases the eventual certainty of success.

The Limits of Planning

Successful competition requires knowing what you can control and what you cannot control. To improve your position, each move must return more than it costs. If you knew which new move were going to be profitable, there would be no need for this set of principles. The truth is that you cannot know how valuable a new position will be before you win it. Therefore, you control what you can, which are the costs.

Competitive environments are dynamic. Within them, people's plans collide continually, creating situations that no one planned. You cannot predict competitive conditions. This limits traditional planning. The longer you try to perfect your plans by gathering more and more information, the more expensive your new move becomes and the more likely it is that the opportunity will pass you by. When you plan, you make decisions in advance. However, in dynamic competitive arenas, it is usually less costly and much safer to test a position in a small way to see what happens and then adapt to the conditions you discover.

Instead of planning, Sun Tzu's Playbooks teaches us to think about testing. You want to get a new venture off the ground as soon as possible. Inertia destroys enthusiasm for any new project. Planning long, careful, drawn-out campaigns drains your limited resources. These campaigns are more likely to fail. Bigger experiments are never better experiments.

People think that the more detailed the plan, the safer a new venture is. This is true in controlled environments, but the opposite is true in any competitive arena. Planning is meaningless without testing your plans. The desire to keep planning creates sluggish organizations. The longer you plan, the more effort you invest. While you are planning, your competitors can test their ideas to see what works. It doesn't matter how smart you think you are. You can't get ahead by falling behind your competitors.

You can sometimes go into a new position too quickly, but you can never start testing too soon. You can continue to plan or your can start testing your venture to see what happens. You can't do both at once.

Do Less, Not More

The goal of all of Sun Tzu's Playbook is to improve your competitive position. In this volume, we learn the power of doing less, not more. When you see an appealing opportunity, you naturally want to pursue it. But your time and efforts are limited. You cannot always do more. You must grow by subtraction. If a new opportunity makes sense, it expands on what you are currently doing. This means that you must decrease what you are doing elsewhere. A decision to do more must be coupled with a decision to do less.

Let me give you an example from my personal experience of how to grow a business by making it simpler.

When we started our software company, we started as general consultants. Our most profitable jobs came from database development, so we slowly stopped doing other projects. By focusing on database projects, our business doubled. Then our most profitable projects were accounting related, so we focused on those projects. We again doubled in size. Then the most profitable accounting sales came from resellers. So we stopped other sales and doubled again. Then the most profitable sales were from large systems. We stopped selling smaller systems. We doubled again. The we saw that our most profitable sales came from order processing. We stopped selling other types of accounting software and doubled in size again.

We became one of the Inc. 500 fastest-growing companies in America not by doing more and more, but by doing less and less. And we did it without any outside financing or borrowing money because we were always working at what was most profitable.

You use every opportunity to further refine and simplify your focus. A focused venture is successful. An unfocused venture fails. Doing one thing better and better is easy. Doing more and more things well is hard. A concentrated effort is powerful. A divided effort is weak. Well-defined positions make you successful. A confused position is costly. Clear-cut goals keep you on track. Confused goals get you nowhere.

The more focused your efforts are, the easier it will be to win competitive comparisons. Still, the best way to win competitive comparison isn't constantly being compared to others. Success comes from avoiding competitive battles. You want to develop positions that stand out from the crowd, that are unique. You win by avoiding comparison.

This is the power of focus.

The Goal is to Win Rewards

The proof of any new positions is getting rewarded for controlling it. You must avoid positions in which the rewards are poorly defined. You must avoid positions in which you are not sure who will reward you for that position. You must avoid ventures in which it isn't clear how you will make money selling your product.

Instead, these principles teach us to choose opportunities where it is easy to know who rewards you for having that position and why. What is the easiest way of assuring that a position's value? Go after positions similar to those that are already being rewarded. In business, these means you concentrate your efforts on the most profitable areas of commerce. Reward your early customers for trusting you. Advertise and promote your success with early adopters. Choose markets that generate repeat business to avoid high sales and marketing costs.

Internal Distractions

You want to improve your position. You are going to be devoting time and resources to improving it. Those resources are taken from elsewhere. Sun Tzu tells us that people are naturally frightened by change. A new venture is always a threat to more established parts of a position, especially when we work within a larger organization.

Internal conflict and political divisions over what is "fair" can undermine your success in several different ways. Ignorant of the need and nature of real opportunities, people in more established part of an organization want to force expansion on their schedule. Ignorant of the dynamic nature of competition, they want to abandon new ventures when they get difficult. Sun Tzu calls this hamstringing the army.

The confusion between controlled and dynamic environments underlies the conflict between an established enterprise and every new venture. An established enterprise exists in a more controlled and predictable space than a new venture. Existing organizations want to plan new ventures like they do proven operations. They think they can manage a new venture according to the same principles that they use to manage established businesses. The goal of a new enterprise isn't to be predictable but to find some way to survive.

New ventures require different priorities and are run by different sets of principles. The demands of a fast-changing, dynamic environment can only be met by good strategy. To survive in a dynamic, competitive market, you must play by the rules of competition. You must ignore internal desires.

If you let internal politics fester in your organization, everyone will become confused about your goals. Others will undermine confidence in your leadership. Politics will tear any organization apart and invite challenges from outside competitors. The more promising the potential of your organization, the more dangerous political conflicts become.

Establishing a clear mission is critical. It unites the different functions within an organization and focuses it on a shared goal. You must not weaken an enterprise's trust in its focus and purpose.

Minimizing the Initial Investment

A major theme continuing through the principles in this chapter is the idea of minimizing investments. A number of concepts cover ways to do this.

These methods flow directly from the problem of knowledge in competitive environments. What can you know for certain? You can know that don't have the resources to invest in every new opportunity. You can know that no one sells an insurance policy that guarantees success. While you cannot know how rewarding a new positions will be, you know for certain that your resources are limited. You know for certain that the efforts that you invest in a new, unproven positions must come from other parts of your life where you know the value.

These competitive principles teach us to think from the perspective on the long term. You cannot think that you can put more and more effort into a new position until it pays off. You must minimize your investments. Instead of investing, think about ways that you can make the position rewarding. Look for easy ways to make a position pay. Once you get more resources from a new position, you have invest more resources in developing that position. Even when you get rewarded, invest your limited resources only in what you absolutely need. This is the way you ensure that this new position will be rewarding.

Experimenting Locally

Many of Sun Tzu's minimization principles apply to distance. In our modern world, better communication and transportation have made the world smaller, but when you are exploring a new area, these principles teach us that is always best to start as close to home as you can. Moving away from your current position is just too expensive. If your experiments with new position are successful, they can always be broadened later.

This chapter's methdos look at the different ways in which distance can be costly. Travel and shipping are the costs of crossing geographic distance. Learning and communication are the costs of crossing intellectual distance. Learning about a new position distant from your own is expensive. Educating a new group of supporters who don't know you or your virtues is costly. High costs make it more difficult for a move to a position to reward us.

You want to test a new position as close to home as possible. Even new position can be close to home geographically or intellectually. Ideally, they are both. If the venture proves rewarding locally, you can then expand geographically as you increase your efficiency. If a new opportunity is too distant—either physically or intellectually—from what you are currently doing, you cannot afford to explore it.

Local Competitive Mismatch

Even though you start small, minimizing the size of your investment, you must be totally committed to the success of your position. Halfhearted efforts are certain to fail. When you work to minimize your mistakes, the only thing you cannot afford to minimize is the quality of your effort. You must persist in trying everything you can think of to make it work. You start small so you can overload the effort with resources.

The biggest danger in starting small is thinking that it doesn't matter if the venture succeeds or not. Just because you have put a minimum at risk never means you can afford to fail. It may take a hundred small failures to find a huge success, but you will never find that success if you don't put your best efforts into each attempt. In creating the light bulb, Edison failed again and again, but not because he was sloppy and disorganized.

Sure, many of these experiments with new positions will fail. You keep them small because of this real possibility of failure. Failure provides the best possible education if done correctly. A hundred productive failures teach you more precisely what works. A million sloppy, halfhearted failures get you no closer to your goal.

In the end, the principles in this volume teach that the overall size of your position or that of your competitors doesn't matter. It is the local mismatch, that is, the immediate comparison, that matters. If you are smaller than your competitors, you can more easily defend a smaller area. Positions with fewer resources are not powerful in comparison to the positions with a wealth of resources, but they can move much more quickly than their larger competitors. Large competitors cannot address the new situations as quickly as small ones can.

The principles in this chapter are important if you want to make all your new ventures pay for themselves as quickly as possible. You cannot plan how new positions will work out in the same way you can the operations of existing positions. These principles determines whether or not your new positions are successful or a threat to your future.

These rules teach us to focus on what you can do best. This means balancing your capabilities against those of your competitors. You may know your capabilities but not those of your competitors. Then for every successful new venture, another venture will fail. You can be ignorant of your abilities *and* those of your competitors. Then every new venture is doomed.

Mostly this volume of Sun Tzu's Playbook is about how you must minimize your mistakes. Success comes from knowing what needs to be done and what you can leave undone. Success comes from focusing your limited resources on new positions of the appropriate size.

5.0.0 Minimizing Mistakes

Sun Tzu's five keys for minimizing mistakes in advancing a position.

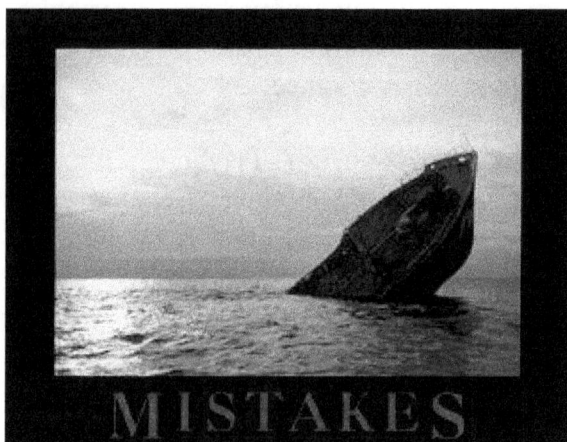

"Make good use of war.
Make the enemy's troops surrender.
You can do this fighting only minor battles."
                                    Sun Tzu's The Art of War 3:3:1-3

"Never mistake motion for action."
                                    Ernest Hemingway

General Principle: Our choice of action must minimize potential mistakes.

Situation:

This article begins a new section of The Playbook dealing with selecting the best way to pursue opportunities. Strategic moves are experiments. Our goal is to experiment safely. No matter how good our information and analysis, competitive environments are always uncertain and potentially treacherous. While we train to pick high-probability opportunities, we cannot delude ourselves about knowing those opportunities before exploring them directly. We must judge probabilities from surface appearances. We cannot understand the nature of an opportunity until we get into it. In using Sun Tzu's methods, nothing is as dangerous as investing too much in what seems like a certain opportunity.

Opportunity:

In choosing how to act to take advantage of opportunities, our first concern must be how we can minimize mistakes. Strategy requires both action and non-action. We must know when to act and when action is not only unnecessary but unwise. When we act, we must know how to increase the likely success of those actions while still minimizing the cost of our failures.

Key Methods:

The general key methods for making successful moves to advance our position are:

1. ***Successful actions serve our goals instead of simply responding to events and discoveries.*** This principle balances the prior one. While we must react to what we discover exploring opportunities rather that follow our plans, those reactions must be guided by our goals, taking us in a consistent direction. In exploring opportunities, we are going to make discoveries and encounter events that do not take us in the direction that we desire. Not all of these events and discoveries require or deserve a response. Not all discoveries demand exploration. Events that don't demand a reaction are merely distractions (5.1 Mission Priorities).

2. ***Successful actions explore opportunities instead of simply following plans.*** We must go where our opportunities lead us, not where we planned for them to lead us. It is easy for individuals and especially organizations to waste time and effort on executing campaign plans that are no longer relevant as more is learned about

a given opportunity. Plans can take on a life of their own if we let them. Plans start as a series of steps toward a goal, but the goal can move but the series of steps remains, offering us a seductive if unproductive path for our effort. Each move to take advantage of an opportunity must be thought of as an experiment. The key is to learn to experiment safely (5.2 Opportunity Exploration).

3. ***Successful actions are fast feedback loops adjusting our course of action.*** Successful actions are quickly chosen, quickly executed, and quickly adjusted. Competitive environments are highly dynamic. We must respond to situations quickly before those situations are outmoded by new developments. These quick adjustments also minimize opposition. Action usually generates resistance. The easiest way to minimize resistance from others is to change direction or reach our goals before opposition forms, ***fait accompli***. The faster we are able to move, the harder it is for opponents to get a fix on our position because the only information they have is outdated information (5.3 Reaction Time).

4. ***Successful actions eliminate waste.*** They use as few resources as possible to accomplish the desired goal. The best strategy is doing less, not more. Choose actions that simplify or minimize current activities rather than making them larger and more complicated (5.4 Minimizing Action).

5. ***Successful actions focus limited resources in a small space and time.*** Smaller, shorter, and quicker moves are always more successful more often than larger, longer, and slower moves. Small investments should prove themselves before investing more. The bigger the investment, the more difficult it is to admit failure. We attempt small, quick steps forward rather than large, long leaps. By choosing small, quick steps, we can sometimes end up making large leaps by getting ourselves positioned to use the force of the environment (5.5 Focused Power).

6. ***Successful actions know when to advance and when to defend.*** Even while we are exploring new opportunities, we must protect our current position. We advance our position on the basis of our strengths, but we must act to defend our position on the

basis of our weaknesses. The result is a balancing act balancing our resources between defense and advance (5.6 Defense and Advance).

Illustration:

The most frequent advance that more people make is getting a promotion at work so let us use that to illustrate these ideas.

1. *Successful actions serve our goals instead of responding to events.* Just because a new position opens up that is a promotion, we do not have to take it if it doesn't lead to the type of job we want.

2. *Successful actions explore opportunities instead of simply following plans.* We might have a certain career path in our heads, but that is not the path our career will follow. When we get out of school and join a company, we may imagine a certain promotion path, but most of our opportunities will not lie on that path.

3. *Successful actions are fast feedback loops adjusting our course of action.* Instead of thinking in formal job titles and pre-defined roles, think of a job in terms of responsibilities that can be added quickly to make others, including those over you, more dependent on your knowledge and skills.

4. *Successful actions eliminate waste.* One of the easiest ways to get recognition and promotion is by saving time, money, and effort by identifying resources that are currently being wasted by the organization.

5. *Successful actions focus limited resources in a small space and time.* The responsibilities don't have to be big ones, but little ones that accumulate over time. The best jobs are those that we define for ourselves over time by doing what is needed where our skills allow us to add the most value.

6. *Successful actions know when to advance and when to defend.* We must not let our expansions on our job get in the way of the core of what people expect from us. Over time, we must have

our new responsibilities formally recognized and get compensated for them.

5.1.0 Mission Priorities

Sun Tzu's five keys for aligning our actions with mission.

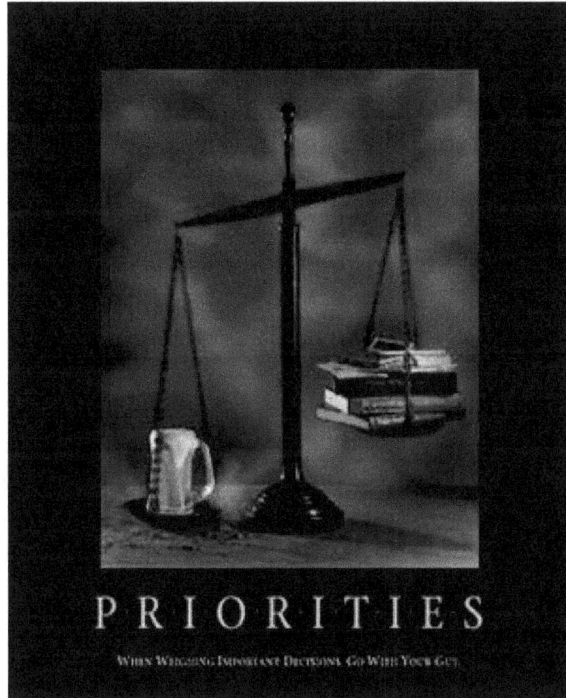

PRIORITIES

WHEN WEIGHING IMPORTANT DECISIONS, GO WITH YOUR GUT.

"Everything depends on your use of military philosophy."
Sun Tzu's The Art of War 2:1:1

"Before you begin climbing that ladder of success, make sure it's leaning towards the window of opportunity you desire!"

Tracy Brinkmann

General Principle: Actions that support our mission can be immediately gratifying but often aren't.

Situation:

Despite using our sophisticated mental models for picking high-probability opportunities, Sun Tzu's strategy cannot predict where an opportunity will lead. The strategic problem here is that, once we start pursuing an opportunity, that pursuit can take on a life of its own. Our choice of actions loses sight of our goals. We can choose actions because they are familiar, comfortable, and because we enjoy doing them. It would be wonderful if we could choose only actions that we enjoy on our path to success, but that is seldom the case.

Opportunity:

While we cannot always choose actions that are familiar, comfortable, and pleasurable, such actions do not necessarily conflict with our mission (1.6 Mission Values). As a matter of fact, we are more likely to make progress if our goals satisfy our short-term desires as well as our long-term values. However, we must also make that choice of action with a clear understanding of our range of our priorities (1.6.3 Mission Priorities). When we choose an action that satisfies many levels of motivation, both our own and our supporters, our chances of success increase greatly.

Key Methods:

The key methods concerning the use of mission to guide our choice of actions offer both serious warning and intriguing possibilities.

1. We must choose actions that conform with our values. This means not only that our actions must move us toward our mission, but it also means that our actions must always be consistent with our values. 2,500 year ago, Sun Tzu taught that the most important thing about our methods is that they must conform with our values. The best time to ask question about the ultimate value of actions is before we begin. Once we have chosen a course of action, it is always more difficult, costly, and sometimes even dangerous to abandon it (1.6 Mission Values).

2. We want to choose actions that address immediate desires and move us toward longer-term goals. Short-term gratification (happiness) and long-term goals (meaning) are not incompatible. Research shows that those who have more of one also find more of the other. Ideally, we want to choose actions that satisfy both at once. There are many levels to the motivations that drive us. Sun Tzu's strategy is, by its nature, a long-term view, but it recognizes our short-term needs. Our longterm success from purposeful action is more certain if we can stay on the right path, but we cannot stay on that path if we make the journey too difficult. We need pleasurable activities as well. We must avoid short-term activities that block our longer-term prospects and we must also avoid choosing long-term courses that are so disagreeable that we cannot sustain our progress (1.6.2 Types of Motivations).

3. We must choose actions that are disagreeable that satisfy our long-term mission. As we move toward our goals, at some point, we are going to get into areas that are unfamiliar, uncomfortable, and unpleasant. This is the price we pay for wanting to advance ourselves. Actively making progress simply is never as easy as drifting where life takes us. Since we have limited resources, we must choose how to invest them. We can either put them into immediately gratification or we can invest them in our longer term goals. Making sacrifices today is a gift that we give our future selves. As actions that were once difficult become familiar, more comfortable, they naturally become more pleasant, decreasing their costs in effort over time (3.1.2 Strategic Profitability).

4. Events are no excuse for forgetting our mission or violating our values. We cannot use events as an excuse. Events are going to continue to happen. We must continually choose which require response, which are external distractions, and which are deadly short-cuts. Our actions have costs but they also have consequences. "Short-cuts" that can seemingly take us toward our goal by cheating on our values run the risk of cutting us off from success completely. Actions that are often the most tempting in terms of potential return are often the most costly in terms of values (5.1.1 Event Pressure).

5. *Existing habits, practices, and procedures must be continually re-evaluated in terms of mission.* Many of our activities are part of our internal system of production. While all our activities originally create some external benefit, these activities can continue past their usefulness. They continue out of internal inertia while external needs change. After a point, they can consume our tlimited resources while producing no benefit satisfying our short-term or long-term goals. To prevent this from happening, we must regularly reevaluate repeated activities to maintain their connection with mission (5.1.2 Internal Distraction).

Illustration:

Let us consider the simplest of all goals, making money. t

1. *We must choose actions that conform with our values*. Even if our goal is making money, we cannot simply lie to get it, steal it from people, or become a politician, but I am being redundant.

2. *We want to choose actions that address immediate desires and move us toward longer-term goals.* If we can make money doing something that we like because people find it valuable, for example, writing and teaching Sun Tzu's strategy, we should do it. We cannot make money enjoying ourselves, say, by writing songs, because too many others are willing to write songs for free.

3. *Often, we must choose actions that are disagreeable that satisfy our long-term mission.* To get to a point where we can make money doing what we like, we have to do certain things that are unpleasant, such as going out and selling ourselves and promoting our work.

4. *Events are no excuse for forgetting our mission or violating our values.* If we get an email offering us millions simply for helping a professional gentleman get some money out of Nigeria a little bit illegally, we shouldn't go for it, no matter how wealthy it will make us.

5. Existing habits, practices, and procedures must be continually re-evaluated in terms of mission. For example, I am working on these articles daily, do they get me closer to my goals? Fortunately, my goal is not simply making money but building a lasting body of work.

5.1.1 Event Pressure

Sun Tzu's eight keys for avoiding mistakes under the pressure of events.

> *"Internal and external events force people to move. They are unable to work while on the road."*
>
> Sun Tzu's The Art of War 13:1:6

> *"When I can't handle events, I let them handle themselves."*
>
> Henry Ford

General Principle: Mission guides us about how to respond to the pressure of events.

Situation:

This article will never be finished because events keep intruding. Just joking. One of the biggest challenges in undertaking actions to pursue opportunities is the pressure of events. Unless we remain focused on our mission, events can rob us of our ability to choose our actions. Events create the "ringing telephone" problem. We cannot know if the call is valuable or not without answering it, but the probability of value is remote while the cost of disruption is certain. We often seem helpless to choose our actions in the face of events. Events come to us, knock on our door and keep demanding our attention. They can even seem to demand specific actions that leave us little choice but to respond. If our lives become a series of ringing phones, we have no time left over to do anything but answer and answer endlessly.

Opportunity:

Good choices about responding or not responding to events can become an automatic reflex. As our training in Sun Tzu's strategy progresses, our focus becomes more fixed on our mission and we develop the appropriate filters to automatically eliminate distractions while noticing what must be noticed. Inaction is a legitimate choice to of response to events. We can train ourselves to recognize which events demand a response and which do not. This is important because, under the pressure of events, we don't have time to consciously decide (6.1.1 Conditioned Reflexes). Just as we can train ourselves to see opportunities that are usually hidden, we can also train ourselves to automatically reject events that do not require a response.

Key Methods:

The following are the key methods for dealing with event pressure, filtering out distractions while responding to events that demand a response.

1. We must always listen to events. Strategy means responding to the outside environment. We cannot cut ourselves off from events, at least not for any meaningful period of time. In the Progress Cycle of listen-aim-move-claim, the listening is constant. We must always be listening so we can always be adjusting to events. We cannot know when the event demanding our attention is a critical one or not unless we at least listen. The choice is when we move, that is, respond to events. (1.8 Progress Cycle).

2. Because we always listen we must constantly choose action or non-action. In the world of production , we are trained to follow orders so listening implies responding. In the competitive world, our success depends on our making our own decisions about when to act. Since we are always listening, we must constantly choose whether or not to respond. In the terminology of strategy, we are always aiming as well. This means that we have to retrain ourselves to recognize non-action as the most common appropriate response (4.2 Choosing Non-Action).

3. The more events we respond to, the more events we will trigger. In some situations, we may want to create more events and interaction with our environment. In other situations, creating more events simply create more distractions. We must filter out fewer events if we want more interaction and filter out more events if we want less interaction. We must constantly be aware if these events and responses are taking us closer to our goals or further away (2.3.1 Action and Reaction).

4. We must filter out events that don't affect us. Inside a productive organization, most messages we receive are aimed at us personally and therefore require a response. Outside, in the larger competitive world, most events have nothing to do with us, our strategic position, and our competitive neighborhood can be safely ignored. While these events may be interesting, satisfying our curiosity is a very short-term desire that needs to conform with our longer term goals (5.1 Mission Priorities).

5. We must filter out events that our actions cannot affect. Even if an event affects us or our position, there are many events where our actions cannot change anything. We cannot use the event to advance our position or defend our position. Events that we cannot use or affect can be ignored (5.6 Defense and Advance).

6. We must notice which events that demand action now. Even if an event affects us and can be used by our actions, those actions usually don't have to be performed immediately. What we cannot ignore are events that demand immediate action. These events fall into two categories 1) attacks or challenges that will get worse with delay and 2) opportunities which will soon disappear (5.6.2 Acting Now).

7. We must filter out events if we lack the resources to respond. Even if events require action now, we don't necessarily have the resources necessary to respond. Often the issue here is the size of the response required. Events that demand a small response are much easier to deal with because the resources are more readily available. The gap between other tasks on our stack gives us little pieces of time to respond to events without distraction. (3.1.1 Resource Limitations).

8. We must balance what we are doing now against the value of responding to the event. This brings us back to the core idea of our mission determining our priorities. Even if an event requires immediate action, responding to it isn't necessarily as important as completing our current task. Even timely events, if they can prevent us from accomplishing anything if we let them. We must balance acting now in response to an event against completing the task (move) at hand. The only way to compare the two actions and decide which best serves our goals (1.6 Mission Values).

Illustration:

Today, we live in a world of communication devices, many of which can create very bad habits in terms of event pressure. Cell phones, texting, email, instant messaging, Internet searches and Twitter all present different challenges. Let us briefly illustrate these principles in the context of modern communication to highlight some of the issue.

1. We must always listen to events. All these tool expand our ability to listen. ringing cell phone demands attention, but caller ID and messaging systems alleviate the pressure of responding now. However, tools such as instant messaging create problems because, by logging in, we are saying we are available.

2. Because we always listen we must constantly choose action or non-action. We do not have to respond to every email or text message. As a matter of fact, doing so can become a time-wasting addiction.

3. The more events we respond to, the more events we will trigger. Respond to every text message increases the number of texts that we get. The same if true of every other form of communication.

4. We must filter out events that don't affect us. A given Twitter stream may be interesting and entertaining, but most are strategically useless.

5. We must filter out events that our actions cannot affect. We may be upset or excited about what celebrities or politicians (am I repeating myself?) are doing, but these "events" are well beyond our arena of action.

6. We must notice events that demand action now. If we get a call from our mother, we better answer because nothing is as important as a mother's love.

7. We must filter out events if we lack the resources to respond. I would really like to help out that guy in Nigeria with all that money stuck in a bank, but my time is limited.

8. We must balance what we are doing now against the value of responding to the event. I found that, as my software company grew to over a hundred employees, I no longer owned the company. It owned me. My time was no longer my own. The issue was which customer, employee, or partner had the most pressing claim on my time. I ended up doing what I felt was important in the evening or when I was traveling.

5.1.2 Unproductive Responsibility

Sun Tzu's seven keys for understanding how our planned activities develop a life of their own.

"Supporting the military makes the nation powerful. Not supporting the military makes the nation weak."
Sun Tzu's The Art of War 3:4:3-4

"Never again clutter your days or nights with so many menial and unimportant things that you have no time to accept a real challenge when it comes along. This applies to play as well as work. A day merely survived is no cause for celebration. You are not here to fritter away your precious hours when you have the ability to accomplish so much by making a slight change in your routine. No more busy work. No more hiding from success. Leave time, leave space, to grow. Now. Now! Not tomorrow!"

Og Mandino

General Principle: Productive responsibilities must be measured against competitive mission.

Situation:

Our existing responsibilities can act as a serious barrier to progress. Unfortunately, in the world of production, we tend to see our responsibilities in terms of a list of specific activities rather than a set of general goals. That list of opportunities can grow until it leaves room for little else. These activities may have value in the larger scheme of things, but they may not. We commit to doing many tasks that have minimal value and tasks that were valuable can cease to have value. Sun Tzu's principles in this area are designed to keep unproductive commitments to a minimum.

Opportunity:

If we keep focused on our mission, finding time to pursue new opportunities should become a regular part of our workload rather than an intrusion upon it. We pursue new opportunities when we have the "excess" resources, but we must continually cultivate those resources (3.3 Opportunity Resources). If we regularly evaluate our activities against our mission, we will have the time and resources when an opportunity comes along (5.1 Mission Priorities).

Key Methods:

The following are the key methods for dealing with the pressure of our daily responsibilities, filtering out low value activities that do not service our mission.

1. An activity can fall within our span of control without being productive. The difference between competition and production is explained in this series of public articles. Competition wins control of ground. Production harvest resources from that ground. However, just because an activity falls within the realm of productive planning , it doesn't automatically mean that that activity itself is productive. Within our span of control, internal routines and procedures are developed that serve the needs of current competition, but as those external needs change, those responsibilities can continue without producing value (1.9 Competition and Production).

2. Planned productive activities must produce resources to defend _and_ advance our position. We not only want to hold our current position but we want to improve it over time. Value is defined by our mission, that is, our goals and values. We plan activities within our span of control to produce value. The ultimate end of strategy is to secure more potential productive capacity. The ultimate end of production is to produce more resources for competition (8.1.1 Transforming Resources).

3. Planned activities and responsibilities can easily lose sight of competitive mission. We can live our lives devoting more and more of our time to our controlled activities. We feel more secure within this bubble of control. From working within this bubble, we develop methods that work to best discharge our responsibilities. This gives us the illusion of control. We start to think that only what happens inside of our span of control is important. We lose sight of the fact that our mission goals always lie outside our control (1.7.2 Goal Focus).

4. Our productive responsibilities can not lose contact with events. Our position is never secure. Events outside of our control constantly affect our position. All existing positions are temporary. We cannot cut ourselves off from responding to events, that is, making strategic moves, at least nto for any meaningful period of time. We must not only pay attention to external events but be prepared to respond to them when necessary (1.1.1 Position Dynamics).

5. We must prioritize planned internal activities by their production of external value. We must use the yardstick of our competitive goals. From those values, we must understand which activities are high-value and which have low value. If we are assigned low-value duties, we must work to get those responsibilities dropped or transferred elsewhere. If we perform even the most routine tasks with a sense of the value they produce, the better we are able to balance our use of time (5.1 Mission Priorities).

6. We must do the most valuable productive tasks first. The production of value follows the law of diminishing returns. We cannot afford to perform every productive activity, no matter how slight its value. Our first priority is defending our current position because our current position provides the starting point for our future progress. So we must do those tasks that maintaining our positions absolutely requires. However, our productive work must also create the excess resources to pursue future opportunities. This means that we cannot use all our time and efforts on value production alone (5.6.1 Defense Priority , 3.3 Opportunity Resources).

7. **Split our limited resources between production and competition based on our opportunities.** Our resources are always limited. During periods of limited opportunities, we must focus more of those resources on maintaining our current position. During period of high-opportunity, we must shift our use of resources to advancing our position. However, we must always split our resources between both arenas. Using the 80/20 Pareto Principle and shifting the 80% in the required direction in a given position is a useful rule of thumb. This means that we should never use less that 20% of our resources on improving our position, serving our long term mission (3.1.1 Resource Limitations).

Illustration:

Let us illustrate these principles by applying them to a internal productive role, accounting, and an external competitive role, selling. The contrast between the two very different types of roles is instructive.

1. *An activity can fall within our span of control without being productive.* Both salespeople and accountant can be required to do certain activities, such as producing specific reports, that once served an important competitive purpose but, over time, have lost their value.

2. *Planned productive activities must produce resources to defend <u>and</u> advance our position.* An accountant primarily works to defend a position by providing information on current financial status and trends, but they must also help advance position by cost controls that save money that make the organization more cost competitive. A salesperson works primarily to advance a competitive position by winning new customers but must also defend position by maintaining existing customers.

3. Planned activities and responsibilities can easily lose sight of competitive mission. An accounting procedure or report can be established to address a given accounting or tax rule but continue after that rule changes. A salesperson can continue to service an existing customer long after that customer has ceased to be profitable.

4. Our productive responsibilities can not lose contact with events. Accountants must know when tax, accounting, and management demands that require account work change. Salespeople must know when a customer or product status changes.

5. We must prioritize planned internal activities by their production of external value. Accountants should know which of their reports are the most valuable for management decisions. Salespeople should know which customers and products are the most profitable.

6. We must do the most valuable productive tasks first. Accountants must first work on getting the most valuable information out quickly and correctly. Salespeople must first focus on selling their more profitable products to their most profitable customers.

7. Split our limited resources between production and competition based on our opportunities. All accountants must spend some of their time evaluating the value of the reports they produce. All salespeople must spend some of their time maintaining existing customers before going after new ones.

5.2 Opportunity Exploration

Sun Tzu's seven keys regarding a mental framework for exploring opportunities.

"Make no assumptions about all the dangers in using military force.
Then you won't make assumptions about the benefits of using arms either."

Sun Tzu's The Art of War 2:2:1-2

"There's an element of exploration. You are always looking over the hill [to] what's next."

James Reilly

General Principle: Exploration of opportunities requires more commitment than planning.

Situation:

Choosing the best way to explore an opportunity is less a matter of planning than experimenting. We can think about various courses our exploration might take, but the actual course that it does take depends on what we find along the way. If we commit ourselves to a specific series of preplanned steps rather than exploration itself, we are making a mistake before we begin. Planning assumes control. Competitive environments are beyond our control because they are complex, dynamic, and chaotic. The thought that we can pre-plan our explorations of competitive environment misses the whole point of exploration.

Opportunity:

When we commit ourselves to exploration, we commit to the unknown. When we explore opportunities, we work in undiscovered territory (3.2 Opportunity Creation). Opportunities are "openings" because no one knows what they contain. By definition, we cannot predict what conditions we will find. We explore opportunities to discover those conditions. Exploration of opportunities takes us beyond the limits of traditional planning.

Key Methods:

The following key methods provide the best mental frame for thinking about activities to explore and opportunity.

1. When an opportunity is explored, no one knows what we will find. Our plans are based upon what we think can happen. Since so much can happen in an unknown environment, our plans naturally expand. We try to consider all possibilities, and that leads to making more alternative plans. The longer we try to perfect our plans, the more costly our new venture becomes in terms of the time and effort we have put into it without learning anything. While we are busy planning, we are not exploring the situation and learning about it (3.1.5 Unpredictable Value).

2. When an opportunity is explored, our activities test the ground. When we explore opportunities, we are just testing them. We take a few steps in a given direction to see if it is viable. Instead of thinking about developing opportunities through a series of activities, the first step is thinking of a way to test their value. The best activity demonstrates simply whether or not an opportunity is worth developing further. The activities we choose should quickly prove only that an opportunity is worthy of further resources (5.4.1 Value Tests).

3. To explore opportunities, we start with the simplest possible experiment. It is never wise to start with a big, complex experiment. Big complex experiments require a lot of resources and have a lot of moving parts. They involve too many variables and require a lot of planning and control. Planning and control are rare in competitive environments. Instead, we start with the simplest possible steps in the direction of the opportunity to see what arises. If those first few steps prove fruitful, we can then scale up our activities (5.0 Minimizing Mistakes).

4. Exploring opportunities requires general deadlines and goals rather than specific ones. In controlled, production environments, we have very specific goals in the form of some-type of product specification. From that specification, we can determine exact resources needed. Since we specify the exact product, we can design, organize our production process, and set firm deadlines for production. Our goals in exploring an opportunity must be more general because an opportunity is never specific. We know only that is is an opening, a hole that we might be able to fill. We must discover its shape by exploration in order to see how we can fill it. From that exploration, we start to put together product specifications not before (3.1.4 Openings).

5. When we are exploring an opportunity, we must make many of our decisions in the moment. Our decisions depend on what we find. Our moves test openings. From a distance, we only know the surface of these openings but we don't know their true shape. We must follow the shape of the opening to understand it. Sun Tzu called this letting the ground dictate our methods (3.2.1 Environmental Dominance).

6. The more we plan opportunity exploration, the more unwarranted assumptions we make. When we think in terms of major expeditions with specific goals, we want to develop more detailed plans. We think that the more detailed our plan, the safer our new venture is. The opposite is true. All of the assumptions that we must make to create those plans are meaningless because they have not been tested. The longer we plan, the more we think of our assumptions as true and the more we expose ourselves to uncertainty (2.1.2 Leveraging Uncertainty),

7. The more we execute a plan instead of freely exploring opportunities, the further we fall behind our competition. While we are planning grand expeditions, our competitors can take simple steps exploring the territory to see what works. It doesn't matter how smart we think we are. We can't get ahead by falling behind. The secret is finding out a little more about the opportunity and quickly adapt our future activities to what we have learned (1.8.3 Cycle Time).

Illustration:

Let us illustrate these principles by applying them to exploring the opportunity for training people in strategy using games instead of traditional classroom education techniques.

1. When an opportunity is explored, no one knows what we will find. People may like the idea of a game. People may not. Useful games may be easy to develop or very difficult. Board games may be better than card games. We simply do not know what the opportunity holds.

2. When an opportunity is explored, our activities test the ground. We want to test this idea by getting some games out for people to try.

3. To explore opportunities, we start with the simplest possible experiment. Instead of developing games from scratch, we want to adapt existing games to teach strategic principles. Since many games teach strategy, we can adapt a few to make those lessons clearer and teach standard terminology.

4. Exploring opportunities requires general deadlines and goals rather than specific ones. We will start looking at various games an how they might simply be adapted. We want to get initial versions into people's hands as quickly as possible but not as finished products as much as tests of the concepts.

5. When we are exploring an opportunity, we must make many of our decisions in the moment. We may be looking at a game that we heard about as useful, but in search for that game, we must find a completely different game that is even better suited to our purposes. The StratUnity Card Game came about in just this way. We were looking at one card game, reading reviews and someone mention an older, similar game that became the basis of Stratunity.

6. The more we plan opportunity exploration, the more unwarranted assumptions we make. While our goals may be to automate our training games, putting them on hand-devices and allowing members to have tournaments on-line, we want to make sure that those games work before making the investment.

7. The more we execute a plan instead of freely exploring opportunities, the further we fall behind our competition. Our primary focus is on first creating a complete set of principles worthy of learning. The more effort we put at this point in developing more sophisticated game platforms, the more that work will be delayed.

5.2.1 Choosing Adaptability

Sun Tzu's five key methods for choosing actions that allow us a maximum of future flexibility.

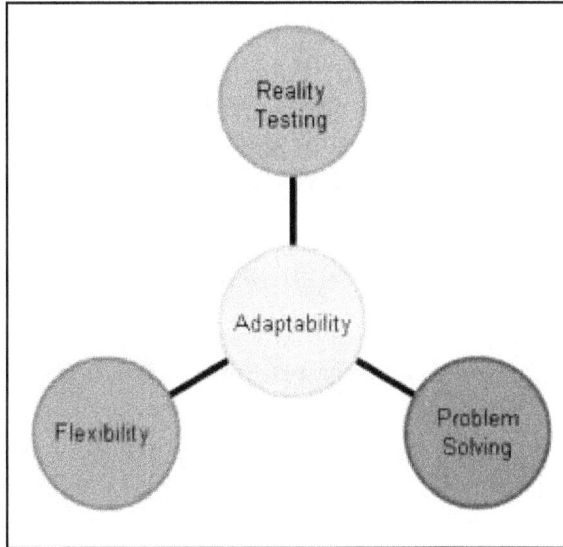

> *"Make war without a standard approach.*
> *Water has no consistent shape."*
>
> Sun Tzu's The Art of War, 6:8:8-9

> *"All fixed set patterns are incapable of adaptability or*
> *pliability. The truth is outside of all fixed patterns."*
>
> Bruce Lee

General Principle: We must choose actions that allow us to best respond to unknown conditions and unforeseen events.

Situation:

Adaptability requires the ability to move in a new direction at any time. Exploring an opportunity means expecting unforeseen discoveries (3.1.5 Unpredictable Value). Exploration takes time so we must be prepared for unforeseen events to occur (2.3.2 Reaction Unpredictability). We must choose our initial actions so that we can easily adapt them to emerging circumstances. Success in moving to new positions requires both our commitment to the goal and flexibility as to our methods. Our goal of exploring an opportunity remains the same, but we want to be free to choose a different path of exploration at any time.

Opportunity:

When we commit ourselves to exploration, we commit to the unknown. When we explore opportunities, we work in undiscovered territory (3.2 Opportunity Creation). Opportunities are "openings" because no one knows what they contain. By definition, we cannot predict what conditions we will find. We explore opportunities to discover those conditions. Exploration of opportunities takes us beyond the limits of traditional planning.

Key Methods:

In choosing how to explore an activity, we must keep the following key methods in mind.

1. To use adaptability, we must expect anything and everything. We have to admit to ourselves that we do not know what we will find when we explore an opportunity. Exploring an opening requires opening ourselves up to the possibilities. Discovery always lies outside of our expectations and assumptions. This is the fun and excitement and terror of real strategy. Any given step may lead onward or to a dead-end. It may lead to fortune of failure. We commit ourselves to taking the next step with this in mind (5.2 Opportunity Exploration).

2. To improve our adaptability, we choose initial activities that give us a better vantage point. From a better vantage point, we can get the lay of the land. Every step forward into an opening is experimental. The goal of the experiment is to discover more about the opportunity. With a broader point of view, we can pick better and better follow-up activities to explore the terrain we discover (2.4.1 Ground Perspective).

3. To maintain our adaptability, we choose activities that allow adjustment to unexpected events. We must prepare ourselves not only for discovering more but for what we already know to change. We must choose initial actions that gives us the greatest possible flexibility to adapt to these unforeseen events. Situations will change in expected ways. Especially when opportunities require us to navigate difficult ground forms, we must choose activities that minimize the common types of problems we will encounter from climate shifts ((1.4.1 Climate Shift , 4.3 Ground Forms).

4. To improve our adaptability, we choose directions that open up new options. Exploration is a learning activity. Every choice closes some doors, but when we have the option, we should pick activities that open more doors than they close. To do this, the best activities usually get us over a small barrier that obstructs other options (4.5.2 Opportunity Barriers).

5. To get the most out of our adaptability, we must leverage the conditions we find. A journey of a thousand miles always starts with a single step, but there is an inherent difference between traveling a well-mapped route and exploring unknown territory. Adapting to an opportunity means taking what the situation gives us. In a sense, our initial steps are experiments to discover the path of least resistance. We only have limited resources and we don't want to waste them tackling challenges until we have looked for a way around them (1.8.2 The Adaptive Loop).

Illustration:

Let us illustrate these ideas with the simple analogy of choosing to right vehicle to explore unknown terrain.

1. To use adaptability, we must expect anything and every-thing. We don't buy a train ticket to explore unknown terrain. We don't want an ordinary car, even if the road looks smooth. We want a rugged four-wheel drive SUV with good visibility all around because we don't know what we will find.

2. To improve our adaptability, we choose initial activities that give us a better vantage point. Since there are no roads, we want to choose a route that works its way up a hill to get the lay of the land.

3. To maintain our adaptability, we choose activities that allow adjustment to unexpected events. We don't go into narrow ravines where a rock fall might block us or a rain storm could flood us. We don't cross rivers where we might get stuck or hit unexpected currents.

4. To improve our adaptability, we choose directions that open up new options. We head for areas where the underbrush looks thinner, rocks fewer, the ground more even, less sticky, and slippery.

5. To get the most out of our adaptability, we must leverage the conditions we find. While we can get over the rocks or fallen trees blocking our path, we first try to find a way around them.

5.2.2 Campaign Methods

Sun Tzu's five key methods describing the use of campaigns and their methods.

CAESAR'S CAMPAIGNS IN GAUL
1st Century B.C.

"Fight five different campaigns without a firm rule for victory."

Sun Tzu's The Art of War 6:8:12

"Life is a campaign not a battle, and has its defeats as well as its victories."

Don Piatt

General Principle: Campaigns use a variety of methods to combine smaller moves toward a longer-term goal.

Situation:

A campaign is a series or group of related actions or moves used to take advantage of an opportunity. In a campaign, we use a series of short-term positions to attain a longer term position that we desire.

Campaigns are necessary because many opportunities cannot be pursued by a single move but rather in a series of stages. The fact that related moves can be tied together, leads, unfortunately, to much of the confusion between planning and strategy. Changing circumstances can easily make both plans and campaigns irrelevant, but that fact cannot let us ignore this powerful tool of strategy.

Opportunity:

As long as we continually re-evaluate the value of a given campaign, campaigns can serve as a powerful tool (6.2 Campaign Evaluation). The use of campaigns allow us to break down our progress toward a goal into a series of smaller, more certain steps (5.5 Focused Power). A good understanding of campaigns can help us identify how to best take advantage of an opportunity and our alternatives when a given move fails.

Key Methods:

The following key methods describe the methods campaigns use to take advantage of an opportunity.

1. A campaign is a series of related actions used to take advantage of an opportunity. The open positions targeted by campaigns cannot be achieved by a single move. They are usually positions that are well-defined, well-established, and persistent. They therefore require a series of related, small actions. The relationships among these moves can take a variety of forms. Though we can think about the potential shape a given campaign *may* take, in the end the actual shape of the campaign will be determined not by our plans, but by the result of each move (5.2.1 Choosing Adaptability).

2. Campaigns are required to cover large distances and/or get around significant barriers. In our daily decision-making, we often filter out opportunities that require large investment in time and effort because those opportunities are less likely to lead to success. Since some well-defined and established positions are more persistent than regular opportunities, the nature of a competitive landscape can simply require a group of related moves to establish these positions (4.5 Opportunity Surfaces).

3. A campaign can divide a large, risky move into a safer series of incremental actions. Using this method, each move depends on the others. Each move gets us a little closer to our goal, building on the progress of all the previous actions in the series. Each move addresses a separate aspect or issue of the opportunity. These issues are defined by the nature of the opportunity, what must be learned and controlled. The exact nature of each action cannot be known precisely beforehand since it depends on the result of the previous action. The series of actions method gets its strength from our ability to focus on single smaller actions at a time (5.4 Minimizing Action).

4. A campaign can break down a large barrier with the cumulative, convergent effect of small actions. Some campaigns rely upon mounting effects separate, independent actions. Each action, by itself, is not sufficient to achieve the desired goal. Indeed, each action may be in many ways considered a "failure" because it appears not to make any difference in our situation. However, the impact of these actions mount over time. While each action doesn't get us measurably closer to our goal in incremental sense, it does build up the pressure that eventually wins the desired position (6.8.2 Strength in Adversity).

5. A campaign can persistently pursue a sequence of alternative paths one after another. Using this method, each move independently explores a different path until we find one that works. Each of these paths, if successful, could get us to our goal by itself. These paths are parallel, not a series of steps or a cumulative effort. We do not to pursue these alternative paths at the same time. Each failure may or may not teach us about where to look for the next.

We try one after a other until we find the one the works (1.9 Competition and Production).

Illustration:

Since we are talking about a variety of different uses of campaigns, let us describe a variety of different types of campaign.

1. A campaign is a series of related actions used to take advantage of an opportunity. We all start our lives with the campaign called "getting an eduction." For some of us, that campaign never stops.

2. Campaigns are required to cover large distances and/or get around significant barriers. Campaigns are required to get a college degree, get licensed in a profession, win elected office, or build a successful company.

3. A campaigns can divide a large, risky move into a safer series of incremental actions. We are developing this Strategic Playbook using this campaign method. First, we created the outline of strategic topics. Then we created the initial articles to fill in that outline. Now we update those articles to detail the principles involved and meet a certain standard. Finally, we can develop training and certification procedures around the resulting body of knowledge. Completing each step was and is necessary before we can proceed to the next.

4. A campaign can break down a large barrier with the cumulative, convergent effect of small actions. The best example of this technique was the political career of Abraham Lincoln. Lincoln ran for a series of offices, losing every election. However, the cumulative affect of his campaigns was to eventually win the presidency.

5. A campaigns can persistently pursue a sequence of alternative paths one after another. This method largely describes Edison's search for the right filament to create the electric light. He simply tried different materials in sequence until he found one that worked.

5.2.3 Unplanned Steps

Sun Tzu's seven key methods distinguishing campaign adjustments from steps in a plan.

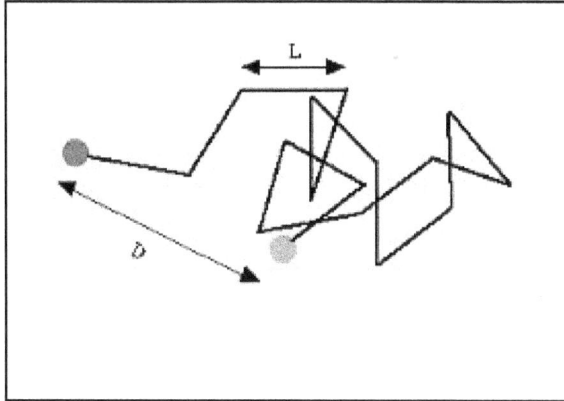

"You must be creative in your strategy.
You must adapt to your opportunities and weaknesses."
Sun Tzu's The Art of War 8:2:1-2

"No battle plan survives contact with the enemy."
Colin Powell

"When we are sure that we are on the right road there is no need to plan our journey too far ahead. No need to burden ourselves with doubts and fears as to the obstacles that may bar our progress. We cannot take more than one step at a time."
Orison Swett Marden

"A good plan violently executed now is better than a perfect plan next week."
General George S. Patton

General Principle: A campaign is a series of separate adjustments not a pre-planned series of commitments.

Situation:

Our plans have gravity. That gravity can capture us. It can trap us without our even being aware of it. Like a planet speeding around a star, we think we are going somewhere when we are really going in circles.The gravity of plans, like the gravity of the stars and planets, is determined by their size. The larger and more massive a plan is, the more it tends to control our direction and shape our view of reality. People mistakenly think that the more detailed their planning is, the more likely it is that their plans will be successful. While this is true in production environments, the opposite is always true in competitive environments.

Opportunity:

While strategic campaigns can require many separate steps, we cannot confuse a campaign with a plan. Our opportunity is to get away from the word "planning" entirely when considering competitive advances. Like the word, "strategy," people use the word "planning," to describe many different types of activities. George Patton, growing up in a less linear era , used the term to mean setting general objectives in a campaign. A campaign sets aside resources to surmount a specific obstacle (6.2 Campaigns). Colin Powell, a product of a more linear education system , sees planning as a series of steps to produce a well-defined result. It is this later approach to planning that works against good strategy as General Powell realized.

Key Methods:

The key methods for making sure we are choosing the best activities based on adaptive strategy rather than planned commitments are as follows:

1. In outlining a campaign, we must see each component as a separate test. Since competitive campaigns can overlap with productive plans, we must distinguish between regions of internal control and regions of external competition. Separating linear planning from adaptive strategy is difficult because we are constantly shifting between the two realms. Working within our areas of control, we often formulate plans beyond the event horizon of our control. We must always question ourselves about just where we are crossing the line (1.9 Competition and Production).

2. Planned steps are comforting tasks while a strategic action is an invigorating challenge. By "invigorating," we mean a little nerve-racking. Strategic action always has an air of uncertainty because it is a probabilistic not deterministic process. If an action seems comfortable and certain, it is a plan, not strategic action. We cannot let the comforting nature of plans draw us into making the wrong competitive decisions in the realm of uncontrolled events. If the way we think about the step leaves open the possibility of failure, it is a strategic activity (1.8.4 Probabilistic Process).

3. *We should not feel pressure to act only to satisfy our own expectations.* This means we shouldn't feel any need to do what we thought we might do. The more we use linear plans, the more invested we become to our plans. The more pressure we feel to perform a certain action simply because we expected to perform it. We must escape from the gravity of planning. Any pressure we feel should come from the external situation, not from our planning (3.2.1 Environmental Dominance).

4. We should feel the pressure of cycle time and events not deadlines. Time pressure should come from the window of opportunity closing and our desire to learn. When we plan, we naturally think about deadlines for synchronizing tasks. In an competitive environment, completing many tasks is beyond our control, as we will soon discover. As we start to execute our plan, we cross into the region outside of our control (3.1.6 Time Limitations).

5. Progress means getting environment feedback not checking off to-do items. Working through a plan, we feel like we are making progress when we finish our to-do list. Strategic actions only recognizes progress in the form of learning about the environment, ideally about how we can make exploration pay. If we commit to a direction without getting rewarding feedback from the environment, we can keep heading in a wrong and potentially fatal direction (1.8.3 Cycle Time).

6. *Each step is based upon the results of the last step.* We constantly update our picture of the situation, adjusting our priorities and time-line to what we learn. The results of all these areas of testing are factored in to the moves that we make. In terms of the listen-aim-move-claim progress cycle, we should listen in all these areas at once before aiming and moving in any of them. Maintaining this flexible and adaptive mindset is the key to our competitive success (1.8 Progress Cycle).

7. *Each step may be revisited based upon the results of the next step.* This is not a linear process. The discoveries in a later step may require us to revisit an earlier activity. The process is a loop and the nature of the loop is based upon all the outcomes involved (1.8.2 The Adaptive Loop).

Illustration:

This article was written largely because most "business plans," such as those taught in business school and encouraged by banks, make mockery of good strategy. To illustrate this principle, imagine that we see an opportunity for opening a new restaurant in a fast-growing neighborhood. What does the campaign to open that restaurant look like?

1. *In outlining a campaign, we must see each component as a separate test.* If we thought that controlled the business environment, we might make a plan that looks like this:

- find a good location,
- decorate the restaurant,
- develop a menu,
- get equipment and supplies, and hire and train a staff.

Looks reasonable, but since we don't control the market for a restaurant, a strategic campaign outline for opening a restaurant looks similar to a linear plan, but it is really a series of adaptive and dependent loops:

- We test the market for a good location;
- We test interior designs against strengths of the location;
- We test the menu against the location;
- We test the marketplace for equipment and ingredients; and
- We test the market for a staff and what training is required.

2. Planned steps are comforting while strategic action should be invigorating. See how reassuring the first list looks? The process seems simply, like building a machine. The second list makes it clear everything is uncertain. There may not be any good location. Many designs may not work in the location we find. The menu depends on the location we find and what the competition in the area already offers. The second list is a list of challenges not tasks.

3. We should not feel pressure to act only to satisfy our own expectations. We might have envisioned opening a fancy Italian restaurant, but the situation may well call for a small neighborhood bistro.

4. We should feel the pressure of cycle time and events not deadlines. We need to find a location, but we cannot control what locations are available. The key question here is: what do we do when none of those available locations seems likely to succeed? The correct strategic answer is that we do nothing. We wait.

5. Progress means getting environment feedback not checking off to-do items. If we can't find a location, we are stuck on dependent tasks such as doing a design, but we can work on independent tasks, such as investing other restaurant menus in the area and getting feedback from locals about what they want on a menu, but we must not take a poor location simply to keep to our schedule. We let dependent tasks, such as decorating the restaurant, wait.

6. Each step is based upon the results of the last step. For example, the location that we find determines our designs. If we find a good location, we want to see what kind of restaurants are already in that area before developing a design or our menu.

7. Each step may be revisited based upon the results of the next step. We may get a good menu, but then have to change it because the ingredients and staff are available.

5.3 Reaction Time

Sun Tzu's five key methods on the use of speed in choosing actions.

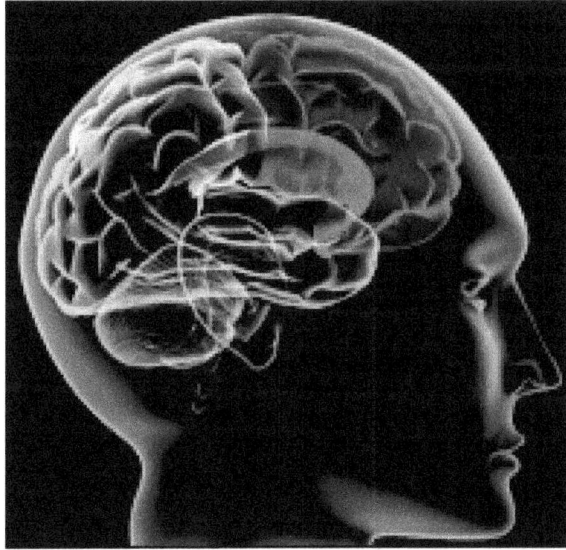

"Mastering speed is the essence of war."
Sun Tzu's The Art of War 12:2:16

"What comes first, the compass or the clock? Before one can truly manage time (the clock), it is important to know where you are going, what your priorities and goals are, in which direction you are headed (the compass). Where you are headed is more important than how fast you are going. Rather than always focusing on what's urgent, learn to focus on what is really important.

Anonymous

General Principle: Actions pursuing opportunities must be chosen quickly.

Situation:

When we choose how we want to pursue and opportunity, our first concern is minimizing mistakes. We don't want to endanger our current position or waste resources. It is natural to think that the best way to minimize mistakes in exploring opportunities is to go slowly and carefully. The problem is that slow reactions are almost always extremely costly in competitive environments. Of course, some forms of speed are extremely dangerous. For example, it is always dangerous to get heavily involved with a new opportunity before we have explored what is holds. Good strategy doesn't promote speed in the sense of a headlong rush.

Opportunity:

In choosing the best way to explore an opportunity, we cannot over estimate the value of speed. Sun Tzu wrote extensively about how and why speed is important. Acting and reacting quickly gives us a advantage in every strategic situation. The definition of a competitive situation is one in which we are compared to others (1.3.1 Competitive Comparison). The definition of a strategic situation is one in which we have to adjust to conditions and events in our environment (1.1.1 Position Dynamics). We are always compared by how quickly we respond. Our reaction time is often the difference between success and failure.

Key Methods:

The following key methods explain why actions that can be taken quickly are always preferable to slower reactions.

1. We can never start exploring an opportunity too soon. The faster we begin our exploration, the faster we can learn what an opportunity holds. As the saying goes, "He who hesitates is lost." This is especially true when it comes to taking advantage of opportunities. Natural forces in the environment open those windows of opportunity, but those openings are closed by other people filling them. The longer we delay in testing our new opportunities, the less likely we are to be successful in exploring and exploiting them (3.1.6 Time Limitations).

2. Any quick action increases our safety by decreasing conflict. If we react quickly to an opportunity, we get ahead of the competition. If we keep reacting quickly to what we discover, we can stay there. When we move quickly and with confidence, we discourage others from competing with us. This decreases the main risk in competition, the cost of conflict (3.1.3 Conflict Cost).

3. We *make fewer and less costly mistakes when we react quickly.* This is especially true if we have honed our strategic instincts through training and exercise. Competitive environments are too complex for us to consciously analyze. Our unconscious gut reactions process a great deal more information than our conscious mind can. If we are trained, we usually come to the right decisions automatically in high-pressure situations. We can easily over-think these if we take to much time. Focusing on unimportant details which we can understand rather than the big picture (2.5 The Big Picture)

4. Faster reaction times gain us more knowledge more quickly. This is not to say that, by acting quickly, we won't make mistakes. We will. However, fast reactions always have an advantage over delay. By acting quickly, even our mistakes quickly win us more knowledge. We can learn more from our mistakes than our successes. The mistakes that we make by hesitating are more expensive because they don't teach us a thing other than to act more quickly the next time (2.6 Knowledge Leverage).

5. Even a series of quick, safe failures dramatically increases our eventual probability of success. The issue of speed brings us face to face with the laws of probability. Our time is limited. Success in strategic environments is always a matter of probability rather than control. While strategic methods improve our chances of success, one of the ways it does that is simply by using speed to give us more tries. The more trials we get, the more likely our success becomes over time as long as none of our failures ends the process. This is why we must understand all the lessons in this section regarding minimizing our mistakes (4.0 Leveraging Probability).

Illustration:

Let us look at the example of going after a new position with a current employer.

1. We can never start exploring an opportunity too soon. If we want a promotion into a specific position, we are better off exploring that positions immediately, even before those openings are available, rather than later.

2. Quick action increases our safety by decreasing conflict. We should let the current position holders know of our interest in their job, and see if we can work with them to get them promoted. This opens the desired position sooner rather than later and we are positioned for it as the heir apparent. Done correctly, others may not even challenge us for the opening.

3. We make fewer and less costly mistakes when we react quickly. We can worry about threatening the current holders of the position, but we will know when we sound them out if they are threatened or flattered by the attention. We cannot guess at the situation without exploring it. If we worry about approaching people and delay, we will probably never do it.

4. Faster reaction times gain us more knowledge more quickly. Even if they are threatened and unwilling to help us, planning to keep their position for years, it is better to know that sooner rather than later.

5. Even a series of quick, safe failures dramatically increases our eventual probability of success. If one potential position proves to be a dead-end, we are better knowing that so we can look elsewhere rather than waiting. Even if we fail many times trying to find future openings and champions, we will certainly find them over time.

5.3.1 Speed and Quickness

Sun Tzu's seven key methods regarding the use of pace within a dynamic environment.

"You can fight a war for a long time or you can make your nation strong. You can't do both."
Sun Tzu's The Art of War 2:1:25

"In skating over thin ice our safety is our speed."
Ralph Waldo Emerson

General Principle: The best actions leverage both speed and quickness and recognize their difference.

Situation:

Not all our explorations of openings are going to be successful. Many, if not most, are going to fail. Our explorations fail because of two major reasons. First, the nature of the opening may not offer any real rewards. Second, we are too slow in finding out how to make that opportunity pay. Being too slow opens us up two types of failure 1) the competition beats us or 2) we run out of resources. The first problem comes from our limited knowledge. The second comes from our limited skill. While some skills may be beyond our capability, the most common cause of the second failure is the lack of focus on speed and quickness.

Opportunity:

We must focus on what we can control. Our resources are always limited (3.1.1 Resource Limitations). We cannot control it making some opportunities pay requires more than we can afford to invest. We can control our pace. Once we master the secret of speed and quickness, we can usually outpace our competitors. If we can fill an opportunity before others do, we dramatically increase our success rate (3.1.6 Time Limitations).

Key Methods:

Let us start with some clear definitions differentiating between speed and quickness.

1. Speed means directly closing the distance between our existing position and an open opportunity. Distance measures the space between positions. Distance exists both in physically space and in intellectual space. Covering physical space requires movement while covering intellectual space requires learning (4.4 Strategic Distance).

2. The best actions use speed to get through difficult ground with a minimum of risk. Tilted, fluid, and soft forms of ground open us up to certain forms of temporary problems. The longer we are on such ground, the larger our risk. This is especially true of soft ground, which gives out over time (4.3 Ground Forms).

3. Quickness is the ability to change directions rapidly. Quickness requires 1) seeing a situation, 2) making a decision, and 3) executing that decision. This is a general function of cycle time (1.8.3 Cycle Time).

4. Speed can work against quickness. Speed increases our inertia in a specific direction. Moving fast can make it harder to change direction. It can prevent us from seeing a situation and changing direction to adjust to it. Going faster and faster when we are going in the wrong direction creates more problems. Going in the right direction is always more important than our speed. We cannot afford to go so fast that we miss our turnoff (1.6.3 Shifting Priorities).

5. Quickness can work against speed. If we constantly worry whether we are going the right direction, we are going to end up going too slow. We must commit to our direction so we can build up speed. Mastering Sun Tzu's strategy gives us confidence in balancing speed against quickness, recognizing when the situation calls for speed and when for quickness (6.4.4 Open Situations). *The best actions use both speed and quickness to get ahead and stay ahead of competitors.* As with all strategic characteristics, both speed and quickness are evaluated only in comparison. We are only relatively faster or slower when compared with other competitors operating within our environment. We want to move faster toward the right solution than anyone else (1.3.1 Competitive Comparison).

6. If we cannot win a position on the basis of speed, we must use quickness. Some competitors are simply faster than we are. They get going first and at a good rate. We should recognize when we cannot catch up on speed alone. In those situations, we must focus on quickness. We must be prepared to change directions when events or the ground offer us an advantage (5.3 Reaction Time).

Illustration:

The critical difference between speed and quickness is most commonly recognized in the world of sports so I initially used baseball to illustrate them. However, in thinking about it, it seems that failures of intellectual speed and quickness are more common and more difficult to understand. Let us use selling as an example of an area where we have to develop intellectual speed and quickness.

1. Speed means directly closing the distance between our existing position and an open opportunity. In sales, the distance that we must close is a gap in knowledge, the gap between our product knowledge and our knowledge of the customer's needs. The more quickly we close that gap, the more sales we can make.

2. The best actions use speed to get through difficult ground with a minimum of risk. The faster we learn about a given customer's needs, the more often we will avoid wasting time describing features and benefits that are meaningless to the sale.

3. Quickness is the ability to change directions rapidly. During the sales process, we eventually focus on a specific set of products and needs. We focus on a group of customers who have those needs. Quickness is our ability to see a better direction in dealing with a specific customer or meeting and change our focus.

4. Speed can work against quickness. If we have learned a lot about a particular set of customer problems, our inertia takes us in that direction. When a given customer situation calls for us to go in a new direction, we can easily miss the signs. Changing directions is often necessary because customers will see where we are going and put up barriers. Even if our direction is correct, we must quickly change direction to get around those barriers.

5. Quickness can work against speed. Customer situations are complex. We cannot learn everything about a customer's business. If we keep shifting directions like a puppy chasing chickens, the customer gets over-loaded with information and the sales process loses focus.

6. The best actions use both speed and quickness to get ahead and stay ahead of competitors. If we can out pace our competitors in identifying and addressing customer needs, quickly adapting to the unique aspect of every situation, we are going to be successful in selling. Our ability to do this speedily and quickly isn't a matter of simply being smarter than our competitors. It depends largely on having better mental models than they do so we can fill in the pieces more quickly.

7. If we cannot win a position on the basis of speed, we must use quickness. This is especially true when we are taking a customer away from a competitor. That competitor has a big lead over us in terms of knowing that customer. We cannot close that gap by speed alone. We must use our quickness to take the sale in directions that put the competitions at a disadvantage.

5.3.2 Opportunity Windows

Sun Tzu's five key methods on the effect of speed upon opposition.

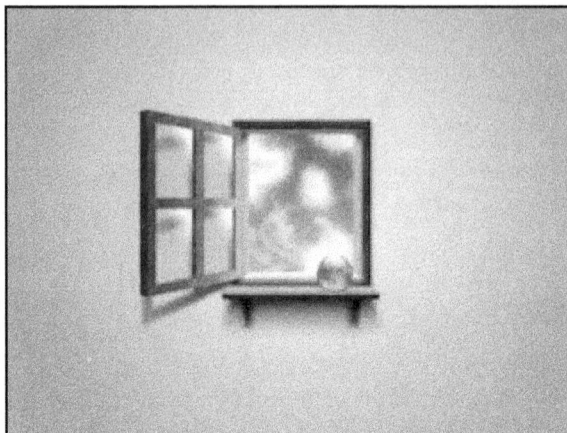

"Never waste an opportunity to defeat your enemy."
Sun Tzu's The Art of War 4:3:23

I was seldom able to see an opportunity until it had ceased to be one."
Mark Twain

"Opportunities are never lost; they are taken by others."
Anonymous

General Principle: Opportunity duration is determined by the environment's speed and quickness.

Situation:

When we choose the way to explore an opportunity, we must ask ourselves how long that opportunity is likely to last. Opportunities only last long enough for the fastest and quickest competitors to take advantage of them, not one moment longer. One opportunity can disappear in a flash of insight during a single meeting. Other opportunities can linger on for decades, as a series of barriers are broached one by one. Fast actions waste resources in slow environments. Slower actions waste resources in faster environments.

Opportunity:

All opportunities are created by others (3.2.1 Environmental Dominance). All opportunities arise because an emptiness, a need, cries out to be filled (3.2.4 Emptiness and Fullness). Our opportunity starts with recognizing that need before others and seeing how our unique resources can fill it (3.4.2 Opportunity Fit). We can conserve our resources by avoiding opportunities that we are not in a position to fill. Speed and quickness affects both how rapidly opportunities emerge and how quickly those opportunities are satisfied. More opportunities emerge in fast environments, but more competitors are are prepared to take advantage of them there as well.

Key Methods:

When choosing the best way to explore an opportunity, we must consider the nature of our window of opportunity.

1. Generally, faster action is better than slower ones because all opportunities are temporary. All positions are temporary. The more temporary the positions that border the opening, the more temporary the opportunity itself. Faced-paced environments arise when everyone focuses on the temporary nature of their positions (1.1.1 Position Dynamics).

2. The pace of action must match the pace of the environment. Opportunities arise more rapidly in environments that welcome change. More competitive environments embrace change. Opportunities are stifled in environments that resist change. More regulated environments resist change. Our speed and quickness are always measured relative to the environment in which we work. We must always be faster than our competition, but we cannot get too far ahead of them. Too much speed within a slow environment will create friction. (1.3.1 Competitive Comparison).

3. Quickness recognizes developing opportunities first. In slower-paced environments, fewer people are open to seeing opportunities so windows of opportunity open more gradually. In fastpaced competitive environments, needs are more quickly recognized. In either case, the recognition of a problem is the firing of the starting gun at the beginning of a race. Quickness allows some people to get the jump on others (5.3 Reaction Time).

4. Speed is required to secure an opportunity. Again, this speed is relative. In a quick environment, we can be more reckless because success depends on speed more than anything else. In slower environments, we must aim for more measure progress because recklessness is heavily penalized. Whatever the environment, we take advantage of the opportunity by learning how to fill the openings more quickly than others (1.8.3 Cycle Time).

5. The larger the organization, the larger window of opportunity it requires. Larger organizations tend to identify opportunities more slowly and start moving more slowly because of the diseconomies of scale, especially slow reaction time. We would think that in the case of large opportunities, large organizations would be able to catch up to their smaller competitors because growth takes time. However, history shows that large organizations can only take advantage of opportunities that are very close to their current position because a fast organization can grow more rapidly than a large organization can move (3.4 Dis-Economies of Scale).

Illustration:

We can see this difference in comparing different environments, for example, the high-tech business environment with the federal government environment. High-tech is one of the environments most open to change because it is highly competitive. The federal government is one of the environments most resistant to change because it has no competition.

1. Generally, faster action is better than slower ones because all opportunities are temporary. In both the high-tech world and government, all opportunities are temporary. More of them are missed in government because of their pace.

2. The pace of action must match the pace of the environment. Try to act too quickly within a slow environment such as the federal government creates more problems than it solves. Unlike the hight-ech environment which embraces creative destruction, rash action creates potential disasters within the federal government because no government entity is allowed to fail. Witness Fanny Mae.

3. Quickness recognizes developing opportunities first. In the federal government, few people are open to seeing opportunities. Changes play out gradually over decades. In the world of high-tech, everyone is on the lookout for new opportunities because businesses and entire industry segments rise up and die out within a few years.

4. Speed is required to secure an opportunity. In high-tech, speed is measured in months. In the federal government, it is measured in years.

5. The larger the organization, the larger window of opportunity it requires. As organizations grow larger in high-tech, they find fewer and fewer opportunities so they are frequently outmoded and replaced. The US federal government, on the other hand, may have outgrown all possible opportunities except in size reduction.

5.3.3 Information Freshness

Sun Tzu's six key methods on the choosing actions based on freshness of information.

"You must have surviving spies capable of bringing you information at the right time."
Sun Tzu's The Art of War 13:4:10

"Life is made up of constant calls to action, and we seldom have time for more than hastily contrived answers."
Billings Learned Hand

" On the plains of hesitation bleach the bones of countless millions who, at the dawn of decision, sat down to wait, and waiting died."
Sam Ewing

General Principle: The best actions are based on the most recent information.

Situation:

A common strategic mistake is waiting to make the decision to act, hoping for better information. No matter how long we wait, our information is always incomplete. But, the longer we delay deciding on action, whatever correct information we have is likely to become outdated.

Opportunity:

The need for speed in choosing an action is based on our need to leverage information (2.6 Knowledge Leverage). We can make good decisions despite imperfect information (2.1.1 Information Limits). We can rely on situations constantly changing rather than battle against it (2.1.2 Leveraging Uncertainty). Once we act, we get immediate feedback about the nature of the situation, improving our actions in a constant cycle (1.8.2 The Adaptive Loop).

Key Methods:

In identifying the best actions, we must consider the following key methods relating to the nature of our information.

1. Timely action based on current information is always more likely to be successful than waiting for better information. All actions are experiments. Only by experimenting can we discover what is real. Information gathering through our information channels is a critical part of strategy, but it only goes so far. After identifying a high-probability opportunity, the best way to gather information about it is through action, not more information gathering (4.0 Leveraging Probability).

2. We must not act when conditions are changing so rapidly that our information is probably already outdated. Acting on the basis of outdated information is usually wasteful. It can also be dangerous, threatening our current position. When a fluid environment is going through dramatic shifts in climate, it is always better to wait then to act (4.3.2 Fluid Forms).

3. All actions must factor in the possibility that even the freshest information can be wrong. Recent information is not any more perfect than any other type of information. While fresh information is less likely to be outdated, we must, still choose actions that minimize our risks. When the information that we have requires action, we are always better off acting, rather than wasting time trying to get better information, but only if we choose actions that allow for our information being wrong (2.1.3 Strategic Deception.

4. New information is more likely to be correct when it is consistent with our situation awareness. We must always test new information against our sense of the big picture of our situation. If the information we get is consistent with our expectations, we can rely on it more heavily. New information that is inconsistent with our expectations can disprove our sense of the situation, but that information must be questioned (2.5 The Big Picture).

5. Even if action doesn't attain its desired goal, a quick response to events improves our subjective position. It demonstrates that we are decisive, improving our position in their eyes. Acting quickly is never acting rashly as long as we know how to experiment safely. By gauging our responses based on our fallibility, we demonstrate that we are not afraid of making mistakes if we can learn from them (5.0 Minimizing Mistakes).

6. We always get the advantage of surprise. We create events that others must respond to rather than passively react to events created by others (2.1.4 Surprise).

Illustration:

Let us illustrate these principles with an example from selling. What should we do if we hear that a customer has just gotten a very low price offer from a competitor.

1. Timely action based on current information is always more likely to be successful than waiting for better information. We must react instantly by contacting the customer rather than wait to see if we can get more specific information about the offer elsewhere.

2. We must not act when conditions are changing so rapidly that our information is probably already outdated. If offering low prices with many special conditions and restrictions is common in our industry, we should wait to see what the pricing really means before acting.

3. All actions must factor in the possibility that even the freshest information can be wrong. We must not react by trying to cut our prices. Our actions should be gauged to open up possibilities not close them down.

4. New information is more likely to be correct when it is consistent with our situation awareness. If this competitor normally tries to undercut prices, the news is probably correct. If this competitor seldom does, we should suspect it, but still react.

5. Even if action doesn't attain its desired goal, a quick response to events improves our subjective position. Our quick response will, at the minimum, show the customer that we are aware of what is happening and care about their business.

6. We always get the advantage of surprise. The response that we make should make price less of an issue rather than more of an issue. It should focus on questions of quality or long-term shared risk rather than price, forcing our competitors to adapt to us.

5.4 Minimizing Action

Sun Tzu's six key methods regarding minimizing waste, i.e. less is more.

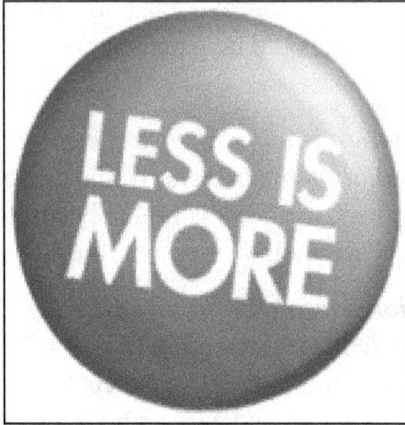

> *"Make good use of war.*
> *Make the enemy's troops surrender.*
> *You can do this fighting only minor battles."*
>
> Sun Tzu's The Art of War 3:3:1-3

> *"Less is more."*
>
> Ludwig Mies van der Rohe

General Principle: To do more with less we must focus on small areas of deep knowledge.

Situation:

Since Sun Tzu defines success in economic terms, we seek to do more with less. Every action we take or resource we use that we can eliminate is waste. In pursuing an opportunity, waste increases our risk of loss. If we try to improve our position by pursuing opportunity after opportunity by doing more and more different activities, our position grows more and more complex and waste multiplies. The result is that our position becomes more and more expensive and difficult to maintain.

Opportunity:

In choosing actions to safely pursue opportunities, we look for ways to eliminate waste. the strongest competitive actions are usually the simplest, most direct, and most economical. Strategic positioning is based on economical action (3.1 Strategic Economics). Since we cannot know the return from any new venture at the beginning, our first goal must be to control our costs. This means that the best strategy is doing less, not more. In choosing action, we must look to every new venture as a means of simplifying our current activities rather than making them more complicated.

Key Methods:

There is a science to Sun Tzu's approach to doing less that comes from choosing doing what is best not second-best.

1. We should choose activities that make our skills deeper rather than broader. When we focus our efforts on a smaller range of activities, we need in-depth knowledge, increasing the value of our capabilities. When we spread our efforts over an increasing range of different activities, we broaden our skills but decrease their value (1.5.2. Group Methods).

2. We should eliminate waste in using resources, movement, stockpiling, mistakes, and delay. These ideas are closely related to the seven mura of lean manufacturing, but they are also related directly to Sun Tzu's points of competitive vulnerability (9.2 Points of Vulnerability).

3. We should choose activities that simplify our external focus. Focus is a key source of power. If we pursue opportunities by becoming less and less focused, we weaken our position even as we seem to be expanding it. We want to broaden our external knowledge but focus that knowledge on smaller and smaller external regions. Spread-out positions and over-extended operations result from choosing to pursue activities by doing more and more instead of less and less (1.7.2 Goal Focus).

4. Whenever possible, we want to grow by subtraction. Doing one thing is easy. Doing many things is hard. A concentrated effort is powerful. A divided effort is weak. A well-defined target makes us successful. A vague target is hard to hit. Clear-cut goals keep us on track. Confused goals get us intro trouble. We must spend more time on activities that meet current demands while exploring new territory and spend less and less time on activities that do not take us into new areas. We should pursue opportunities as a way to escape from the lowest valued activities we are currently performing. To start a new venture, we need excess resources. These resources should be pulled away from our least profitable activities. We want to build our position up by focusing more narrowly on what we are already doing (3.3 Opportunity Resources):

5. We can direct existing activities to take advantage of new opportunities. One of the best ways to explore an opportunity is to use existing activities. We want to kill two birds with one stone. We can use existing skills for meeting our current commitments while exploring new territory at the same time. If two sets of activities are of equal value in maintaining our current position, we should choose those activities that allow us to move into new areas at the same time (2.6 Knowledge Leverage). For example, if a business sees a product line as a potential new opportunity, it is best to talk to existing customers in the regular course of business about its potential rather than seeking out new customers in new markets.

6. We choose activities that decrease internal and external competition. We must always remember that the most profitable moves are those that face the least competition. Competition can come from others, or it can come from competing internal activities. When choosing among potential ways of exploring an opportunity, we should pick the ones that decrease conflict because they will always be less expensive. Less conflicted activities are always more profitable ones (3.1.3 Conflict Cost).

Illustration:

The example that I always use for this in my lectures is the way that we built our software company, growing it an average of 40% a year from our profits alone for over a decade.

1. We should choose activities that make our skills deeper rather than broader. When we started our software company, we started as general consultants. Our most profitable jobs came from database development, so we slowly stopped doing other projects. By focusing on database projects, our business doubled. Then our most profitable projects were accounting related, so we focused on opportunities that were accounting related.

2. We should eliminate waste in using resources, movement, stockpiling, mistakes, and delay. Our least profitable activities were eliminated as waste since the resources that they used could be better applied to more profitable activities.

3. We should choose activities that simplify our external focus. We started selling any type of services to any type of company. By working more and more on accounting, we eventually developed a basic modifiable accounting package that other developers wanted to use and resell. Since selling software was more profitable than running projects, we gradually stopped our own projects and concentrated on reseller sales. Then, the most profitable sales through those resellers started coming from larger system installations, with division of Fortune 500 companies. We began to concentrate our efforts on only those types of systems and resellers that could support them. Then we saw that our most profitable sales came from order processing companies. We stopped selling other types of accounting software and concentrated on companies with complex order-processing problems.

4. Whenever possible, we want to grow by subtraction. We became one of the Inc. 500 fastest growing companies in America not by doing more and more, but by doing less and less, at least in terms of our range of skills and customers. And we did it without any outside financing or borrowing money because we were always working at what was most profitable.

5. *We can direct existing activities to take advantage of new opportunities.* In making each of these transitions, we did not develop a new base of activities or skills. We simply make our knowledge deeper and narrowed our focus.

6. *We choose activities that decrease internal and external competition.* We ended up where we did, selling order-processing systems to sales-oriented divisions of large companies because there was less external competition for those projects and because they were consistent with the skill set in developing software.

5.4.1 Testing Value

Sun Tzu's five key methods on choosing actions to test for value.

"When you fall behind, you must catch up."
Sun Tzu, Art of War 7:1:11

"Simplicity and repose are the qualities that measure the true value of any work of art."
Frank Lloyd Wright,

General Principle: Choose the smallest action that tests the value of an opportunity.

Situation:

It is always a mistake to think that by spending more and more money, we can some how force an opportunity to produce the results that we want. Most of us realize that such an approach is simply throwing good money after bad. Only those expending other people's resources, i.e. those in government, can afford to continue programs that return little or no value to the investors.

Opportunity:

We cannot control the underlying, fundamental nature of an opportunity. The ultimate costs and benefits of controlling a given position are determined by the larger environment (3.2.1 Environmental Dominance). Our job is simply to choose the right positions. In improving our position, we therefore must seek to control what we can: our own expenditures. The more we minimize those expenditures, the more likely it is that a given move to a new position will be profitable (3.1.2 Strategic Profitability).

Key Methods:

Choosing the best activities must be constantly guided by the overarching and demanding economics of strategic profitability.

1. Our exploration of any opportunity must be designed as a test of our value assumptions. We pursue opportunities because we think they are likely to be valuable. We identify high probability opportunities by testing their surface characteristics from a distance. However, we cannot know the real value of that opportunity before exploring it directly. The principle of unpredictable value is the foundation of much strategy. Any assumptions we make about either the cost of benefits of a given opportunity are unproven. (3.1.5 Unpredictable Value).

2. We must limit our opportunity exploration to activities that directly determine whether or not an opportunity will pay. Doing less is better than doing more because doing less requires less investment. Fewer costs mathematically improve our likelihood of making a profitable move. At its root, all strategy is based on these simple economics (3.1 Strategic Economics).

3. If we can use cost-effective methods to explore opportunities, the more of them we can afford to explore. Since no given move is certain to be profitable, we must take a probabilistic approach, minimizing our failure and maximizing our successes. We limit our costs to focus our efforts on what really matters: making victory pay. In other words, we must find the shortest, simplest route possible to see if a given opportunity can pay for itself (1.8.4 Probabilistic Process).

4. Only a precious few opportunities we pursue will prove to be as beneficial as we hope. Even using the many strategic techniques for identifying high-probability opportunities, "high-probability" is a relative term. These opportunities are worth pursuing compared with what most people mistake for opportunities, but they are far from certain. Only by exploring many such opportunities do we make our success certain over time (4.0 Leveraging Probability).

5. All tests of value must gauge our mission against our methods. Our mission is what defines value. Our methods dictate our costs. In terms of costs,we always want to minimize our investment in exploring new territory. Small steps are not only safer but more powerful. However, smallness alone is not the measure for success. All exploration activities must identify the ways in which a new position can bring us closer to our goals (8.0 Winning Rewards).

Illustration:

For example, when I ran a software company, there were always many directions in which we could develop our software. We used Sun Tzu's techniques to identify which of those directions were best before we started a development project.

1. Our exploration of any opportunity must be designed as a test of our value assumptions. We would undertake only new development that we suspected that people would find valuable. Actually, we cheated a little. Most of our development projects were financed by customers so we knew that there was some value in the project.

2. We must limit our opportunity exploration to activities that directly determine whether or not an opportunity will pay. In designing that project, we asked ourselves only one question: what is the minimum product that we can sell? What is the minimum product for which a customer will pay?

3. If we can use cost-effective methods to explore opportunities, the more of them we can afford to explore. In our environment, we always saw the key limited resource as time to market. When we undertook speculative development products--those not funded by customers--we made sure that the people on the team understood the limits on risk. To make sure that newly developed product was the minimum product, we often set a deadline of three months to bring something to market. The team understood that if the product couldn't be passed off to sale in that span of time, it wouldn't get more time.

4. Only a precious few opportunities we pursue will prove to be as beneficial as we hope. Only the market, that is, the real world of our software customers, could tell us if we were on the right track or not. The sooner we could start asking people for money, the sooner we would know if we were on the right track or not. Many projects swallowed up our time, but they are forgotten. What we remember our successes because they became part of our position.

5. All tests of value must gauge our mission against our methods. No projects were approved unless they met the basic criteria of our mission: developing software that was modifiable-by-design, easily changed to adapt to a constantly changing environment.

5.4.2 Successful Mistakes

Six key methods regarding the advantages in learning from our mistakes.

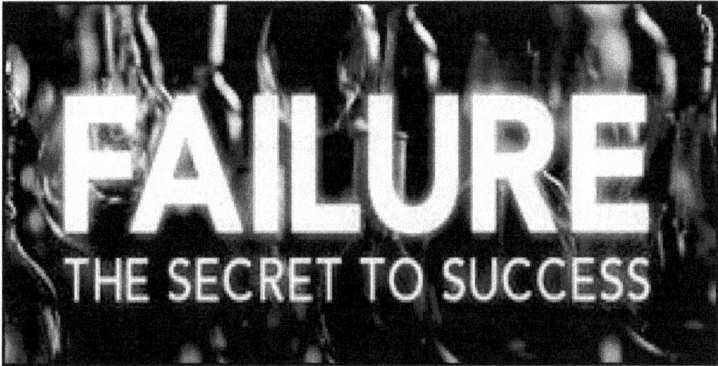

"You can be stopped and yet recover the initiative.
You must use your days and months correctly.
If you are defeated, you can recover.
You must use the four seasons correctly."
                    Sun Tzu's The Art of War 5:2:7-10

Your future takes precedence over your past. Focus on
your future, rather than on the past."
                    Gary Ryan Blair

"Some of the best lessons we ever learn are learned
from past mistakes. The error of the past is the wisdom
and success of the future."
                    Dale E. Turner

General Principle: Choose actions to secure benefits rather than to prove past decisions correct.

Situation:

We come to each choice of action based on our past choices. When we explore what looks like an opportunity, we are often going to be disappointed by our initial choices. The challenge arises from our reactions to that disappointment. There are two opposite mistakes that we can make. On one hand, we can throw good money after bad, increasing the size of our loss by simply expanding on our initial efforts. On the other hand, we can abandon a good opportunity by failing to follow up after a poor initial choice. The question is how we find the right balance of persistence.

Opportunity:

We come to each choice of action based on our past choices. When we explore what looks like an opportunity, we are often going to be disappointed by our initial choices. The challenge arises from our reactions to that disappointment. There are two opposite mistakes that we can make. On one hand, we can throw good money after bad, increasing the size of our loss by simply expanding on our initial efforts. On the other hand, we can abandon a good opportunity by failing to follow up after a poor initial choice. The question is how we find the right balance of persistence.

Key Methods:

The key methods for choosing the appropriate actions to learn from our mistakes are:

1. Avoid investing in any actions to prove past decisions correct. The error of "throwing good money after bad" in economics is called the problem of sunk costs , investing more on the basis of unrecoverable past expenditures. It arises because people are loss averse. We have a stronger desire to avoid known losses than to make unknown gains. Without training, we are naturally sucked into investing more and more in opportunities, even when their value has been disproven. When we are responsible for a decision, we will tend to invest more to support that decision, even when we are disappointed in the results (1976 Staw and Fox) because we desire to prove our first decision correct. We can never make choices based upon past actions but on their future potential (4.1 Future Potential).

2. Loss aversion makes sense in defending positions but not in advancing them. There is a great deal of scientific research devoted to mapping the nature of loss aversion. As always, we see this natural bias as appropriate in the right framework. The research shows that we become more optimistic about an outcome after we have invested in it (1968 Knox and Inkster). This means that the more we invest, the more optimistic we become. This works for us when we are developing an existing position that is producing value. It works against us when trying to establish a new position where the value is unproven (1.9 Competition and Production).

3. The best action is never simply more of the same. Einstein defined insanity as repeating the same action expecting a different result. Since we are taught to think of size as an advantage, we can easily fall into thinking that our failure requires simply doing more. This is a dangerous approach in competitive environments where so much is unknown. Even if we can overcome the barriers that we discover with more resources, by investing more we decrease any likelihood of an opportunity being worth what it costs. The more time and resources we waste trying to make our original approach work, the fewer resources we have to find success along another path. The most important casualty of investing on the basis of sunk costs is the cost of wasting our other opportunities at finding success. (5.4 Minimizing Action).

4. We must base future actions on the knowledge gained from failure. Every failure teaches us something about the boundaries of an opportunity and the barriers to exploiting it. The opening that defines an opportunity exists for a reason. Failure to exploit an opportunity tells us something about the nature of the opportunity. If we think of each move as an experiment, every action helps us because we learn more about the shape, size, and character of the opportunity. Because of the limits of information, we may know after a single action where the flaw lies, but we do know that there is a problem (4.5.2 Opportunity Barriers).

5. We persist only as long as the opportunity meets the test of being our high-probability opening. Our basis of choosing actions is always the same at every iteration of the adaptive loop: our probability of winning awards. After each failure, we measure what we have learned about the principles that define high-probability opportunities. If the opportunity still measures up as our best option, we must continue pursuing it (4.0 Leveraging Probability).

6. We must choose actions that explore more of the opportunity's boundaries. We must change our approach based upon what we have learned. Only by coming at an opportunity--AKA problem--from different angles do we learn its dimensions. If the opportunity is real, we will see progress in getting around the barriers that block the filling of an opportunity (4.5.2 Opportunity Barriers).

Illustration:

Let us look at the invention of the electric light bulb as an illustration of these principles. In that process, Thomas Alva Edison failed many times to find a filament that would work but continued on until he finally found a workable action. As Thomas Alva Edison said in his search for a good electric light filament, *"I have not failed. I've just found 1,000 ways that won't work."*

The difference between Edison's repeated experiments and throwing good money after bad is that after all, Edison had no assurances that a viable filament existed. After testing a thousand materials that didn't work, he found himself making progress. Some materials worked better than others and, over time, he was able to identify the characteristics of the ideal material. He learned the dimensions of the opportunity space through his failures and, over time, was able to find materials that brought him closer and closer to his goal. In doing this, we seek to verify that the opening is real and that the problems it poses have an economical solution.

1. Avoid investing in any actions to prove past decisions correct. Over his career, Edison abandoned scores of ideas that did not prove out. He persisted with the electric light because he knew the need was real and the technology was conceptually correct.

2. Loss aversion makes sense in defending positions but not in advancing them. Edison's part in the War of Currents between Edison's direct current-based systems and Westinghouse's alternating currents was based mostly on Edison's loss aversion, but both sides had established companies.

3. The best action is never simply more of the same. To create the electric light, Edison tried over 3,000 different approaches to solving the problem of creating a usable light.

4. We must base future actions on the knowledge gained from failure. As Thomas Alva Edison said in his search for a good electric light filament, *"I have not failed. I've just found 1,000 ways that won't work."*

5. We persist only as long as the opportunity meets the test of being our high-probability opening. Some materials worked better than others. Making an element glow to create light was never an issue. The utility of electric light over gas lighting was never an issue. The issue was always one of functional design, how bright and how long.the light lasted.

6. We must choose actions that explore more of the opportunity's boundaries. Over time, Edison was able to identify the characteristics of the ideal material. He learned the dimensions of the opportunity space through his failures and eventually was able to find a couple of different materials that produced both enough light and lasted (persisted?) for a long time.

5.5 Focused Power

Sun Tzu's five key methods about size consideration in safe experimentation.

> *"Where you focus, you unite your forces."*
>
> Sun Tzu's The Art of War 6:4:3

> *"Simplicity means the achievement of maximum effect with minimum means."*
>
> Dr. Koichi Kawana

General Principle: Small steps are more certain and powerful.

Situation:

We cannot be successful if we fail to understand the critical relationship between safety and power. Most people confuse size with power. Large efforts seem more powerful even when they entail taking greater risks. This gets the formula for power exactly backwards. Properly understood, small moves are not only safer but more powerful. We cannot confuse a small, concentrated action with a weak, half-hearted one. The problem is that many of us do not know how to concentrate our actions to create power and minimize risk simultaneously.

Opportunity:

Powerful actions are concentrated. The safest way to test the potential of new opportunities is also the most powerful. The easiest way to minimize our risks is to limit the size of our experiments. The easiest way to create powerful actions is to concentrate our efforts in size. The most powerful actions are small, local, and quick.

Key Methods:

The following key methods define how we create focused power.

1. Competitive power comes from focused, concentrated activity. Power comes from focus and unity. Since size works against focus and unity, it creates weakness. The most powerful moves are those that concentrate intense, united effort in a small area of space and time. Diffusing our concentration of effort in larger groups, areas, and time period makes it less likely we will be successful (1.7 Competitive Power).

2. The more people involved, the less likely the move will be profitable. Number of people is the first dimension for measuring activity size. People have to be coordinated to pursue an opportunity. The larger that effort, the more costly the action will be. Large groups are simply more difficult to work with in exploring new opportunities. Costs often grows logarithmically as more and more people get directly involved in the project (5.5.1 Force Size).

3. The greater the distance to be covered, the less likely the move will be profitable. Strategic distance is the second dimension measuring the size of an action. Long moves require more resources so they are less likely to be profitable. In using Warrior's Playbook, we measure distance both in physical space and mental space. This means "distance" also measures the amount of information to be learned to complete a move. A local move requires us to cover territory that we already know (5.5.2 Distance Limitations).

4. The greater the time it takes to get results, the less likely the move will be profitable. The feedback loop is the circulatory system of strategy. Without feedback, we have nothing. With sluggish feedback, we must spend more time going in a direction before finding if we are off course or not. One of the easiest ways to control costs is to set deadlines for exploration activities to produce results (5.5.3 Evaluation Deadlines).

5. All three dimensions of activity also affect speed. Larger forces are slower; longer distances take more time, and slower feedback loops are, well...slower. The time value of resources means that longer moves are more expensive and therefore less likely to be profitable. Smaller actions measured in these three dimensions are always better. One of the ways we do this is to gravitate toward actions that are the smallest possible steps in these three dimensions (5.3 Reaction Time).

Illustration:

Let us think about these lessons from the perspective of developing a new product. We will use SOSI's philosophy of developing strategic training games for download.

1. Competitive power comes from focused, concentrated activity. We initially develop our games as manual games with playing cards, boards, and pieces. They are developed as downloads PDFs where the users "manufacture" the game by printing it. This takes much less time than our manufacturing the game and, given current technology, than developing them as a computer game, even though we would prefer that form long-term.

2. The more people involved, the less likely the move will be profitable. Games, like books, are developed by one person. When we have tried to develop games in groups, it just leads to endless discussion instead of a product.

3. The greater the distance to be covered, the less likely the move will be profitable. There are a lot of principles in strategy. A game that teaches many of them would create a lot of distance in the game. Such a game would be difficult to design and to learn to play. We limit our games to teaching just a handful of strategic principles. This makes our games easier to learn. To further reduce the learning distance, our games are either based on existing games or designed to be self-explanatory.

4. The greater the time it takes to get results, the less likely the move will be profitable. We develop our initial versions around the idea that the game can be extended over time by the addition of new rules over time. This allows us to easily improve the game and extend its lesson content, based on the interest that we get from our customers.

5. All three dimensions of activity also affect speed. We should be able to upgrade existing games several times a year while adding new games. More importantly, as the games get more refined and popular, we can convert them into a digital form. Ideally as the technology for creating portable phone apps matures and prices come down.

5.5.1 Force Size

Sun Tzu's eight key methods about limiting the size of force in an advance.

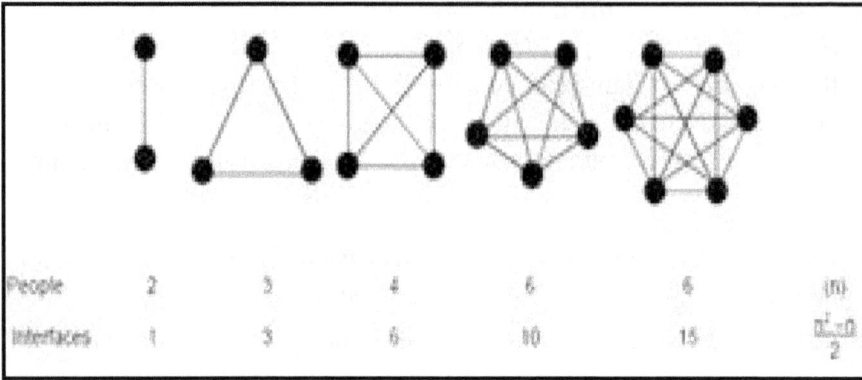

People	2	3	4	6	6	(n)
Interfaces	1	3	6	10	15	$\frac{n^2 - n}{2}$

"Using a huge army in battle success is very expensive. Long delays create a dull army and sharp defeats."
Sun Tzu The Art of War 2:1:12

"Force is all-conquering, but its victories are short-lived."
Abraham Lincoln

General Principle: To explore opportunities, choose actions that require a minimum of force.

Situation:

While there are competitive situations where we must use all of our resources to survive, choosing our actions for exploring opportunities is never one of them. Exploring new opportunities requires a minimum rather than maximum use of force. When we constantly invest too much in each opportunity, we soon find ourselves out of resources. Large forces take more time to organize and they always move slower since, to stay together, they are tied to the pace of their slowest component.

Opportunity:

We learn to separate the concept of "force" and "strength" from that of "power." Strategic power comes from unity and focus (1.7 Competitive Power). Strategic strength arises when we target an opposing weakness (3.5 Strength and Weakness). Both depend on leveraging the situation. Force, on the other hand, is simply using an abundance of resources to overpower a challenge or problem.

Key Methods:

These are the key methods defining the use of strategic force.

1. Competitive power comes from focused, concentrated activity. Po*Force is a matter of the size of effort.* When we talk about the size of a strategic force, we are talking about the size of the investment we make in a move. These investments are made in whatever resources are appropriate to the situation: manpower, money, reputation, relationships, emotion, and so on (3.3 Opportunity Resources).

2. Force is successful at too great a cost. This is based on the simple economics of opportunity. We use minimum force in exploring opportunities to reduce our costs. The bigger the investment we make, the more difficult it is for any opportunity to return more benefits than its costs (3.1 Strategic Economics).

3. The use of force limits the opportunities that we can explore. Our resources are always limited. The more force we use, the fewer opportunities we can afford to explore. Too much use of force eventually depletes the resources that we need to defend our existing position (3.1.1 Resource Limitations).

4. Even with force, most opportunities produce limited returns. We can hope each opportunity will provide a huge step forward, but we know that most will disappoint us. Most advances that we make in our position are small. Often all we gain from our efforts is a better picture of our situations (3.1.5 Unpredictable Value).

5. *The use of force alone often generates an escalation of opposing force.* This is Newton's Third Law: "To every action there is an equal and opposite reaction." In competitive situations, the use of force tends to create wars of attrition where both sides expend resources instead of leveraging strategy (2.3.1 Action and Reaction).

6. *Small advances can be profitable if we limit our use of force.* Each small advances can be profitable if we don't risk too much on any one of them. Over time, the accumulation of small advances dramatically improve our position over time. The small moves ideally put us in the right position at the right time to catch a major wave of climate change, but even if we are never that fortunate, our progress is constant and secure (3.1.2 Strategic Profitability).

7. *Amassing and using a large force take too much time.* The larger the force we use, the slower it takes us to respond to an opportunity. The more difficult it is to move that force, since all groups are limited by their slowest member. Since all opportunities are limited in time, the larger the force involved, the more likely the opportunity is to get away from us (3.1.6 Time Limitations).

8. *Even potentially large opportunities are better tested by small, exploratory forces.* These forces can gather information and discover the lay of the land much more quickly and efficiently than large forces. While we may need much more resources to fill a position, we have to remember that exploring a position is not the same as developing it. If an opportunity proves to have a very large potential, we will have time to increase the size of force. Ideally, we let the opportunity itself pay for its own development (8.2 Making Claims).

Illustration:

Using large forces is a lot like going "all in" in Texas Hold'em. Let's use that idea as our example.

1. Force is a matter of the size of effort. Going "all in" is the maximum effort, what Sun Tzu calls a "fight," that is, investing everything in the effort.

2. Force is successful at too great a cost. As they say, going "all in" works every time but the last one.

3. The use of force limits the opportunities that we can explore. If we use this tool all the time, it is just a matter of time until we run into a hand that beats us.

4. Even with force, most opportunities produce limited returns. All-In usually scares off opponents from calling when the pot is small, but then we can only win a small amount. When we eventually get unlucky and an opponent has a strong hand, possibly even the "nuts," we will almost always get called and likely lose everything for a usually small potential gain. The larger the pot-- and the more desperate the opponent--the more likely it is that we will be called. Even when we go into the All-In with a strong hand, often winning is simply a matter of luck, since in any given show-down, the odds can go against us. Eventually our straight will meet another flush.

5. The use of force alone often generates an escalation of opposing force. The more often a player uses the All-In, the more likely it is that he will get called because others will assume he is frequently bluffing.

6. Small advances can be profits if we limit our use of force. We do not have to go All-In to get other players to drop out. A series of small raises often looks more threatening because it seems to invite a call.

7. Amassing and using a large force take too much time. A large stack takes a great deal of time to accumulate but can be lost in a single moment with the "All-In". It takes even longer if we are gambling with our earnings in the normal business of the real world, outside of the poker table. y.

8. Even potentially large opportunities are better tested by small, exploratory forces. Since the rules of Hold-em eventually force an All-In, it is best to set up the All-in by a history of more conservative betting. Even within a given hand, the play works best after escalating from a series of smaller bets that test an opponent's resolve and build up potential winnings if the All-in forces the opponent out.

5.5.2 Distance Limitations

Sun Tzu's eight key methods on the use of short steps to reach distant goals.

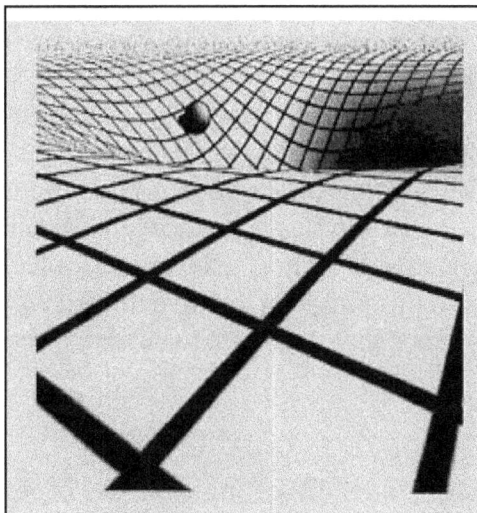

"Stay close to home to await the distant enemy."
Sun Tzu's The Art of War 7:5:13

"Whoever wants to reach a distant goal must take small steps."
Saul Bellow

General Principle: When exploring opportunities, choose actions that minimize the distance covered.

Situation:

The danger here is the romance of distance. The grass always seems greener somewhere else. The problem is that the further we travel, the bigger our investment in effort and time. The bigger our investment, the more costly it is for us to explore opportunities. The more costly exploration is, the less of it we can afford to do and the less we will profit in general from advancing our position.

Opportunity:

This principle of using short moves is based on the simple economics of exploring opportunities (3.1 Strategic Economics). To identify the best opportunities, we look for openings that are close to home (4.4 Strategic Distance). In choosing the best actions to explore any opportunity, we use our closeness to the situations to our advantage. This means picking actions that minimize both the physical distance (4.4.1 Physical Distance) and the intellectual distance (4.4.2 Intellectual Distance) that we must travel. If our move to a new position requires others to move toward us, we must also minimize the distance that they have to cover as well.

Key Methods:

These are the key methods defining the use of strategic force over distance.

1. Short steps are more powerful. This means we not only look for opportunities that are nearby, but we also move toward those opportunities by the shortest possible <u>open</u> route. The longer the route we choose, the more chances there are that we will encounter unforeseen problems. The ideal moves forward are always local ones. We must learn to prefer opportunities that are physically close to where we are now and intellectually close to what we already know (<u>4.4 Strategic Distance</u>).

2. We also want to shorten the distance our supporters must cover. While we tend to talk about exploring opportunities in terms of how far we must go, it is always the reaction of others that determines our success or failure. If we want the support of others, we must find ways to shorten their route, making it easier for them to do so. The closer we can get to them, the easier it is for them to support us (<u>2.3.1 Action and Reaction</u>).

3. Minimizing distance means simplifying our moves. In terms of testing the ground for value, simple tests are always better than more complicated ones. They are easier to execute and their results are easier to understand. While it is true that there are no shortcuts to success, we should always be looking for shortcuts when it comes to exploring opportunities. It is easier to test ground that we mostly understand rather than ground that is more foreign to us. (5.4.1 Testing Value).

4. The shortest route is that most in line with our current mission. Our mission sets the direction. While conditions and the nature of the ground can make a detour the shortest route, our mission is the compass that guides us (1.6 Mission Values)

5. The shortest route follows the dominant trends of climate. Change can bring the future to us so that we don't have to go to it. Having the wind at our backs makes every journey shorter ((1.4.1 Climate Shift).

6. The shortest route goes around obvious barriers. Going around barriers is usually easier than going over them. We do not want to fight gravity any more than we want to fight the wind (4.5.2 Opportunity Barriers).

7. The shortest route demands decisions that are easier to make. If a decision is difficult to make the problem is knowledge and information. Difficult decisions are a clear sign of intellectual distance (1.5.1 Command Leadership).

8. The shortest route utlizes skills that we already have. This is the methods aspect of intellectual distance. The more skills we must master or the more systems we must develop, the longer and less favorable the route (4.4.2 Intellectual Distance)

Illustration:

Let us explain these principles using the illustration of developing a new product.

1. Short steps are more powerful. A small simple product is better than a large complex one.

2. We also want to shorten the distance our supporters must cover. An inexpensive, easy-to-buy, and easy to use product is better than an expensive and difficult one.

3. Minimizing distance means simplifying our moves. Before developing a more sophisticated version, we should create a simpler prototype.

4. The shortest route is that most in line with our current mission. Make sure that the product unifies and focuses the business rather than spreading it out.

5. The shortest route follows the dominant trends of climate. The product should utilize popular technologies and relate to what is new and exciting.

6. The shortest route goes around obvious barriers. If there are obvious difficulties implementing a given feature, find an alternative feature that addresses the problem in a different way.

7. The shortest route demands decisions that are easier to make. If it is difficult to choose one feature at the expense of another, compromise.

8. The shortest route utilizes skills that we already have. We develop for existing "off-the-shelf" assembly and distribution methods rather than ones that have to be developed from scratch.

5.5.3 Evaluation Deadlines

Sun Tzu's six key methods for setting deadlines for evaluating progress.

Each day passes quickly.
A month can decide your failure or success.

Sun Tzu's The Art of War 6:8:14-15

"A goal is a dream with a deadline."

Napoleon Hill

General Principle: When exploring opportunities, set the quickest possible deadlines for evaluating progress.

Situation:

While small amounts of force and moving short distances can save time, saving time alone is not our goal. Using a small amount of force and moving short distances has advantages in safety and power, but such moves can be too small to have any effect. A move can have so little force that it creates no results. A move can cover so little distance that we do not gain any new perspective on an opportunity. In choosing actions to take advantage of an opportunity, we can waste time both by doing too much and by doing too little.

Opportunity:

Setting deadlines for evaluation is a powerful tool for focusing the power of our competitive moves. When pursuing opportunities, we must choose actions that can be evaluated quickly. The key to success is getting feedback (1.8.3 Cycle Time). Using the smallest amount of force is quicker than assembling and organizing large ones. The smaller our forces the quicker they move but the action uses time effectively only when it gets feedback (5.5.1 Force Size). The closer our target, the sooner the move is completed but completing a move means getting actionable information (5.5.2 Distance Limitations). This means that we choose actions that have a stopping point for evaluation.

Key Methods:

The following key methods describe the value of an aggressive approach to setting deadlines.

1. Since each action has an end, it allows us to set a deadline for its completion. Taking an action on an opportunity is a discrete, time-limited event. Unlike analysis and observation, which are continuous processes, each competitive move to explore an opportunity should have a beginning, middle, and an end. To act on an opportunity, we have to physically do something, not just think about doing something. (5.4 Minimizing Action).

2. An evaluation deadline isn't the end of exploration, but a stopping point for evaluating our progress. In picking the right ways to The faster that we can get feedback about our success or failure in exploring an opportunity, the more successful we will be over time. Exploration is best performed in a series of stages, where each stage justifies the next (5.2 Opportunity Exploration).

3. We choose actions that can be executed rapidly and evaluated quickly so we can adapt to what we learn. This learning allows us to better explore an opportunity. This rule is the practical implementation of the principles teaching the importance of fast reaction times, speed, quickness, and short cycle times in executing strategy (5.3 Reaction Time).

4. Deadlines not only help us keep in touch with our environment, they often improve our performance. The most successful actions in competitive environments are those which we begin immediately and complete quickly. The more time we take, the less likely we are to be successful. Unlike production, where adding time can improve control and quality, competition never benefits from slowing down the process. They specifically help us avoid project creep where we get caught up in the infinite loops that are so common in competitive environments (2.3.5 Infinite Loops).

5. Setting aggressive deadlines forces us to learn the maximum pace of our environment. As we discussed in predicting the duration of opportunity windows, different environments work at different paces. An aggressive deadline is one that is unusually short for the environment in which we work, but not so short that results are impossible given the pace of the environment (5.3.2 Opportunity Windows).

6. Wildly optimistic deadlines are better for choosing actions than more practical ones. When we first started setting deadlines in a new competitive arena, our expectations for seeing results will often prove to be wildly optimistic given the pace of the environment. Though we may initially miss most deadlines in terms of getting feedback from our environment, through the practice of setting them, we eventually learn how to take action that gets the fastest possible feedback. The practice of setting deadlines is itself an adaptive loop where we learn how to do it better and better over time. One of the reasons we stay close to home is so we can learn realistic feedback times (1.8.2 The Adaptive Loop).

Illustration:

Let us use examples from businesses in which I have personally worked, the software industry, publishing, and developing on-line content.

1. Since each action has an end, it allows us to set a deadline for its completion. Developing a software product, writing and publishing a book, and creating on-line content are all discrete events for which we can set deadlines.

2. An evaluation deadline isn't the end of exploration, but a stopping point for evaluating our progress. Software has multiple versions, books multiple editions, and web content is continually updated. Within each of these processes, there are a series of smaller deadlines where we can evaluate progress.

3. We choose actions that can be executed rapidly and evaluated quickly so we can adapt to what we learn. We can only know how well a software product, a book, or web contents will be received by releasing it. But we can judge how easily more complicated products such as software or books are coming together at earlier stages. If a software product or a book runs into problems, we want to learn it as soon as possible.

4. Deadlines not only help us keep in touch with our environment, they often improve our performance. Software development is especially prone to mission creep because there are an infinite number of features that might be valuable, but writers can also suffer writer's block. The best cure for such blocks is the need to get something out at a given deadline.

*5. Setting aggressive deadlines forces us to learn the maximum pace of our environment. T*here is a huge difference between the pace in the software industry and the pace in the book publishing business. In software, we could release new products whenever we wanted, coming up with new ideas and selling them as soon as we could put together a demonstration to see if they were financially viable. However, in the book publishing business, the major book chains require six months notice and it usually requires a year of cycle time to get real feedback to learn how well a book is selling. Of course, the web-environment is both faster, because we can bring out new content continuously, but also it is more patient, since old material is always new to those who are just discovering it.

6. Wildly optimistic deadlines are better for choosing actions than more practical ones. In software development, our standard for new products was three months from assigning a developer (usually only one) to a version our salespeople could demonstrate. In books, our standard deadline from start to sending to the printer was less than ten weeks, even though the releases were planned a year ahead of time. In web content, we have committed to producing new Principle a Day articles every day and new game download products every month.

5.6 Defensive Advances

Sun Tzu's six key methods on balancing defending and advancing positions.

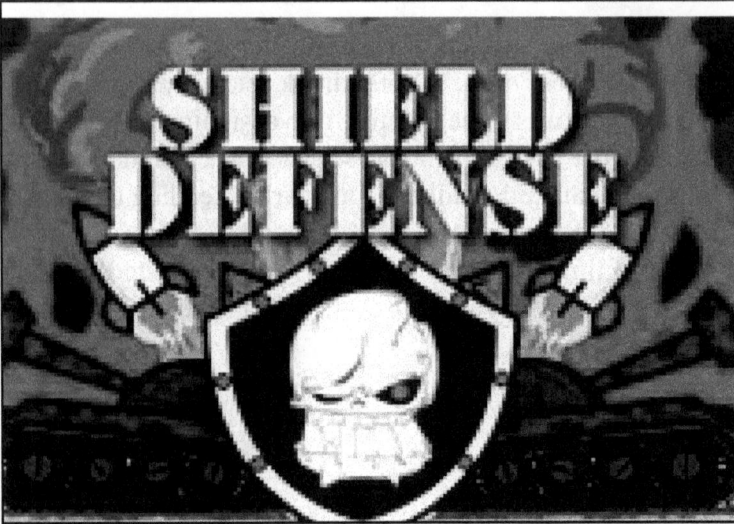

"Defend when you have insufficient strength.
Attack when you have a surplus of strength."
Sun Tzu's The Art of War 4:2:5-6

"The best defense is a good offense."
Carl von Clausewitz

General Principle: Defend on the basis of weaknesses, advance on strength, and do both when possible.

Situation:

It is commonly said that the best defense is a good offense, but this idea can easily be misunderstood. Defense means protecting our ability to exploit our position. It is the opposite of offense, which means exploring new opportunities for advancing our position. If we are always exploring opportunities and never exploiting them, we get no advantage from exploration. We can get into serious trouble when we do not clearly understand how defending positions relates to advancing them.

Opportunity:

Before committing to an action to explore an opportunity, we must balance defense against advance. We usually defend out of weakness and advance out of strength, with defense having the priority. The best actions, however, can sometimes do both at once. Our opportunity is to clearly connect exploring new positions with exploiting our existing position.

Key Methods:

The following key methods describe how we balance defending and advancing positions and how we can occasionally do both at once.

1. Exploiting an existing position requires defending that position. All our resources come from our existing position. If we lose any part of our position, we have fewer resources, making it more difficult to find opportunities to advance. Defense requires a special set of skills. Those skills start with recognizing our vulnerabilities and knowing how to defend them (9.0 Understanding Vulnerability).

2. The balance between defense and advance depends on the stability of our current position. Correctly understood, all advances are somewhat defensive because our existing position is only temporary, naturally decaying over time. We must therefore advance our position at some point in order to keep it from getting worse over time. Normally, most positions are fairly stable, decaying slowly, allowing us plenty of time to advance our position. However, when our current position is collapsing due to environmental conditions beyond our control, we must divert resources from defense to advance (1.1.1 Position Dynamics).

3. We normally defend existing positions based on our weaknesses. If we have vulnerabilities, our resources must first be spent creating a defense. If we leave others no openings, they are discouraged from attacking us and defending our existing position is easy. However, openings are a matter of opinion as well as fact. If people perceive openings, we can be attacked even if that perception is unjustified. If we leave openings undefended, real or imaginary, an attack by others is inevitable. Our first responsibility is therefore always to shore up our vulnerabilities (5.6.1 Defense Priority).

4. We must avoid actions exploring opportunities that expose our weaknesses. We gain credibility by our incumbency, that is, by our holding our current position. People assume that we have our position for good reasons, even without knowing us. We can maintain their good opinion if we don't violate this assumption. When we pursue opportunities with actions that highlight our weaknesses, we call our current position into question, making it more vulnerable instead of less so (1.2 Subobjective Positions).

5. We advance by choosing actions that emphasize our strengths. Opportunities are openings that we can fill, needs we can satisfy, and weaknesses that are complemented by our strengths. The excess resources that we use to pursue opportunities are an excess of strength. We cannot win a better position unless we demonstrate our abilities. We can only do this by pursuing opportunities in a way that highlight our strengths. Any demonstration of strength improves an existing position by justifying people's confidence in us (3.4.2 Opportunity Fit).

6. The gap between reality and perception allows us to both defend and advance positions at the same time. Though we defend on the basis of weakness and advance on the basis of strength, we can accomplish both at once when people perceive a weakness where there is really strength. By choosing activities that defy people's expectations, we both strengthen our existing position while advancing it. The best actions for pursuing opportunities are those that utilize resources that others did not realize we had (3.6 Leveraging Subjectivity , 5.4 Minimizing Action).

Illustration:

Let us look at these principles using the simple illustration of defending and advancing a job position.

1. Exploiting an existing position requires defending that position. We cannot get a promotion if people do not think we are doing a good job at our current position.

2. The balance between defense and advance depends on the stability of our current position. If our current employer is failing, we have to use our current position to find a new position with a different employer.

3. We normally defend existing positions based on our weaknesses. If we want to bolster up our current position, we must focus on erasing the doubts that people have about our abilities.

4. We must avoid actions exploring opportunities that expose our weaknesses. If we look for a change of position within a company because we are failing at our current job, we further undermine our existing position.

5. We advance by choosing actions that emphasize our strengths. Normally, we look to expand our responsibilities and authority in areas where we have had success.

6. The gap between reality and perception allows us to both defend and advance positions at the same time. If our employers have made bad judgments about our capabilities in a given area, we should dispel those opinions by seeking a promotion based upon our strengths in those areas of presumed weakness. We use the opportunity to make our case and extol our virtues that others are missing. Even if we do not win the new position, we shore up the vulnerabilities affecting our current position.

5.6.1 Defense Priority

Seven key methods regarding why defense has first claim on our resources.

"You can divide the ground and yet defend it.
Don't give the enemy anything to win."
Sun Tzu's The Art of War 6:3:14-15

"First, do no harm. (Primum nil nocere.)"
Auguste François Chomel

General Principle: Choose only actions that strengthen rather than risk a current position.

Situation:

We explore opportunities to identify how to advance our position. These explorations are experiments. We never know if they will work or not. To experiment safely, we must always consider the effect of our actions on our current position. The problem is that certain types of actions are incompatible with certain types of positions. We endanger our position when we take actions without considering their effect on our position.

Opportunity:

The basis of all opportunity is in preserving existing positions until our advances are successful (1.1.2 Defending Positions). In attempting to advance our position, we change it, even if we are merely extending our existing position in a small way. This is true whether the transition is successfully or not. Any move temporarily decreases our resources so we cannot move when we don't have resources needed for defense (3.3 Opportunity Resources). We avoid danger by putting our first priority on defense, foreseeing any actions potentially deleterious effects on our existing position.

Key Methods:

The key methods describing the logic and method for putting defense first are as follows.

1. Every position has weaknesses. We must choose actions that ideally alleviate those weaknesses rather than exacerbate them. We pick actions that leverage our current strengths. Indeed, our strengths cannot help but create weaknesses because strength and weakness are complementary opposites, two sides of the same underlying condition (3.5 Strength and Weakness). Going back to our rock climbing example, we must pick new holds that make our existing hold stronger. We must *never* try for new untested holds that pull us away from our current position.

2. Weakness is not the same as vulnerability. Simply because we have weaknesses doesn't mean that our existing position is vulnerable to attack. A vulnerability is an opening that allows opponent can undermine a key resources of our position. Vulnerabilities arise when we leave key resources needed to maintain our position undefended (9.0 Understanding Vulnerability).

3. *Actions pursuing opportunities should never create key vulnerabilities.* This means that they should never endanger the five key points of vulnerability--personnel, short and long-term resources, transportation/communication, and organization. Before committing to any action, we must make sure that we are not opening these five areas to attack (9.2 Points of Vulnerability).

4. *Actions pursuing opportunities should never move against the form of our current position.* While we normally use "form" as a way of evaluating potential opportunities, we must also consider the form of our current position. We should not choose actions that violate the gravity, current, and stability of our current position (4.3 Opportunity Forms).

5. *Actions pursuing opportunities must not over-extend our position's area.* There is a point at which a position becomes too spread-out to defend. Before pursuing some opportunities, we must eliminate other areas of activity to prevent this (4.6.1 Spread-Out Conditions).

6. *Actions pursuing opportunities must not erode barriers protecting our position.* If our actions damage some of the barriers of entry currently protecting our position, we should not undertake them. We must find actions that protect the existing barriers that protect us (4.6.4 Wide-Open Conditions).

7. *Actions pursuing opportunities must consider our current position's holding power.* There is a reason why Sun Tzu described the characteristics of holding power as dangers. Moving from a fixed position means that we are giving up a local peak position, which is seldom a good decision. Moves from sensitive position are risky because they mean giving up our existing position and not returning to it (4.6.5 Fixed Conditions , 4.6.6 Sensitive Conditions).

Illustration:

We can compare advancing a position to rock climbing. We move up one hold at a time. We must use our current position to support our weight while we find a new hold that will support us. We transfer gradually from an existing hold to the new one. We reach out and test several holds to find the one that works best.

1. Every position has weaknesses. In climbing a mountain, we cannot stay in any position forever. We must move up or down.

2. Weakness is not the same as vulnerability. Just because each hold is temporary, it doesn't mean that it is a weak hold. It cannot give way too soon.

3. Actions pursuing opportunities should never create key vulnerabilities. We must pick new holds that make our existing hold stronger. We must *never* try for new untested holds that pull us away from our current position.

4. Actions pursuing opportunities should never move against the form of our current position. If the angle of our existing position utilizes gravity, it holds us down. We cannot choose a new hold with an angle that pulls us away from that downward pressure.

5. Actions pursuing opportunities must not over-extend our position's area. Our arms and legs can only reach so far. Overreaching, using holds that are too far apart makes us weaker and can easily get us stuck or dislodged.

6. Actions pursuing opportunities must not erode barriers protecting our position's area. If a outcropping is blocking the wind, we do not want to take a hold that suddenly exposes us to it.

7. Actions pursuing opportunities must consider our current position's holding power. If we have to jump to a new hold, we must be absolutely, positively certain that it will take our weight.

5.6.2 Acting Now

Sun Tzu's eight key methods on acting on opportunities immediately.

"You must know the time of battle."

Sun Tzu's The Art of War 6:6:2

"So never lose an opportunity of urging a practical beginning, however small, for it is wonderful how often in such matters the mustard-seed germinates and roots itself."

Florence Nightingale

"Procrastination is the fear of success. People procrastinate because they are afraid of the success that they know will result if they move ahead now. Because success is heavy, carries a responsibility with it, it is *much easier to procrastinate and live on the 'someday I'll' philosophy."*

Denis Waitley

"Procrastination is, hands down, our favorite form of self-sabotage."

Alyce P. Cornyn-Selby

General Principle: Given an opportunity, excess resources, and a viable action, we must act immediately to explore opportunities.

Situation:

Though there are many principles for choosing the best action, we must internalize those principles so that our decision for action can become automatic and instantaneous. This may seem impossible because there are such a large number of interconnected principles that guide us to choose both the best opportunities to pursue and the best action to pursue them. The reason that most of us are not more successful is simply because we don't have the right mental models and that lack creates a commonplace failure to act on our opportunities.

Opportunity:

Though we can describe the principles of strategy in a list of principles, these principles are not a to-do list, but a description of a series of related mental models. We train our instincts to instantly gravitate toward the best possible actions so we can take immediate action. Our mental models work on a subconscious level to process a complex array of conditions that defy the linear reasoning that we have been taught to use consciously. Our goal is not choosing a perfect action eventually but a viable action instantly. Our instant actions are seldom brilliant, exciting, or impressive. They usually seem insignificant and dull. What makes this series of little, small actions so powerful is our insistence on doing them now so that their effects accumulate quickly over time.

Key Methods:

To master the habit and power of acting instantly, we must master the following:

1. We must develop a prejudice toward taking immediate action to explore opportunities. Immediate actions requires only three ingredients 1) any opportunity, any opening, no matter how small 2) excess resources of time, money, etc., 3) any small action that tests that opportunity with those resources. When the three ingredients are present, our instinctual response should be to use them (4.0 Leveraging Probability).

2. We must internalize the mental models for choosing opportunities and actions. This means that we must practice them until they become second nature. Though there are many different principles, these mental models describe a few underlying related concepts from a variety of perspectives. We link principles to each other to train minds in the general concepts rather than specifics of terminology or condition (2.2.2 Mental Models).

3. As long as an action does not damage our existing position, we should try it. If it *does* damage our current position, we should reject it so we can come to an action that doesn't hurt our position *(*5.6.1 Defense Priority).

4. A single action will not likely make a difference, but a pattern of action will. The chances are that any one action won't seem to make a huge difference in our lives, at least not at first. Exploration takes time. Most of these actions will amount to little or nothing. However, over time, if we are constantly exploring opportunities, we cannot help but be successful. Patterns of success breed more successes while patterns of failure to act breed more failures. If we continue to act on them, we will continually find new opportunities to advance our position in small ways until we end up making huge progress (5.2 Opportunity Exploration).

5. Choosing small actions make acting now much easier. The best action is *never* a major commitment of effort. By definition, it is small, local, and quick. We do not make instant decisions about undertaking campaigns to get around barriers but about the small focused efforts that work best in pursuing windows of opportunity (5.5 Focused Power).

6. We cannot act now if we are constantly executing plans or distracted by new events. We don't work on our opportunities because we get locked into plans and because we are distracted by events that have nothing to do with our goals. We do what we had planned to do instead of what we should be doing. Instead of focusing on simple actions to explore simple opportunities, we diffuse our efforts in dozens of different directions (5.2.1 Choosing Adaptability).

7. In delaying action, even for a day or an hour, windows of opportunities will close. Conditions will change. Others will take advantages before we do, closing the opening. Our information gets outdated (5.3.2 Opportunity Windows).

8. Given the proper ingredients for action, acting now will be successful more often than delay. We must practice to improve our reaction time. If we do develop a prejudice for action, we will develop a reputation for speed and quickness. We will impress our supporters and discourage our adversaries (5.3 Reaction Time).

Illustration:

Let us use an illustration from an area we don't often address, the strategy of making a purchase in a hot market, in this example, purchasing a new house in the hot retail market of a decade ago. This illustration comes from a real-life mistake.

1. We must develop a prejudice toward taking immediate action to explore opportunities. If after exploring the market, we find a house that meets our complex criteria at a great price, we must buy it, even if it isn't perfect.

2. We must internalize the mental models for choosing opportunities and actions. We will know the right house when we see it. We will feel it in our gut. We must not let our conscious mind's reasonable doubts prevent us from acting when time is critical.

3. As long as an action does not damage our existing position, we should try it. Any house that seems like a great deal will almost certainly be better than our current house.

4. A single action will not likely make a difference, but a pattern of action will. After rejecting a very good house at a great opportunity, we will likely reject future houses because they are not as good.

5. Choosing small actions make acting now much easier. Though there is not small action in buying a house, it starts with simply signing an agreement and risking a deposit.

6. We cannot act now if we are constantly executing plans or distracted by new events. We may have planned to look at twenty different houses before making a purchase, but if we find the right house within the first five, we have a problem. In our case, the third house was the best that we have found in all the years of looking since.

7. In delaying action, even for a day or an hour, windows of opportunities will close. If we wait, maybe even for a day, a good house at a great price will certainly be sold.

8. Given the proper ingredients for action, acting now will be successful more often than delay. We still live in the same house that we bought twenty-five years ago because we didn't act immediately when we found a great house to move to fifteen years ago.

Sun Tzu's Playbook

Volume 6:
Situations

About Responding to Situations

Competitive environments are uncertain. Competitors will always do something unexpected. Successful strategies must constantly adjust to these unpredictable conditions. Fortunately, the science of strategy lays out the most common ways situations change and how you should adjust your responses to them. This is the focus of this volume of Sun Tzu's Playbook.

We cannot completely understand any competitive situation. This is the information problem at the heart of all competition. The goal therefore is simply to understand the changing situation better than your competitors do. You can then use the dynamics of situations to control your opponents' behavior. This requires understanding the principles for identifying and reacting appropriately to changing conditions.

The Power of Choice

When you explore an opportunity, you cannot know what exact conditions you will encounter. Not only that, but those conditions will change as your venture continues toward its goal. Progress itself forces changes in the situation. A competitive campaign is like driving. You know where you want to go, but you have to deal with a wide variety of traffic conditions on the way. You constantly adjust the way you drive to accommodate the traffic you encounter.

You cannot succeed in pursuing any opportunity unless you can surmount the challenges you meet along the way. Consistent progress requires different types of adjustments. Every situation offers challenges, but you can always find a good response if you understand the deeper nature of those challenges and the general approach it requires. This knowledge allows you to react quickly to changing conditions.

Competitive situations may not follow a plan, but they do follow a pattern. The principles in this volume teach us that pattern. In each evolving situation, a different response is required. These key methods teach you those responses. Sometimes the right response is speed. Sometimes it is cooperation. Sometimes it is an act of desperation. You use the key methods in this volume to correctly diagnose the situation. This enables you to know generally how to respond. Adapting to situations in the appropriate way is the key to success.

The Nine Common Stages

This volume introduces you to nine predictable situations or stages that arise naturally in a competitive campaign. These situations can be described as early, middle, or late stages. Early on, you run into dissipating, easy, and contentious situations. Later on, you run into open, shared, and serious situations. Toward the end of a campaign, conditions become more challenging leading to difficult, limited, and, finally, desperate situations.

This volume, the principles for identifying each of this nine situations are explained in detail, but let us define these stages generally here to provide you some perspective:

- Before a campaign starts, you have to defend against outside threats and criticism. This is the dissipating stage.
- When you begin a new campaign, the idea can seem novel and exciting. This is the easy stage.
- When you start to see some success, competitors and rivals can want to take it from you. This is the contentious stage.
- When you can make progress while competitors are also finding their way, this is the open stage.
- Over time, you can discover that good partnerships are needed to support your position. This is the shared stage.

- As the project makes progress but without paying, critics can start sniping at your back. This is the serious stage.
- As time passes, you can run into unforeseeable barriers to making progress. This is the difficult stage.
- When a campaign is close to success, you can come to a key transition point. This is the limited stage.
- In the end, your success may require you to quickly commit all your resources. This is the final desperate stage.

There is nothing new in any of these situations. They have occurred a million times in competition, but every situation will not occur in every campaign. You cannot predict if or when they will occur.

Every change is a new opportunity to make the right decision. If you run into a problem at the beginning of a campaign, you can still succeed in the end. If you are challenged at the end, you will succeed if you started out on the best possible way. If you are threatened in the middle of a campaign, you succeed by starting well and finishing strong.

Adapting to Change Instantly

At each of the nine situations or stages covered in this volume, the general response is fairly simple but there are detailed key methods for executing each response. Again, to give you some context, we list those responses generally here.

- You avoid the dissipating stage by distracting critics by attacking them instead of defending yourself.
- During the easy stage, you cannot be satisfied with what is accomplished easily and work as hard as you can.
- During the contentious stage, you avoid getting into battles, and avoid competitors as much as possible.
- In the open stage, you keep up with your competitors and copy whatever they do.

- In the shared stage, you form partnerships, even with competitors.
- In the serious stage, you focus on generating rewards any way you can, even if only for the short term.
- In the difficult stage, you keep going, no matter how slow your progress becomes.
- In the limited stage, you must do the unexpected. You must get creative and unpredictable.
- In the desperate stage, you bring all your resources to bear as quickly as possible.

The faster you recognize and respond to these situations, the more certain your success becomes. You must respond to these situations automatically. This is only possible through drills and training. You want to act on instinct.. If you over-think these situations, you may question your judgment. This delays your response in a situation where you must act. The secret to success is making the right decisions quickly. The longer you delay, the less likely success becomes.

Controlling Expectations

To lead people, you must welcome challenges discussed in this volume. If you follow these rule, they give you an opportunity to show your abilities and win the confidence and support of others. People come together when they are threatened. This is a part of sharing a mission. People work together when they are in the same boat during a storm. When people share adversity, one person rescues the other just as naturally as the right hand helps the left.

This part of Sun Tzu's Playbook teaches us instant decision-making as the basis of confident leadership. You must recognize and explain the conditions you are in. You must know how to use each stage correctly. If you demonstrate that you know exactly what you are doing, you make it impossible for people not to trust you.

As a campaign continues, you must prepare people for situations becoming more difficult. Many of the principles in this volume cover the worst-case scenarios. A new position can stabilize and start producing rewards at any point in a campaign. If it does, great, but you need to prepare others for what may happen if it does not. When campaigns go perfectly, the situation takes care of itself. When they don't, you must take care of the situation. Few campaigns go perfectly from beginning to end.

Each stage of a campaign requires the appropriate reaction from others. Again, there are a lot of detailed key methods for preparing the expectations of others, but below we offer a general outline:

- To succeed in the dissipating stage, you need the commitment of others before a project begins.
- In the easy stage, you must let others know that you plan to go as far and as fast as you can. In the contentious stage, you use others to create obstacles for your competitors.
- In the open stage, you must get people to focus on your business, not your competitors.
- In the shared stage, you must get others to join you as partners.
- In the serious stage, you need to generate income from people in any way you can.
- In the difficult stage, you must give everyone a sense that you will not be discouraged.
- In the limited stage, you must make sure that your competitors do not know that you are vulnerable.
- In the desperate stage, you must prove yourself by putting an end to the crisis.

Your general goal in each situation is to make other people feel like they are winners for working with you. If you show them that you can respond to both blessings and difficulties, they will follow you. People will have no choice but to give you all they have. This is how you win their commitment.

Leverage Your Values

Your core mission acts as a stabilizing force as your new campaign passes through different stages and take you into different markets. The shared values defined by your mission unite you with others and give you strength. You must know to utilize this mission as you adapt to unexpected changes.

Your values cannot be just words and ideas. They must be part of the tangible value in your efforts. People must be proud of the value it puts in their products, services, and standards. If you use people's pride correctly, you will always beat the competition. Honesty and directness will always lend an advantage to your campaign. Your strength is built on trust and dependability.

Know When to Pause

Sun Tzu's Rulebook emphasizes that advancing a position requires resources. In any situation, you must have the resources to respond correctly. If you run low on resources, a response is impossible. This means you must know when to pause in an advance.

All people and organizations have temporary limits that restrict what they can do to meet their goals. You do not test these limitations. Leave yourself plenty of room for error. Give your ventures a margin of safety. You want to force your competitors to their limits. You must know and respect your own limitations. Your competitors can ignore their limitations. There is no need for you to make the same mistake.

Making great progress takes you into unknown areas. You don't want progress to trip you up. Problems can hide in the shadows of your business. A successful fashion can quickly become a worn-out fad. Your success can lead to confusion. You may not see that you are going against the changing trends. The confusion of markets can always surprise you. You must pause to reanalyze your market position. You never want to be surprised.

When your resources are stretched to the limit, you must develop more resources or do less . You must increase the size of your resources over time. To grow, you need to hold onto your current position and develop its resources. You shift from a competitive focus to a productive one.

6.0.0 Situation Response

Sun Tzu's eight key methods on selecting the actions most appropriate to a situation.

"You must develop these instant reflexes."
Sun Tzu's The Art of War 11:3:3

"When a warrior learns to stop the internal dialogue, everything becomes possible; the most far-fetched schemes become attainable. "
Carlos Castaneda

General Principle: We must drill ourselves to instantly recognize and respond to situations automatically.

Situation:

When we move to pursue an opportunity, we cross a critical threshold from simple decision-making to executing decisions. Sun Tzu called this movement "armed march" but we understand it more broadly as a competitive move or action. To pursue an opportunity, we must move into a region outside of our control. Once outside of controlled areas, we must respond instantly to the situations that we encounter. As important as reaction time is quickly deciding how to pursue opportunities, it is many times more important in responding to the immediate situations in which we find ourselves. Our range of potential actions collapses because the situation limits our options. If we don't know the best responses to these situations, we are going to get into serious trouble.

Opportunity:

Starting this new section, we move our discussion to the Move skills of Sun Tzu's Progress Cycle (1.8 Progress Cycle). Aim skills choose the highest probability opportunities (4.0 Leveraging Probability) and the best actions to explore them (5.0 Minimizing Mistakes). Move skills execute our aim decisions. Sun Tzu described in detail how they do this through situations response. These responses are required by situations that arise in the course of our move. There are nine classes of competitive situations that we encounter. Each of these classes has one best response. It gets even easier. While any of these classes of situations can arise in any move, they are most commonly found at certain stages of a competitive campaign.

Key Methods:

The following key methods guide the way that we respond to situation.

1. We must train ourselves to instantly recognize our situation. At this stage, the emphasis shifts from thought to action, from decision to execution. Our actions in a competitive environment are not executed like the steps in a plan. The job of making good strategic decisions gets more intense and demanding. We get information more quickly and we have to respond to it much more quickly as well (6.1 Situation Recognition).

2. We must also distinguish between simple moves and moves as a part of a larger campaign. A *campaign* describes longer term changes in position that consists of a sequence of moves. Campaigns are executed in smaller actions since smaller steps are more powerful. Within a campaign, we can recognize situations more easily because campaigns and the situations within them develop in a predictable, logical way (6.2 Campaigns).

3. Campaigns usually go through three stages. Each stage reveals more about the nature of the opportunity and has certain implications as far as creating situations. Understanding the stage of our campaign helps us better recognize the situation in which we find ourselves. Campaigns have beginning, middle, and end stages. Situations in each stage proceed logically from the nature of that stage (6.3 Campaign Patterns).

4. We must instantly separate competitive situations into one of the nine common classes. While every competitive situation has its unique characteristics, most fall into one of these nine categories. These nine situation classes are defined by differences in: 1) the true nature of the opportunity, 2) our position versus that of potential rivals, and 3) the depth of our commitment to the move (6.4 Nine Situations).

5. Once we recognize a situation, we must immediately know the one and only correct response. To reflect the fast pace of decision-making in making competitive moves, the best decisions are *responses* that arise from reflex rather than contemplation. Experience has demonstrated there is one, best response that works a high percentage of the time in each of the common situation. These responses have been proven over thousands of years of experience since they were first developed by Sun Tzu (6.5 Nine Responses).

6. We must pause our campaign when we run low on responses. The nine common situation responses are triggered by external developments. A growing lack of resources is an internal state that must also be monitored. While situation response requires us to focus externally on our situation, we cannot let ourselves lose sight of our internal need for resources (6.6 Campaign Pause).

7. Our dominant response must be tailored to three categories of unique characteristics. This is where the unique aspects of a position come into play. While our dominant response is dictated by standard situations, these same situations arise over and over again but they are never exactly the same. Every occurrence involves a unique constellation of conditions. We look at three categories of arena, relative size, and strength conditions *(*6.7 Special Conditions of Opposition).

8. Instant situation response creates key psychological advantages. By responding quickly and appropriately to challenging situations, we create confidence in our supporters and fear in our rivals. We improve the subjective dimensions of our position regardless of the objective rewards of our moves (6.8 Competitive Psychology).

Illustration:

The illustration that we usually use in our seminars to demonstrate these key aspects of situation response is a simple one of driving to the store to buy groceries. The decision that getting groceries is the best use of our time and that we are going to use a car are behind us. What happens when we get out on the road? This illustration makes solving these problems seem simple and indeed they are once we can apply them to every area of our competitive life as naturally as we do driving to the store.

1. We must train ourselves to instantly recognize our situation. If we don't run into problems, no responses are necessary. On this particular trip, we are going to run into problems. No strategic knowledge is necessary if we don't face challenges in our move. These key methods are for meeting challenges.

2. We must also distinguish between simple moves and moves as a part of a larger campaign. Let us assume that getting bread is part of a larger campaign of making special dinner for guests, which has certain deadlines.

3. Campaigns usually go through three stages. This is an early stage of a campaign, so we expect three potential situations and prepare mentally for them.

4. We must instantly separate competitive situations into one of the nine common classes. An early stage has three possibilities and let us assume we hit them all. An intrusion threatens to interrupt us before we get out the door. We initially find no problems on the road. Then we hit a serious traffic jam.

5. Once we recognize a situation, we must immediately know the one and only correct response. We must know to 1) evade the intruder, 2) not get distracted and go quickly on the open road, and 3) know how to get around the traffic.

6. We must pause our campaign when we run low on responses. Running low on gas after getting out the door? Don't ignore it and hope you don't hit more problems. We'll be in a world of hurt when we hit traffic. We stop and get gas.

7. Our dominant response must be tailored to three categories of unique characteristics. We have to adjust our responses depending on how far it is to the store, how big the traffic jam, and road conditions. For example, if the road is icy and slippery, we don't choose the same alternatives as we do when the roads are bare and dry.

8. Instant situation response creates key psychological advantages. By navigating the challenging road conditions, we become come confident that our dinner party will go well.

6.1.0 Situation Recognition

Sun Tzu's seven key methods on situation recognition in making advances.

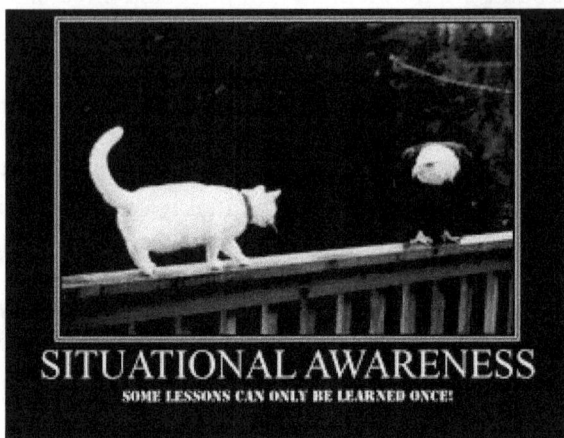

"See the time to move.
Don't try to find something clever."
                              Sun Tzu's The Art of War 4:3:8-9

"Repetition of the same thought or physical action develops into a habit which, repeated frequently enough, becomes an automatic reflex."
                              Norman Vincent Peale

General Principle: Competition generates common classes of situations where we can know the appropriate response.

Situation:

Sun Tzu saw that every competitive situation had unique aspects. This diversity of conditions creates many problems for those trying to execute strategic decisions. The details of situations can easily confuse and distract us. Without a system for instantly recognizing different classes of competitive situations, we will often respond inappropriately. There are more than a thousand conditions important to competitive situations. Recognizing them all on a conscious level would be totally overwhelming. In situations where we must respond quickly and confidently, we cannot question every aspect of our situation.

Opportunity:

Another of Sun Tzu's common complementary opposites is the alternating use of expansion and contraction. When we look for opportunities, we expand our awareness. When we focus on pursuing one, we must know how to concentrate our efforts. If we can focus on the key elements distinguishing different classes of competitive situations, we can recognize the major categories of situations instantly. That recognition automatically triggers our situation response. We limit ourselves to recognizing the nine major classes of situations because we have techniques for drawing clear lines separating them (6.4 Nine Situations).

Key Methods:

The following warrior's key methods help us understand the nature and demands of situation recognition.

1. Competitive situations are event-driven changing relationships among competitors, rivals, and their environment. The triggering event is the pursuit of an opportunity. We cross a border from controlled territory to explore an opportunity. That event takes us into a new area and changes the relationship that we have with our rivals. This nature of relationship is what we call a situation (5.2 Opportunity Exploration).

2. As we get information more quickly, we must recognize situations instantly. In the course of making a move, the requirements of progress are more intense and demanding. Crossing a border puts us in immediate contact with new ground, potentially creating new rivalries. In listening and aiming phases of progress, time presses but it doesn't threaten to overwhelm. When we are executing a move, we are under much pressure to respond to conditions as they arise. In most situations, if we don't recognize what is happening almost instantly, the situation will quickly get out of control (6.1.1 Instant Reflexes).

3. Recognition must be geared to triggering a response. To reflect the faster pace, decisions at this stage are best understood as *responses*. These responses arise from reflex rather than contemplation. Recognition of situations to which we do not know how to respond is worse than useless. Such recognition simply creates confusion. We focus on broad categories of recognition to eliminate gray areas and confusion, which are often even more destructive than the situation itself (6.0 Situation Response).

4. Recognition must be limited to relatively few generic situations. While we can pursue an infinite number of different types of opportunities using an infinite number of activities, recognizing situations requires a much narrower focus. While we could theoretically define a hundred generic situations and craft a hundred good responses to them, we could not execute them. The demands of time require us to limit our scope. We do so by limiting ourselves to recognizing those nine situations in which our instant response is critical to success. While limiting our focus to the nine most important situations is somewhat arbitrary, some limit is necessary, at least as a starting point. Over time, we can incrementally extend this list into more specific areas (5.0 Minimizing Mistakes).

5. Recognition must pick out key details to categorize a situation. The skill of situation response requires recognizing the key characteristics of situations. We must discern the difference between general conditions and the specific conditions that affect our responses. We cannot contemplate all conditions or even all relevant conditions. We must focus only on those dominant conditions which dictate the specific type of situation in which we find ourselves (6.1.2 Dominant Conditions).

6. Recognition must be unambiguous. We cannot know how to respond to ambiguous situations. Vacillation can not only eliminate our best option but create a more difficult situation. One of the key benefits of mastering the nine common situations is that they are unambiguous and exclusive. While other situations can arise out of our current situation, one situation always dominates our position (6.4 Nine Situations).

7. The skills of situation recognition can only be learned over time by practice. Situation recognition develops over time. This is true both in terms of our personal skills and in the course of a given move or campaign. We can adapt to situations correctly, sometimes without even recognizing them, but skill as situation recognition takes work to develop. While we can write and read about this situation, recognition is not an academic exercise. Our training programs are built around constant exercise in decision-making because it is only through those exercises that we can develop these types of skills. Our StrateSition Board Game was specifically designed around teaching the nine common situations and their responses in an environment based on building positions (1.8 Progress Cycle).

Illustration:

To put this idea in everyday terms, let us use the example of driving to the store to buy groceries (6.0 Situation Response).

1. Competitive situations are event-driven changing relationships among competitors, rivals, and their environment. The situation is the series of conditions we encounter on the road, culminating in a traffic jam.

2. As we get information more quickly, we must recognize situations instantly. The longer it takes us to recognize the formation of a traffic jam, the more likely it is that we will be trapped within it.

3. Recognition must be geared to triggering a response. If we are on a freeway and do not know the best response to the traffic jam, our recognition is useless.

4. Recognition must be limited to relatively few generic situations. Though traffic jams didn't arise until two thousand years after Sun Tzu, they fit nicely into his nine classes of situations.

5. Recognition must pick out key details to categorize a situation. To react appropriately to the traffic jam, we must know what the key differences are. In one type of situation, we can get off the freeway (6.4.3 Contentious Situations) while in another situation, when we are not near an exit, we must simply be patient (6.4.7 Difficult Situations). Both require very different responses.

6. Recognition must be unambiguous. Do we try to get off the road or should we be patient? Vacillation between the two on the road can lead to a worse situation, an accident.

7. The skills of situation recognition can only be learned over time by practice. Most new drivers are bad drivers simply because they lack the skills of situation recognition. What an experienced driver sees automatically from the signs, they miss entirely.

6.1.1 Conditioned Reflexes

Sun Tzu's four key methods on how we develop automatic, instantaneous responses.

"A daring soldier asks:
Can any army imitate these instant reflexes?"
We answer:
It can."

Sun Tzu's The Art of War 11:4:8-12

"It's all about hand-eye coordination, reflexes, timing,
strategy, being quick on your feet, being able to think
fast."

Johnathan Wendel

"The wise man does at once what the fool does at last."

Baltasar Gracian

General Principle: We can only develop instant reflexes through drill and practice.

Situation:

In making a move to advance our position, Sun Tzu taught that we are not executing a plan but exposing ourselves to events. The realm of strategy is the realm of uncontrolled events. We don't execute plans, but we still must think ahead and rehearse our possible responses. Sun Tzu taught that strategy demands more practice than production because we don't know what is coming next. Without practice, we cannot develop those instant reflexes. Our reflexes determines our success and failure. Without rehearsing our playbook, the more slowly we will react, and the less success we will have.

Opportunity:

Sun Tzu put together a detailed playbook. When asked if instant response were possible, Sun Tzu responded that they were a necessity. The faster we react correctly, the more successful we will be. Instant reflexes unite our seeing signs to situation recognition to knowing right responses to confident execution. This connection is only forged through practice. The research shows that the difference between experts and amateurs is simply in their depth of practice in developing instant reflexes. With more and more practice, we learn to pick out key conditions, connect them to situations, know their responses, and execute those responses automatically. An expert or master is simply one that is skilled at this.

Key Methods:

There are only four key methods we must follow to develop instant competitive reflexes.

1. We must practice recognizing key conditions instantly. We do not have time to analyze. Events are complex. Every event represents a unique combination of conditions. We do not have time to parse every aspect of every event. Even amid a chaotic, complexity of conditions, we can filter out all but the most important conditions in a given situation. We look for key condition in 1) the campaign stage, 2) the campaign class, 3) the form of ground, 4) the size of opposition, and 5) the strength of opposition (6.2.1 Dominant Conditions).

2. We must practice instantly connecting key conditions to identify our situation. Once we recognize these key conditions, we must instantly know which situation we are in. Since situations have exclusive conditions, it should take absolutely no analysis to connect conditions to situations any more than it takes analysis to decide if nine is more than five (6.4 Nine Situations).

3. We must practice instantly correlating the situation with its appropriate response. Each situation requires a single, known, definite response. The recognition of the situation and its response must be instantaneous. The beauty of instant reflexes is that, after we are trained, we don't have to reason our way to the right conclusion. We simply know it. We see the condition and respond without having to think (6.5 Nine Responses).

4. We must practice the instant, skilled execution of responses. Knowing what to do is not the same as being able to do it. Execution requires practice. The more we practice, the more skillful we become. The human brain is malleable. It learns by doing. The more often we do something, or attempt to do something, the better we get at doing it. We progress from initial clumsiness to professional polish. Our goals should be to practice our responses to common strategic challenges until they become effortless. Our on-line training, especially our Warrior Class Lessons, are designed with that idea in mind. Only by continually challenging ourselves, can we develop the instant responses to conditions that situations require (5.6.2 Acting Now).

Illustration:

An illustration from sports is the best here. Since this is being written in playoff season, let us consider American football.

1. We must practice recognizing key conditions instantly. Though plays are learned from a book, recognition is learned on the field through practice. Players always know where they are on the field and what the down is. A player must pick out the few key tells that indicate what their opponent's play is going to be. Some, like the alignment of the players, happen before the play. Others, such as how hard the linemen block, actually happen during the play. Coaches drill their players in this recognition.

2. We must practice instantly connecting key conditions to identify a standard situation. As the play unfolds, the knowledge about down and distance connects with sound and movement. Sometimes, you can tell just by the sound of the blocking what is happening. To those who have played football, the sounds made when linemen try to create a passing pocket or open a running lane are very different sounds. Trained players instinctively recognize a running play or a passing play. They feel which way the play is flowing, indicating more specifics. Though football may have more or less than nine general classes of plays, players are able to distill the complexity to a handful of common situations, a run to the right, left, or middle, a screen pass, a short pass, pr a long-pass.

3. We must practice instantly correlating the situation with its appropriate response. Through practice, recognition of the situation immediately leads to recognition of personal responsibility. In a given situation, you know the man for which you are responsible or the lane for which you are responsible.

4. We must practice the instant, skilled execution of responses. Your feet start moving in the right direction in less than a second.

6.1.2 Prioritizing Conditions

Sun Tzu's six key methods for parsing complex competitive conditions into simple responses.

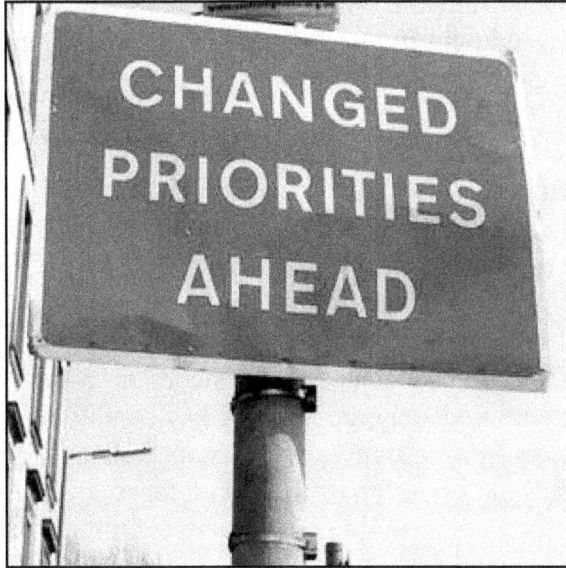

*"Your first actions should deny victory to the enemy.
You pay attention to your enemy to find the way to win."*
Sun Tzu's The Art of War 4:1:2-1

"Priority is a function of context."
Stephen R. Covey

*"Control your own time. Don't let it be done for you. If
you are working off the in-box that is fed you, you are
probably working on the priority of others."*
Donald Rumsfeld

General Principle: We tailor our response to five categories of conditions defining a situation.

Situation:

Underlying all of Sun Tzu's work is a respect for human limitations. A perfect system that is too complicated for most people to use is not really perfect at all. He saw that we are easily overwhelmed by the complex array of conditions that make up competitive situations. Different conditions suggest a variety of responses. Unfortunately, without training, most of us can easily come up with the wrong response because we lack the perspective on the overall objectives of the system.

Opportunity:

Situation response is Sun Tzu's play book. Along with it, he developed a systematic way of tailoring just the right kind of moves to fit a situation. In making a move, we are not executing a plan but navigating through the events that we encounter in the environment. We do this by immediately recognizing key conditions that suggest a single, specific response (6.1.1 Instant Reflexes). Assuming we never lose sight of our goals (6.2.2 Guidance by Goals), we need clear principles for prioritizing our responses from among a range of possibilities to make instant decisions.

Key Methods:

We can dramatically simplify the task of tailoring our responses to very specific conditions using the following key methods.

1. Five categories of conditions are the key to our situation. These categories of the conditions are:

- 1) the stage of our campaign (6.3 Campaign Patterns,
- 2) the nine situations or stages (6.4 Nine Situations),
- 3) the form of the situation we are in (6.7.1 Form Adjustments),
- 4) the relative size of our opposition (6.7.2 Size Adjustments), and

- 5) the relative strength of our opposition ([6.7.2 Size Adjustments](#)).

2. Each category of conditions defines an exclusive aspect of a situation. In a given campaign, we can only be at one stage, in one common situation, on one form of situation, and meeting one opponent. The conditions within each category are exclusive. The campaign stage is either early, middle, or late. As the situation can be only in one of the nine common classes: dissipating, easy, etc. It occurs on only one form of various grounds: inclined, fluid, uncertain, or neutral. The opponent has only one size and strength even if it is an alliance of many separate individuals or groups. One situation can evolve into another as time goes on, but at any given point in time, we only respond to the specific situation that we currently face ([6.0 Situation Response](#)).

3. The dominant response is dictated by the nine classes of situations. The campaign stage helps us understand which classes of situations are the most likely. After that, we use the characteristics of the situations themselves to parse them. Knowing the standard situation dictates the dominant response ([6.5 Nine Responses](#))

4. The dominant response is adjusted to fit details of form and relative size and strength. We adjust our responses for the gravity, currents, or uncertainty of the ground. Our relative size and strength--or lack of it--determines how we adjust our responses against specific competitors when their presence shapes the situation ([6.7 Tailoring to Conditions](#)).

5. If our response doesn't work as expected, we must spot where we went wrong and adapt. We are only human. As with every strategic endeavor, situation response is adaptive. If we get one part of the recognition wrong, we recognize our mistakes, learn of what parts are working, refine our actions, and try again ([1.9 Competition and Production](#).

6. If we run out of resources, we must stop. Continuing beyond the limits of our responses is inherently dangerous, leading to almost certain defeat. ([6.6 Campaign Pause](#)).

Illustration:

To illustrate these key methods, let us imagine a specific business situation, a simple case study. Imagine you are in a meeting. In the meeting is a decision-maker, a person with all the authority and three people are working together against you. The topic under discussion is a critical business issue about which there is a disagreement. You take one side of the question and your rivals take another but they are not personally close. The decision-maker has shown no preferences on the question but his general character is well known to everyone in the meeting. The discussion is well-advanced and should be approaching a decision, but there are a number of difficult obstacles that must be worked through to arrive at that decision. There is a firm deadline for the meeting to end because the decision-maker is needed elsewhere.

Snap decision, what do you do?

1. Five categories of conditions are the key to our situation. Trained in Sun Tzu's system, we would instantly think about the stage, the nature of the situation, the form of the situation, and the size and unity of your opponents.

2. All five categories of conditions define exclusive aspects of situations. The campaign for decision is in a late stage. The situation is one defined by obstacles that slow progress. The form of the situation is dominated by a key single decision-maker. Opponents outnumber us but they are not tightly united.

3. The dominant response is dictated by the nine classes of situations. The stage and nature of the situation indicate that we are in a difficult situation. This situation requires persistence. Our primary focus must be on the obstacles not our opponents. We persistently work through those obstacles, taking our time rather than rushing.

4. The dominant response is adjusted to fit details of form and relative size and strength. The form of the situation is inclined, dominated by the decision-maker. We therefore slant our arguments to favor his or her known opinions and prejudices, especially try to position ourselves on his side against our opponents. Our opponents outnumber us, so we cannot attack them but they are not an over-whelming number so we can easily defend when they attack. However, they are divided so if they give you an opportunity, you work on their differences.

5. *If our response doesn't work as expected, we must spot where we went wrong and adapt.* We may see from the way the decision-maker reacts to something we said that we misunderstood his or her opinions. We immediately adjust our statements to fit our new understanding of his or her position.

6. *If we run out of resources, we must stop.* Though we are being persistent, when we come to the end of the meeting, we must stop.

6.2.0 Campaign Evaluation

Sun Tzu's five key methods on how we justify continued investment in an on-going campaign.

"Make war without a standard approach. Water has no consistent shape.
If you follow the enemy's shifts and changes, you can always find a way to win."
Sun Tzu's The Art of War 6:8:8-10

"I believe in the battle-whether it's the battle of a campaign or the battle of this office, which is a continuing battle."
Richard M. Nixon

General Principle: Campaigns must be evaluated in terms of length, mission, continuing cost and benefits.

Situation:

Campaigns involve a series of related moves toward a longer-term goal. Without understanding campaigns and the Playbook about their nature, we have a much more difficult time identifying and classifying the various competitive situations in which we find ourselves.

Opportunity:

Campaigns tie a group of related moves together (5.2.2 Campaign Methods). As a series of moves, campaigns have emergent properties that are not part of any given move (1.2.3 Position Complexity). The competitive situations in which we find ourselves are predictable because our movements have a history (1.1 Position Paths). Certain histories lead to certain types of development. Competitive positions interact in complex ways, but complexity can lead to order. We capture that order in our mental models to foresee situations (1.2.3 Position Complexity). Seeing campaigns as the frame for how and why situations develop is a simple and powerful tool.

Key Methods:

The following key methods describe the specific strategic challenges that commonly affect campaigns.

1. The longer time spans of campaigns permit more learning and more environmental change. In a dynamic environment, conditions continue to change throughout the course of a campaign. We learn more about the nature of the opportunity that we are pursuing. We inevitably discover barriers and problems that we didn't expect. Our position continues to change, changing its relative value to the position we are pursuing. New opportunities can arise that depreciate the benefits of the current campaign (1.1.1 Position Dynamics).

2. During a campaign we must not lose track of our larger mission. As we learn and conditions change, the original goal can lose its appeal, but we will still tend to continue the campaign because it has its own inertia. As campaigns continue, they, like all systems, can take on a life of their own. It is hard to get out of a campaign, even when the goal of the campaign no longer suits our purposes (1.6.2 Types of Motivations).

3. In campaigns, new investments must be evaluated only in terms of future returns not past investments. This rule applies to all actions, but it is especially important in evaluating campaigns. Campaigns last so much longer than most actions that they simply accumulate more sunk costs. In evaluating the benefits of well-defined and established positions, we must forget about past investments. We cannot change them. If we include them in our calculation, we will always over value the benefits of a campaign, throwing good money after bad. We cannot consider the benefits of a campaign without considering the value of learning more about the nature of the opportunity that they represent (5.4.2 Successful Mistakes).

4. The discovery of new opportunities must force us to reconsider an existing campaign. We must always consider the cost of not pursuing other opportunities. These costs are unavoidable if we stay the course of a campaign. These opportunity costs are built into every campaign in a way that makes them easy to overlook. Our environment can change well-defined and established positions into low-opportunity probability despite anything we do or fail to do. In moving, we can also discover new and better opportunities. If either of these conditions occur, we must make a conscious decision either to continue or abandon our campaign because other opportunities offer a better potential return on our time. We only have a limited amount of time and must invest it as wisely as possible despite being caught in a campaign (3.1.1 Resource Limitations).

5. We must never abandon a campaign simply because it becomes difficult. Campaigns typically go through a pattern where the penultimate stages are the most difficult. We must expect this going into a campaign. All campaigns are more difficult than we anticipated at first. We are always the most optimistic at the beginning of a campaign,. We don't discover the challenges until we get further into them. However, simply having more knowledge about the difficulties about a campaign alone cannot discourage us from continuing. We can never compare the known challenges in explored opportunities to the unknown challenges in unexplored opportunities. We must know exactly how to respond to the most common challenges. That way we are not frustrated by each new challenge (6.3 Campaign Patterns).

Illustration:

We have military campaigns, political campaigns, campaigns to find a job, and campaigns to graduate from college. While all face challenges, the campaign to get a college degree is one of the most commonly wasted.

1. The longer time spans of campaigns permit more learning and more environmental change. Fifty percent of college students change their major at least once and often several times. We must always be open to new conditions as they arise. Since I wanted to learn the law, during my first year as an undergraduate, I took a job doing legal research for a local legal firm.

2. During a campaign we must not lose track of our larger mission. While the law was academically interesting, from my work experience I found the actual practice of law a deadly bore.

3. In campaigns, new investments must be evaluated only in terms of future returns not past investments. Despite the past investment in a college education, I just didn't see continuing that investment, so I dropped out. I was already studying Sun Tzu and wanted to get into a more interesting competitive environment, one not so dominated by personal connections.

4. The discovery of new opportunities must force us to reconsider an existing campaign. I was also working in retail during summers and got promoted to a department manager. I had people with PHDs in political science and English literature working for me. At that point, I decided a business career simply made more sense. A better example of this, however, might be Bill Gates leaving Harvard to start Microsoft.

5. We must never abandon a campaign simply because it becomes difficult. For me, the easier thing would have been to stay in school. I had an academic scholarship. The academic work was easy and fun. I was also exposed to the emerging computer technology at Stanford, which was important to may later career.

6.2.1 Campaign Flow

Sun Tzu's six key methods for seeing campaigns as a series of situations that flow logically from one to another

"Your war can take any shape.
It must avoid the strong and strike the weak.
Water follows the shape of the land that directs its flow.
Your forces follow the enemy, who determines how you win."

Sun Tzu's The Art of War 6:8:1-7

"Take time to deliberate; but when the time for action arrives, stop thinking and go in."

Andrew Jackson

"Reality is that which, when you stop believing in it, doesn't go away."

Philip K. Dick

"We win some and we learn some."

Gary Gagliardi

General Principle: Control the flow of campaigns by leveraging the flow of one event into another.

Situation:

There are dangers in the flow of events during a campaign. Following Sun Tzu's logic, campaigns must accept the course of events and, at the same time, resist their course when they lead us into danger. To most of us, this appears to be a contradiction. This is because we don't understand how to use the balancing forces of complementary opposites. Guiding the course of a campaign is not like driving a car where our path is passive. It is like riding the rapids of a river. The path is turbulent with many hidden currents. We must both accept that turbulence and know how we can struggle against it.

Opportunity:

Sun Tzu taught that the flow of campaigns must be directed by the flow of events. Events create situations. The way we react to situations determines our success. Like riding a river, we use the flow of events to take us where we want to go. To do this, we must adjust from moment to moment to shifts in the current situation. We cannot simply follow the course of least resistance nor can we dictate the course of events. We shape our flow of actions in a campaign not by trying to control our environment but by mastering the skills of interacting with it (6.2 Campaign Evaluation).

Key Methods:

We master Sun Tzu's perspective for seeing competitive situations by remembering these five key methods.

1. Though we deal with events one at a time, it is best to think of them as a stream. Each action, especially responses to events, can have a distinct beginning and end, but they are not really separated. Each action and reaction flows from one situation to the next. In using Warrior's Playbook, we harness this perspective of flow as a part of our situation awareness. Situations are arising from nothing and returning to the void. They are flowing from one into the next, endlessly. Competitive landscapes are like kaleidoscopes where new situations are created from the reflections of the last (1.1 Position Paths).

2. We cannot control the natural flow of events during a campaign. An event is any action by any agent in our competitive landscape or any interaction of actions that creates unexpected conditions. Competitive landscapes are defined by the freedom of people to act in their own-self interest. This creates a steady stream of events that must be dealt with during a campaign (3.2.1 Environmental Dominance).

3. We cannot make progress if we fight against the flow of events. We must engage our environment. We cannot ignore events because they dictate our course as much as our own actions do. We cannot fight events because there are limits to our resources of energy and effort. There are no limit to the number of events that can affect the course of a campaign. (3.1.1 Resource Limitations).

4. We affect the flow of events by skilled responses to individual events. We don't have to respond to every event. When we do respond, we must do so because we recognize the best response. We leverage individual events in the flow of events. Our responses use the particular nature of a given event to our best advantage. We deflect events at the best angle to take us where we want to go. When people talk about "spinning" events, they are describing this process (2.3.1 Action and Reaction).

5. In reacting to the current event, we must be looking forward toward the next event. This means that we must be living in the moment. As we react, we are changing the situation but never decisively. Our actions are still a relatively small part of the environment. Most of our actions are quickly swallowed by the flow of events (1.2.1 Competitive Landscapes).

6. In a stream of events, the effects of our responses are cumulative. A single response to a single event never takes us exactly where we expect. We can recover from disasters as long as we survive. The turbulent nature of competitive environments come from the interaction of actions and reactions. As our responses interact with our environment, we discover what is needed for future moves. The course of a campaign is never straight, it is a result of the turbulence of events combined with our efforts to utilize them (1.9 Competition and Production).

Illustration:

Let us illustrate these principles in terms of a political campaign.

1. Though we deal with events one at a time, it is best to think of them as a stream. A candidate cannot get "stuck" on any one event during the campaign. A good campaigner takes both the good and bad in stride. The campaign moves on even if he or she doesn't.

2. We cannot control the natural flow of events during a campaign. The situations that can be controlled--rallies, mailings, ads-- are never as important as events in the environment--what political opponents do and say, economic and international crises, the breaking news, and so on.

3. tWe cannot make progress if we fight against the flow of events. No matter how hard he or she works at controlling perceptions, a politician that isn't engaged with the flow of events is going to seem out-of-touch and disconnected. People will see these politicians as disconnected from the electorate, as though they are in a bubble.

4. We affect the flow of events by skilled responses to individual events. A skilled politician must know when and when not to respond to a rival's actions. For example, if a political rival makes a mistake, it is often best to let the media and the public dissect it rather than jump on the situation, getting directly involved.

5. In reacting to the current event, we must be looking forward toward the next event. In a sense, nothing is ever forgotten in a political contest. The politician who keeps moving forward creates a bigger impression than one that never lets go of one event and moves onto the next.

6. In a stream of events, the effects of our responses are cumulative. Winning an election depends on overall position. The politician that improves his or her position the most during a race is always going to be the one who responds the best to events during the campaign.

6.2.2 Campaign Goals

Sun Tzu's five key methods for assessing the value of a campaign by a larger mission.

"Methods shape systems to the authority of our mission."
Sun Tzu's The Art of War (Ancient Chinese Revealed version)
1:1:30-32

"If you don't know where you are going, any road will get you there."

Lewis Carroll

"I have found that great people do have in common an immense belief in themselves and in their mission."
Yousuf Karsh

General Principle: Campaigns are navigated by measuring progress toward our goals.

Situation:

Sun Tzu saw that campaigns can easily take on a life of their own. Since they cover long spans of time, months and even years, it is easy for us to lose sight of their ultimate purpose. This is especially difficult because campaigns involve more or less constant interaction with our environment. As we interact with our environment, it is easy to get turned around. As the flow of events take us in unanticipated directions, layer upon layer of short-term goals can eventually bury the original purpose of the campaign.

Opportunity:

Sun Tzu taught that the most important thing about the methods that we use is that they must be consistent with our mission (1.6 Mission Values). We must remember our mission not only in choosing how to explore an opportunity but throughout the entire series of activities we choose during the course of a campaign (5.1 Mission Priorities). Clarity of purpose is critical as we must react to what we find in the environment. For that to work, our values must be clear enough that we can never lose site of them.

Key Methods:

Let us contrast a couple of analogies to help us understand how we navigate our campaigns.

1. Every campaign has a larger mission than simply reaching the end. The goal of a campaign is to achieve a well-defined and established position, but that position is only valuable because it serves our larger mission. The problem is that campaigns continue for such a long time that simply finishing can become more important that the larger mission. This is why we must continually evaluate campaigns (6.2 Campaign Evaluation).

2. Our mission values provide a compass to keep our campaigns on track. A mission is more than a goal. It is a complete set of priorities. Those priorities include a set of values. Mission goals and values are not so much a restraint as a resource. As we are buffeted by events, only our values help us prioritize our often conflicting options. Clear values and outr need to make our values clear eliminate many choices that we would have to consider simply on the basis of completing the mission (6.2.2 Campaign Goals).

3. Our choice of methods during a campaign clarifies our mission values, making them more tangible. Values start as a guiding concept, but our choices during a campaign give them form and substance. The clearer our mission is, the more powerful it is. By putting our values into practice, they become more readily understood and shared by others 1.7.2 Goal Focus).

4. Campaigns create commitments to other people that impact our mission. One of the ways that missions take on a life of their own is that they involve commitments to other people. Honoring our commitments must be part of our values, but this potentially sets up a serious dilemma. When our mission values require us to abandon a campaign, we must sometimes find a way to honor our commitments outside of completing the campaign itself (1.6.3 Shifting Priorities).

5. We cannot let ourselves confuse satisfying our pride with satisfying our mission. Even when our mission is totally humanitarian and altruistic, it is based on our own personal interpretation on what is valuable to others. We can only base our goals and values on our unique, individual position, perspective, and consciousness. Because of this, it is very easy for us to confuse our mission with our personal pride. During the length of a campaign, we develop a natural pride of ownership over what we have achieved. It can be difficult to give up a mission that no longer serves our larger goals simply because of that pride. We must question all our decisions regarding mission to see if we are not confusing pride with mission (1.6.2 Types of Motivations).

Illustration:

Let us illustrate these principles with SOSI's campaign to build a comprehensive Sun Tzu's Playbook based on Sun Tzu's principles.

1. Every campaign has a larger mission than simply reaching the end. The Playbook is a means to an end. We want to make it must easier to learn and apply Sun Tzu's rich and complex competitive system.

2. ***Our mission values provide a compass to keep our campaigns on track.*** As each article of the Playbook is developed, we can measure it against the larger goal of making Sun Tzu's ideas more readily understood and broadly accepted.

3. ***Our choice of methods during a campaign clarifies our mission values, making them more tangible.*** We seek to provide concrete and tangible explanations and illustrations in the Playbook. They provide a practical standard against which people can evaluate the depth of their competitive knowledge and skill. Over time, we want to make the Playbook even more concrete by developing exercises in our training programs that illustrate the working so of these principles in simple forms of competition.

4. ***Campaigns create commitments to other people that impact our mission.*** Because of our commitment to publish an article on Sun Tzu's Playbook every day, we work to update and standardize our Playbook every day. At some point, our priorities will shift from developing articles to developing related training material. At that point, we may have to shift our commitments as well.

5. ***We cannot let ourselves confuse satisfying our pride with satisfying our mission.*** Our Rule Book is based on a conviction that mastering Sun Tzu's methods are important. These principles not only help people to become more successful individuals but a world trained in his system of "winning without conflict" will be less dangerous and wealthier in all senses of the word. Since creating the Playbook is a commitment that requires months and years, with no real compensation, there is a certain amount of ego involved, so I have to question whether this is really valuable to others or not and gladly solicit feedback.

6.3.0 Campaign Patterns

Sun Tzu's seven key methods on how knowing campaign stages gives us insight into our situation.

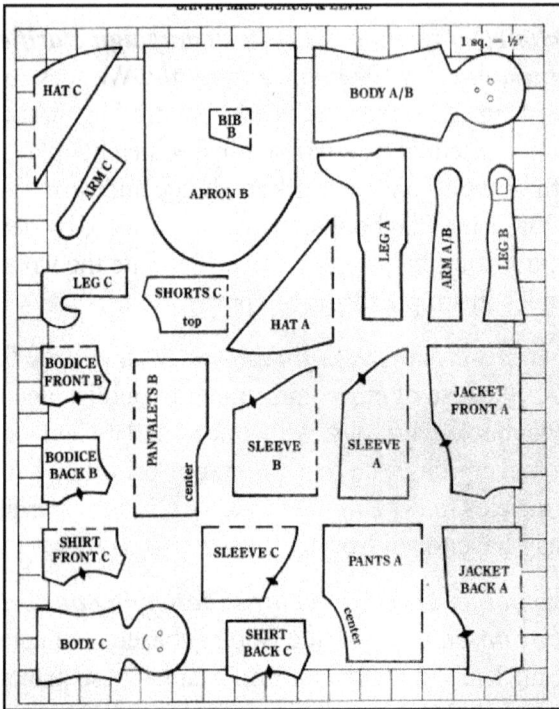

"You must control chaos.
This depends on your calculations."
Sun Tzu's The Art of War 5:4:10-11

"What we call chaos is just patterns we haven't
recognized. What we call random is just patterns
we can't decipher. What we can't understand we call
nonsense. What we can't read we call gibberish ."
Chuck Palahniuk

General Principle: Knowing what can happen in the course of a campaign is the key to controlling expectations.

Situation:

Through the course of a campaign, the competitive situations that arise appear chaotic, but, as Sun Tzu pointed out 2,500 years ago, the chaos of competition is not random. There is a deeper order underlying it. We cannot see the patterns in it because we haven't been trained where to look. Today we know this type of chaos as complexity, the patterns that arise from the interactions of independent, adaptive agents. The emergent properties that arise in these environments cannot be predicted from their elements, but we can learn them from observation and training.

Opportunity:

Our success in campaigns depends on patterns, the patterns that we see in situations and the patterns that others see in our handing those challenges. This is a game of expectations (7.2.2 Preparing Expectations). To navigate all the challenges that occur over the course of a campaign, we must expect certain classes of situations to arise in a pattern. Through preparation and training, we know which developing conditions to look for, selecting the key signs from the complex conditions of the competitive landscape (1.2.1 Competitive Landscapes). Most people cannot see these patterns, but they can see our pattern of reacting appropriately to them.

Key Methods:

The following eight key methods describe how we can use the stages of a campaign to determine our situation.

1. The confidence with which we handle challenges during the course of a campaign determines the depth of our support. The strength of competitive positions is determined by the strength of our support. Our supporters opinions form over time. While first impressions are important, the depth of our support can develop only over the course of a campaign, as others witness our handling of a series of challenges (1.7.1 Team Unity).

2. In meeting challenges, we have an opportunity to demonstrate our ability to see what is hidden. We handle situations with confidence when we know what to expect beforehand. Most people cannot see the same signs that we do, but they can see how easily we respond to different situations. Nothing increases confidence--our own or that of others--more than our ability to make successful predictions about how situations are likely to unfold. This same confidence and ability also discourages opposition from forming (3.2.2 Opportunity Invisibility).

3. We see these patterns by knowing that campaigns usually go through three general stages. At each stage, we can know what conditions to look for. From those conditions, we can know what class of situation we are in. From those situations, we can know how to respond. To help us understand the different stages that campaigns go through, we think of a campaign in terms of its beginning, middle, and end. By developing the appropriate conditioned reflexes to respond to each situation, we create an objective pattern of success others can observe (6.1.1 Conditioned Reflexes).

4. These classes of situations don't only appear in campaigns, but it is more important to identify them when they do. Campaigns require more investment and more support. When these situations arise in the pursuit of an ordinary opportunity, we lose that opportunity if we don't respond to them correctly, but when they arise in a campaign, the consequences of not handling them correctly are much more serious (6.2.2 Campaign Goals).

5. We prepare ourselves and our supporters for the appropriate classes of situations at each stage of a campaign. Of course, not every venture goes through all or even more of these situations or stages. A new venture *can* end successfully at any point in the process, running smoothly from start to finish. When things go smoothly, we don't have to worry about meeting these challenges. The point of this training is to prepare for situations that arise when our pursuit of a new position does not go smoothly (6.0 Situation Response).

6. The beginning stages arise when we cross our borders into new territory. This is the initial stage of discovery. In the initial stages, we first learn the basic position of potential rivals and the nature of the battleground, but the situations are relatively simple. The only difficult form of beginning stage is when we are forced to pursue a new position because our current position is directly threatened. Other than that, the easiest and most open stages of a campaign are when we first start to explore new territory (6.3.1 Early-Stage Situations).

7. In the middle stages, campaigns take on a deeper, more serious character. In these stages, competitors are more deeply committed, not only to exploring the territory but to a specific course of action. As we try to meet those challenges, three things happen. First, opportunities to develop significant advantages arise,. Second, resources get stretched more thinly. Third, your supporters can begin to waiver (6.3.2 Middle-Stage Situations).

8. The most difficult stages arise at the end of the campaign. If a campaign ends successfully before this point, all is well and good, but we have to be prepared for the problems that often arise at the end of many campaigns. At that point, we are totally committed to the success of a campaign and have fewer and fewer options. Our rivals are often in the same situation. In the end, the situation often gets desperate (6.3.3 Late-Stage Situations).

Illustration:

Let us illustrate these issues from the perspective of a project manager whose company has been hired to create and deliver a product, such as a software application, to a client company.

1. The confidence with which we handle challenges during the course of a campaign determines the depth of our support. As a project manager, everyone involved is looking to us for guidance. Those in our organization whom we control want to be protected from the customer from chaos so that they can get the work done. Those in the client organization are usually skeptical about the project simply because it represents change.

2. In meeting challenges, we have an opportunity to demonstrate our ability to see what is hidden. As the project goes forward, we are continually preparing the expectations of those involved. By letting them in on the potential problems that lie ahead, we are demonstrating that we are not approaching this project naively.

3. We see these patterns by knowing that campaigns usually go through three general stages. We should lay the potential issues out, both for our own people and our client's so that everyone knows what to expect. This can prevent problems and panic simply because everyone understands that we are prepared for what is likely to happen.

4. These classes of situations don't only appear in campaigns, but it is more important to identify them when they do. Because of the sunk costs involved, dealing with each subsequent situation becomes more important in terms of potential loss.

5. We prepare ourselves and our supporters for the appropriate classes of situations at each stage of a campaign. We should explain the three stages of a campaign, or in this case, a project. We assure everyone that we will make it clear which stage we are in and that each stage requires a change in response. This means that our priorities can change though the course of the project.

6. The beginning stages arise when we cross our borders into new territory. At the beginning, we should make it clear that the early stages, difficult or not, are the most transitory. Though challenges can arise at this stage, we can deal with them directly and quickly.

7. In the middle stages, campaigns take on a deeper, more serious character. As we arrive at this stage, we should again get everyone together and explain where we are. The issue is not just the project work that has gotten done, but the normal problems with integrating changes into the organization. We should explain specifically what class of situation we are encountering and what situations are the most likely to arise.

8. The most difficult stages arise at the end of the campaign. We should prepare everyone on both our side and the client's side for that stage from the beginning of the project. We should cast any terminal difficulties as a good sign rather than a bad one.

6.3.1 Early-Stage Situations

Sun Tzu's six key methods describing the common situations that arise the earliest in campaigns.

"Your first actions should deny victory to the enemy."
Sun Tzu's Art of War 4:1:23

"The ultimate wisdom which deals with beginnings, remains locked in a seed. There it lies, the simplest fact of the universe and at the same time the one which calls faith rather than reason."

Hal Borland

"Well begun is half done."

Aristotle

" ...a practical beginning, however small, for it is wonderful how often in such matters the mustard-seed germinates and roots itself."

Florence Nightingale

General Principle: The three early-stage situations arise from our most basic discoveries about conditions.

Situation:

Sun Tzu taught that there are three common situations that arise when we begin to explore an opportunity. These situations represent our most likely initial discoveries when exploring a new area. We might assume the entire campaign will assume the character of its earliest stages, but this perspective is simply wrong. Sun Tzu taught that the initial classes of conditions are the most temporary. Reacting inappropriately to these three situations and the campaign simply ends in failure. However, reacting correctly usually means that the current campaign stage evolves into a new situation.

Opportunity:

Beginnings are the most delicate times. Good responses at the initial stages of a campaign have more to do with preventing disaster than securing success. Bad decisions can lead to quick defeats that could have been avoided. On the other hand, good decisions at this juncture seldom lead to quick successes. Success comes from sustaining the campaign long enough to transform the initial stages of a campaign into another type of situation.

Key Methods:

The following key methods describe Sun Tzu's approach to handling the beginning of a campaign.

1. The initial situations in a campaign are defined by the discovery of basic conditions. Prior to undertaking a campaign, we observe from a distance. As we begin the campaign, we learn more about conditions by seeing the situation from the inside. We instantly learn the nature of the landscape and the disposition of our potential rivals. These two components define our initial situation (5.2 Opportunity Exploration).

2. These three classes of situations arise from the creation of a boundary situation. As we cross a boundary to explore an opportunity, we not only learn more, but we introduce ourselves into that the situation. We not only discover conditions, but our presence can change them. The nature of the opportunity has changed because of our presence. It will continue to change because others will respond to our presence (2.3.1 Action and Reaction).

3. The three initial classes of competitive situations are known as 1) dissipating, 2) easy, and 3) contentious. At the risk of terribly oversimplifying them, we can describe these three classes of situations fairly simply. Dissipating situations are those in which we are attacked. Easy situations are those where we make good progress. Contention situations are those where we meet immediate opposition (6.2 Campaign Evaluation).

4. Campaigns cannot be planned because, when we encounter these situations, we must respond appropriately. The situation is either invisible or doesn't exist until we cross the boundary to learn about it. We cannot plan our response. We are ignorant about what we will find. Hindsight bias leads us to think after the fact that these situations are more predictable than they really are. Good strategy starts with the assumption that we must react to events rather than plan them (5.2.1 Choosing Adaptability).

5. Initial campaign situations quickly evolve into more advanced situations. They can turn into other more advanced initial situations or they can turn into middle-stage or later-stage situations. Their order given by Sun Tzu, 1) dissipating, 2) easy, and then 3) contentious represents that standard order of development. Dissipating situations can turn into easy or contentious situations but the reverse is seldom true. Thus, recognizing our current situation not only helps us respond correctly to it, but we must be prepared for it to transform into something else, requiring instant reflexes (6.1.1 Conditioned Reflexes)

6. Middle-stage and late-stage situations cannot arise initially in campaigns because they need time to develop. Middle-stage situations can only arise from reactions to previous situations so we cannot start with them. Late-stage situations are so difficult and risky that they would be filtered out by any sensible process of choosing high probability opportunities (5.0 Minimizing Mistakes).

Illustration:

One way to understand these initial stages is to think about what can happen at the beginning of a plot of a science fiction movie.

1. The initial situations in a campaign are defined by the discovery of basic conditions. As the movie opens, we discover characters and the situations that they are in. In our science fiction movie, a space ship visits an alien world where sensors show that there are needed resources.

2. These three classes of situations arise from the creation of a boundary situation. The action starts once the exploration team goes down to the surface of the planet.

3. The three initial classes of competitive situations are known as 1) dissipating, 2) easy, and 3) contentious. There are only three possibilities. The explorers discover a big, dangerous alien horde already preparing to attack their ship or planet (dissipating situation). A non-threatening but alien environment that must be searched (easy situation). Aliens who are potential opponents (contentious situation).

4. Campaigns cannot be planned because, when we encounter these situations, we must respond appropriately. Our explorers could not have known which of these situations would occur until they began their exploration. They must react as situations develop.

5. Initial campaign situations quickly evolve into more advanced situations. What initially seems to be a non-threatening alien environment suddenly turns into contentious one when aliens are discovered.

6. Middle-stage and late-stage situations cannot arise initially in campaigns because they need time to develop. On a dramatic level, placing characters in the more complex middle-stage or late-stage situations is just confusing. Middle-stage situations arise from a series of actions and reactions, while believable characters wouldn't choose to go into the most series late-stage situation without some earlier reason to do so.

6.3.2 Middle-Stage Situations

Sun Tzu's six key methods on how progress creates transitional situations in campaigns.

"Learn from the history of successful battles.
Victory goes to those who make winning easy."
Sun Tzu's The Art of War 4:3:11-12

"You don't develop courage by being happy in your relationships everyday. You develop it by surviving difficult times and challenging adversity."
Epicurus

"People who have lost relationships often wonder why they can't just let it be "water under the bridge." It is water under the bridge - the trouble is we do not live on

the bridge but in the river of life with its many twists and turns."

Grant Fairley

"It seems essential, in relationships and all tasks, that we concentrate only on what is most significant and important."

Soren Kierkegaard

General Principle: Middle-stage situations arise from the different relationships created by different knowledge and resources.

Situation:

Sun Tzu's Warrior's Rulebook methods teach us that more is not just more but often different. This is especially true of the progress in a campaign. People often expect campaigns to continue as they began, but they never do. Situations do not just repeat themselves. They evolve over time. This means what works at the beginning of a campaign will stop working. Different situations require different responses. Certain situations arise as we become more deeply committed to an opportunity.

Opportunity:

These three situations all describe the condition of our relationship with others, specifically how relationships change as we get more deeply involved pursuing an opportunity. Our involvement in pursuing an opportunity cannot help but change our relationships with others. These situations include relationships with our rivals and supporters and illustrate how easily those roles can change. While it seems like relationships can develop in an infinite number of directions, there are only three directions that are common.

Key Methods:

The following key methods explain the situations that develop in the middle of a campaign.

1. The middle situations in a campaign are defined by the evolution of relationships. This evolution is not driven by personality. It is driven by the nature of the ground and the nature of the opportunity. As time goes on, we learn more about the nature of the competitive landscape. Middlestage situations arise directly from that knowledge (1.2.1 Competitive Landscapes).

2. These three classes of situations require a deeper commitment to the campaign. We only progress to the middle stages if the campaign isn't an instant success or instant failure. We must discover enough promise that we want to continue and problems that require more work. To continue, the project requires more commitment. The nature of that commitment is what separates these different situations (2.3.3 Likely Reactions).

3. The middle three classes of competitive situations are known as 1) open, 2) intersecting, and 3) serious. Though it oversimplifies them, let us offer some simple descriptions of these three situations. An open situation is a race that isn't determined by speed. An intersecting situation is a joining of forces. A serious situation is a cut-off of resources that is determined by lack of support. (6.2 Campaign Evaluation).

4. We must know instantly how to react when we get into these situations. These situations arise because everyone involved must adapt to the situation. We cannot plan our response, but we can know how to respond. We must react appropriately from instinct rather than doing what we want (5.2.1 Choosing Adaptability).

5. Middle campaign situations evolve more slowly into other middle-stage or end-stage situations. The challenges represented by middle-stages are deeper, representing our deeper knowledge of the situation. This means that they take more time to resolve, evolving more slowly. Open situations can develop into intersecting situations, but serious situations are a wild-card, arising at any time (6.1.1 Conditioned Reflexes).

6. Middle-stage situations are all concerned with resource management. Because this situation takes time to evolve and more time to resolve, they focus in different ways on getting the most return possible from what the situation offers (3.1.1 Resource Limitations).

Illustration:

Let us think about these situations from the perspective of managing a professional sports team through a long season.

1. The middle-stage situations in a campaign are defined by the evolution of relationships. Over the course of the season, the relationship among the various teams vying for the title develops gradually.

2. These three classes of situations require a deeper commitment to the campaign. While teams can switch players around at the beginning and end of seasons, the middle stages reflect a commitment to a given lineup of players.

3. The middle three classes of competitive situations are known as 1) open, 2) intersecting, and 3) serious. Teams at the top of their division tend to be in an open situation. Those in the middle tend to be in an intersecting situation. Those at the bottom tend to be in a serious situation.

4. We must know instantly how to react when we get into these situations. Their positions in team standing are not certain because they change every week. A team at the bottom of the standings can rise. A team at the top can fall. Everything depends on them reacting appropriately to their current situation.

5. Middle campaign situations evolve more slowly into other middle-stage or end-stage situations. Team situations can change dramatically between the middle of the season and the end, but those changes will go much more slowly than at the beginning or the end.

6. M*iddle-stage campaign situations are all concerned with resource management*. Professional players play a long season. They must know how to make the most of their resources given their particular situation.

6.3.3 Late-Stage Situations

Sun Tzu's six key methods for understanding the final and most dangerous stages of campaigns.

"Avoid the enemy's high spirits.
Strike when his men are lazy and want to go home.
This is how you master energy."
Sun Tzu's The Art of War, 7:5:7-9

"Though no one can go back and make a brand new start, anyone can start from now and make a brand new ending."
Carl Bard

"It is better to spend one day contemplating the birth and death of all things than a hundred years never contemplating beginnings and endings."
Buddha

"If you want a happy ending, that depends, of course, on where you stop your story."

Orson Welles

General Principle: Final stage situations are always the most challenging.

Situation:

These final situations are the most difficult challenges the we face in the course of a campaign. They are the riskiest, with the highest probability of loss. We would prefer to conclude our campaigns without passing through these stages. Unfortunately, experience teaches that few things of value are won easily.

Opportunity:

If a campaign ends prior to these final stages, we obviously avoid their worst-case scenarios. All of our earlier decisions attempt to avoid them. Unfortunately, no matter how we tip the odds in our favor, strategy is a probabilistic process. That means that there is always a chance we will find ourselves in the most challenging situations (1.8.4 Probabilistic Process). Actually, given enough campaigns, it is only a matter of time. If we are wise, we train for these worst case scenarios. Because of their danger, we must understand them more clearly than all other situations. Recognizing and knowing how to respond to them is literally a matter of life and death. Responding to these situations correctly provides us with the greatest upside, saving ourselves from complete disaster.

Key Methods:

The following key methods explain the challenges of late-stage situations.

1. These final three classes of situations are the most difficult and dangerous. We do not get to this stages if our campaign is successful. Because these situations are the most challenging, the mistakes we make during them are the most costly. Since mistakes are so costly, knowing the right responses is valuable (5.0 Minimizing Mistakes).

2. The final three classes of competitive situations are known as 1) difficult, 2) limited, and 3) desperate. Though it oversimplifies them, let us offer some simple descriptions of these three situations. Difficult situations encounter obstacles that slow progress. Limited situations describe a transition that must be made secretly. Desperate situations are do-or-die situations where our goal is survival (8.7.2 Abandoning Positions).

3. We run into these situations when our goal is near. The proximity of our goal makes going through these situations worthwhile. By resolving these final stage problems, we can claim the rewards offered by the entire campaign (8.0 Winning Rewards

4. Failure is certain if we do not know how to react to these situations. These three situations all describe different types of problems that must be resolved before a campaign can be concluded. Missteps are easy. Each requires us to do something that is against our instinct (5.2.1 Choosing Adaptability).

5. Late-stage campaign situations require the right character. They all certainly require courage and confidence, but character plays a more subtle role involved with timing. The response to each of these situations requires a certainty about how we can use time in our favor (1.5.1 Command Leadership)

6. Improperly handled, one of these situations can easily lead to another. These situations can form a kind of chain reaction. Slower progress can be followed by a difficult choice, which itself can be followed by a desperate situation. Needless to say, Sun Tzu's principles of response are designed to avoid these situations whenever possible, but even then, there is a potential connection. All we can do is cope in the best way possible with what the environment gives us (3.2.1 Environmental Dominance).

Illustration:

Think of these stages as arising when fighting a fire.

1. These final three classes of situations are the most difficult and dangerous. If everyone gets out of the building and the fire gets put out, no problem. However, the longer the fire fight goes on, as long as people are trapped, the more likely these situations are to arise.

2. The final three classes of competitive situations are known as 1) difficult, 2) limited, and 3) desperate. The fire is persistent. We save someone from a tight situation taking a risk. We are trapped by the flames.

3. We run into these situations when our goal is near. The last person saved is always in the most serious situation.

4. Failure is certain if we do not know how to react to these situations. People will die.

5. Late-stage campaign situations require the right character. We cannot be panicked into rushing or frightened into going too slow.

6. Improperly handled, one of these situations can easily lead to another. The hard to put out fire will turn into a life-or-death situation.

6.4.0 Nine Situations

Sun Tzu's ten key methods defining the nine common competitive situations.

"A commander provides what is needed now.
This is like climbing high and being willing to kick away your ladder.
You must be able to lead your men deeply into different surrounding territory.
And yet, you can discover the opportunity to win."
Sun Tzu's The Art of War 11:5:12-15

"It is a challenge. I spoke about things being uncomfortable sometimes. It's not always going to be a situation where it's going to be convenient for you."
Rubin Carter

General Principle: Before responding to a situation, we must know its general nature.

Situation:

Sun Tzu's system recognizes that competitive situations are complex and constantly changing. As we pursue opportunities, our progress itself naturally changes our situation. Every situation is unique, but they have characteristics in common. Situations occur on the similar forms of ground. Our rivals can take certain types of positions against us. Our commitment to the venture can vary. Still, none of these conditions always dictate the same response. Our response depends on the larger situation in which we find ourselves.

Opportunity:

The secret is in knowing how situations combine these characteristics. Sun Tzu's Playbook defines nine common classes of situations. These classes combine different types of ground, opposing postures, and levels of commitment. The power of recognizing these situations is that each has one and only one correct response. When we recognize the situations, we know exactly what to do. When a situation doesn't meet the situations criteria, we know what not to do. Our skills at situation response depend upon instant recognition of these situations.

Key Methods:

We list these nine common classes of situations below to give a basic understanding of what they are and how they develop naturally out of the current situation. Any situation can arise with any move and usually many will arise during the course of a campaign.

1. The nine classes of situations both qualify and disqualify a given situation from a given response. These classes of situations provide templates for action. As we will see, the definitions of these situations get very specific. These specifics are important. If a situation does not meet all the specific conditions of its type, the missing conditions point to the proper response (6.5 Nine Responses).

2. We are sometimes forced to find an opportunity because our existing position is threatened. In a lesser form, this situation takes the form of natural pressure against pursuing a new venture as an opportunity, but in its specific form, something more is required. We call this a dissipating situation (6.4.1 Dissipating Situations).

3. Campaigns get off to an easy start as we stay close to what we know. Frequently just the novelty of getting into a new territory gives us certain advantages. This is an easy situation (6.4.2 Easy Situations).

4. If a new opportunity is very appealing, other competitors and rivals will discover it as well. Sometimes, our initial success in the opportunity gives them the idea. This is a contentious situation (6.4.3 Contentious Situations).

5. We and our opponents can make quick progress along different routes without conflict. We can build our position while competitors can also build their positions in different ways. This is an open situation (6.4.4 Open Situations).

6. Over time, we and potential rivals pursue an opportunity along the same lines. None of us have all the skills and resources needed to establish a dominant position. These different groups bring different forms of value to create a complete solution. This is a intersecting situation (6.4.5 Intersecting Situations).

7. Our investment to establish our position gets larger and larger. At this point, even our supporters can become critics of the new venture, threatening to cut off funding. This is a serious situation (6.4.6 Serious Situations).

8. As we explore the opportunity more deeply, we discover barriers that slow progress. We must overcome these barriers to make the venture successful. This is a difficult situation (6.4.7 Difficult Situations).

9. When a move gets close to a conclusion, we reach a key transition point. During this time, our options are severely limited. The transition is delicate and can be derailed if opposition arises. This is a limited situation (6.4.8 Limited Situations).

10. As we get to the very end of the campaign, we can succeed only if we commit all our resources. We must do this quickly because our venture will fail if we delay. This is a desperate situation (6.4.9 Desperate Situations).

Illustration:

Let us illustrate these ideas with a scenario about starting a business as a hairdresser as a friend of ours once did have quitting a big salon.

1. The nine classes of situations both qualify and disqualify a given situation from a given response. Going into a new business, the new owner doesn't know what situations he or she will encounter but must pick the best responses and avoid damaging ones in order to survive, given that 80% of new businesses do not survive.

2. Sometimes we are forced to pursue any new opportunity because our existing position is threatened. We must start our own business because we lost our job and cannot find a new one. In this example, let us say that we are a hairdresser.

3. Campaigns get off to an easy start as we stay close to what we know. We start a business using our existing skills by making contact with our existing customers and offering to visit them in their homes to do their hair.

4. If a new opportunity is very appealing, other competitors and rivals will discover it as well. Our "at-home" service is very popular, so we start working with other hairdressers who work as freelancers. Some of the hairdressers start their own competing businesses. "At home" service is popular. It attracts other hair-dressers and salons into offering it.

5. We and our opponents can make quick progress along different routes without conflict. There are a lot of different types of customers in different areas of town so direct competition is limited. Different at home providers concentrate on different groups of customers and types of services-coloring, perms, etc.

6. Over time, we and potential rivals pursue an opportunity along the same lines. As our business grows, we spread out through town and expand our services. Other successful organizations do as well. We start having problems with consistent standards and quality from our free-lance work force.

7. Our investment to establish our position gets larger and larger. Since we have been growing so quickly, we have had to borrow money from the bank. However, despite our growth, we don't seem to be making a profit and the bank cuts us off.

8. As we explore the opportunity more deeply, we discover barriers that slow progress. In making the transition from a hairdresser to a business owner, we are forced to master a whole new set of management skills.

9. When a move gets close to a conclusion, we reach a key transition point. The market has reached a saturation point and poor management has forced us to change our original model. We are going to change from using free-lancers to hiring and training our own hairdressers who are employees, but the transition will take time.

10. As we get to the very end of the campaign, we can succeed only if we commit all our resources. Our free lancers revolt against the transition, starting their own competing organization. We must respond quickly or lose everything.

6.4.1 Dissipating Situations

Sun Tzu's five key methods on situations where defensive unity is destroyed.

"Warring parties must sometimes fight inside their own territory.
This is scattering terrain."
Sun Tzu's The Art of War 11:1:11-12

"Divide and rule, the politician cries; unite and lead, is watchword of the wise."
Johann Wolfgang von Goethe

"Words divide us, actions unite us."
Tupamoros Slogan

General Principle: Dissipating situations arise when defensive unity is clearly threatened by an attack.

Situation:

A competitor or rival is mounting a large, well-organized attack on our existing position. Given its size and power, this invasion is very likely to be successful. At the very least, the confrontation with this opponent will be difficult and expensive. We are forced to defend our existing position within our own territories. The main problem here is not the rival, but the internal division that the threat causes.

Opportunity:

This is called a dissipating situation because it dissipates our strength. In Sun Tzu's system, strength comes from unity (1.7 Competitive Power) , especially in defense (1.7.1 Team Unity). Joining with others doesn't mean that we all don't have our separate interests. It measn that our shared mission is more important and more defensible (1.6.1 Shared Mission).

Key Methods:

We use the following principles to clearly identify the conditions that create a dissipating situation.

1. An opponent forces us into the campaign by creating a dissipating situation. A dissipating situation arises at the beginning of a campaign because the situation creates the campaign. We do not create these situations ourselves, at least not by our choice of immediate actions. These events are outside of our control (3.2.1 Environmental Dominance).

2. In a dissipating situation, the attacking force must be large enough that we cannot defend our existing position. Since it is easier to defend than attack, the attacking force must be so large that we cannot defend against it. Given the principles of force size, the force must be many times larger than our defending force (6.7.2 Size Adjustments).

3. In a dissipating situation, the attacking force must be well-organized. This means that there are no internal divisions within the group attacking us. If these internal fractures exist, we should attempt to divide the force to reduce it to a size against which we can defend (9.2.5 Organizational Risk).

4. In a dissipating situation, the attack must be on our territory, on our span of control, rather than on our competitive forces. The attempt must be to take away our existing position not simply undermining our attempts to win a new position. Since we are being attacked in our own territory, we cannot evade the larger force by the principles of force size (5.6.1 Defense Priority).

5. Because the threat is to our existing position, our supporters are likely to abandon us in a dissipating situation. While they may support our position, they are more concerned with maintaining their own positions. In other situations, they might normally support us, but under the nature of the threat here, most will likely desert us to protect themselves. They put a higher priority on defending themselves than on helping defend our position (1.6.3 Shifting Priorities).

Illustration:

Let us illustrate these key methods with a case study where a large, well-known company announces that it is targeting a market niche that is occupied by a much smaller, local company.

1. An opponent forces us into the campaign by creating a dissipating situation. No actions at the smaller company could have avoided triggering this event. Indeed, it is the success of the small company's position that attracted the tact.

2. The attacking force must be large enough that we cannot defend our existing position. The large, well-known company moving "down market" sets aside an overwhelming amount of resources and money given the size of the market.

3. The attacking force must be well-organized. There is no internal conflict created by their decision to go after the smaller company's market.

4. The attack must be on our territory, on our span of control, rather than on our competitive forces. The large company is not simply trying to take away new customers, they are specifically targeting the smaller company's existing customers, trying to take them away.

5. Because the threat is to our existing position, our supporters are likely to abandon us. In this case, supporters include the smaller company's existing employees, service providers, suppliers, and their customers. This attack throws people into chaos. Employees start looking for jobs elsewhere, possibly with the invader. Customers and suppliers who have worked with the smaller company for years are suddenly divided. Each is concerned about how the change will affect their particular positions.

6.4.2 Easy Situations

Sun Tzu's five key methods for recognizing situations of easy initial progress. .

"When you enter hostile territory, your penetration is shallow.
This is easy terrain."

Sun Tzu's The Art of War 11:1:13-14

"Almost everything in life is easier to get into than out of."

Anonymous

"There's no thrill in easy sailing when the skies are clear and blue, there's no joy in merely doing things which any one can do. But there is some satisfaction that is mighty sweet to take, when you reach a destination that you thought you'd never make."

Spirella

General Principle: Easy situations sow the seeds of future difficulties.

Situation:

The "easy situation" arises when we first begin a move or a campaign and have a minimal commitment to it. It defines a situation where we can seemingly make progress easily. As a result, we form our expectations regarding the future of the move. The problem is both our lack of commitment and a set expectations based on minimal experience. Without making a commitment, it is easy to get distracted. Our set of expectations are almost certainly wrong.

Opportunity:

Our perception of progress comes from our expectations compared to reality (1.3.1 Competitive Comparison). Before making a move or starting a new campaign, we usually have a number of concerns and worries. As we begin to actually act, there is a kind of relief of pressure. We often discover that many of our concerns were unwarranted. When this happens, it is a tremendous opportunity if we know how to take advantage of it, but because of the special nature of our easy situation, we often do not.

Key Methods:

The kyey methods for identifying an easy situation are:

1. An easy situation can occur only at the beginning of a move or campaign. Other situations can resemble an easy situation because they lack significant barriers, but the ease of an easy situation is of a special kind. It is easy both in the sense of representing few significant barriers but also easy in the sense that it causes no real concern (6.3.1 Early-Stage Situations).

2. In an easy situation, we lack commitment because the move or campaign is just beginning. The more we invest in a move or campaign, the more committed we become to making it work. Though sunk costs should not influence our commitment to pursuing an opportunity, the fact is that they often do ([6.2 Campaign](#) [Evaluation](#)).

3. In an easy situation, we have no challenges that slow us. When we stay close to what we know, as we are at the beginning of all moves, we make quick progress, both in learning and in physically moving. This easy initial progress is easy to take for granted. Only as our distance from our current position increases, do we usually encounter the challenges of establishing a new position ([4.4](#) [Strategic Distance](#)).

4. In an easy situation, we are easily distracted because of our lack commitment. This is the second, perhaps more important sense in which these situations are easy. Easy progress is easy to take for granted. Our choice of pursuing a given opportunity is made moment-to-moment. Since the easy situation arises early in a campaign, before we have made any significant commitment to the opportunity or been engaged by any serious challenges, events can easily distract us from them ([5.1.1 Event Pressure](#)).

5. The easy situation sows the seeds for its own future difficulties. Most campaigns that are easy at first naturally grow more difficult over time. We are easily distracted in an easy situation. We think that we will continue making easy progress even if we take a break to do something else more pressing. We always think that the opportunity represented by an easy situation will keep. But our fast progress will naturally create opposition. We are mistaken if we think of an easy situation as friendly territory. The easy situation leaves us poorly prepared to these situations as they naturally reverse themselves ([3.2.4 Emptiness and Fullness](#)).

Illustration:

A group is given the task of designing a product for a specific market. The product development deadline is three months away at the beginning of the project.

1. An easy situation can occur only at the beginning of a move or campaign. Once the analysis is finished and the group starts working, the product comes together quickly. After a week, the project seems about half done. What could go wrong?

2. Because the move or campaign is just beginning, we lack commitment to it. Management is happy with the progress, but since things are going so well, the energies are naturally focused elsewhere.

3. We often meet no challenges that slow us at the earliest parts of a move. At this point, the project seems trivial. People are not losing sleep over it. They look at their schedule and the project and feel only complacency.

4. Because of our lack of commitment, we are easily distracted in these situations. Since the project is so far ahead of schedule, it is easy to pull people off of it when other needs naturally arise. Even if management doesn't do this, people find it much easier to put their time into personal matters since the project seems well in hand.

5. The easy situation sows the seeds for its own future difficulties. Time passes and deadlines grow nearer when the inevitable problems and barriers are encountered. There is much less time and resources to address those problems because of the project's initial easy situation.

6.4.3 Contentious Situations

Sun Tzu's four key methods for identifying situations that invite conflict.

"Some terrain gives you an advantageous position. But it gives others an advantageous position as well. This will be disputed terrain."

Sun Tzu's The Art of War 11:1:15-17

"The well-meaning contention that all ideas have equal merit seems to me little different from the disastrous contention that no ideas have any merit."

Carl Sagan

"Such democracies have ever been spectacles of turbulence and contention; have ever been found incompatible with personal security or the rights of property; and have in general been as short in their lives as they have been violent in their deaths."

James Madison

General Principle: Contentious situations offer obvious rewards that tempt people into conflict.

Situation:

The contentious situation arises when we discover that an opportunity is very rewarding, but others discover it as well. Because of an opportunity's obvious potential, it attracts competitors. The opportunity initially looks like an opening, but because others react to it as we have, the opening is not closed but it is contested. While no one has yet established a position taking advantage of the opening, there are a number of competitors vying to do so.

Opportunity:

The contentious situation arises because the opportunity's abundant benefits seem equally available to all contenders. None of them have established positions. If the benefits were not abundant, it would be easy to leave the opportunity because of its potential for conflict. Unfortunately, the benefits are real. Big opportunities are rare, hence, the strategic problem (4.0 Leveraging Probability).

Key Methods:

The following principles identify the conditions of a contentious situation.

1. In a contentious situation, the area of opportunity quickly demonstrates that it offers rewards or advantages. If there were no rewards, there would be no basis for contention. If the rewards were not fairly obvious fairly quickly, the area would not draw adversaries into contention (8.0 Winning Rewards

2. In a contentious situation, the extent of the rewards and the costs of harvesting them are unknown. Since this is an early-stage situation, those involved have not had time to learn the deeper nature of the territory. As more is learned, different non-conflicting paths or ways to share in the benefits of the territory may be discovered (2.1.1 Information Limits]).

3. In a contentious situation, those rewards seem equally available to all of those pursuing them. In other words, no one has control of them and no one has a clear advantage in getting control of them. Conflict is usually avoided by someone demonstrating a superior position. In a contention situation, no one has had time to develop such a position (6.3.1 Early-Stage Situations).

4. The contentious situation tempts those vying for the opportunity to fight each other over it. No one wants to leave the field of competition because of the potential that it offers. Those involved focus on the rewards of the situation, which are readily apparent, rather than the costs of conflict, which are not (3.1.3 Conflict Cost).

Illustration:

A great example of a contentious situation is the early stages of a presidential campaign where a number of candidates are still in contention for their party's nomination.

1. The area or opportunity being explored quickly demonstrates that it offers rewards or advantages. The advantage of a nomination for the president are well known.

2. The extent of the rewards and any restrictions on harvesting them are not yet known. Early in the campaign, before the primaries, the candidates do not know which of them will draw the most votes or even the most funds in the contest.

3. Those rewards seem equally available to all of those pursuing them. All the candidates see themselves as positioned equally in terms of winning the contributions of supporters and the votes of primary voters.

4. This contentious situation tempts those vying for the opportunity to fight each other over it. The candidates naturally meet to debate the issues, setting up a situation where they are encouraged to fight it out. As Sun Tzu predicts, this fight weakens all candidates so that, when running against an incumbent, the challenger seldom wins.

6.4.4 Open Situations

Sun Tzu's five key methods for recognizing situations of that are races without a course.

"You can use some terrain to advance easily. Others can advance along with you.
This is open terrain."

Sun Tzu's The Art of War 11:1:18-20

"Plodding wins the race."

Aesop

"The trouble with the rat-race is that even if you win, you're still a rat."

Lily Tomlin

General Principle: Open situations create a race without a clear route.

Situation:

The challenge in an open situation is finding the best way to utilize a given opportunity. The open situation puts us in a contest where the best methods for winning the contest are uncertain because they depend upon the as-yet-unknown potential of the ground. We are forced to choose among alternative routes with the clear probability of choosing the wrong such path.

Opportunity:

There are two opportunities for learning in an open situation. One is to learn more about the nature of the ground and how to secure its benefits. The second is to learn from our rivals, by observing their progress along the paths that they have chosen.

Key Methods:

We use the following mehods to clearly identify when we are in an open situation.

1. A open situation occurs only in the middle of a campaign. In a sense, it defines the conditions that separate the beginning of a campaign from its middle. It is based on a deeper but incomplete understanding of an opportunity. In the beginning of a campaign, our understanding and that of our rivals, isn't deep enough to create an open situation. At the end of a campaign, that understanding is more complete and positions have solidified to a degree to close off an open situation (6.3.2 MiddleStage Situations).

2. In an open situation, competitors have different options about how to pursue the opportunity. Our situation is uncertain in terms of which direction will yield the best results. There are alternative paths and methods that can be used to establish a position on the basis of the same opportunity. The best route depends upon the still evolving nature of the situation, that is, what others do, and the deeper nature of the environment, which remains to be discovered (3.2.1 Environmental Dominance).

3. In an open situation, there is a race among competitors to discover the complete solution. Not everyone will end up with a winning position. We may be ahead in some aspects of developing a position, but we may be behind in others. The challenge is to be among the first competitors to discover the right formula for a complete and productive position (1.3.1 Competitive Comparison).

4. In an open situation, competitors are making different types of progress by using different methods. No single, superior path toward success has yet been identified. Such a single path may or may not exist. It is a situation that no one yet dominates. A number of alternative routes to exploiting the opportunity and a number of different positions may remain viable indefinitely. When one superior path is identified, the situation evolves into an intersecting situation (6.4.5 Intersecting Situations).

5. In an open situation, each competitor is forced to choose among alternative routes. We must choose where we put our efforts and how much to invest in developing a position. Since we have limited resources, we cannot pursue all the possible alternatives involved. We must commit to one or the other of them (3.1.1 Resource Limitations).

Illustration:

Let us consider an open situation for the promotion to a new position at work. You are being considered for a job promotion. Others are also being considered. You still have time to prove yourself, but you don't know what the selection criteria will be. When you ask your boss directly what she is looking for, she tells you, "I don't know exactly, but I will know it when I see it."

1. A open situation occurs only in the middle of a campaign. The contest for the open job cannot exist without a group of potential candidates and some criteria, as yet unknown, for selection.

2. In an open situation, competitors have different options about how to pursue the opportunity. Candidates can emphasize a range of different types of skills and abilities in positioning for the job opening.

3. *In an open situation, there is a race among competitors to discover the complete solution* . A decision must be made in a limited amount of time. Only one candidate will best identify and best demonstrate a match for the job during that period of time. The contest is not the identification of the perfect person, but the best among the alternatives.

4. *In an open situation, competitors are making different types of progress by using different methods*. Candidates can have different strengths and weakness, but the relative value of those strengths and weakness in terms of filling the job are unclear and uncertain.

5. *In an open situation, each competitor is forced to choose among alternative routes*. Candidates must choose which of their various strengths to emphasize, which requires understanding the field of competitors, and a way of promoting those particular strengths as the most valuable for the job opening, which requires understanding the job and the decision-maker.

6.4.5 Intersecting Situations

Sun Tzu's five key methods for recognizing situations that bring people together.

"Everyone shares access to a given area.
The first one to arrive there can gather a larger group
than anyone else.
This is intersecting terrain."

Sun Tzu's The Art of War 11:1:21-23

"Thought is the organizing factor in man, intersected
between the causal primary instincts and the resulting
actions."

Albert Einstein

"One never reaches home, but wherever friendly paths
intersect the whole world looks like home for a time."

Hermann Hesse

General Principle: Intersecting situations force people to move on the same path.

Situation:

The challenge here is almost the opposite of that in the open situation. In the open situation, no one knows which path leads to a successful position. In the intersecting situation, everyone agrees on what a successful position is, but no one has the resources needed to create it. What we have discovered in the intersecting situation is that our path to success requires more resources than we have alone.

Opportunity:

All competitors vying for position have gathered enough information to see clearly what has to be done to successfully take advantage of an opportunity. Our opportunity here is that none of our rivals have the resources or skills needed to establish a successful position. This creates an opening within the opportunity, an opening within an opening (3.1.4 Openings).

Key Methods:

We recognize an intersecting situation by the following set of conditions.

1. An intersecting situation occurs only in the middle of a campaign. It is based on a more complete understanding of what is required to take advantage of an opportunity but the limited ability to execute based upon that understanding. In the beginning of a campaign, our understanding isn't complete enough to create an intersecting situation. The campaign ends when competitors are able to execute based on this understanding (6.3.2 Middle-Stage Situations).

2. In an intersecting situation, competitors share the same view of how to pursue the opportunity. Everyone agrees that there is only one path and set of methods that can be used to establish a position on the basis of the opportunity. Though everyone seeks to improve their own individual position, they realize that they share a mission in terms of the position that they want to establish (1.6.1 Shared Mission).

3. In an intersecting situation, no individual competitor has all the resources needed to establish a viable position. We all have limited resources. In this situation, each competitor's individual resources are not sufficient to establishing a position that can be successfully defended (3.1.1 Resource Limitations).

4. In an intersecting situation, competitors are tempted to join with others to create a complete solution and/or a dominant position. This is the natural result of seeing a shared mission. In this situation, no one yet dominates but everyone sees domination as possible. Sun Tzu describes this situation in terms of a "crowd under heaven," which I rendered rather clumsily as a "larger group than anyone else." This concept infers both completeness and relative superiority. 1.3.1 Competitive Comparison).

5. In an intersecting situation, there is a race among competitors to complete the solution. Those parties in the winning combination will succeed. The challenge is to be among the first competitors to establish a complete and productive position (5.3.1 Speed and Quickness).

Illustration:

As an illustration, let us use a common example that recurs frequently in high-tech. Several companies are bringing a new electronic device to market. The device requires complete integration among hardware, software, distribution, and service components. Hardware companies, software companies, device distributors, and service companies are all developing similar products for this market because they all see its potential. Each is ahead in their own area, but success will be determined by who will be able to create a complete product. Think about the recent, competition between Blu-Ray and HD-DVD as standards for the new generation of DVD player, a competition that Blu-Ray eventually won.

1. An intersecting situation occurs only in the middle of a campaign. The situation had to evolve to the point that there were competing technological camps promoting two different standards.

2. In an intersecting situation, competitors share the same view of how to pursue the opportunity. Everyone generally agrees about what the device requires in terms of capacity.

3. In an intersecting situation, no individual competitor has all the resources needed to establish a viable position. Sony (Blu-Ray) and Toshiba (HD-DVD) couldn't establish a standard on their own. They needed the support of other machine makers and those offering movie content.

4. In an intersecting situation, competitors are tempted to join with others to create a complete solution and/or a dominant position . Everyone saw the value of joining one camp or the other rather than having a divided market forever.

5. In an intersecting situation, there is a race among competitors to complete the solution. The question was, which one will get there first?

6.4.6 Serious Situations

Sun Tzu's six key methods for identifying situations where resources can be cut off.

"You can penetrate deeply into hostile territory.
Then many hostile cities are behind you.
This is dangerous terrain."
Sun Tzu's The Art of War 11:1:24-27

"The essential support and encouragement comes from
within, arising out of the mad notion that your society
needs to know what only you can tell it."
John Updike

"Support from a lack of new supply will be short-lived."
Makoto Yamashita

General Principle: Serious situations arise when distance and opposing forces makes it impossible to get more resources.

Situation:

The serious situation is not serious only in the sense of "grim" but also in the sense of "significant," as in a serious opportunity. In the serious situation, we have learned a great deal about the opportunity we are exploring. If the situation did not show the potential for more rewards, we would simply stop our move or campaign when our resources ran out. The fact that the situation evolves into a serious situation means the opportunity's potential has been, at least to some degree, verified.

Opportunity:

All competitors vying for position have gathered enough information to see clearly what has to be done to successfully take advantage of an opportunity. Our opportunity here is that none of our rivals have the resources or skills needed to establish a successful position. This creates an opening within the opportunity, an opening within an opening (3.1.4 Openings).

Key Methods:

There are six key methods for identifying serious situations.

1. A serious situation occurs when we are in the middle of a campaign after significant investments have been made in it. Time must pass to create a serious situation. The original resources we started with must have time to be exhausted. However, from that investment, we have learned enough about the potential reward to justify our desire to invest more (6.3.2 Middle-Stage Situations).

2. A serious situation requires distance between our position and the source of our resources. This distance is the central problem creating the serious situation. We encounter this situation when we are distant from our source of resources. We can only carry so many resources with us in making a move. Additional resources are needed from supporters over time. We are separated from those supporters because we have left them too far behind in our pursuit of an opportunity 4.4 Strategic Distance.

3. This distance can be either physical or intellectual. Physical resources require transportation over physical distances, but intellectual distance has perhaps a bigger affect our support. Our supporters require communication, which becomes more difficult as distance separates our perspective from theirs. Given our different perspectives, our supporters are less able to see the value of the campaign.(2.0 Developing Perspective).

4. The serious situation can only arise when we have verified some aspect of the opportunity's potential. In other words, we must know that the situation offers serious rewards and as well as a serious need for resources. If the nature of the opportunity didn't balance the additional costs, the move or campaign would simply end (8.0 Winning Rewards

5. A serious situation requires some lack of control over our supply lines. Distance alone raises the costs of transportation and communication, but it doesn't threaten it. The threat comes from our lack of control. If we had complete control of our supply lines, the serious situation could not develop. However, our control in this situation is limited due to some opposing force, whether a force of nature or conscious rival. This opposing force can cut-off our supply lines because of the distance involved (8.1.2 Reward Boundaries).

6. Serious situations often arise simply because campaigns continue longer than expected. This is often the case when our resources for a continued campaign rely on our supporters. Supporters naturally weary of campaigns and lose sight of the potential rewards. As campaigns continue, it often disappoints their expectations for a quick pay-off (8.1.3 Reward Timing).

Illustration:

The most famous historical example of the serious situation was Hannibal's campaign against Rome. Because Hannibal lost his support in Carthage, he eventually had to leave Italy without being defeated. Rome was given time to recover from the invasion, building up its army and eventually destroying Carthage entirely.

1. A serious situation occurs when we are in the middle of a campaign after significant investments have been made in it. This campaign took years, starting with the famous invasion over the Alps, but it continued up and down the Italian peninsula for years, through a series of battles.

2. A serious situation requires distance between our position and the source of our resources. Carthage was in northern Africa and Rome was in Italy. Hannibal required continued support from Carthage in order to continue the campaign.

3. This distance can be either physical or intellectual. The most important resource Hannibal needed was political. Over time, Hannibal's perspective grew more and more distant from that of the people in Carthage.

4. The serious situation can only arise when we have verified some aspect of the opportunity's potential. Hannibal saw both the wealth of Rome and the ease with which their armies were defeated. The Carthaginians saw only the continued costs of the campaign.

5. A serious situation requires some lack of control over our supply lines. Despite military success after military success against the Romans in Italy, Hannibal's political opponents in Carthage used Hannibal's absence to turn his supporters against him, cutting off any further support for his campaign.

6. Serious situations often arise simply because campaigns continue longer than expected. Hannibal's political opponents did not have a significant defeat to point to. Their problem was was simply the length and continued cost of the campaign.

6.4.7 Difficult Situations

Sun Tzu's six key methods for recognizing situations where serious barriers must be overcome.

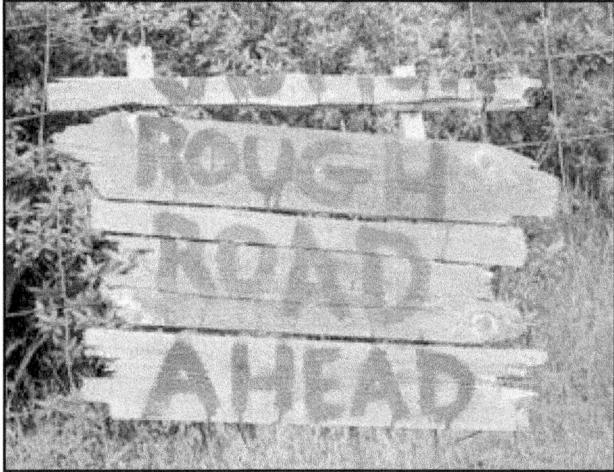

"There are mountain forests.
There are dangerous obstructions.
There are reservoirs.
Everyone confronts these obstacles on a campaign.
They make bad terrain."
                              Sun Tzu's The Art of War 11:1:27-31

Difficulties are things that show a person what they are.
                              Epictetus

"As we advance in life it becomes more and more
difficult, but in fighting the difficulties the inmost strength
of the heart is developed."
                              Vincent Van Gogh

General Principle: In difficult situations, progress slows down so much that we want to give up.

Situation:

The difficult situation is the something of the opposite of the Easy Situation (6.4.2 Easy Situations). Difficult situations arise when we encounter serious obstacles to success. They occur relatively late in a move or campaign, when we have completely explored an opportunity. The difficulties discovered can be a big problem central to the opportunity or a number of problems blocking all our different routes to success.

Opportunity:

In a difficult situation, we have the opportunity to establish a protected position (4.6.3 Barricaded Conditions). If the difficult situation doesn't stop us completely, we get through barriers that will hinder prospective competitors from following us.

Key Methods:

The following six methods help us clearly identify difficult situations.

1. *A difficult situation can occur only toward the end of a move or campaign.* Other situations can resemble a difficult situation because we encounter challenges or barriers, but the difficulty in a difficult situation is of a special kind. It is difficult both in the sense of representing significant barriers and also difficult in the sense that it causes us to worry about losing what we have invested in the move (6.3.3 Late-Stage Situations).

2. *In a difficult situation, we are committed because the move or campaign is close to a successful ending.* We are committed for two reasons. First, we know enough at this point to know that the opportunity has potential, which wins our commitment. Second, the more we invest in a move or campaign that has potential, the more committed we become to making it work. Though sunk costs should not influence our commitment to pursuing an opportunity,

those costs combined with the clearer view of potential creates commitment (6.2 Campaign Evaluation).

3. ***Difficult situations are challenging because progress slows to a crawl.*** A difficult situation arises from a dramatic slowdown in the pace of progress. Slower progress consumes resources, starting with our time, and discourages supporters. Supporters naturally weary of campaigns that are making little progress. They tend to lose sight of the potential rewards. As campaigns continue, it often disappoints people's expectations for a quick pay-off (8.1.3 Reward Timing).

4. ***Difficult situations are often created by earlier easy situations.*** Many campaigns that are easy at first naturally grow more difficult over time. The easy situation creates an expectation of continued quick progress. The subjective perception of slow progress is relative to our comparison with the earlier fast progress (6.4.2 Easy Situations).

5. ***In a difficult situation, the challenges engage us.*** If the problems were simply incomprehensible, the move would end, but in the serious situation, we appreciate the nature of the problem. Through the course of the move, we develop a deeper knowledge of an opportunity. As our distance from our initial position increases, we increase our knowledge of the new terrain. We learn more about the challenge of winning a position in it. The problem occupies our minds (4.4 Strategic Distance).

6. ***A difficult situation can arise when a variety of different obstacles block different potential paths.*** This usually happens when a difficult situation evolves from an open situation. In open situations, we can take a variety of paths to get to our goal. We and our different competitors can try a variety of paths. When we find these different paths blocked by different types of problems, the open situation changes into a difficult situation (6.4.3 Contentious Situations).

7. ***A difficult situation can arise from a single, large obstacle that was once hidden.*** This usually happens when a difficult situ-

ation evolves from an intersecting situation. In intersecting situations, everyone sees one, correct path to success. Since there is only one path to success, it can be blocked by a serious barrier, one that is perhaps impossible to overcome (6.4.5 Intersecting Situations).

Illustration:

As an illustration, let us consider a situation where you have been looking for a new job. You still have a job, but you think you see an opportunity to find a better one at another firm in the larger job market.

1. *A difficult situation can occur only toward the end of a move or campaign.* The situation is difficult because it has gone on for awhile and you are tiring of the process. The psychological effect of rejection is taking its toll. Your current job is looking better and better.

2. *In a difficult situation, we are committed because the move or campaign is close to a successful ending.* You have found that there are better jobs out there, but if something doesn't happen soon, you will give up the search. You have made it to the final interviews several times and have been told a number of times that you were the second choice, but you never get the job. You have been so close that you can taste it.

3. *Difficult situations are challenging because progress slows to a crawl.* You have already contacted all the likely prospects for employing you. It is becoming more and more difficult to find new prospects to contact.

4. *Difficult situations are often created by earlier easy situations.* You were initially surprised by how much demand there was for your skills set and job experience. When you sailed through to the final interview, you thought that the process would be much easier than it turned out to be.

5. *In a difficult situation, the challenges we discover truly engage us.* You find yourself thinking about the job hunt all the

time. You wonder why people don't want you. Even though you are still employed, the continuous rejections are eating at you.

6. *A difficult situation can arise when a variety of different obstacles block different potential paths.* In every situation, the problem seems to be different.

7. *A difficult situation can arise from a single, large obstacle that was once hidden.* You have the experience people are looking for, but the normal job qualifications for the position require more formal education than you have.

6.4.8 Limited Situations

Sun Tzu's six key methods for identifying situations defined by a bottleneck.

"In some areas, the entry passage is narrow. Y
ou are closed in as you try to get out of them.
In this type of area, a few people can effectively attack
your much larger force.
This is confined terrain."
Sun Tzu's The Art of War 11:1:32-35

The margin is narrow, but the responsibility is clear."
John F. Kennedy

"It keeps changing all the time, ... The narrow paths get
wider, the vistas open up as you walk through."
Ted Nierenberg

General Principle: In difficult situations, progress slows down so much that we want to give up.

Situation:

The Limited Situation marks a transition point when we depend on a narrow set of resources. In limited situations, we are constrained by our environment or surrounded by our opponents, making access to additional resources impossible. A limited situation occurs towards the end of a campaign where we are making the final transition to the desired position. This limited situation arises in an area where we cannot bring all our resources to bear because the transition point is a bottleneck.

Opportunity:

As in the difficult situation, a limited situation gives us the opportunity to establish a protected position (4.6.3 Barricaded Conditions). If we can get through the limited situation, we can, with very little work, create a barrier that will hinder prospective competitors from following us.

Key Methods:

The following six key methods are used to identify limited situations.

1. A limited situation can occur only toward the end of a move or campaign. A great deal of knowledge is required to get into a limited situation. We would not undertake the risks of a limited situation if we didn't know for certain that it was our only option and that the potential rewards of the opportunity were worth the risk. (6.3.3 Late-Stage Situations).

2. In a limited situation, the completion of a move is limited to a single path or a single type of resource. This is typically known as a "bottleneck." This bottleneck represents a transition point. The larger the total force making the transition, the more difficult the limited situation becomes(5.5.1 Force Size).

3. Competitive strength cannot exist at a limited situation's transition point. We create focused power by using *all* our available resources at once on a given move. In the limited situation, the nature of the situation prevents this. We can use only a fraction of our resources at a time of the transition point (5.5 Focused Power).

4. In a limited situation, we are vulnerable to relatively small challenges focused at the transition point. Bottlenecks limit production in a manufacturing environment but bottlenecks are vulnerabilities in a competitive environment. This is because opposition can oppose us at a transition point in the competitive environment. A challenge is any opposition to our move. Since we cannot bring all our resources to bear, even a relatively minor challenge can prevent our success (9.0 Understanding Vulnerability).

5. In a limited situation, our specific point of vulnerability is determined by the limited resource. There are five classical points of vulnerability. The nature of our vulnerability is determined by the people or the other materials that we need to complete the transition (9.1 Climate Vulnerability).

6. In a limited situation, the place and time of transition is known to us but not others. This transition point represents an opportunity window for our opponents, but as in all competitive situation, the information regarding that transition point is limited. If it was public, the point of transition would certainly be blocked and the situation would be either difficult or desperate (2.1.1 Information Limits]).

Illustration:

Let us illustrate this situation with an imaginary case study from the business world. A company has introduced a new product, but one of the components needed for that product is in short supply.

1. A limited situation can occur only toward the end of a move or campaign. The new product proves very popular on its introduction but because the supply of the needed component is limited, the manufacturer cannot ramp up production quickly enough, keeping the product from being a true success.

2. *In a limited situation, the completion of a move is limited to a single path or a single type of resource.* The component is currently available only from one small volume supplier. Others could make it but currently do not. There are no alternative components that will work in the current design.

3. *Competitive strength cannot exist at a limited situation's transition point.* The current supplier has little capability to expand, and, because of the component's limited supply, the product manufacturer has no leverage in negotiating with them.

4. *In a limited situation, we are vulnerable to relatively small challenges focused at the transition point.* If the product's popularity is discovered, many other companies can come out with competing products. Potential competitors will have enough time to do so if the original maker cannot get enough of their products onto the market to establish a standard and leadership.

5. *In a limited situation, our specific point of vulnerability is determined by the limited resource.* There are many components in the product, but only the one that is in limited supply matters. Both the component maker and potential competitors can use that vulnerability against the product maker.

6. *In a limited situation, the place and time of transition is known to us but not others.* At this point, neither the component manufacturer or competitors know about the product's potential popularity or the limited supply of the needed component.

6.4.9 Desperate Situations

Sun Tzu's three key methods for identifying situations where destruction is possible.

There is sometimes no place to run.
This is always deadly ground."
Sun Tzu's The Art of War 11:6:14-15

"When matters are desperate we must put on a desperate face."
Robert Burn

"Courage enlarges, cowardice diminishes resources.
In desperate straits the fears of the timid aggravate the
dangers that imperil the brave."
Christian Nevell Bovee

General Principle: Desperate situations arise when everything is at risk.

Situation:

The Desperate Situation represents the class of situations where our position is deteriorating rapidly. A desperate situation occurs at the very end of a campaign when time, alternatives, and favorable conditions are all running out. Also known as the deadly or do-or-die situation, the desperate situation arises in an area where the forces opposing our success are rapidly mounting.

Opportunity:

The opportunity in a desperate situation is simple: to survive. Surviving a desperate situation is a form of "trial by ordeal," which proves the quality of the survivors. Surviving a desperate situation give us more credibility than the average person.

Key Methods:

The following three key methods allow us to recognize the desperate situation.

1. A desperate situation occurs only at the very end of a move when no other options are left. A desperate situation arises when we run out of other options. We would not get into a desperate situation if we had other alternatives (6.3.3 Late-Stage Situations).

2. In a desperate situation, conditions are deteriorating rapidly. We find ourselves in a desperate situation when conditions rapidly deteriorate. This negative shift in conditions may arise from environmental factors or from the actions of our rivals and opponents (1.3.1 Competitive Comparison

3. In a desperate situation, delaying our response is fatal. These conditions pose a threat to our existing established position as well as to the campaign. In the desperate situations, we must instantly recognize the threat and just as immediately respond appropriately (5.3 Reaction Time).

Illustration:

Let us illustrate the desperate situation with a health situation, one that actually happened to me personally.

1. A desperate situation occurs only at the very end of a move when no other options are left. You go to the doctor for what you think is a sinus infection. The doctor does some tests and discovers that you have cancer.

2. In a desperate situation, conditions are deteriorating rapidly. The cancer is in stage two, already spreading to other parts of your body.

3. In a desperate situation, delaying our response is fatal. If you do not pick the right treatment, you will die.

6.5.0 Nine Responses

Sun Tzu's twelve key methods for using the best responses to the nine common competitive situations.

*"To be successful, you must control scattering terrain by avoiding battle. Control easy terrain by not stopping.
Control disputed terrain by not attacking.
Control open terrain by staying with the enemy's forces.
Control intersecting terrain by uniting with your allies.
Control dangerous terrain by plundering.
Control bad terrain by keeping on the move.
Control confined terrain by using surprise.
Control deadly terrain by fighting."*

Sun Tzu's The Art of War 11:1:39-48

*"A wise person does at once, what a fool does at last.
Both do the same thing; only at different times."*

John Dalberg Acton

"He who hesitates is lost."

Proverb

General Principle: Instantly know the right responses to meet the nine common situations.

Situation:

The nine classes of competitive situations develop naturally over the course of a move or campaign. While their development is natural, our successful resolution of these situations depends entirely on our choice of action. Our instinctual responses only lead us from one situation to the next, ending eventually at the desperate situation. This is the path we seek to avoid by training our responses. We can only successfully advance our position in these situations if we apply the right responses. The problem is that most of us simply do not understand those responses, at least not enough to use them instantly as a trained reflex.

Opportunity:

The faster we recognize and respond to these situations, the more certain our success becomes. Instantly recognizing these situations is the beginning of our training, but we must also know what response each common situation requires (6.4 Nine Situations). Reading about these responses is also just the beginning. We need to internalize the worldview required in order to develop instant strategic reflexes. You must respond to these situations automatically. We act best when we have correctly retrained our instincts.

Key Methods:

Let us start with the key methods of response and a simple list of the nine responses to the nine classes or situations.

1. We must use proven responses instead of doing what we feel like doing in the nine situations. Responding by how we feel simply leads us into more and more difficult situations. The appropriate responses have been proven over thousands of years of experience. These situations have occurred millions of times in competition and will recur again and again. We must be prepared to react appropriately when they arise by dealing with the situation pragmatically instead of emotionally (2.2.2 Mental Models).

2. We must respond appropriately to the nine situations instantly as a reflex. The longer we delay, the less likely our success becomes and the more likely it is that our current situation will evolve into another type of situation. The secret to our success is taking the right actions as a matter of reflex (6.1.1 Conditioned Reflexes).

3. The more creatively the nine responses are applied, the better they work. The responses themselves are specific, eliminating most other forms of action, but they allow for a wide variety of application. If we want to succeed consistently, we have to instantly know what each situation requires (7.0 Creating Momentum).

4. We respond to a dissipating situation by avoiding a meeting with the larger, attacking force. We cannot simply evade them because they are attacking our position, so we must defend by distracting them from the attack (6.5.1 Dissipating Response).

5. We respond to an easy situation by pressing forward with our advance. We avoid being easily satisfied with easy gains. Instead, we must be even more aggressive (6.5.2 Easy Response).

6. We respond to a contentious situation by avoiding challenging rivals for positions. We avoid getting drawn into direct confrontations (6.5.3 Contentious Response).

7. We respond to an open situation by keeping up with our competitors. We gauge our progress against theirs and copy whatever they do that is working (6.5.4 Open Response).

8. We respond to an intersecting situation by quickly forming partnerships. If we are the first to

9. form alliances, even with potential competitors, we can create the dominant position (6.5.5 Intersecting Response).

10. We respond to a serious situation by getting our resources from the opportunity. We make the new venture pay in any way that we can, even if only for the short term (6.5.6 Serious Response).

11. We respond to a difficult situation by continuing to move. No matter how slow and difficult our progress becomes, we cannot stop moving. We keep on, trying new angles for direction on the problem (6.5.7 Difficult Response).

12. We respond to a limited situation by keeping our move a surprise. Our actions during these transitions must be unexpected by being creative and unpredictable (6.5.5 Intersecting Response). **We respond to a desperate situation by committing everything.** We bring all our resources to bear as quickly as possible, holding nothing in reserve. (6.5.9 Desperate Response).

Illustration:

In the article on the nine situations (6.4 Nine Situations), we illustrated the classes of situations with a hairdresser opening a new salon. Let us extend that illustration here.

1. We must use proven responses instead of doing what we feel like doing in the nine situations. A hairdresser might want to just cut hair rather than respond to strategic conditions, but that simply doesn't work.

2. We must respond appropriately to the nine situations instantly as a reflex. No matter when one of these situations arises, the salon owner must deal with it immediately before it gets worse.

3. The more creatively the nine responses are applied, the better they work. Knowing the right response is a good beginning, but a creative response is much more powerful in terms of creating strategic momentum.

4. We respond to a dissipating situation by avoiding a meeting with the larger, attacking force. In this example, we played the role of hairdressers who started a salon because of a bad job market.

Starting a business works because it avoids expending resources on looking for jobs for which there is too much competition.

5. *We respond to an easy situation by pressing forward with our advance.* We started this business without a salon by visiting past customers in their homes to do their hair. Though we may find enough customers to make a decent income easily, we should continue to contact past customers, continuing to build the business.

6. *We respond to a contentious situation by avoiding challenging rivals for positions.* As our "athome" service attracts rivals, we should look for niches in the market that others have difficulty covering.

7. *We respond to an open situation by keeping up with our competitors.* If a rival finds a novel way of providing services that gives them an advantage, we should quickly copy it in our own niche.

8. *We respond to an intersecting situation by quickly forming partnerships.* As competition heats up, advertising becomes important, but the businesses in this market are too small to advertise. We should start an association of "home haircare providers" that can advertise and direct those interested to members of the association.

9. *We respond to a serious situation by getting our resources from the opportunity.* As a move takes more time, we have to get compensated for the time it takes. You start billing each member for a referral fee.

10. *We respond to a difficult situation by continuing to move.* In making the transition from a hairdresser to business owner to an association owner, we keep moving, slowly evolving our business role to fit evolving market needs.

11. *We respond to a limited situation by keeping our move a surprise.* We must make a decision, choosing between being a hairdresser and running the association. We choose to focus on the association but don't tell our hairdressing customers until the new business is established and stable.

12.   ***We respond to a desperate situation by committing everything.*** Some members start a competing association. We must respond quickly, devoting all our resources to bring them back into the original group because the market will not support two competing organizations.

6.5.1 Dissipating Response

Sun Tzu's five key methods for responding to dissipation by the use of offense as defense.

"To be successful, you must control scattering terrain by avoiding battle."

Sun Tzu's The Art of War 11:1:39

"Divide and rule, the politician cries; unite and lead, is watchword of the wise."

Johann Wolfgang von Goethe

"Words divide us, actions unite us."

Tupamoros Sloga

General Principle: In dissipating situations, we put our opponents on the defensive to rally our supporters.

Situation:

The Dissipating Situation arises when we are targeted for an attack by a capable foe and, as a result, our supporters are likely to desert us to protect themselves. The response must both protect an existing position while avoiding meeting an overpowering opponent. The critical danger of the dissipating situation is that it undermines the unity of our supporters (1.7.1 Team Unity).

Opportunity:

Our opportunity here starts with correctly identifying a dissipating situation, which helps us identify whether or not we can defend our position directly (6.4.1 Dissipating Situations). In a dissipating situation, our opportunity is to quickly change the priorities of our larger opponent by taking a quick and unexpected action. Therefore the real purpose of our response is to demonstrate leadership that unites our people by giving them a task to focus on (1.5.1 Command Leadership).

Key Methods:

These are the key methods for responding to a dissipating situation.

1. In a dissipating situation, we must identify unprotected resources that are valuable to our attacker. We discover what our attackers prize dearly. It can be their reputation, a relationship, a physical resource, or any other resources. This resource must have more proven value for them than the unproven value of fighting us for position. When someone focuses on attacking, they overlook what they must defend (1.1.2 Defending Positions).

2. In the dissipating situation, we advance toward the valued resource and away from the forces attacking us. In this situation, evading our attacking opponent is not enough. Since our position is threatened, we must advance toward something. Of course, a clever attack is better than a poor one, but the real issue is time: we must put together the best attack that we can launch immediately (6.1.1 Conditioned Reflexes).

3. In a dissipating situation, we must make sure that our opponents know exactly what we are threatening. While this move is not what our opponent expected, we don't make this advance in secret. The point here is not to win the targeted resource but to force our opponents to shift from an attack on our position to a defense of their own. Psychologically, people fear loss more than they value gain (loss aversion). This is the one situation where the best defense is a good offense (5.6.1 Defense Priority).

4. In a dissipating situation, we seek to make attacking us more trouble than it is worth. Whatever our attackers hoped to gain from attacking us is less important to them than losing something that they already have and value. By attacking what they prize, we are making ourselves more trouble than we are worth (1.6.3 Shifting Priorities).

5. In a dissipating situation, going on the attack rallies our supports and unifies them. If our supporters face an overwhelming threat, they will desert us, each giving a priority to their own personal defense. People naturally run away from danger. We harness this desire and, at the same time, provide them with a focus for their movement. People would rather move toward a goal than away from a threat. The job of the leader in this situation is to provide their supporters with a clear goal, increasing their strength and unity (1.7.2 Goal Focus).

Illustration:

In our article, on recognizing dissipating situations, we used the example of a large company threatening a smaller company's niche. Let us continue this illustration.

These are the key methods for responding to a dissipating situation.

1. In a dissipating situation, we must identify unprotected resources that are valuable to our attacker. We immediately identify what the invading organization is most proud of in their company's performance, standing, relationships, history, etc.

2. In the dissipating situation, we advance toward the valued resource and away from the forces attacking us. We then find a way to turn the attack against us into a direct threat to what they value. For example, if their organization publicly acclaims a value such as honesty, we find ways to demonstrate how the attack on our market is, above all, dishonest.

3. In a dissipating situation, we must make sure that our opponents know exactly what we are threatening. We make it clear that though they could probably win our market, we will use that battle to attack their reputation, fighting the battle in the media rather than in the market.

4. In a dissipating situation, we seek to make attacking us more trouble than it is worth. Their reputation for honesty must be more valuable to them than our niche of the market.

5. In a dissipating situation, going on the attack rallies our supports and unifies them. By making it clear how we are going to put the larger opponent on the defensive, we encourage our supporters,

6.5.2 Easy Response

Sun Tzu's five key methods regarding overcoming complacency.

"Control easy terrain by not stopping."
Sun Tzu's The Art of War 11:1:41

"Almost everything in life is easier to get into than out of."
Anonymous

"There's no thrill in easy sailing when the skies are clear and blue, there's no joy in merely doing things which any one can do. But there is some satisfaction that is mighty sweet to take, when you reach a destination that you thought you'd never make."
Spirella

General Principle: In easy situations, we make as much progress as quickly as we can.

Situation:

Of course, we must first know for certain that we are in an easy situation. If not, we can make a serious mistake in our response.

We describe the Easy Situation generally as when we first begin a move or campaign and make progress easier than we expect (6.4.2 Easy Situations). As a result, we form our expectations and attitudes about the future of our progress. These attitudes work against us as our move progresses. The danger is that these expectations lead us into patterns of behavior that set us up for failure.

Opportunity:

The easy situation is, by its nature, a tremendous opportunity if we can take it seriously. Of all the nine classes of situation, it offers us the most progress in advancing our position at the least cost. All we need to take advantage of this situation is to realize that it is a limited time offer (5.3.2 Opportunity Windows).

Key Methods:

When we start any campaign or project, we can never be surprised if our initial progress comes easily, and we must never let our initially easy progress change our behavior. The successful response to the easy situation requires us to instantly do the following:

1. In an easy situation, we must focus exclusively on making as much progress as quickly as we can. We keep going. We don't stop. We especially don't want to get distracted. This lesson goes back to Aesop's tale of *The Tortoise and the Hare*. The hare lost for one reason. He got so far ahead he felt that he could afford a break. The real danger of the easy situation is that it creates an expectation that we will not have to press hard to succeed. This lack of pressure leads to a lack of focus because it gives us time to get distracted (1.7.2 Goal Focus).

2. In an easy situation, we communicate our increasing control of the ground and concern about future problems. Our continued, *visible* progress creates the subjective impression that we own the position. Our expressions of concerns are taken more seriously because of our increased pressure. If we pause, we give others time to see an opportunity in what we have left undone. We want people to perceive our position as even more advanced than it is rather than have them doubt our enthusiasm. The subjective perception helps create the objective reality by changing the actions of others as well as our own (1.2 Subobjective Positions)

3. *In an easy situation, we want to offer a moving target.* Since we are making progress, others will be tempted to duplicate our efforts. They are more likely to be tempted into competition if they feel that they can catch up to us. This will allow them to make our lives difficult in any number of ways. (5.3.1 Speed and Quickness).

4. *Until the easy situation ends, we press forward until we can reap rewards from our progress.* Sun Tzu's strategy is not just about advancing our position but making our advances pay. We do not really control a position until our move pays for itself in tangible advantages. We want the easy situation to end with the reality of getting rewarded from our rapid progress (8.0 Winning Rewards)

5. *Until the easy situation ends, we keep putting more resources into the move.* Ideally, those resources come from winning rewards from the new opportunity, but this rule holds even if the position doesn't yet pay for itself. If we are not putting all our resources into an easy situation, where we are making the greatest progress, we are making a mistake. We want to put more resources into what is working so we are not tempted into putting more resources where we are not making progress. We will naturally find other outlets for our excess resources (3.3 Opportunity Resources).

Illustration:

We will continue the example we started in our discussion of identifying easy situations (6.4.2 Easy Situations). A group is given the task of designing a product for a specific market. The product development deadline is three months away at the beginning of the project. A group is given the task of designing a product for a specific market. After three weeks, they seem to have completed half of their project's goals.

These are the key methods for responding to a dissipating situation.

1. In an easy situation, we must focus exclusively on making as much progress as quickly as we can. In response to this easy progress, the team leader presses the team even harder toward completion.

2. In an easy situation, we communicate our increasing control of the ground and concern about future problems. The team leader communicates the team's fast progress to management but also voices concerns about the project hitting a future serious problem. The pressure on the team arises out of that concern.

3. In an easy situation, we want to present a moving target. In pressing forward, the team leader resists the pressure to expand the features being developed in the product.

4. Until the easy situation ends, we press forward until we can reap rewards from our progress. Instead of feature creep, the leader instead expands the scope of his project to include a market test, which will generate revenue.

5. Until the easy situation ends, we keep putting more resources into the move. The project leader seeks more resources, ideally from the market test, as a way of perfecting the design again based on feedback from the market test.

6.5.3 Contentious Response

Sun Tzu's five key methods for responding to contentious situations by knowing how to avoid conflict.

"Control disputed terrain by not attacking."
Sun Tzu's The Art of War 11:1:42

"The well-meaning contention that all ideas have equal merit seems to me little different from the disastrous contention that no ideas have any merit."
Carl Sagan

"Such democracies have ever been spectacles of turbulence and contention; have ever been found incompatible with personal security or the rights of property; and have in general been as short in their lives as they have been violent in their deaths."
James Madison

General Principle: In contentious situations, hamper your opponents, don't fight them.

Situation:

The contentious situation arises when we find that an opportunity is very rewarding, but, as a result, others are attracted to it as well (6.4.3 Contentious Situations). Contentious situations tempt us into conflict with others. If the opportunity being explored didn't offer potentially rich rewards, the risk of costly conflict would mean simply that it wasn't really worth pursuing (3.1.3 Conflict Cost). However, the potential for rich rewards changes not only our response, but what we can expect from others.

Opportunity:

Our primary goal is to further explore the situation while avoiding costly conflict. Since this is an early stage situation, we want to give the situation time to develop (6.3.1 Early-Stage Situations). If given the time, these situations often develop in open situations (6.4.4 Open Situations) or intersecting situations but only if we are able to avoid costly conflict (6.4.5 Intersecting Situations).

Key Methods:

In this specific situation, the following key methods govern our responses:

1. In contentious situations, we must respond instantly but against our basic impulses. We respond instantly to make fast progress because these situations naturally quickly degrade over time. Unfortunately, our two instinctual responses, the flight or fight reflex, both work against us in this situation as we explain below. Instead, we react instantly not on instinct but on the basis of training (6.1.1 Conditioned Reflexes).

2. In contentious situations, we cannot abandon the area of opportunity. The fact that the opportunity shows promise so early in the process, long before any positions are established, means we must focus on exploring it further, looking for a way to establish a position (5.2 Opportunity Exploration).

3. In contentious situations, we must go out of our way to avoid conflict with potential rivals. Conflict defines situations where a meeting is damaging to all participants. The easiest way to avoid conflict is to avoid such meetings on contentious ground (3.1.3 Conflict Cost).

4. In contentious situations, we seek to make ourselves less visible and threatening than opponents. We must not only avoid meeting potential opponents, but we must give them as little incentive as possible to come after us as a potential opponent. We need to keep a low profile in our exploration, attracting a minimum of attention (2.7 Information Secrecy).

5. In contentious situations, we hamper the progress of others in any way that we can. This rule is subordinate to the previous one. We must do this anonymously. We only do this in ways that cannot draw retaliation. With that in mind, we do not want to pass up any opportunities to slow our rivals down. One primary method is to use misdirection while working behind the scene (2.1.3 Strategic Deception).

Illustration:

The example that we discussed earlier in identifying a contentious situation was the early stages of a presidential campaign where a number of candidates are still in contention for their parties nomination (6.4.3 Contentious Situations). Let us continue with this illustration. In this case, let us assume we are the candidate.

1. In contentious situations, we must respond instantly but against our basic impulses. We must react quickly to the crowded field. In this case, we should have expected it.

2. In contentious situations, we cannot abandon the area of opportunity. We must not abandon the field simply because it is crowded.

3. In contentious situations, we must go out of our way to avoid conflict with potential rivals. During debates and other appearances, we must go out of our way not to attack any of our rivals. We can ignore them or even say nice things about them, but we must go out of our way not to damage them.

4. In contentious situations, we seek to make ourselves less visible and threatening than opponents. We should work as much as possible beneath the surface, raising money and putting together local organizations. Even in public forums, like debates, we should not attempt to be the star. If we shine before we have established our position, we will draw the fire of all the other candidates. We want to appear solid rather than threatening. It would be great if we could make all the other candidates think that we were actually running for the number two spot, with them as number one.

5. In contentious situations, we hamper the progress of others in any way that we can. Again, working behind the scenes, we should create challenges and problems for the other candidates when we can do it secretly. For example, if we find damaging information, we should not use it ourselves or even have our supporters use it. We should leak it to the press, or even better, to another rival.

6.5.4 Open Response

Sun Tzu's five key methods to help us keep up with the opposition.

"Control open terrain by staying with the enemy's forces."

Sun Tzu's The Art of War 11:1:42

"Plodding wins the race."

Aesop

"The trouble with the rat-race is that even if you win, you're still a rat."

Lily Tomlin

General Principle: In open situations, keep up with opponents.

Situation:

The Open Situation arises in the middle of a campaign when we are in a race with other competitors but the best route to success is not clear (6.4.3 Contentious Situations). Open situations challenge our ego on one hand and our herd mentality on the other. Ego is dangerous if the situation develops into a intersecting situation

(6.4.5 Intersecting Situations). A herd mentality forgets the basic rule about opportunities being openings (3.1.4 Openings). These two attitudes can easily create a lagging position, which can degrade quickly in a serious situation (6.4.5 Intersecting Situations).

Opportunity:

Our primary goal in the open situation is not to get left behind (1.3.1 Competitive Comparison). As long as we can stay close to the race, our position is viable. Our opportunity is to remain within striking distance as these contests develop. Since this is a middle-stage situation, we must still explore the terrain. The end is not yet in sight (6.3.2 Middle-Stage Situations).

Key Methods:

We respond to the challenging realities of the open situation by following the following key methods:

1. In an open situation, we must quickly pick the route that seems best. Middle-stage situations are all different forms of a race. Speed is important in all strategic moves, but it is more important as we get into the middle stages of moves and campaigns and most important in the open situation where speed determines the winner (5.3.1 Speed and Quickness).

2. If several routes in an open situation seem equal, we must pick the path furthest from the others. This is the path in the the least popular area of exploration. If our route proves successful, we are actually in a better position because our path is less crowded and others will have more of a tendency to ignore us rather than their more proximate rivals (3.2.4 Emptiness and Fullness)

3. In an open situation, we keep in touch with what everyone else is doing. Responding to an open situation is like navigating a maze where we cannot know the right route. Chance plays a critical role in chaotic competitive environments. Anyone might stumble on the right route or many different routes may prove equal. When they do so, we need to know it as soon as possible. Though we hope our distance will help them ignore our progress, we cannot overlook theirs (1.8.4 Probabilistic Process).

4. If our progress in an open situation is equal to that of others, we must keep on the path that we have chosen. We must *not* switch our route even if the majority takes another route. If our progress along our alternative path is equal to that of others, we are better on our own path. This is not an intersecting situation where we get an advantage by joining with others (6.5.4 Open Response)

5. If others find an area in the open situation where progress is faster, we must instantly switch to that area. We must keep up with the leaders. We cannot stubbornly defend our path after we clearly fall behind others. This mistake is just another form of conforming to the pressure of our plans (5.2.1 Choosing Adaptability).

Illustration:

Let us continue the illustration that we started in discussing the identification of open situations (6.4.3 Contentious Situations). We are being considered for a job promotion. Others are also being considered. We still have time to prove ourselves, but we don't know what the selection criteria will be. When we ask our boss directly what she is looking for, she tells us, "I don't know exactly, but I will know it when I see it."

1. In an open situation, we must quickly pick the route that seems best. We must choose a course of action, say, increasing sales, that we think will impress our boss.

2. If we have several routes that seem equal, we must pick the route furthest from the others. If most of our rivals are working to develop one category of products, we pick another category of products that seems to have equal potential but as far away from them as possible.

3. In an open situation, we keep in touch with what everyone else is doing. We must track their progress and especially keep in contact with our boss to gauge how he feels about our progress relative to that of our rivals.

4. If our progress in an open situation is equal to that of others, we must keep on the path that we have chosen. We stick to our original choice of increasing the sales of a different category of products as long as our progress seems equal to the others in terms of making an impression on our boss.

5. If others find an area where progress is faster in an open situation we must instantly switch to that area. If another category of products becomes more important, especially in the mind of our boss, we immediately redirect our sales efforts. We publicly recognize our shift and how it is a response to the situation. We learn from our rivals' successful methods and try to improve on them.

6.5.5 Intersecting Response

Sun Tzu's five key methods on the formation of situational alliances.

"On intersecting terrain, you must solidify your alliances."

Sun Tzu's The Art of War 11:1:43

"Thought is the organizing factor in man, intersected between the causal primary instincts and the resulting actions."

Albert Einstein

"One never reaches home, but wherever friendly paths intersect the whole world looks like home for a time."

Hermann Hesse

General Principle: In intersecting situations, create the right alliances to quickly create a dominant situation.

Situation:

The Intersecting Situation arises when an opportunity takes all rivals to the same path, but none of those rivals have the size and strengths necessary to develop a winning position on it (6.4.5 Intersecting Situations). In this situation, being better than other competitors (1.3.1 Competitive Comparison) is not enough to be successful. The situation demands a particular set of skills and resources and it will take too long for anyone to develop those skills on their own (5.3.1 Speed and Quickness).

Opportunity:

Our opportunity in the intersecting situation is to put together the skills and resources needed to dominate the single path to success. Where no single competitor can dominate the situation, the first group of competitors to create a working alliance will always dominate the intersecting situation. The alliance only works if it is successful in establishing a new position and making that position pay (3.1 Strategic Economics). Intersecting situations leverage our herd mentality in a positive way.

Key Methods:

There are five key methods that define our response in an intersecting situation.

1. In an intersecting situation, we must start thinking about others in terms of shared goals. Since Sun Tzu's strategy is about improving position, rather than defeating enemies, the idea of an "enemy" is simply the idea of someone close to us with whom our position is compared. The fact that others are close to us in an intersecting situation creates the basis for a shared mission (1.6.1 Shared Mission).

2. In an intersecting situation, we look at the strengths *and weaknesses of our potential competitors in terms of potential fit.* Responding to the intersecting situation requires that we instantly form alliances with those with whom we might normally consider rivals or competitors. We must understand how our strengths and weakness fit with those of others around us (3.4.2 Opportunity Fit).

3. In an intersecting situation, we quickly join with others. The key here is speed. Since time is of the essence especially in middle-stage responses, we must make our choice of partners quickly. As in the school yard, those who pick first get the best choices (5.3 Reaction Time).

4. In an intersecting situation, we keep joining with others until we create a dominant position. A dominant position can be defined in terms of either the right combination of skills to make a complete product or simply by size. We want to create the type of force needed to clearly dominate the intersection (1.3.1 Competitive Comparison).

5. In an intersecting situation, we trade a smaller slice of the pie for more certainty. To make the alliance work, we must be willing to give up our personal preferences for the group goal. Within that larger mission, we can focus our own smaller area of control to create unity within the group (1.7 Competitive Power).

Illustration:

As an illustration, we used the common version of the intersecting situation that recurs over and over again in high-tech that we used when discussing how to recognize this situation (6.4.5 Intersecting Situations). Several companies are bringing a new electronic device to market. The device requires complete integration among hardware, software, distribution, and service components. Hardware companies, software companies, device distributors, and service companies are all developing similar products for this market because they all see its potential. Each is ahead in their own area, but success will be determined by who will be able to fill in the gaps in their offering to create the complete product. Think the recent, competition between Blu-Ray and HD-DVD as standards for the new generation of DVD player, a competition that Blu-Ray eventually won.

1. *In an intersecting situation, we must start thinking about others in terms of shared goals.* While everyone else is thinking how they can dominate this market, we start thinking about why some of these companies might want partners.

2. *In an intersecting situation, we look at the* strengths *and weaknesses of our potential competitors in terms of potential fit.* If we represent a software company, we are looking for hardware, distributors and service providers who would make good partners.

3. *In an intersecting situation, we quickly join with others.* We want to be the first company soliciting partners with whom to work.

4. *In an intersecting situation, we keep joining with others until we create a dominant position.* We make it clear that these are not exclusive partnerships, but that our association wants to help each member by creating a dominating market presence. Each member gets stronger by adding new members. The new members are not competitors. The real opponent is invisibility in the marketplace.

5. *In an intersecting situation, we trade a smaller slice of the pie for more certainty.* We want to keep dividing the pie to grow it until we push out any competing position in the market.

6.5.6 Serious Response

Sun Tzu's six key methods for responding to serious situations by finding immediate income.

"Control dangerous terrain by plundering."
Sun Tzu's The Art of War 11:1:44

"The essential support and encouragement comes from within, arising out of the mad notion that your society needs to know what only you can tell it."
John Updike

"Support from a lack of new supply will be short-lived."
Makoto Yamashita

General Principle: In serious situations, refocus on finding local resources for survival.

Situation:

The Serious Situation arises when we lose our original source of support for a campaign or project. In a Serious Situation, we get further from our original sources of resources because we have gotten more deeply involved in the project. This positions us so that our support gets pinched off (6.4.6 Serious Situations).

Opportunity:

Our only opportunity in the serious situation is to work on resources generation (8.0 Winning Rewards1.8 Progress Cycle). While we c do only one thing at a time, we can switch our focus at any time to the claim step to get a partial award based on a partial move (8.2 Making Claims).

Key Methods:

In a serious situation, we must instantly move to get local resources in any way that we can. We respond to serious situations by:

1. As with all middle-stage situation, we must act quickly. Middle-stage situation are all different types of races. In this case, the race is to find more resources before our current supplies run out. The faster we adapt to our situation, the further ahead we will be (6.3.2 Middle-Stage Situations).

2. In a serious situation, we put our original targets on hold. If we are short on resources, we are no longer a serious competitor for the larger rewards of the opportunity. The first requirement for exploring an opportunity is the availability of resources (3.3 Opportunity Resources).

3. In a serious situation, we keep our shortage of resources a secret if possible. Resource shortage is a vulnerability. If others in our competitive arena know about our weakness, it will invite attack (2.7 Information Secrecy).

4. In a serious situation, we must identify any ways in which our current position can generate resources. This means looking for resources in the immediate vicinity, even if only for the short term. The resources must be strategically nearby because speed is critical here (4.4 Strategic Distance).

5. *In a serious situation, we must shift from longer-term exploration to short-term local exploitation.* A serious situation demands that we shift our internal mindset from the adventure of adaptive exploration to the boring nuts and bolts of scrabbling for resources. This requires a shift in mindset. Sun Tzu describes this as plundering or pillaging, but in modern competition, this isn't stealing resources from the local area as much as providing value to the local area in exchange for resources (1.2.2 Exploiting Exploration).

6. *In a serious situation, we must often get creative.* This is one of those situations where we must leverage adversity into creativity, doing something novel, new, and different (6.1.2 Prioritizing Conditions).

Illustration:

In our original explanation of how to recognize these situations, we used the most famous historical example of the serious situation, Hannibal's campaign against Rome. We will use this illustration to demonstrate both where he took the correct steps and why he failed to do so.

Hannibal's response to being cut-off from resources by Carthage was to rely more heavily upon his brother in Spain, develop alliances with local Italian tribes who were unhappy with Roman domination and with Philip V of Macedon. None of the sources provided enough resources to succeed in his campaign, especially after his brother, Margo, was defeated in Liguria and the breakdown of his alliance with Phillip. This returned him to Carthage in 203 BC.

In a serious situation, we must instantly move to get local resources in any way that we can. We respond to intersecting situations by:

1. *As with all middle-stage situations, we must act quickly.* Originally, Hannibal did act quickly to raise local resources which was why his campaign in Italy lasted for years. However, his biggest mistake was developing new channels of supply that were still too distant, in Spain and Greece.

2. In a serious situation, we put our original targets on hold. He failed here as. Psychologically, he was still dependent on support from Carthage. He did not secure his new channels of supply.

3. In a serious situation, we keep our shortage of resources a secret. This was difficult because his two main supply channels were too distant.

4. In a serious situation, we must identify any ways in which our current position can generate resources. Again, Hannibal was too dependent on his past position, as the leader of Carthage, rather than his new position and the occupier of Italy. He never really transitioned to a local ruler from an external conqueror.

5. In a serious situation, we must shift from longer-term exploration to short-term local exploitation. When he developed his local alliances, he should have worked more methodically at politically balancing his Italian allies against each other than relying on his own military control. He needed to use the politics of Italy in his favor rather than simply making alliances that could be easily betrayed, positioning himself as a necessary component in that balance. He should have promised the various city-states the extension of their local dominion at the expense of Rome while protecting them against each other. He had demonstrated his ability to defeat the Roman armies. He needed to position himself as the military champion of the local city-states. Instead, he presented himself as an alternative external ruler instead of simply a liberator and peace keeper.

6. In a serious situation, we must often get creative . The raw materials for victory were all there, but as a general rather than a politician, Hannibal couldn't put them together. He was unable to switch his competitive skills from the battlefield to the realm of politics.

6.5.7 Difficult Response

Five key methods regarding the role of persistence.

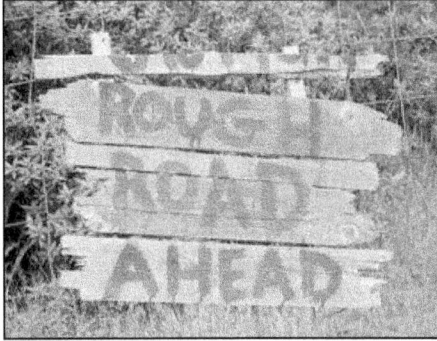

"Control bad terrain by keeping on the move."
Sun Tzu's The Art of War 11:1:45

"Winners never quit and quitters never win."
Vince Lombardi

"As we advance in life it becomes more and more difficult, but in fighting the difficulties the inmost strength of the heart is developed."
Vincent Van Gogh

General Principle: Overcome difficult situations through persistence and creativity.

Situation:

Difficult situations arise at the end of a campaign when we encounter obstacles that make progress much slower and more difficult than expected (6.4.7 Difficult Situations). While we are always interested in finding the path of least resistance to our goals, no path that takes us anywhere worth going is easy the entire way. The danger of the difficult situation is that it causes us to think that the grass must be greener somewhere else. Since beginnings are almost always easier than endings, it is always tempting to start a new project rather than finish an existing one (6.4.2 Easy Situations). People who skip from one thing to another without finishing anything are never successful.

Opportunity:

As we approach the successful end of a campaign, the clearest signs that we are succeeding is often mounting resistance and opposition (3.2.4 Emptiness and Fullness). The fact that we are getting more resistance is a symptom of the fact that we are getting close to success. Opponents redouble their efforts to stop us as we approach our goal. Our reaction to that opposition is the key. When we are not discouraged and press on, our persistence gives others the impression that our success is inevitable (1.2 Subobjective Positions).

Key Methods:

The following five key methods are key to winning a difficult situation.

1. We must keep our goal in sight during a difficult situation. A difficult situation is a late-stage situation where we have learned a great deal about the opportunity and its payoff. It is very different from a low-probability or any early-stage situation where the goal is distance and payoff uncertain. Lombardi's advice about "winners never quit," only applies to the difficult situation. It is a waste of resources if applied to situations where it is inappropriate (6.3.3 Late-Stage Situations).

2. In a difficult situation, we focus on making progress no matter how slowly. Notice the difference here between the late-stage difficult situation and a middle-stage situation where speed is a primary requirement for all responses. Speed is impossible in a difficult situation. Instead, we rely on focused power, taking one step at a time no matter how small (5.5 Focused Power).

3. In a difficult situation, we cannot turn back on the progress that we have made. A difficult situation is very different from an open situation where we are still choosing among various paths. This late in a campaign, the path is clear. We cannot abandon our progress to look for another path. We get rewarded faster by persisting through a difficult stretch at the end of a path than we do by abandoning that path (4.5.2 Surface Barriers).

4. In a difficult situation, we try different angles and invent creative ways to go forward. Sometimes we don't have to tackle the barrier directly. We can often find a faster, easier path, not by going back, but by trying different directions forward. Often we need to meet the challenge of a difficult situation in order to spark the creativity needed to create momentum. As with all late stage situations, innovation is especially important (7.3 Strategic Innovation).

5. In a difficult situation, we use our actions to eliminate doubts about our enthusiasm and commitment. The barriers in a difficult situation are both physical and psychological. We can often speed our progress by winning the support of others. When we persist, we create the perception that we are in control of the situation and win the support of others to help us through (9.3 Crisis Leadership).

Illustration:

In our illustration of how to correctly recognize this situation, we considered a situation where you have been looking for a new job. You still have a job, but you think you see an opportunity to find a better one at another firm in the larger job market (6.4.7 Difficult Situations).

1. We must keep our goal in sight during a difficult situation. In this example, you have discovered that people are looking for your talents and experience, but the standard job qualifications for the position require more formal education than you have. You must see the employer's need as more important than the obstacle, your lack of formal education.

2. In a difficult situation, we focus on making progress no matter how slowly. You persist in searching for the job you want by contacting more and more organizations. In making these new contacts, you bring up the problem, your lack of standard qualifications, at the beginning of the process to save time and to get decision-makers to eliminate the barrier early rather than using it as a tie-breaker later.

3. In a difficult situation, we cannot turn back on the progress that we have made. While you are making new contacts, this doesn't mean you forget about the companies where you were the second choice because of your formal training. You keep in touch with them in case their first choices do not work out.

4. In a difficult situation, we try different angles and invent creative ways to go forward. If you are creative, you can find a way to turn your more unique set of qualifications into a positive instead of a negative. If most of their people have those qualifications, your different success profile broadens their organization's spectrum of skills rather than duplicating the same skills that they already have.

5. In a difficult situation, we use our actions to eliminate doubts about our enthusiasm and commitment. While most organizations will stick to the formal standard, there will be a percentage who do not. That percentage will appreciate your persistence in facing the problem directly rather than trying to hide the problem or giving up when faced with it.

6.5.8 Limited Response

Sun Tzu's four key methods on the need for secret speed in tight situations.

"Control confined terrain by using surprise."
Sun Tzu's The Art of War 11:1:46

"Whoever can surprise well must Conquer."
John Paul Jones

"It is surprising what a man can do when he has to, and how little most men will do when they don't have to."
Walter Linn

General Principle: In limited situations, we must secretly invent a surprise.

Situation:

The Limited Situation marks a transition point when we depend on a narrow set of resources. In limited situations, we are constrained by our environment or surrounded by our opponents, making access to additional resources impossible (6.4.8 Limited Situations).

Opportunity:

Our opportunity in a limited situation exists in our ability to use secrecy (2.7 Information Secrecy). Even if they suspect that our options or resources are limited, we can use that fact to set them up for a surprise, leveraging unpredictability against them (2.3.2 Reaction Unpredictability).

Key Methods:

A limited situation puts us in a highly vulnerable position in a late stage of our campaign. As we pass through the transition involved, we can be easily stopped. With this in mind, we respond to limited situations by:

1. In a limited situation, we keep our situation a secret. When we can only bring limited resources to defend or advance, our primary goal must be to keep others from recognizing our vulnerability (9.0 Understanding Vulnerability).

2. In a limited situation, we must give every appearance of being calm. When we are hemmed in and surrounded, we often give ourselves away because we panic. We don't want to be the rabbit that panics jumps up and exposes its hiding place at the approach of a coyote. If we remain calm in what appears to be a limited situation, our opponents must wonder what we know that they do not (2.1.1 Information Limits]).

3. In a limited situation, we use creativity to make the path of transition less predictable. All latestage responses require more creativity than other situations. In this situation, surprise is absolutely required. In limited situations, our actions seem predictable so we must use methods that are not predictable (7.0 Creating Momentum).

4. In a limited situation, we complete the transition out of our limited situation before others can block us. This is different from speed in the "race" situations of a campaign's middle-stages because we must finish our move before our opponents suspect it.

We must keep our hurry from attracting attention and triggering a reaction (5.3.1 Speed and Quickness).

Illustration:

We will extend the illustration we used in discussing how to identify these situations using an imaginary case study from the business world. A company has introduced a new product, but one of the components needed for that product is in short supply (6.4.8 Limited Situations).

1. In a limited situation, we keep our situation a secret. In purchasing negotiations with potential suppliers, the company should be discussing other, ideally much different, broader, and longer-term supply needs. These needs could be for totally fictitious future products, whose component demands are ideal for each vendor to whom they are talking.

2. In a limited situation, we must give every appearance of being calm. The company must not display any excitement about the success of their new product that requires the component in limited supply. The discussion of this component should only be brought up casually and tangentially, as a possible immediate test of suppliers' ability to deliver on the fictitious larger, longer term need.

3. In a limited situation, we use creativity to make the path of transition less predictable. By opening discussions with a number of different suppliers, we put pressure on existing suppliers who will hear about those discussions. We can discuss the needed component with the supplier who presently provides the required component based, not upon our desperate need, but upon their limitation in production, putting them on the defensive.

4. In a limited situation, we complete the transition out of our limited situation before others can block us. This approach will prevent suppliers from taking advantage of our immediate needs. The monopoly supplier cannot overcharge and competitors cannot use their existing relationships with potential alternative suppliers from undercutting the needed purchase.

6.5.9 Desperate Response

Sun Tzu's five key methods on when to use all our resources.

"Control deadly terrain by fighting."
Sun Tzu's The Art of War 11:1:47

"On deadly terrain, you must show what you can do by killing the enemy."
Sun Tzu's The Art of War 11:6:24

"Fight till the last gasp."
William Shakespeare

"It is surprising what a man can do when he has to, and how little most men will do when they don't have to."
Robert Louis Stevenson

General Principle: In desperate situations, we must use every resource we have.

Situation:

The Desperate Situation arises when our position is deteriorating rapidly and everything is at risk. The desperate situation is characterized by its lack of alternatives. We must make sure we identify our situation correctly, eliminating every other possible situation and response--which is why it is last in this series (6.4.9 Desperate Situations). The real risk of the desperate situation is that we delay making the difficult decision. The only alternative is that we simply give up, roll over, and die (6.8 Competitive Psychology). Unfortunately, more are killed running away from a losing battle, than fighting their way through it.

Opportunity:

This drastic response is an opportunity because it dramatically increases our chances of survival and success. The response required is so drastic that it can only be used in truly desperate situations. Since we have nothing to lose through conflict, but our opponents do, we can turn our weakness into a strength (3.5 Strength and Weakness) Our strength comes from knowing we are in a desperate situation before our opponents do so that our ferocity of response catches them unprepared and unwilling to take the risk of meeting us.

Key Methods:

The desperate situation is the exception that proves the general rule about avoiding conflict. In the desperate situation, everything is at risk. With this in mind, we respond to desperate situations by following the five key methods:

1. In a desperate situation, we instantly and directly engage the opponents who have trapped us. When we are in a desperate situation, our opponents grow in strength against us, making our demise inevitable. This is a situation where we want our opponents to clearly understand the threat we pose. We must not only fight with everything we have, but we must do so instantly and very visibly (5.3.1 Speed and Quickness).

2. *In a desperate situation, we focus all our resources to the single point of engagement, holding nothing back*. The goal here is to create a maximum of focused power in a minimum burst of time (5.5 Focused Power).

3. *In a desperate situation, we seek to damage those who oppose us as much as possible.* Our response must give opponents something to fear, something to lose. We make it clear that meeting us will be very expensive, hoping to raise the risks so that they are no longer worth the rewards. When we demonstrate our willingness to bring down our opponents with us, they have to reconsider their plans (3.1.3 Conflict Cost).

4. *In a desperate situation, we seek to suprise our opponents with our ferocity*. As with all latestage situation, surprise is always important. By surprising our opponents, we seize the initiative in the situation, forcing them to deal with our response. They not only have to reconsider their plans, but they must do so quickly, choosing their course in an instant because we leave them little time to do otherwise. People prefer avoiding loss over seizing gain so they will have a tendency to want to back down (7.4.2 Momentum Timing).

5. *In a desperate situation, we must not press our luck*. If our opponents blink and we get some breathing room, we must not press forward, hoping to turn a surprise into a big victory. We would not be in a desperate situation if a big victory was possible. In these situations, our definition of success means simply surviving so that we can evade defeat and find a more defensible position (3.1 Strategic Economics).

Illustration:

To use the same situation we did to illustrate how to recognize the desperate situation, a health challenge where you go to the doctor for what you think is a sinus infection. The doctor does some tests and discovers that you have cancer. This is a desperate situation that I personally survived.

1. In a desperate situation, we instantly and directly engage the opponents who have trapped us. You must instantly dedicate all your time and resources to fighting the cancer. You cannot avoid the problem. In my case, I quickly found out who the best doctors were, what the best treatment was regardless of monetary or other costs, and instantly committed to that course of treatment.

2. In a desperate situation, we focus all our resources to the single point of engagement, holding nothing back. You must be willing to sacrifice your comfort, your wealth, and accept long-term disability in order to survive.

3. In a desperate situation, we seek to damage those who oppose us as much as possible. You must not surrender your decisions to whatever doctor you happen to have, insurance companies, and, God forbid, the government bureaucracy. No one cares as much about your life as you do.

4. In a desperate situation, we seek to surprise our opponents with our ferocity. We must not be shy about questioning our doctor and expressing our willingness to make sacrifices. In my case, despite the pain associated with my radiation treatment, I challenged my doctors to do more, upping my radiation regardless of the pain.

5. In a desperate situation, we must not press our luck. When you get cleared of the cancer, you must avoid any activities that create more potential dangers. After getting cured of my cancer, I am much more careful about my health than I was before.

6.6.0 Campaign Pause

Sun Tzu's five key methods on knowing when to stop advancing a position.

"If you are too weak to fight, you must find more men. In this situation, you must not act aggressively.
You must unite your forces.
Prepare for the enemy.
Recruit men and stay where you are."
Sun Tzu's The Art of War 9:6:1-5

"The sword outwears its sheath, and the soul wears out the breast. And the heart must pause to breathe, and love itself have rest."

Lord Byron

General Principle: Know the key situations in which campaigns must be paused.

Situation:

While our movement to improve our position never stops, we must sometimes take a pause. We can only take what we have the strength to grasp. We get into trouble when we reach beyond our capabilities. When our resources are spread too thin, we become vulnerable. We reach barriers that we don't have the resources to overcome, we must regroup. The problem is that it is often difficult to recognize our situation. Mistakes in monitoring resources are easy while we are making progress. The faster we are going, the easier it is to forget to monitor our limited resources (3.1.1 Resource Limitations). The more we focus on fighting the battle, the easier it is to run low on ammunition.

Opportunity:

The opportunity when we reach our limits is to consolidate our gains. We must reset and focus on our internal situation rather than the external. This is our switch from winning new ground to better controlling it (1.2.2 Exploiting Exploration). It means making the mental transition from competitive positioning to production management (1.9 Competition and Production). and work on improving its organization. We leverage the natural force of a situation but within our always limited capacity.

Key Methods:

The following five key methods define different pausing situations and how we must deal with them.

1. When we grow low on resources, we build up our existing position rather than extend or advance it. The most important internal resources are: 1) temporary resources, 2) physical resources, 3) condition recognition, and 4) message communication. We must have excess resources to explore opportunities. We always want to advance our position, but if we use more resources than we have, we endanger our current position. While we pause, we organize our operations. We work to become more internally productive. We build up our resources (3.3 Opportunity Resources).

2. When the situation changes too quickly to get feedback, we pause and wait for change to slow. During chaotic conditions, a right decision can turn into a wrong decision in a second. Under these conditions, it is better to find a safe port and do nothing for awhile. These situations usually arise on fluid situations, where we described them earlier as "change storms" (4.3.2 Fluid Forms).

3. When the conditions around us require skills that we don't have, we pause to acquire those skills. Making great progress eventually takes us into unknown areas. We have to realize when we are getting out of our depth. When we don't understand what the situation requires, we cannot know where we are or see where we are going (1.5.2. Group Methods).

4. Pausing situations temporarily take priority over the other classes of strategic situations. When we reach these limits, either in our internal resources or the external environment, we must pause. In some situations, such as dissipating and desperate, the pause will be as short as possible. Fortunately, in these serious situations, external conditions affect our opponents as much as they do ourselves. There may be more to gain. It may be right in front of us, but we cannot reach out to take it without endangering our position (1.6.3 Shifting Priorities).

5. When we are in a pausing situation, we must not challenge our opponents. We must do as little as possible to attract the attention of our rivals. We must make the minimum adjustments necessary to keep up with our rival's movements and wait until we have excess resources again and see the path to pursue clearly (1.3.1 Competitive Comparison).

Illustration:

A common illustration that we use for explaining strategic movement is navigating traffic. To reach our goal, we still have to deal on a case-by-case with the traffic we encounter on the path.

1. When we grow low on resources, we build up our existing position rather than extend or advance it. In this analogy, this principle says simply that we must not forget to check our gas tank during the trip. Even if it looked like plenty when we started out, it can run low if we get stuck in traffic.

2. When the situation changes too quickly to get feedback, we pause and wait for change to slow. If we have to make a turn, we have to wait for an opening in the traffic to do so.

3. When the conditions around us require skills that we don't have, we pause to acquire those skills. We cannot use the high-capacity lanes unless we stop and pick up a passenger.

4. Pausing situations temporarily take priority over the other classes of strategic situations. We have to deal with other standard situations in traffic, such as traffic jams, but we have to deal with these pausing conditions first.

5. When we are in a pausing situation, we must not challenge our opponents. We shouldn't push it to see how far we can get without running out of gas or force on-coming traffic to brake in order to make a turn.

6.7.0 Tailoring to Conditions

Seven key methods regarding overcoming opposition using conditions in the environment.

"Some military commanders do not know how to adjust their methods. They can find an advantageous position. Still, they cannot use their men effectively."
Sun Tzu's The Art of War 8:1:19-21

"The one who adapts his policy to the times prospers, and likewise that the one whose policy clashes with the demands of the times does not."
Niccolo Machiavelli

General Principle: Certain specific conditions determine how we adapt to overcome opposition.

Situation:

Movement often naturally generates opposition. Many of the nine common classes of strategic situations are defined by our position relative to opposition (6.4 Nine Situations). These same types of situations arise over and over again but they are never exactly the same. Every occurrence involves a unique constellation of conditions. As with all aspects of situation response, the devil is in the details.

Opportunity:

To minimize the impact of opposition, we have the opportunity to leverage the most specific conditions in our general situation. In addition to knowing the basic response a given situation requires, we can also know how to leverage certain conditions to our advantages (6.5 Nine Responses). Remember, our goal is never simply beating the opposition. Our goal is improving our position. In facing opposition, we must get past it to get to our goal. We must do this as easily and quickly as possible to accomplish our mission.

Key Methods:

The following seven key methods defined the major types of conditions to which we must adjust.

1. Dominant conditions are primarily determined by the physical form of a competitive arena. There are four primary forms: tilted, fluid, soft, and ideal. Three forces determine the key conditions of these forms of ground: gravity, currents, and solidity. (6.7.1 Form Adjustments).

2. Gravity is the most important condition on tilted forms of ground. These are areas where the force of gravity favors one relative direction is over another. We always want the gravity on our side (4.3.1 Tilted Forms).

3. Current direction is the most important condition on fluid forms of ground. These are areas where the force of change favors one direction over another. We want to move with the current and not against it (4.3.2 Fluid Forms).

4. Solidity is the most important condition on soft or uncertain forms of ground. Some locations and situations are much more solid and dependable than most locations around them. Here, we want the sparse support that is available, such as solid information, on our side (4.3.1 Tilted Forms).

5. Relative size and strength are the most important conditions on ideal forms of ground. Ideal forms are those in which the forces of gravity, currents, and solidity do not create a clear advantage. On this ground, it is the nature of the meeting forces, not our location on the ground, that determines our success (4.3.4 Neutral Form).

6. Relative size is the most important condition at the moment of meeting. This relative comparison is used to choose the exact best behavior to minimize the cost of dealing with opposition. Both large and small forces have certain advantages and disadvantages. How we respond when we have an overwhelming force is different than how we respond when we have a merely dominant force. Even if we are overwhelmed or dominated in size of force, we can turn the situation around by using the weaknesses of size (6.7.2 Size Adjustments).

7. Relative strength is the most important condition over the course of the contest. Strength conditions arise from the relative breadth, depth, and clarity of competing philosophies, goals, or missions. Strength comes from the uniting and focusing power of a mission. Different types of mission have different types of power. In each of these areas defining strength, the issue is not just recognizing what conditions are but in knowing how which advantages are on our side (6.7.2 Size Adjustments).

Illustration:

Let us illustrate these ideas using examples from product marketing.

1. Dominant conditions are primarily determined by the physical form of a competitive arena. When we are running a business, we tailor our responses to adjust to the conditions of our marketplace, that is, the customers and potential customers to whom we sell.

2. Gravity is the most important condition on tilted forms of ground. When a marketplace is dominated by a few large customers, positions supported by one of those customers is much more important than a position supported by a lot of the small ones.

3. Current direction is the most important condition on fluid forms of ground. In fast-changing marketplaces such as high-tech, we must not position ourselves against the dominant trends in the standards of the industry. If our customers are currently adopting certain standards, we must lead the trend and not follow it.

4. Solidity is the most important condition on soft forms of ground. In marketplaces that are very fickle and uncertain, such as the marketplace that is constantly changing where no one really knows what the trend is, we use a rare verifiable fact to support our marketing. For example, in the book market, most new book sales are uncertain and most fail. The only solid areas are popular authors, such as Sun Tzu, who sell year after year.

5. Relative size and strength are the most important conditions on ideal forms of ground. These are marketplaces with lots of similar customers. In these markets, one year's sales are very much like the previous year's. Change in them follows predictable cycles.

6. Relative size is the most important condition at the moment of meeting. In ideal markets, when the products of two competitor's meet in the marketplace, the companies selling those products must choose their distribution methods depending on their relative size. Large companies can try to be everywhere, surrounding the competition. Small companies must look for small niches evading the competition.

7. Relative strength is the most important condition over the course of the contest. After the initial meeting, the success of our marketing depends on: 1) focusing on customers' needs and 2) developing relationships with customers.

6.7.1 Form Adjustments

Sun Tzu's four key methods on adapting our responses based on the form of the ground.

"To win your battles, never attack uphill."
Sun Tzu's The Art of War 9:1:4

"Never face against the current."
Sun Tzu's The Art of War 9:1:13

"You must keep on the water grasses. Keep your back to a clump of trees.
This is how you position your army in a marsh."
Sun Tzu's The Art of War 9:1:18-20

"The gravity is the first thing which you don't think."
Albert Einstein

"Time is a sort of river of passing events, and strong is its current; no sooner is a thing brought to sight than it is swept by and another takes its place, and this too will be swept away."

Marcus Aurelius

"Although our intellect always longs for clarity and certainty, our nature often finds uncertainty fascinating."

Karl von Clausewitz

General Principle: When meeting opposition, know how to leverage the character of the ground.

Situation:

As we are moving to a new position, we meet opposition. To make our responses more effective, we want to leverage the the physical, persistent conditions of our environment, known as the "ground" (1.3.2 Element Scalability). Where we meet that opposition, that is, the type of ground that we are on, is critical to making the best decisions about how to respond. Different forms of ground offer us different types of advantages. We cannot leverage the different forms of ground unless we understand where its force lies.

Opportunity:

When we meet opposition, we can be on three forms of ground: a) highly uneven ground, b) fast changing ground, or c) very uncertain ground (4.3 Leveraging Form).

Key Methods:

The following four key methods describe how we use the form of the ground to improve our responses.

1. The force of the ground arises from the form of the ground. There are three valuable ground forces: gravity, currents, and solidity. They become important on tilted, fluid, and soft forms of ground, respectively. On these three forms of ground, their related forces give an advantage to one location over another (4.3 Leveraging Form).

2. On tilted ground, we get the gravity on our side. Inequality defines tilted forms. On tilted ground, the physical or psychological conditions favor certain locations over others. We get these forces on our side or get on the side of these forces (4.3.1 Tilted Forms).

3. On fluid ground, we must move with the current of change. This means avoiding the dominant, stable fixtures in the environment and siding with the changing ones. Dynamics define fluid forms. On fluid ground, the physical or psychological force of change favors a flow that avoids stable points (4.3.2 Fluid Forms).

4. On soft ground, we must get the islands of stability on our side. This means avoiding areas where the direction of change is uncertain. Uncertainty defines soft forms. On soft ground, the force favors physical or psychological points of stability. The key to using this ground is to identify those rare, stable features in the environment and using them. (4.3.1 Tilted Forms).

Illustration:

Let us use a variety of different examples to illustrate the different forms of grounds and how we tailor our responses.

1. The force of the ground arises from the form of the ground. Business and political situations arise on different ground. While business always depends on customers and politics always depends on voters, customers and voters are very different based on their geographical and demographic area. Knowing these differences allows us to work with the right forces.

2. On tilted ground, we get the gravity on our side. Inequality defines tilted forms. One form of uneven ground is a market dominated by a few large customers. If challenged by a rival in such a market, find the positions supported by these dominant customers that your rival has opposed. Use those positions to stand (keep existing customer) and move (win new customers) against these rivals.

3. On fluid ground, we must move with the current of change. One form of fluid ground is the personal technology hardware market, where the coming thing always dominates the established thing. If challenged by a rival in such a market, leverage the coming thing against their support of the established thing; netbooks over notebooks (see this article on Acer's rise over Dell) or a Pre, Droid, or Nexus One over iPhone.

4. On soft ground, we must get the islands of stability on our side. One form of soft ground is today's financial markets. Given the uncertain financial future--depression or recovery, inflation versus deflation, etc--we must focus our investments on what little that we know for certain: Government spending and US deficit is going through the roof.

6.7.2 Size Adjustments

Sun Tzu's seven key methods regarding adapting responses based on the relative size of opposing forces.

> *"The rules for making war are:*
> *If you outnumber enemy forces ten to one, surround them.*
> *If you outnumber them five to one, attack them.*
> *If you outnumber them two to one, divide them.*
> *If you are equal, then find an advantageous battle.*
> *If you are fewer, defend against them.*
> *If you are much weaker, evade them."*
>
> Sun Tzu's The Art of War 3:3:12-18

> *"Though your enemy is the size of an ant, regard him as an elephant."*
>
> Danish Proverb

General Principle: When meeting opposition, the relative size of force suggests the appropriate response.

Situation:

The problem is that the size of force, that is, the number of our supporters, can be a complicated topic. The relative size of forces are easily miscalculated because we know our resources much better than those of others (2.1.1 Information Limits). The result is that we overestimate what we can do. The result is costly conflict where even the "winner" can lose.

Opportunity:

The appropriate use of force is dictated by economics of strategy (3.1 Strategic Economics). Our first goal is to minimize the mistakes in using force that create conflict (3.1.3 Conflict Cost). Size has both value and costs. These costs include the dis-economies of scale.

Key Methods:

There are seven key methods describing the correct methods of dealing with the relative balance of forces.

1. Both we and our opponents are likely to overestimate the relative size of our supporting forces. We should assume both mistakes in our calculations. These mistakes will result in misjudgments. All the other principles are designed to avoid making mistakes based on this fundamental error (2.1.1 Information Limits]).

2. Rather than attacking with overwhelming force (10 to 1), we simply surround our opponents. We hem them in so that they must confront the futility of their situation. Our goal is to get them to surrender without a fight (2.6 Knowledge Leverage).

3. Using dominant force (5 to 1), we go directly after our opponents leaving them a clear outlet for retreat. This size advantage is so large that opponents are not likely to want to stand and battle.

Our goal is to win our position with a minimum of costly conflict ([3.1.3 Conflict Cost](#)).

4. Using larger forces (2 to 1), we divide our opposition. This advantage is small enough that either we or our opponents might miscalculate the situation. We therefore seek to handle smaller groups of opponents one at a time. Our larger force is not in itself sufficient to chase a relatively smaller opponent from the field ([5.4 Minimizing Action](#)).

5. Using equal forces (1 to 1), we avoid meeting the opponent until we can find the right situation. With equal forces, we must seek to leverage the ground against our opponents. We need to lure our opponents into ground positions where they are at a serious disadvantage ([6.7.1 Form Adjustments](#)).

6. Using a smaller force, we only meet opponents in defense of a well-fortified position. Defending always requires fewer resources than attacking. We concentrate our forces in a highly defensible position, resisting the opponent's attempt to draw us out ([1.1.2 Defending Positions](#)).

7. Using a much smaller force, we evade the opposition. We use our relative advantage in speed against their relative advantage of size. We strike where they are unprepared and fall back before they can mount a response ([3.4 Dis-Economies of Scale](#)e-alone link]).

Illustration:

Let us illustrate these key methods with a battle of office politics where we are opposing a policy that a rival is attempting to introduce.

1. Both we and our opponents are likely to overestimate the relative size of our force. We and our rival within an office probably both think that we have more support in the office than we really have.

2. Rather than attacking with overwhelming force (10 to 1), we simply surround our opponents. If virtually everyone is on our side, we set up an "intervention" where we force our rival to confront our universal opposition.

3. Using dominant force (5 to 1), we go directly after our opponents leaving them a clear outlet for retreat. We are going to have a showdown but, before we do, we make sure of two things. We must make sure that they can see how large our support is and give them a way to save face and back down.

4. Using larger forces (2 to 1), we divide our opposition. Since our opponent has a significant number of supporters, we keep them from getting together. We stage separate meetings consisting of all of our supporters with a few of our opponent's supporters.

5. Using equal forces (1 to 1), we avoid meeting the opponent until we can find the right situation . We could set up a meeting on tilted ground. We set up our showdown with a big boss in the meeting, who we know supports our point of view. The supporter of our opponent will be afraid to voice their support.

6. Using a smaller force, we only meet opponents in defense of a well-fortified position. We do not get into any open battle with our opponent. Instead, we keep to areas of responsibility where we clearly have that authority to decide and our opponent does not.

7. Using a much smaller force, we evade the opposition. We do not engage in direct opposition. Instead, we fight a guerrilla action, opposing the policy behind the scenes. We work secretly to disrupt the decision.

6.7.3 Strength Adjustments

Sun Tzu's nine key methods on how to adapt responses based on relative strength of opposing missions.

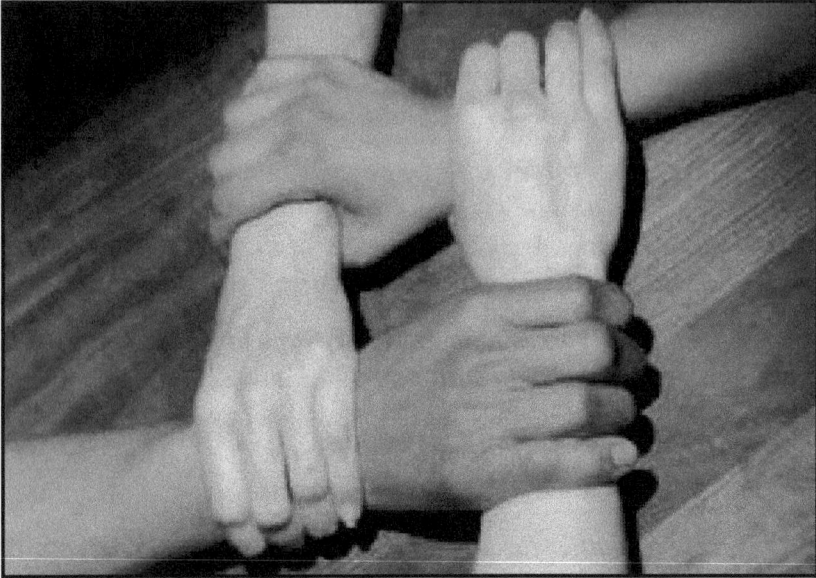

"You must control your field position. It will always strengthen your army."
Sun Tzu's The Art of War 10:3:1-2

"Only one who devotes himself to a cause with his whole strength and soul can be a true master. For this reason mastery demands all of a person."
Albert Einstein

"We confide in our strength, without boasting of it; we respect that of others, without fearing it."
Thomas Jefferson

General Principle: When meeting opposition, the relative strength of opposing missions tells us the best response.

Situation:

When we meet opposition, we also have to consider our relative strength versus our opponent's. Strength comes internally from our mission and externally from how well our mission fits a given position. Position strength is a very different strategic concept from size of forces, but it relates directly to our shared dedication to a mission.

Opportunity:

Our opportunity is to use our internal strength to create external strength. We can compare the internal strength of organizations in three different dimensions: 1) dedication to mission (1.6 Mission Values and 1.7 Competitive Power), 2) unity (1.7.1 Team Unity), and 3) focus (1.7.2 Goal Focus). External strength arises in the fit between these dimensions of mission and the opportunity dimension of a given position (4.6 Six Benchmarks).

Key Methods:

There are nine key methods describing how we adjust to conditions of relative strength.

1. Broad missions provide the strength needed for broad positions. Area breadth describes how inclusive or exclusive a position, an opportunity, or a mission are. A broad mission is generally a low level mission that most people share, for example, the desire for economic gain. A narrow mission is one that appeals to a smaller, more specialized group of people. The extremes of area are *spreadout* and *constricted* positions (4.5.1 Surface Area).

2. Deep missions provide strength to surmount high barriers. Deep missions are required to overcome serious barriers. Depth of mission describes how heavily committed people are to a particular mission. The level of commitment can be either deep or shallow. Often, the greater the breadth of a mission, the shallower its depth.

High-level missions both require and instill in people a deeper commitment. The two extremes of barriers are the barricaded position and the wide-open position (4.5.2 Surface Barriers).

3. Clear missions provide strength for positions that require holding power. Clarity describes the ease with which a mission, an opportunity, or a position are understood. Mission clarity describes how concise, transparent, and believable a set of goals are. Clear goals have an advantage when we want to increase a position's holding power. Clear goals have an advantage in depth, but fuzzy goals have an advantage in breadth. The extremes of holding power are *fixed* positions--extremely sticky-and *loose* positions--extremely loose (4.5.3 Surface Holding Power).

4. Spread-out positions must be supported by larger groups of people, which require a broader mission. Broad missions appeal to larger groups of people. Spread-out positions cannot be held by narrow groups, no matter how deep their commitment. In spread-out positions, we must broaden our mission to attract allies (4.6.1 Spread-Out Conditions).

5. Constricted positions can be defended by relatively small groups with narrow missions. These positions can survive on narrow missions appealing to smaller groups. Broad groups cannot access constricted positions. Confined positions cannot be accessed by broad groups. In confined positions, we must narrow our mission to our elite core (4.6.2 Constricted Conditions).

6. Wide-open positions are more easily captured by shallow missions. These positions are more popular, but they are always difficult to defend. In wide-open positions, we must emphasize the most shallow aspect of our mission to generate support that is easy to hold (4.6.3 Barricaded Conditions).

7. Barricaded positions require a depth of dedication to capture and are always easily defended. In barricaded positions, we must narrow our mission to its most dedicated core (4.6.4 Wide-Open Conditions).

8. Fixed positions are more easily captured and defended by clear missions. Clear missions are easier to understand and remember. These characteristics are part of the holding power of a fixed position. In fixed positions, we must clarify and simplify our mission so people understand and remember it (4.6.3 Barricaded Conditions).

9. Loose positions are better suited to fuzzy missions. These positions have little holding power so we have to be prepared to move on from them. Fuzzy positions can be more easily adapted to changing circumstances. In loose positions, we must keep our mission flexible so we can adapt it when we are forced to move (4.6.6 Sensitive Conditions).

Illustration:

All of these key methods are easily illustrated by the types of positions taken by politicians.

1. Broad missions provide the strength needed for broad positions. A politician running for national office must have a broader mission and take broader positions than one running for local office. "Make the world safe for Democracy" during WWI.

2. Deep missions provide strength to surmount high barriers. A politician hoping to make serious changes to well-established policies must have deeper support than one who is willing to go with the flow. "All men are created equal" in the Civil war.

3. Clear mission provides strength for positions that require holding power. If a politician takes a clear stand on an issue, he will get deeper support, but it is much harder for him to change that position later. "Read my lips, no new taxes" was very clear.

4. Spread-out positions must be supported by larger groups of people, which require a broader mission. The broadest missions are economic. "It's the economy, stupid!" works in almost every age.

5. Constricted positions can be defended by relatively small groups with narrow missions. Legalization of marijuana is easier to establish in a city than in a state or the nation.

6. Wide-open positions are more easily captured by shallow missions. National campaigns are usually conducted on the basis of a very general mission such as "Hope" and "Change."

7. Barricaded positions require a depth of dedication to capture and are always easily defended. There were many historical obstacles to eliminating slavery or expanding voting to women, but, once it was abolished, defending the new position was easy.

8. Fixed positions are more easily captured and defended by clear missions. Conservative politicians defend well-established economic and social norms with missions that make clear distinctions between right and wrong.

9. Loose positions are better suited to fuzzy missions. Progressive politicians prefer vague positions because they seek to change society and the results are often hard to define other than in general terms such as "fairness" and "social justice."

6.8.0 Competitive Psychology

Sun Tzu's nine key methods for improving competitive psychology even in adversity and failure.

"You must control your soldiers with esprit de corps.
You must bring them together by winning victories.
You must get them to believe in you."
Sun Tzu's The Art of War 9:7;7-9

"What counts is not necessarily the size of the dog in the
fight; it's the size of the fight in the dog."
Dwight David Eisenhower

General Principle: Responding quickly and appropriately to situations creates a psychological advantage.

Situation:

Responses that are inappropriate to our situation fail no matter how completely we are committed to them. However, half-hearted and uncertain responses can fail even if they are technically correct. Psychology is a critical component to all success. Making a serious commitment to a response focuses our efforts. Lack of commitment dissipates our efforts. If we are decisive in making the wrong decisions, we are simply reckless and undermine people's respect in us.

Opportunity:

Our ability to respond quickly and appropriately to challenging situations creates confidence in our supporters and fear in our rivals. To lead people, we must welcome challenges. Challenges give us the opportunity to demonstrate our ability to others. We must always make our supporters feel like they are winners. We do this by knowing what the psychology of the situation requires. If we show others that we can respond to both good and bad turns of events, they will support us. People will have no choice but to give us their respect. This is how we win the commitment of supporters and deference of opponents.

Key Methods:

At each stage of a campaign, we have to understand the psychology of creating supporters instead of opponents. No matter how difficult a situation gets, if we know what we are doing, we can use those difficulties themselves to bring people together rather than abandon us. The following nine key methods describe the psychological goals of each of the nine classes of common situations.

1. To succeed in the dissipating situation, we need to win the commitment of our supporters. The response to this situation is designed to unite people by giving them a mission (6.5.1 Dissipating Response).

2. In an easy situation, we use rapid progress to excite our supporters. We keep that progress going because making progress together unites people (6.5.2 Easy Response).

3. In a contentious situation, we pit our rivals against each other. We support everyone in their battles against every one else (6.5.3 Contentious Response).

4. In an open situation, we win supporters by pioneering a unique path. We win supporters away from rivals who are competing along similar paths (6.5.4 Open Response).

5. In an intersecting situation, we must get others to join us as partners. We do this by creating a shared mission to which everyone can contribute (6.5.5 Intersecting Response).

6. In the serious situation, we find ways to immediately create value for which others will reward us. Our psychological focus must shift to the needs of others (6.5.6 Serious Response).

7. In the difficult situation, we must give our supporters confidence. As our progress slows down, we must assure them that slow but sure wins the race (6.5.7 Difficult Response).

8. In the limited situation, we make a show of confidence while we focus on secrecy. We make sure that our competitors do not know that we are vulnerable (6.5.5 Intersecting Response).

9. In a desperate situation, we must focus our supporters on taking action. We prove ourselves by succeeding in the face of crisis (6.5.9 Desperate Response).

Illustration:

In the article on the nine situations (6.4 Nine Situations), we illustrated the nine classes of situations with a hairdresser opening a "hair cuts at home" business. We continued that example in the article on responses (6.5 Nine Responses). Let us finish that illustration here.

1. To succeed in the dissipating situation, we need to win the commitment of our supporters. We must directly ask our customers to support our business, getting them to commit to at least try our service. Once they do, they are less likely to waiver.

2. In an easy situation, we use rapid progress to excite our supporters. We must involve our customers in our success. We must communicate with them as our new business moves forward. We must thank them for their contribution, giving them ownership in our success.

3. In a contentious situation, we pit our rivals against each other. As others copy our methods, we should welcome them and offer to advise and help them against their competitors, that is, each other. We make them feel friendly toward us while hostile toward others.

4. In an open situation, we win supporters by pioneering a unique path. We must emphasize to our customers how our business is taking a different path than our new competitors. We make them feel special for choosing us.

5. In an intersecting situation, we must get others to join us as partners. We build on the friendships we have formed to create our advertising association. By asking them to join us, we acknowledge their worth and what we have in common.

6. In the serious situation, we find ways to immediately create value for which others will reward us. We create fear among members of our association that they will fail if the association cannot support itself.

7. In the difficult situation, we must give our supporters confidence. Though progress is slower, we praise everyone for their persistence, assuring them that it cannot help but be successful.

8. In the limited situation, we make a show of confidence while we focus on secrecy. Though we are making a secret transition, we are careful not to "go silent," making people suspicious.

9. In the desperate situation, we must focus our supporters on taking action. We must elevate the mission to an almost spiritual

level as we ask for our supporters for their last full measure of commitment.

6.8.1 Adversity and Creativity

Sun Tzu's nine key methods for how we can use competitive challenges to spark our creativity.

ADVERSITY
Impossible odds makes achievements even more satisfying.

"To command and get the most out of proud people, you must study adversity."
Sun Tzu's The Art of War 12:4:12

"Necessity is the mother of invention, it is true, but its father is creativity, and knowledge is the midwife."
Jonathan Schattke

"Adversity reveals genius, prosperity conceals it."
Horace

General Principle: Facing competitive difficulties pressures us into increasing our capacity for creativity.

Situation:

There is a seeming paradox at the heart of Sun Tzu's strategy. His system teaches us to seek easy victories, avoiding difficulties, but he also teaches that only by facing difficulty can we reach our true potential. If an advance goes easily, we don't need to be inventive. If we minimize our mistakes, our efforts fail painlessly (5.0 Minimizing Mistakes). That failure leaves us somewhat wiser, but it doesn't thrust greatness upon us. Fortunately, this paradox goes away when we realize that difficulties, no matter how hard we try to avoid them, always find us.

Opportunity:

Our opportunities come from openings but those openings exist because of the unavoidable difficulties of life. As we make progress, our challenges inevitably become more difficult. It is only a matter of time until our advance becomes so difficult that we need to make a real breakthrough. This section of The Playbook deals with responding to situations (6.0 Situation Response). The next section deals with the role of creativity in Sun Tzu's strategy (7.0 Creating Momentum).

Key Methods:

In a campaign, we face a succession of challenges (6.3 Campaign Patterns). As these situations become more challenging, the role of creativity becomes more critical, as the following nine key methods demonstrate.

1. In dissipating situations, we learn what our attacker values and create a way to threaten it. We invent a response that exposes their weaknesses to our speed over their size(6.5.1 Dissipating Response).

2. In easy situations, we learn to control our expectations and create as much progress as possible. We invent a response that prevents us from relaxing (6.5.2 Easy Response).

3. In contentious situations, we learn how to avoid conflict and create obstacles for others. We invent a response that prevents others from relaxing (6.5.3 Contentious Response).

4. In open situations, we learn where our opponents are and create our own unique path. We invent a response that separates us from others (6.5.4 Open Response).

5. In the intersecting situation, we learn the skills and goals of others and create partnerships. We invent a response that brings us together with others (6.5.5 Intersecting Response).

6. In the serious situation, we learn about local resources and create a way to harvest them. We invent a response that brings us more local resources (6.5.6 Serious Response).

7. In the difficult situation, we learn the nature of the obstacles and create a path through them. We invent a response that moves us slowly forward (6.5.7 Difficult Response).

8. In the limited situation, we learn our limitations and create a surprise based on them. We invent a response that moves us secretly forward (6.5.5 Intersecting Response).

9. In the desperate situation, we learn to let go and create chaos. We invent a response that uses all our resources to threaten damage to opponents (6.5.9 Desperate Response).

Illustration:

Below are some inventions that came out of each of these different classes of situations.

1. In dissipating situations, we learn what our attacker values and create a way to threaten it. Google Apps were designed to threaten Microsoft's desktop dominance when Microsoft went after Google's search business.

2. In easy situations, we learn to control our expectations and create as much progress as possible. Apple's progress with the iPod, leading to the iTunes and the App Store are great examples of not resting on your laurels.

3. In contentious situations, we learn how to avoid conflict and create obstacles for others. The creation of various new technological standards are often designed to give one group an advantage over another.

4. In open situations, we learn where our opponents are and create our own unique path. In building their airplane, the Wright brothers kept track of developments in Europe but based their approach primarily on their background in bicycle making.

5. In the intersecting situation, we learn the skills and goals of others and create partnerships. William Durrant in starting General Motors brought together a number of small car companies to compete with Ford.

6. In the serious situation, we learn about local resources and create a way to harvest them. After years of growing famous for inventing great ideas that other companies capitalized on, XEROX finally made its PARC laboratory an independent company in 2002, forcing it to pay its own way, selling not only to XEROX but other companies as well.

7. In the difficult situation, we learn the nature of the obstacles and create a path through them. Years of failure in Iraq finally lead to the "surge" strategy, which brought an end to the war there and which now seems to be working in Afghanistan.

8. In the limited situation, we learn our limitations and create a surprise based on them. The transition of IBM from a mainframe computer company to a computer service company after the biggest financial loss in history was done so smoothly that most people never even realized that it was taking place.

9. In the desperate situation, we learn to let go and create chaos. The Tet Offensive by North Vietnam was a huge military disaster, but it was just as huge a PR bonanza, creating history's first successful in "media war," turning the US media against the success of their country on the battlefield.

6.8.2 Strength in Adversity

Sun Tzu's seven key methods on using adversity to increase a group's unity and focus.

"Use adversity correctly.
Tether your horses and bury your wagon's wheels.
Still, you can't depend on this alone.
An organized force is braver than lone individuals.
This is the art of organization.
Put the tough and weak together."
　　　　　　　　Sun Tzu's The Art of War 12:4:15-20

"In prosperity, our friends know us; in adversity, we know our friends."
　　　　　　　　John Churton Collins

"Sweet are the uses of adversity."
　　　　　　　　William Shakespeare

General Principle: The shared threat of adversity can draw people together creating the unity that is the basis of group strength .

Situation:

The pressure of opposition, as William Shakespeare observed, can be used by wise leaders. One of its uses is to bond people together in the face of a shared threat. Under dire circumstances, people naturally cling to the relative safety of groups. However, when put under certain kinds of pressure, groups can also fall apart (6.4.1 Dissipating Situations). To understand how adversity can create strength or weakness in a group, we have to understand the underlying principles by which Sun Tzu's strategy defines strength.

Opportunity:

That fear of loss is greater even than the desire for gain. Since adversity threatens individuals with loss, they naturally join with others who share their problems, challenges, and risks. Revolutions and political movements are born of adversity, not prosperity.

Key Methods:

The following seven key methods describe how adversity creates strength within organization when leaders know how to respond.

1. The strength of a group under adversity comes from shared goals. This sense of mutual danger and risk during times of adversity binds the group together. (1.7 Competitive Power).

2. Adversity can be used to close the gaps between self-interest and group interest that cause division. Weakness results from any influence that causes a group's members to put their own personal interests above those of the group. We use outside pressure, a common enemy, to draw people together (6.4.1 Dissipating Situations).

3. Adversity makes it more dangerous for members to leave the group. We must make it so their personal situation is more dangerous if they do. No form of motivation is stronger than our desire to protect ourselves. People feel more protected in a group (2.1.2 Leveraging Uncertainty).

4. Under pressure, we organize group members so that they have to rely on each others' strengths. Sun Tzu describes this as putting the weak with the strong and the experienced with the inexperienced (3.5 Strength and Weakness).

5. During times of stress, we control information so everyone gets the same message at the same time. Gaps between self-interest and group interest arise naturally when people are working from different information. The more people share information, the stronger the group becomes (2.2 Information Gathering).

6. We use adversity to move members closer together physically and psychologically. Again, weakness comes from the space between people. Separation in mind and body leads to division in goals (4.4 Strategic Distance).

7. Properly communicated, adversity gives more meaning to people's actions within the group. Everyone can have their own individual goals, but it is the commander's job to connect all the individual contributions to the whole. This is easier when there are common dangers and everyone can see each others contribution clearly (1.6.3 Shifting Priorities).

Illustration:

Let us apply these key methods to a business during a time of economic recession.

1. The strength of a group under adversity comes from shared goals. If people within the business understand that their job security depends on their business's profitability rather than the general economy, they will be stronger in a recession.

2. Adversity can be used to close the gaps between self-interest and group interest that cause division. If some employees see that they are making valuable contributions while others are just coasting, they will realize that the weak employees are threatening them personally, not just the company's profits.

3. Adversity makes it more dangerous for members to leave the group. During a recession, not even the more marketable members of the firm want to look for another position. Instead, they can be focused on making the company more successful.

4. Under pressure, we organize group members so that they have to rely on each others' strengths. We want to make the employees themselves responsible for each others' productivity. If they each understand that they must create value to justify their jobs, they will help each other do that and help identify the weak links that cannot contribute.

5. During times of stress, we control information so everyone gets the same message at the same time. We should make incomes and expenses more visible to everyone so everyone can understand where their paycheck is coming from. People should understand that companies don't print their own money, but that they can only survive from customer sales. If the sales aren't there, then expenses must be cut somewhere, eventually threatening them.

6. We use adversity to move members closer together physically and psychologically. We can use this as an opportunity to close separate offices or outlying businesses, moving people into less space focusing on fewer products, so people work more closely physically and mentally.

7. Properly communicated, adversity gives more meaning to people's actions within the group. Everyone should be challenged to relate their contribution to increasing sales, decreasing costs, and retaining customers.

6.8.3 Individual Toughness

Sun Tzu's eight key methods on how failure develops character.

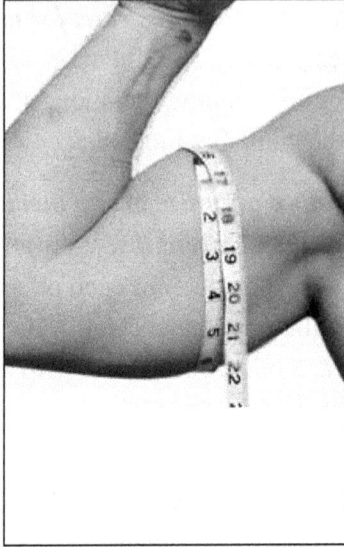

"You can be weakened in a deadly battle and yet be stronger afterward."

Sun Tzu's The Art of War 12:4:15-20

"All the adversity I've had in my life, all my troubles and obstacles, have strengthened me...You may not realize it when it happens, but a kick in the teeth may be the best thing in the world for you."

Walt Disney

"We acquire the strength we have overcome."

Ralph Waldo Emerson

General Principle: Only by facing adversity do we develop the individual strength of confidence.

Situation:

We must explore the borderlands between what is safe and what is foolhardy to be successful. The end result of opening ourselves to the world of possibilities is eventually meeting adversity. No matter how good our training in strategy, our encounters with adversity cannot always result in progress. If failure becomes a habit, we learn little from it. Those who drift wherever life takes them never learn from adversity and failure. Only a dead fish floats downstream.

Opportunity:

We can learn from our failures, but only if we have the right perspective and take action. Sun Tzu's principles work to make failure the exception rather than the rule by building position. Adversity and failure offer valuable resources that we can get nowhere else. We develop resilience and toughness only by meeting adversity and failure. Those for whom everything comes easily are poorly prepared for serious campaigns, which usually grow progressively more difficult over time (6.3.3 Late-Stage Situations).

Key Methods:

There are eight key methods for developing personal toughness from adversity and failure.

1. To develop personal toughness, we must expect the unexpected. The world is not under anyone's control. Life is not only unfair, but it is unpredictable and uncertain (2.3.2 Reaction Unpredictability).

2. To develop personal toughness, we must see success over time as likely. Sun Tzu's principles are all based on probabilities, not certainties, but they are essentially optimistic. They view progress as increasingly certain if we work to improve our position in reasonable ways. The world is not a deterministic machine. The world is an array of complex stochastic processes. We rely on high-probabilities over the long-term but know that many setbacks must occur over the short term (1.8.4 Probabilistic Process).

3. To develop personal toughness, we seek to minimize our maximum loss and maximize our minimum gain. We must expect failures and only seek to minimize them (5.0 Minimizing Mistakes).

4. To develop personal toughness, we restrain ourselves during a crisis. Overreacting to difficulties only makes them worse (4.2 Choosing Non-Action).

5. To develop personal toughness, we must prepare for situations to reverse themselves. This is true both for good and bad situations when they are outside of our control. As conditions reach their extremes, the more likely they are to reverse (3.2.4 Emptiness and Fullness).

6. To develop personal toughness, we must preserve our resources for future challenges. We avoid going "all in" except in the most desperate situations. We regularly accept little failures so that we always survive to fight another day (5.6.1 Defense Priority).

7. To develop personal toughness, we use repeated practice to lose our fear of failure. Fear is the mind killer. While we never accept failure, we can learn to take it in stride. We can do this only through exercises that retrain our normal emotional reactions (6.8 Competitive Psychology).

8. To develop personal toughness, we develop the courage to try again differently. Courage is a critical ingredient to decision-making. It describes our ability to accept uncertainty and take reasonable risks in pursuing our goals (1.5.1 Command Leadership).

Illustration:

Let us illustrate these key methods with how their reverse is being promoted today through the media. Much of this media message arises out of the messenger's desire to promote a certain form of politics.

1. To develop personal toughness, we must expect the unexpected. When a hurricane like Katrina strikes, the message is that such events should always be predictable and even controlled. Nothing is further from the truth.

   2. To develop personal toughness, we must see success over time as likely. If we watch the news, we *know* the world is getting worse. But the reality is that by any objective analysis, as John Stossel's demonstrated in a recent show on "Life is Getting Better." The "man-bites-dog" bad news stories get reported while the "dog-bite-man" stories of every day success do not, giving everyone an upside-down view of life.

   3. To develop personal toughness, we seek to minimize our maximum loss and maximize our minimum gain. What gets promoted in the media are the big gambles that pay-off, making life seem a matter of simple luck. This viewpoint is fueled by Hollywood, where the most successful realize that luck plays a major part in their success and therefore think that it must be a large component in everyone else's success as well. The truth is that there are very few areas, show business being one of them, where chance plays such a major role.

   4. To develop personal toughness, we restrain ourselves during a crisis. During a crisis, the media always promotes the idea that the government must take action and then more action. Any idea of limited resources, priorities, and restraints are pushed out the window. The media never reports on the costs in lives and fortune that such extremes of action actually entail. When the debt bomb explodes from taking unnecessary actions, we will all pay for it.

   5. To develop personal toughness, we must prepare for situations to reverse themselves. Human society is resilient and people adjust to change as a group without being directed to do so. In science, we say that complex, adaptive systems are inherently stable because we learn. The net effect is Sun Tzu's view of a world created of balancing complementary opposites. In such a world, crisis tend to right themselves at a minimum of costs as long as government or the media does not force individuals to make choices that they would not otherwise make on their own.

6. To develop personal toughness, we must preserve our resources for future challenges. We must save resources so we have extra resources to deal with the inevitable reversals of fortune. The idea that government or insurance companies can protect us from anything ever going wrong discourages such saving. This creates what is known as "a moral hazard," where we are willing to take risks that others must pay for.

7. To develop personal toughness, we use repeated practice to lose our fear of failure. The media encourages our fear and helplessness in the face of forces too large for us to control. Instead of acting and practicing decision-making, we are encouraged to become arm-chair critics, critiquing the imperfect judgments of others with 20/20 hindsight. By going through decision exercises, such as those we use in our Warrior Class Training, we learn that perfect judgment is not possible in every situation and that judgment can only become better when we are allowed to fail.

8. To develop personal toughness, we develop the courage to try again differently. The media doesn't celebrate the idea that people should be and are personally rewarded for their courage. Indeed, courage is only portrayed in the media as a selfless act. What this actually encourages is fear and uncertainty because no one can understand the personal benefits of courage over time.

Sun Tzu's Playbook

Volume 7:
Momentum

About Creating Momentum

Adjusting to changing conditions advances a campaign only so far. The secret is knowing how to use innovation and surprise to create competitive momentum and excitement. That is the focus of the concepts in this volume of Sun Tzu's Playbook. The principles here teach you to use momentum to win new positions and grow your resources. Creating excitement from innovation is not that difficult.

Innovation is never in limited supply. Sun Tzu puts it this way:

> *You must use surprise for a successful invasion.*
> *Surprise is as infinite as the weather and land.*
> *Surprise is as inexhaustible as the flow of a river.*
>
> The Art of War, 5:2:4-7

Momentum combines what people expect with what they don't expect. Momentum comes from setting up pleasant surprises and timing those surprises to win positions.

The Chaos of the Marketplace

Sun Tzu's principles teach us that competition is never neat and tidy. We all want to work through a neat to-do list when sitting at our desk in our little protected environment. This isn't how success works.

Success comes from momentum. Momentum comes from balancing two opposite forces—organization and innovation—against one another.

People are confused by the chaos and disorder in any competitive situation. People cannot know what they want because they do not know what they can get. This confusion requires you to be organized. You must create orderly procedures and systems. All organizations must create islands of order amid the competitive chaos. Human uncertainty is thereby turned into confidence. Satisfying peoples' expectations gives you credibility in your competitive arena.

However, there is a limit to what you can gain this way.

Predictability is boring. People like visiting islands of order, but people don't like being confined to islands of order. Eventually they grow tired of the islands they know and stop visiting them. This is what creates new opportunities. People crave new experiences, but, at the same time, they fear the unknown. People appreciate high standards, but standards are eventually taken for granted. The world is changing so fast because people always want more and are always looking for new experiences.

Well-run organizations are not necessarily successful organizations. Successful organizations need something more to establish dominance over their competition.

Establish Standards to Create Order

The first principles in this volume define the need for standards and order. You must understand how people experience your competitive position. They are always comparing you to your competitors. You must organize what is confusing. When they visit your island of order in the confusing sea of the competition, they must know what to expect. To create a satisfying experience, you need to establish quality standards. You must use systems that have proven to be dependable.

Once they know you, people want consistency. They need predictability. You can't help that the world is chaotic, but you can eliminate any uncertainty within your operations. You create expectations and must know how to satisfy them.

You cannot make a profit and use resource efficiently without standard procedures. Chaos isn't profitable. It wastes time, effort, and resources. Organizing saves time, effort, and resources. This is where planning works. You perfect systems, practice procedures, train people, eliminate mistakes, and tighten up operations.

Good organizations create order to get value out of their resources. Great organizations create order to better satisfy other people to get value out of their resources. You cannot undermine how people experience your position. People must understand the basics of what you offer. Make it easy for people to work with you. They don't want to work to work with you. You must provide consistency quickly, with a minimum of effort.

Create Realistic Expectations

You cannot base your position simply on being different. You establish quality standards to set the expectations of others. You then use surprise to win them over. When you use surprise at the wrong time, people see you as a nut. Nuts get attention, but they don't win supporters. People cross the street to avoid a nut because nuts are just too unpredictable.

Before you can surprise people, they need expectations about who you are and what you offer. They must know that you aren't just a nut. Even in crowded competitive conditions, it is a mistaken to think that you first have to get people's attention.

The context can teach people to expect "a surprise." For example, if you are watching the Super Bowl, a crazy commercial cannot surprise you. Everyone expects loony commercials during the Super Bowl, and everyone also know that those commercials cost millions. They aren't really nuts. Of course, because you are expecting it, a crazy Super Bowl commercial isn't a surprise either.

For a surprise to work, the context has to frame your position correctly. When I give a keynote speech on strategy at a convention, I always start my presentation with something that the audience doesn't expect. Surprise works because their expectations have already been set. They know I am not a nut because the organization is paying several thousand dollars for me to talk to them.

An innovation cannot create a dominant position unless it is built on a solid foundation. Standards come first. The latest new electronic gadget is designed according to set standards, made mostly of proven components, built in factories by systems, and marketed and distributed by well-established procedures. For something "new" to work, it has to have a lot of old in it.

People can't relate to concepts that are too new. Personal computers didn't catch on until software makers realized that they needed to put more "old" into them. There were hundreds of calculating programs for personal computers before the first "electronic spreadsheet" was introduced. The fact that the electronic spreadsheet was modeled after something old, the standard accounting spreadsheet, was the key to its success, and, to a large degree, the whole success of the personal computer itself.

The simplest application of Sun Tzu's principles for creating momentum is to combine old and new product ideas together into a single package. The old idea part of the formula provides the context. This is a standard that people can understand. It creates their expectations. The new part is the surprise. It gets their attention and stimulates them with something new.

Rearrange Existing Components

Sun Tzu's system puts a big burden on creativity. You must plan some type of innovation every time you start a new campaign. You use the nature of your opportunity, your opportunity space, and the stage of the campaign to guide your choice of innovations. If you don't use surprise and innovation, your competitors will. Innovation harnesses the flow of change in the business environment to your benefit.

Where do you get these creative ideas? As always, today's problems are the seeds for tomorrow's inspiration. You always use your time to think of ways to improve your products and systems. If you think about the components of products and processes, you will come up with new ways to arrange them to create surprise and momentum.

Rearranging parts is the key. Just think about what the parts are, how they can be rearranged, and the implications of making changes. You just break everything down into its components and rearrange those components. In sales and marketing, there are only a few basic messages for selling products. In manufacturing, there are only a few key components to any product. In operations, there are only a few basic steps in any business processes. Just mix them up in your mind and see what happens.

What was the process of buying a cup of coffee before the half decaf, low fat venti mocha latte? How did Starbucks change it to create a dominant position? Coffee was one size fits all, but Starbucks added a million options. Now, you give your order to a clerk. The clerk writes it on a cup, repeats it the way you should have said it, and passes it to the coffee maker—barrista, if you prefer. I find this process annoying because, when the clerk repeats the order, I feel like I am being corrected for not using the official coffee terminology and proper word order.

How could you reinvent the process that Starbucks reinvented? Just rearrange things a little. Let your customers grab the size of cup they want, check off the little boxes themselves, and pass it to the coffee person. Voilà! No need to worry about terminology! No corrections! No mistakes!

You may not think you are creative, but you can always just rearrange things. Rearrange messages for marketing. Rearrange parts for new products. Rearrange steps for new processes. Just by rearranging, you come up with a new perspective. Do customers usually pay at the end of the process? How could they pay at the beginning? Starbucks moved paying to the middle.

Not all new ideas will work at first, but you can learn from your mistakes. It takes time to get innovations working. Frequently, the reason your innovation didn't work is that you didn't include enough "old" in your formula. Standards come first. Proven ideas that meet people's expectations are always the major ingredient. Innovation and proven practices are mutually dependent on each other. Standards inspire creativity, which inspires new standards. Using both, you can continually improve your business.

Without first establishing a baseline of standards, innovation and surprise are just chaos and confusion. Without innovation, standards are boring and just fall behind a marketplace that is constantly moving forward. You must combine standards with surprises to make the leap into a dominant position.

It is the addition of surprise to a solid position that creates the momentum toward a dominant position. Momentum never comes from consistency alone. The sense of momentum is created by a surprise—changes that get attention.

To offer a sports analogy, a team that is expected to win doesn't develop any momentum by scoring. Everyone expects the dominant team to score. Everyone expects the dominant team to be ahead in the game. When is momentum created? When something surprising happens in the game. This momentum is psychological and real. When expectations are exceeded, abilities are enhanced. When expectations are disappointed, abilities decline. A surprise opens up entirely new possibilities.

How many times have we witnessed this in sports? The underdog scores and momentum changes. Suddenly the favorite can't do anything right and the underdog can't make a mistake. Unless something else surprising happens, momentum doesn't change. The favorite can score, but momentum is still against them. They have to score in a surprising way, doing something that they don't normally do, for momentum to shift again.

You cannot control the chaos of your competitive environment. You can, however, control your momentum. You can do something surprising to change the situation. The change puts your competitors on the defensive. When you get momentum on your side, your competitors have to copy you. You can move from one innovation to another, abandoning them when they are no longer surprising. You can keep opponents following behind you. You don't have to worry as much about competitors when competitors are worrying about you. Your momentum with supporters forces competitors to keep up.

Time Innovation for Maximum Advantage

Together, the shift between standards and surprise creates momentum toward a dominant position, but timing is critical in securing that position. The chaos of competition is your target. You want changes to have an impact on the market. You can defuse the power of innovation by releasing changes at the wrong time or in the wrong way. Bundle small changes together to give them weight. Save up changes to release them to leverage.

The constant creativity of innovation, if hidden, builds up pressure. Timing reveals those surprises, releasing that pressure at the right time. Timing introduces a critical amount of control into the chaos of battle. It is this control that does the most to affect competitive attitudes.

You cannot release changes too soon, but you also cannot go too long without making changes. One step should follow another quickly. This type of continual progress can wash away any obstacles in a business and frustrate your competitors. This is the power of momentum.

Time surprises to impact those you want to influence. People's decisions take place in an instant. You must make an impact to win their support. Prepare your surprises for people in advance but keep them a secret. Release them at the right time to get the decisions that you want. This requires timing.

You must invest only in efforts that win supporters for your position. The shift from standards to surprise must have an impact. You must time your surprises precisely. A change from what is expected creates tension. You must time your surprise to create excitement among other people.

From the viewpoint of potential supporters, the excitement of change gives them the emotional impetus to make a decision. From the competitors' viewpoint, releasing an innovation at the right time increases their confusion and decreases their confidence. Even a small change from expectations can be enough to tip the balance if it is introduced at the right time.

The world of competition is chaotic and confusing. You create expectations to give people the sense that they are in control. You create pleasant surprises to stimulate people and to control them. These same surprises give your opponents the sense that you are in control. Since you and your people are more prepared for the change than others, especially your competitors are, you do attain more control the over chaos of the competition than your competitors do.

If competitors have a sense that you are in control, you have secured a dominant position. If they panic, they will make mistakes. These mistakes create new opportunities to advance.

You create a dominant position for momentum. You do not create it by asking yourself or your people to work harder. You must innovate the ways you handle the way people experience interactions with your position. You shape people's expectations to move them. People move forward when they know what to expect. Make people comfortable and they will support you. You use surprise to challenge them to act in a new way. Give people a sense of belonging and they will stay with you. Bring people together and they will move forward.

You use momentum to control people's thinking. You use people's thinking to control competitors. You want to shape the process so both your supporters and your competitors rush forward without stopping.

Summary

The principles in Volume Seven teach us how to give people a refuge from the chaotic world of competition by using standards that produce a consistent result. Start by giving people clear expectations about what they will get from dealing with you and satisfy those expectations.

These principles then explain how people get bored with having their expectations met. Give them something new and exciting in the way that you operate. They will keep coming back for more.

Finally, these principles teach you how to time your surprises to win supporters. Force your competitors to continually play catch-up. Give your competitors the sense that you are in control of chaos. They will continually feel at a disadvantage. This will pressure them into making mistakes. Their mistakes will open new opportunities for you.

7.0.0 Creating Momentum

Sun Tzu's seven key methods on how momentum requires creativity.

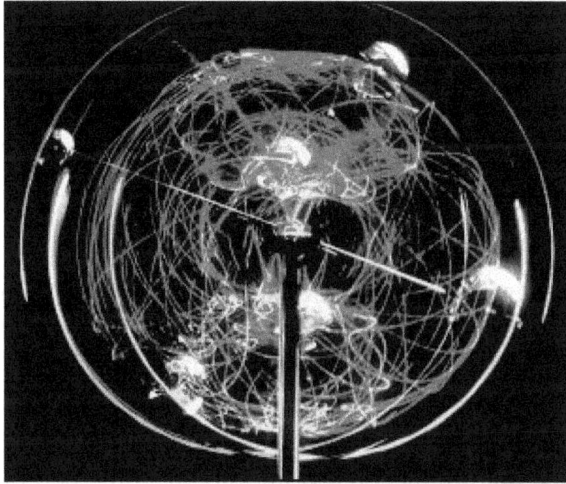

"You must develop these instant reflexes."
Sun Tzu's The Art of War 11:3:3

"When a warrior learns to stop the internal dialogue, everything becomes possible; the most far-fetched schemes become attainable. "
Carlos Castaneda

General Principle: We must drill ourselves to instantly recognize and respond to situations automatically.

Situation:

When we move to pursue an opportunity, we cross a critical threshold from simple decision-making to executing decisions. Sun Tzu called this movement "armed march" but we understand it more broadly as a competitive move or action. To pursue an opportunity, we must move into a region outside of our control. Once outside of controlled areas, we must respond instantly to the situations that we encounter. As important as reaction time is quickly deciding how to pursue opportunities, it is many times more important in responding to the immediate situations in which we find ourselves. Our range of potential actions collapses because the situation limits our options. If we don't know the best responses to these situations, we are going to get into serious trouble.

Opportunity:

Starting this new section, we move our discussion to the Move skills of Sun Tzu's Progress Cycle (1.8 Progress Cycle). Aim skills choose the highest probability opportunities (4.0 Leveraging Probability) and the best actions to explore them (5.0 Minimizing Mistakes). Move skills execute our aim decisions. Sun Tzu described in detail how they do this through situations response. These responses are required by situations that arise in the course of our move. There are nine classes of competitive situations that we encounter. Each of these classes has one best response. It gets even easier. While any of these classes of situations can arise in any move, they are most commonly found at certain stages of a competitive campaign.

Key Methods:

The following key methods guide the way that we respond to situation.

1. We must train ourselves to instantly recognize our situation. At this stage, the emphasis shifts from thought to action, from decision to execution. Our actions in a competitive environment are not executed like the steps in a plan. The job of making good strategic decisions gets more intense and demanding. We get information more quickly and we have to respond to it much more quickly as well (6.1 Situation Recognition).

2. We must also distinguish between simple moves and moves as a part of a larger campaign. A *campaign* describes longer term changes in position that consists of a sequence of moves. Campaigns are executed in smaller actions since smaller steps are more powerful. Within a campaign, we can recognize situations more easily because campaigns and the situations within them develop in a predictable, logical way (6.2 Campaigns).

3. Campaigns usually go through three stages. Each stage reveals more about the nature of the opportunity and has certain implications as far as creating situations. Understanding the stage of our campaign helps us better recognize the situation in which we find ourselves. Campaigns have beginning, middle, and end stages. Situations in each stage proceed logically from the nature of that stage (6.3 Campaign Patterns).

4. We must instantly separate competitive situations into one of the nine common classes. While every competitive situation has its unique characteristics, most fall into one of these nine categories. These nine situation classes are defined by differences in: 1) the true nature of the opportunity, 2) our position versus that of potential rivals, and 3) the depth of our commitment to the move (6.4 Nine Situations).

5. Once we recognize a situation, we must immediately know the one and only correct response. To reflect the fast pace of decision-making in making competitive moves, the best decisions are *responses* that arise from reflex rather than contemplation. Experience has demonstrated there is one, best response that works a high percentage of the time in each of the common situation. These responses have been proven over thousands of years of experience since they were first developed by Sun Tzu (6.5 Nine Responses).

6. We must pause our campaign when we run low on responses. The nine common situation responses are triggered by external developments. A growing lack of resources is an internal state that must also be monitored. While situation response requires us to focus externally on our situation, we cannot let ourselves lose sight of our internal need for resources (6.6 Campaign Pause).

7. Our dominant response must be tailored to three categories of unique characteristics. This is where the unique aspects of a position come into play. While our dominant response is dictated by standard situations, these same situations arise over and over again but they are never exactly the same. Every occurrence involves a unique constellation of conditions. We look at three categories of arena, relative size, and strength conditions (6.7 Special Conditions of Opposition).

8. Instant situation response creates key psychological advantages. By responding quickly and appropriately to challenging situations, we create confidence in our supporters and fear in our rivals. We improve the subjective dimensions of our position regardless of the objective rewards of our moves (6.8 Competitive Psychology).

Illustration:

The illustration that we usually use in our seminars to demonstrate these key aspects of situation response is a simple one of driving to the store to buy groceries. The decision that getting groceries is the best use of our time and that we are going to use a car are behind us. What happens when we get out on the road? This illustration makes solving these problems seem simple and indeed they are once we can apply them to every area of our competitive life as naturally as we do driving to the store.

1. We must train ourselves to instantly recognize our situation. If we don't run into problems, no responses are necessary. On this particular trip, we are going to run into problems. No strategic knowledge is necessary if we don't face challenges in our move. These principles are for meeting challenges.

2. We must also distinguish between simple moves and moves as a part of a larger campaign. Let us assume that getting bread is part of a larger campaign of making special dinner for guests, which has certain deadlines.

3. Campaigns usually go through three stages. This is an early stage of a campaign, so we expect three potential situations and prepare mentally for them.

4. We must instantly separate competitive situations into one of the nine common classes. An early stage has three possibilities and let us assume we hit them all. An intrusion threatens to interrupt us before we get out the door. We initially find no problems on the road. Then we hit a serious traffic jam.

5. Once we recognize a situation, we must immediately know the one and only correct response. We must know to 1) evade the intruder, 2) not get distracted and go quickly on the open road, and 3) know how to get around the traffic.

6. We must pause our campaign when we run low on responses. Running low on gas after getting out the door? Don't ignore it and hope you don't hit more problems. We'll be in a world of hurt when we hit traffic. We stop and get gas.

7. Our dominant response must be tailored to three categories of unique characteristics. We have to adjust our responses depending on how far it is to the store, how big the traffic jam, and road conditions. For example, if the road is icy and slippery, we don't choose the same alternatives as we do when the roads are bare and dry.

8. Instant situation response creates key psychological advantages. By navigating the challenging road conditions, we become come confident that our dinner party will go well.

7.1.0 Order from Chaos

Sun Tzu's seven key methods teaching the value of chaos in creating competitive momentum.

```
⚠ CAUTION

CHAOS FIELD
ESTIMATED STRENGTH: 47 KrZ

LIMIT EXPOSURE TO THIS AREA
AND REPORT ABNORMALITIES
IN YOUR LIFE AFTER EXPOSURE
```

"War is very complicated and confusing.
Battle is chaotic.
Nevertheless, you must not allow chaos."
Sun Tzu's The Art of War 5:4:1-3

"Chaos in the world brings uneasiness, but it also allows the opportunity for creativity and growth."
Tom Barrett

General Principle: Only momentum from creativity can break through the chaos of competition.

Situation:

Chaos describes our inability to see a pattern. Order may exist in situations that appear chaotic, but we cannot see their order. Dynamic natural systems evolve in complexity until we can no longer see any underlying order. In a psychological sense, chaos is the cognitive dissonance that arises from reality failing to match our expectations. We are wired to find patterns even in meaningless noise. As patterns dissolve in the overwhelming complexity of a situation, we perceive chaos even as we cling to our original expectations. This conflict between what we see and what we expect creates confusion, frustration, and fear.

Opportunity:

We experience chaos in competitive events, but so does everyone else. We can use the uncertainty in chaotic environments to our advantage (2.1.2 Leveraging Uncertainty). Success is never neat and tidy. We can work through a neat to-do list while sitting at our desks, but this isn't how we create success in the larger world. Real success comes from getting in the middle of messy, chaotic situations and exploring their potential.

Key Methods:

The following key methods describe how we need to think about using chaos in competitive situations.

1. We use proven mental models to create some order in chaos. Our confusion creates the desire for predictability. Sun Tzu's science of strategy provides certain standard methods for responding to common situations. In using these responses, we earn the respect of others. In advancing our position, we capture territory and create islands of control amid the competitive chaos. Those who create order, get the support of those who want to escape from competitive chaos to an island of order (6.8 Competitive Psychology).

2. As order increases from proven responses, it creates the need for more chaos. Order and chaos are complementary opposites, balancing against each other. As a competitive arena becomes more controlled, the value of introducing more chaos increases. This is true even in our use of Sun Tzu's standard responses. Over time, people adapt to these responses. Some copy what we have been doing. Others prepare against us. We become predictable. As environments become more predictable, they become more boring. We yearn for novelty. Our proven standard responses make less and less progress (3.2.3 Complementary Opposites).

3. As our environment or methods grow more ordered, unexpected methods start working better. In a sense, we must stop making sense, at least in the same ways everyone else does. The need for novelty is a special form of the openings on which all strategic moves are based, but this opening comes from the expectations created by our own use of standards. Given that others have expectations of us, we can go beyond them. We can invent new moves that increase the natural chaos. We can make the most of an opportunity only by surprising others (3.1.4 Openings).

4. We can select unexpected, unproven methods that have a high-probability success. Sun Tzu's methods of using standards as the basis for innovations increases the likelihood that these unproven methods work. Proven methods might work better, except they don't because they are expected. If we add a pinch of innovation to a proven formula, the new formula will sometimes fail, but it will usually work, at least to some degree (7.1.3 Standards and Innovation).

5. The use of unproven methods always gives us the advantage of surprise. Our use of innovation is primarily designed to increase chaos in the situation. This is different than natural chaos in one key respect: we are prepared for it while others are not. The confusion, uncertainty, and fear arising naturally from chaos does not affect us in the same way that it affects others, giving us an advantage (7.1.2 Momentum Psychology).

6. Only by using unproven methods can we discover new methods that work better than proven methods. We cannot depend on this, but we cannot discount it either. Every innovation is an exploration of possibilities. Only through that exploration is discovery possible. Only new methods can reveal the emergent properties in the chaotic environment, which are the source of completely new forms of order. This discovery of new, previously unknown resources, are the basis of our large leaps forward in position (7.6.1 Resource Discovery).

7. Our discovery of new methods, opens up entirely new realms of chaos. Using Sun Tzu's methods, we can create surprises in a systematic way, but the results of some of that innovation are only predictable in limited ways. We always get the advantage of the temporary surprise. We occasionally, get the additional advantage of discovering a better method. Rarely, we also get the advantage of discovering new areas of chaos that we can tame (7.3 Strategic Innovation).

Illustration:

Let us illustrate these ideas by exploring the history of television.

1. We use proven mental models to create some order in chaos. At first, television was a media that no one knew how to use. There was no clear idea of schedules, formats, or even a clear separation between the shows and their commercials. The first television shows were simply video broadcasts of shows that had been popular on radio or in vaudeville in which the commercial sponsors played a dominant role.

2. As order increases from proven responses, it creates the need for more chaos. These early television shows became more predictable. Commercials became standardized. The most popular shows, such as the vaudeville of Milton Berle quickly became boring and fell out of popularity.

3. As our environment or methods grow more ordered, unexpected methods start working better. A wider variety of television shows began to appear, inventing new forms such as the sit-com with "I Love Lucy" (1951).

4. We can select unexpected, unproven methods that have a high-probability success. While new shows were developed for television, they used the same organization and dramatic structures that had been proven earlier in radio broadcasting. Most shows are inherently derivative, simply adding a set of new personalities to a proven format: sit-com, crime drama, medical drama, etc.

5. The use of unproven methods always gives us the advantage of surprise. The most popular shows are those that provide something unique. The Tonight Show breaks new ground as a late night format, starting in 1954 with Steve Allen. Bonanza is the first color series. Archie Bunker brought in contemporary values. The Simpsons was the first cartoon show for adults.

6. Only by using unproven methods can we discover new methods that work better than proven methods. While most television formats had their roots firmly in the past, certain new formats, such as the reality series, were completely new to the medium. Because of their economic advantages, such shows may be the dominant form of programming.

7. Our discovery of new methods, opens up entirely new realms of chaos. There are now so many television shows available that we need technologies from DVRs such as TIVO to help organize it.

7.1.1 Creating Surprise

Sun Tzu's five key methods for creating surprise using our chaotic environment.

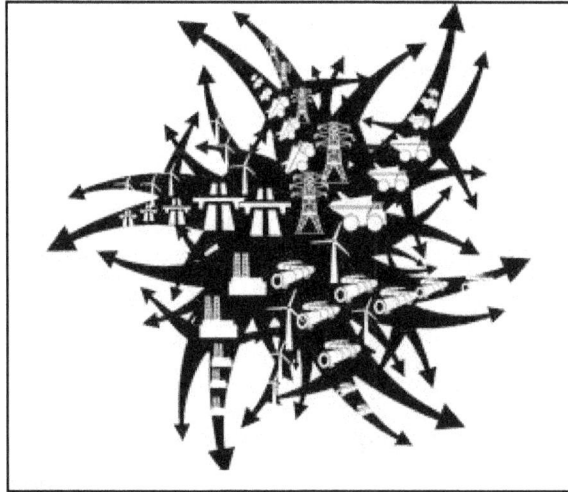

> *"You fight with momentum.*
> *There are only a few types of surprises and direct*
> *actions."*
>> Sun Tzu's The Art of War 5:2:20-21

> *"Apprehension, uncertainty, waiting, expectation, fear of*
> *surprise, do a patient more harm than any exertion."*
>> Florence Nightingale

General Principle: Surprise requires chaos, expectations, and an unambiguous, intentional action.

Situation:

Though competition is inherently chaotic, we still expect it to make sense. We are wired to find patterns even in meaningless noise. Despite the overwhelming complexity of competitive environments, we still cling to our expectations of order. Admitting that we cannot understand a situation creates cognitive dissonance, especially since we have been trained in linear thinking rather the than adaptive methods of Sun Tzu's strategy. We cling to our expectation. We are surprised when situations fail to develop according to those expectations. The reality of chaos affects us emotionally on a subconscious level. The unrecognized chaos makes us feel tense, frustrated, and even fearful.

Opportunity:

Our reaction to chaos makes surprise possible. When we use surprise, we take advantage of the inherent chaos of the situation. Since people are looking for patterns, they shift their focus to us. As the author of a surprise, we are different from everyone else in the situation. We alone are assumed to be in control of the event, and, by proxy, of the situation. This changes the expectations of everyone with whom we deal. They grant us power over a situation that everyone else sees as outside of their control. Everyone gauges their reactions based upon that perception of power.

Key Methods:

We create surprise using the following five key methods.

1. We leverage people's sense of expectations in a chaotic situation. Chaos is a necessary ingredient to creating surprise. Competition is chaos, but we fool ourselves into thinking it is controlled. Chaos creates a secret unease within us. Despite the rising feeling of uncertainty created by competition, expectations about the future are also necessary to create surprise. We can only be surprised if we think we know what is happening and how events should unfold. This means that the chaos cannot be so great that all expectations get thrown out the window. An action must have expectations to work against for it to be surprising (7.1.3 Standards and Innovation).

2. We must use a set-up action that seems to violate expectations while secretly satisfying them. We need to take an action that violates apparent expectations but which really satisfies those who are expecting a surprise. In competitive situations, we only pretend to know what to expect. Deep down, we know they are chaotic. The set-up satisfies our secret expectation of the unexpected. However, it creates a deeper tension, as opponents try to respond to the set-up action correctly (2.0 Developing Perspective).

3. We must then use a follow-up action to create the surprise that gives us momentum. The setup is the unexpected for which others are prepared. It is the follow-up that creates surprise and from it, momentum. The unexpected puts others off-balance, but the surprise pushes them over. When we witness an event that violates our expectations, we start to worry about what we are missing. If the set-up was an accident, it has no meaning. We don't have to worry about it. The follow-up action proves that the set-up was intentional. The follow-up demonstrates our control over the situation, giving us the desired momentum (3.6 Leveraging Subjectivity).

4. Both set-up and its follow-up must be significant enough to force attention. If either action is minor, we will either overlook it or simply take the action in stride, without reassessing the situation. However, if the action is significant, we react differently. We cannot take it in stride because of its impact on our perceptions of the situation. We are forced to reassess the situation as a whole. Our new perception of the situation centers around the surprising event (2.3.1 Action and Reaction).

5. Both set-up and its follow-up must appear suddenly out of secrecy. This is a matter of good timing. Under the subtle tensions of a secretly chaotic situation, our first reaction is to fit all actions within our expected narrative. If the action can be interpreted as something expected, it will be interpreted as something expected, no matter how mistakenly. This can actually help us in early stages of preparing a surprise because it enables us to disguise the "set-up" as something familiar. If we use the action too soon or too late, it will lose most of its impact (7.4 Competitive Timing).

Illustration:

We can illustrate these ideas by using the way that a magic trick is constructed.

1. We leverage people's sense of expectations about a chaotic situation. The first part of a magic trick is called "The Pledge". The magician shows you something ordinary: a deck of cards, a bird or a man. He shows you this object. Perhaps he asks you to inspect it to see if it is indeed real, unaltered, normal. However, underlying the Pledge of ordinariness is the sense of something coming, a hidden secret, the beginning of tension.

2. We must use a set-up action that seems to violate expectations while secretly satisfying them. The second part of a magic trick is called "The Turn". The magician takes the ordinary something and makes it do something extraordinary. However, while the Turn seems extraordinary, it is really expected because people are watching a magic act.

3. We must then use a follow-up action to create the surprise that gives us momentum. This is the third part, called the Prestige. Making something disappear isn't enough; you have to bring it back. The Turn was expected, almost promised by the Pledge. It is the Prestige that finalizes the surprise, making us realize that the Turn was itself another Pledge.

4. Both set-up and the follow-up must be significant enough to force attention. Neither the Turn nor Prestige can be subtle. They must command our attention. They force us to figure out what is really going on. Together, they reinforce our attention. At first we were looking for a secret, but before we could resolve that quest, we are confronted with another. We won't find the secret, because we know we are looking in the wrong place.

5. Both the set-up and the follow-up must appear suddenly out of secrecy. Both the Turn and Prestige must happen suddenly, ideally when we aren't expecting it. Since we are expecting something from the Pledge, but the Turn relieves those expectations only to be confronted with the Prestige, this sudden revelation that causes us to recognize control.

7.1.2 Momentum Psychology

Sun Tzu's five key methods on the psychology of surprise.

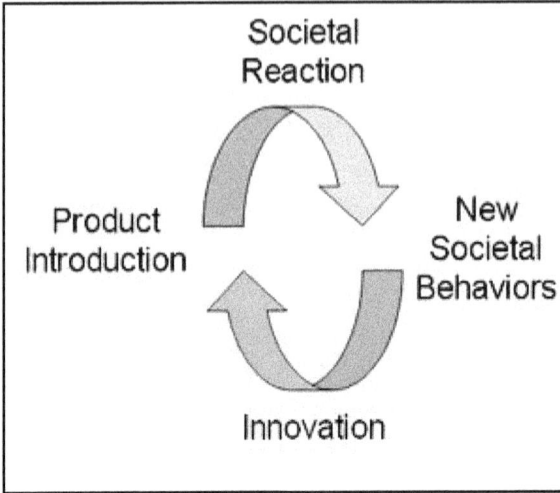

"You fight with momentum.
There are only a few types of surprises and direct
actions."
                                    Sun Tzu's The Art of War 5:2:20-21

"Demoralize the enemy from within by surprise, terror,
sabotage, assassination. This is the war of the future."
                                    Adolf Hitler

General Principle: Momentum amid chaos creates a psychological competitive advantage.

Situation:

In the generally chaotic conditions of competition, no one's actions truly control the situation. The situation as a whole is determined by the complex, unpredictable interactions of actions and events in the environment (3.2.1 Environmental Dominance). However, when we perceive that someone has momentum within a chaotic situation, that perception alone creates a psychological advantage. For those who understand its nature, that short-term subjective advantage can be transformed into longer-term, objective gains in position.

Opportunity:

A psychological divide separates those who have used a surprise from those who were taken by surprise. Those who use surprise are seen on both sides of this divide as 1) understanding and controlling the situation, 2) being prepared for the surprising event, and potentially having other surprises in addition to the followup. This situation increases the uncertainty and fear for those who have been surprised. Their worry about what may happen next, diffusing their focus and increasing the chances that they will leave an opening (3.1.4 Openings). Meanwhile, those who used surprise focus on its results looking for an opening to exploit (1.7.2 Goal Focus). This focus is the difference between having and lacking momentum.

Key Methods:

The following key methods describe how we leverage the psychological nature of surprise to create momentum.

1. The gap between having and lacking momentum is subjective. This subjective difference can be easily transformed into objective differences in position. This depends on our ability to create the proper mental states in others and take advantage of them (1.3.1 Competitive Comparison).

2. Those who have been surprised must leave an opening for us. As always, our actions to create surprise do not create momentum. Those actions must work through others, who create the opening for us. If the opening is left, as it usually is, we can make huge gains, However, as always, this is a matter of probability not certainty. If our opponents are not truly surprised, they may still adjust in time to stop us (3.2 Opportunity Creation).

3. We must immediately move to exploit the opening created by the surprise of others. Our response must assume that an opening will be created. By starting on our followup *before* the opening is there, we set the stage for building momentum. Our hope is that our speed will not give others the time to recover (5.3 Reaction Time).

4. Our move must consume our opponent's psychological resources rather than our physical ones. It cannot endanger our existing position by using resources vital for our defense. Instead, it should be designed to exhaust our opponents psychological resources as they try to understand the situation. If an opening is not left, we lose little. If one is left, we keep up the competitive psychological pressure on opponents (5.4 Minimizing Action).

5. The move must objectively improve our competitive position. We change subjective perceptions because it is less costly than changing objective positions, but that work is wasted unless our actions transform that subjective advantage into objective ones. Momentum is confirmed when people can confirm those objective gains (3.6 Leveraging Subjectivity).

Illustration:

Let us illustrate these ideas with an illustration from American football.

1. The gap between having and lacking momentum is subjective. During a sports contest, a play can result in a surprising turn of the tide such as an interception in football.

2. Those who have been surprised must leave an opening for us. The sudden change of offense and defense puts the intercepted team at an immediate disadvantage, emotionally unprepared for the next play.

3. We must immediately move to exploit the opening created by the surprise of others. The offense often takes advantage of this weakness by attempting a big play, for example, a long touchdown pass.

4. Our move must consume our opponent's psychological resources rather than our physical ones. This play works much more often than it would under normal circumstances. This is not because the defending team is physically less capable but because it is still recovering psychologically from the surprise.

5. The move must objectively improve our competitive position. If the turnover results in a score, the change in momentum is confirmed. If no score results from the surprise, the momentum of the intercepting team is neutralized.

7.1.3 Standards and Innovation

Sun Tzu's seven key methods on the methodology of creativity.

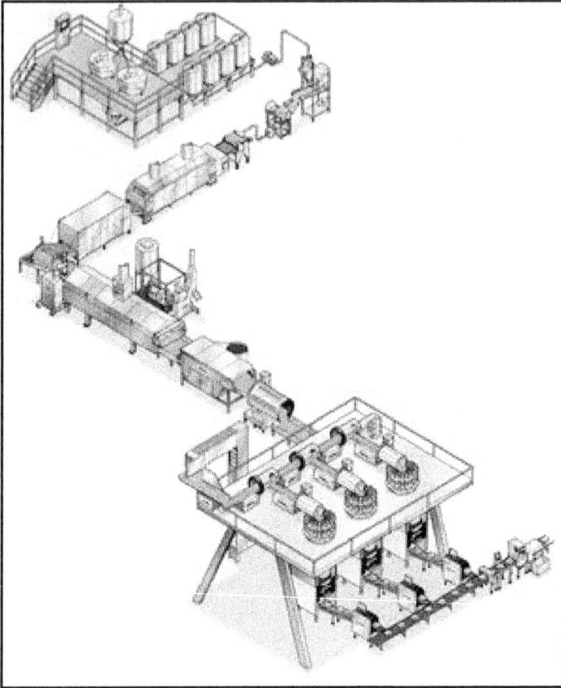

"It is the same in all battles.
You use a direct approach to engage the enemy.
You use surprise to win."
Sun Tzu's The Art of War 5:2:1-3

"Innovation distinguishes between a leader and a follower."
Steve Jobs

General Principle: The best balance of standards and innovation in competition is the opposite of the best balance in production.

Situation:

We live in an age of linear thinking where we are taught to rely on systematic pre-planned steps to address problems. Within the controlled environments of our schools, we are taught to obey instructions. Workers on the production line repeat standard steps. In production environments, innovation occurs relatively rarely. It usually comes from decisions outside those doing the work. Constant creativity by the workers on the line would disrupt the process of standard production. The problem is that this balance of standards and innovation is completely different in competitive environments.

Opportunity:

In competition, innovation is never external to the strategic process. It is an inherent part of it. Our opportunity is that most people do not realize this, at least at first. Standards are the basis of our creativity. Our creativity is the basis for developing our new standards (3.2.3 Complementary Opposites). Creativity can never disrupt competition. It always enhances it. Without the use of both standards and creativity, direct action and surprise, we can never create the strategic momentum necessary to win success. While production favors standards over innovation, competition favors innovation over standards. Both are still required, but in the competitive environment, everyone is a decision-maker, responsible for improving the process.

Key Methods:

The following key methods describe the roles of standards and innovation in competition.

1. Competitive creativity is necessary because every competitive situation is more unique than the same. We learn standard competitive methods to address the many aspects of competitive situations that repeat themselves, but each of these standard approaches also requires creativity. Creativity addresses the unique content in every situation (7.3 Strategic Innovation).

2. Strategic standards require instantly responding appropriately to conditions. Standards give us speed because we don't have time to craft every response from scratch. Our basic responses must be automatic, learned from drill and practice. The faster we recognize situations and respond, the more often we will be successful (6.0 Situation Response).

3. Our use of creativity and surprise must be reflexive as well. We must automatically implement all of our generic responses to conditions in a creative way. Creativity in using standard responses can also be practiced (6.1.1 Conditioned Reflexes).

4. Situations contain multiple conditions whose responses must be creatively combined. Situations are unique because they combined different sets of conditions in different ways. The combination of responses required is itself a unique prescription for the situation (6.2.1 Campaign Flow).

5. As others learn our patterns of response, we must creatively adjust our responses to their evolving reactions. We act in competition in order to get a set of desired responses. The standard responses work because they get the responses we desire. When we understand why they work, we can keep one step ahead of everyone by adapting those methods to their learning curve (2.3.1 Action and Reaction).

6. We must creatively adapt to the continual changes of climate and position. Shifts in climate change our position automatically. Our ability to spot the opportunities and new resources from our competitive arena (1.3.1 Competitive Comparison).

7. The more creative our responses, the more productive our competitive moves will be. The more creative we are, the more we are perceived as having momentum. Others will find it difficult to predict our moves making it difficult for people to hinder our progress. Being seen as unpredictable is always a competitive advantage (2.3.2 Reaction Unpredictability).

Illustration:

Let us illustrate these ideas with an illustration from a sales presentation.

1. Competitive creativity is necessary because every competitive situation is more unique than the same. A salesperson that simply repeats the same sales pitch to every client is not going to be successful.

2. Strategic standards require instantly responding appropriately to conditions. A salesperson must know how to instantly respond with the best proven answers to the common objections that he or she hears from customers.

3. Our use of creativity and surprise must be reflexive as well. The most successful salespeople automatically use the unique perspectives and situations of clients in their sales presentations.

4. Situations contain multiple conditions whose responses must be creatively combined. Great salespeople are like medical diagnosticians, able to separate different symptoms into a prescription that makes the best possible sense.

5. As others learn our patterns of response, we must creatively adjust our responses to their evolving reactions. A salesperson realizes that the more established the customer, the more something new and different is required to interest and hold them.

6. We must creatively adapt to the continual changes of climate and position. Great salespeople always start with what is changing as the basis for their sales presentation because they realize that it is change that both worries us and captures our imagination.

7. The more creative our responses, the more productive our competitive moves will be. A great salesperson is like an entertainer. The customer never knows what to expect but is always stimulated by the result.

7.2.0 Standards First

Sun Tzu's seven key methods on the role of standards in creating connections with others.

> *"You win a war by first assuring yourself of victory.*
> *Only afterward do you look for a fight."*
> Sun Tzu's The Art of War 4:3:24-25

> *"First impressions are often the truest, as we find (not*
> *infrequently) to our cost, when we have been wheedled*
> *out of them by plausible professions or studied actions."*
> William Hazlitt

General Principle: We must use the standard, proven methods to initiate a competitive move.

Situation:

All moves have a beginning. At the beginning of a move, we have the least information about the situation into which we are getting involved (2.1.1 Information Limits]). When our move brings us in contact with new people, we know little about them and how they will react. Among potential supporters, a bad initial impression is costly to overcome. Since these people know little about us and our intentions, they are likely to be suspicious since everyone's first reaction should be to defend.

Opportunity:

When we make initial contact with others, we have an opportunity to control their first impressions. We have the opportunity to create a good impression. That impression provides a leverage point, creating expectations that we can use to advance our position. Our initial actions have a disproportionate effect, a leveraging effect, on how people react to us and how we are likely to proceed. Initial contact is a natural leverage point, if we know how to use it.

Key Methods:

The following key methods determine how we should act in making our initial contacts with people.

1. Standards are the foundation of all contact and connection. This is true whether we are talking about connections among people or among communication systems. Without shared standard, no communication is possible. This communication starts with a common language, which provides the lowest common denominator of connection, but it includes layer after layer of cultural context that ties people together, including standard of courtesy and professionalism (7.2.1 Proven Methods).

2. We must initiate all contacts by invoking standards. In practical terms, these standards are both social and professional. In the world of technology, we call the initiation of communication between systems a "handshake." The same ideas applies to personal communication. If we start by being so different that others simply don't know what to expect from us, we will have a difficult time making any connections. If we want to connect with others, we get started on the right foot by doing what is expected. Objectively, we use standard methods because they are proven to work. Subjectively, we use standards because human psychology requires a standard reference point around which to form an impression (1.2 Subobjective Positions).

3. When we first connect with others, we must minimize chaos. The initiation of contact is chaotic and novel enough. In today's networked world, new contacts are often interruptions in the expected order of events. Chaos creates work and stress for us, wasting time, effort, and resources. We increase our chances of connecting by minimizing the work required. While we no longer require a formal introduction to meet new people, we can expect better responses if we use every social and professional standard (2.3.1 Action and Reaction).

4. This question of standards quickly becomes a question of shared values. After the initial handshake, people quickly move to questions about goals and motivation. We build on a shared acceptance of our mutual self-interest. While we don't have to share all our values, we have to share our respect for our different resources and that our differences for the basis for a mutually rewarding exchange (1.6 Mission Values).

5. We generate strong initial impressions by using existing expectations. We form our first impressions with a minimum of information. First contact is a leverage point where a little information goes a long way. We must play an expected role to generate the type of impression that we desire. We attempt to duplicate a typical experience that is easier for others to categorize. This first impression then becomes a commonly understood point for the rest of the relationship (1.1 Position Paths)

6. We can shape future expectations more easily starting with a clear first impression. Sun Tzu's strategy requires controlling other people's expectations. If we don't know people's first impressions, we have a much more difficult time shaping their future opinions. We surprise people by exceeding their expectation. For this method to work, people must think they know what to expect. People simply cannot relate to concepts that are too new and different (7.2.2 Preparing Expectations).

7. Sun Tzu's mental models give us a simple set of standard starting points for competitive situations. Sun Tzu's strategy is based on the archetypal concepts of comparing positions and relationship. Despite its depth of detail and specialized language, it maps to a basic model of the world that most people already carry in their minds. It is easy to explain Sun Tzu's concepts using analogies in so many different competitive areas because people start with many of its preconceptions without knowing it (2.2.2 Mental Models).

Illustration:

Let us illustrate these ideas discussing the importance of user interface in introducing new technologies.

1. Standards are the foundation of all contact and connection. New technologies must be build on existing understanding. For example, personal computers sold only to a small technical segment of the population until software such as word-processing and electronic spreadsheet created an easy starting point for regular people to connect with computers.

2. We must initiate all contacts by invoking standards. Hundreds of calculating programs for computers came and went before the first "electronic spreadsheet" like today's Excel was introduced. Modeled directly on the existing accounting spreadsheets, it gave people an easy entry point into using computing to address problems.

3. When we first connect with others, we must minimize chaos. When computer operating systems required users to master a new language, responding with cryptic error messages, people quickly rejected the experience. As user interfaces became more graphic, they allowed users to understand the computer environment by connecting them to more physical environments.

4. This question of standards quickly becomes a question of shared values. A given user interface design results from a set of values, often unconsciously expressed. The original cryptic computer interfaces placed their value on arcane knowledge of users. That knowledge created a private, exclusive club. The modern, graphical designs put a premium on simplicity and clarity.

5. We generate strong initial impressions by using existing expectations. When we encounter a new device, we rely on our knowledge of similar devices to figure out how to use it. We use visual and other cues to understand the underlying template used for design. When the controls and words used are unfamiliar, making it hard to know what to do, we form a negative first impression that is very difficult to overcome. When they are familiar working in ways we already understand, we get a positive first impression.

6. We can shape future expectations more easily starting with a clear first impression. Devices can lead us to new capabilities more easily when they start from familiar starting points. Leading software companies all realize this by designing their family of products around familiar formats. No matter what desktop browser you are using now, it probably has a menu that starts "File Edit View" following the original design of Microsoft applications.

7. Sun Tzu's mental models give us a simple set of standard starting points for competitive situations. User interface design falls within the realm of production and control rather than competition and strategy, but the market for under interface design is competitive. Designs for interfaces must minimize barriers to usability (4.5.2 Surface Barriers) and create easy situations for users (6.4.2 Easy Situations) are always going to be more popular than those that don't.

7.2.1 Proven Methods

Sun Tzu's eight key methods for identifying and recognizing the limits of best practices.

		Effective Competition	
		Winners	Losers
Efficient Production	Valuable	**Best Practices**	No Difference
	Costly	No Difference	**Worst Practices**

"Influence events.
Think about opportunities in terms of methods you can control."

Sun Tzu's The Art of War 1:3:4-5

"It's all very well in practice, but it will never work in theory."

French Proverb

General Principle: A given set of proven methods combine a formula for production with a formula for competition.

Situation:

Leveraging the forces of our environment without know-how is impossible. Our world works because it is built on thousands of years of accumulated human knowledge. It requires work to prove which techniques, methods processes, and activities work best to accomplish a certain set of goals. As our technical knowledge has grown more complex, we each master a smaller and smaller piece of the whole. As our success at manipulating our environment has grown, more and more of us are isolated from the hard realities of nature. Complexity leads to chaos if the connections tying together our know-how are not preserved and passed down from generation to generation.

Opportunity:

Sun Tzu's system of innovation is based upon knowing how the world works, both in production and in competition. The value of competition is that it naturally separates what works from what works better. If we focus on what has been proven to work, progress using innovation is much easier. When we must base our creativity on the thousands of years of strategic learning, it becomes fairly easy to do.

Key Methods:

The following eight key methods describe what we must understand in order to use proven methods as a basis for innovation.

1. Proven methods represent techniques, processes, and activities that are more effective at delivering a desired outcome than alternatives methods. This rule means that there is an objective reality whose natural laws are best leveraged with some actions over others. While our knowledge of these laws is always limited, the effectiveness of a given set of actions is not merely a matter of belief or perspective but based on an underlying reality (1.2 Subobjective Positions).

2. Best methods are proven by comparing the results of alternative approaches. We cannot determine best practices merely by our intellectual analysis, which is always based solely on our limited knowledge. Superior methods can only be determined in the arena of competition where they outperform less effective methods (1.3.1 Competitive Comparison).

3. Best practices represent a snapshot of our limited knowledge not complete knowledge about what is possible. Over time, better practices are discovered through the competition of ideas. Most new approaches are proven not to work, but eventually better methods are discovered (1.2.2 Exploiting Exploration).

4. Proven methods combine a set of competitive methods with a set of production methods. What is proven in any given case is the combination. The comparative advantage of any given combination can lie at either side of this equation or emerge from the combination of both. As complementary opposites, these two separate realms of skills are two sides of the same coin (1.9 Competition and Production).

5. Small advances to proven methods are more likely to be successful than big ones. This rule is the basis for successful innovation. If we start with a large base of knowledge about strategy, we need to add only a small drop of creativity. Strategically, the best innovations are those that leverage the most existing knowledge. (5.5 Focused Power)

6. Any attempt to innovate too many aspects of a best practice is extremely likely to fail. A working process works like the links in a chain. It works because each link supports the others. Any attempt at innovation that replaces too many links in that chain depends upon too many unproven links. While large innovation can rarely succeed, their rate of success conforms to the power law distribution, which calls for a great many small advances for every large one (1.8.4 Probabilistic Process).

7. Proven production methods require less innovation than competitive methods. Models of production are relatively easy to understand because they exist in areas where we have greater knowledge and control. Production methods are based on duplication so they are by their very nature, more easily duplicated (1.9.2 Span of Control).

8. Proven competitive methods require an innovation to deal with unique conditions. Unlike production environments where conditions are controlled, competition exists in an environment that is beyond our control. While some general aspects of competitive methods can be proven to work in similar conditions, the unique and shifting nature of competitive environments require constant adaptation (1.9.1 Production Comparisons).

Illustration:

Let us illustrate these key methods by discussing the introduction of a successful new electronic product.

1. Proven methods represent techniques, processes, and activities that are more effective at delivering a desired outcome than alternatives methods. No matter how revolutionary it seems, a product must be built with familiar controls. Inside, it consists primarily of proven components.

2. Best methods are only proven by comparing the results of alternative approaches. Think about everything that goes into making that device work. All have been chose because someone thought they would work best, but only the success of the product on the market proves those decisions correct.

3. Best practices represent a snapshot of our limited knowledge not complete knowledge about what is possible. Each generation of products represents an advance over previous ones. No generation of products is so perfect that it cannot be improved over time.

4. Proven methods combine a set of competitive methods with a set of production methods. The product is assembled in factories using standard methods. It is marketed in existing media based on existing brand images in ways previous products have proven. It is distributed by existing product channels. 99.9% of what makes a product successful both in production and competition is standard, proven technology.

5. Small advances to proven methods are more likely to be successful than big ones. What makes the product "new" is perhaps 1% of innovation added to make it different from previous generations of product.

6. *Any attempt to innovate too many aspects of a best practice is extremely likely to fail.* For that "new" product to work, it must have a lot of old in it. Products that involve too much innovation fail either in production, because they cannot be made efficiently, or in competition, because they cannot be effectively understood by their potential customers.

7. *Proven production methods require less innovation than competitive methods.* Almost all new successful electronic products require very little less innovation in their production methods.

8. *Proven competitive methods require an innovation to deal with unique conditions*. Almost all new successful electronic products require an innovative take on the customer needs that they must address.

7.2.2 Preparing Expectations

Sun Tzu's eight key methods on how we shape other people's expectation.

"Chaos gives birth to control.
Fear gives birth to courage.
Weakness gives birth to strength."
Sun Tzu's The Art of War 1:3:4-5

"The quality of expectations determines the quality of
our action."
A. Godin

General Principle: We shape people's expectations by leveraging the certainty of hope against the confusion of fear.

Situation:

When we participate in a controlled process, our expectations are nothing more than assuming everyone else involved will do their job. In the chaotic arena of competition, the term "expectation" takes on a different meaning. We have no overall specification of anyone's responsibilities before we come to an agreement with them. Everyone's decisions regarding their commitments depend upon their own individual goals and the conditions that affect them over time. What do we expect them to do? Only to behave in accordance with their own best interests as they see those interests.

Opportunity:

Since people long for predictability, our opportunity is in controlling their expectations, that is, giving them what they long for. In chaotic competitive environments, we want to know what to expect from others. We realize that we can only learn what to expect from our interactions with them. We gravitate toward those whose interests we can understand. We prefer those who promote their interests in a consistent and dependable way. Though individual actions cannot be predicted, we develop expectations developed upon our experience. These expectations take the form of probabilities (1.8.4 Probabilistic Process).

Key Methods:

The process of setting expectations is a feedback loop that depends on eight key methods.

1. Controlling people's expectations is valuable whether or not we expect to confirm them. Sometimes, we control people's expectations so that we can confirm their beliefs. Other times, we control expectations to set people up for a surprise. We can use either approach to win supporters or frustrate opponents depending on the situation (2.3.1 Action and Reaction).

2. People want events or results in an external, competitive environment to be as predictable as those in controlled internal environments. This desire is a result of our education for working in a linear, controlled environments. The truth is that the our expectations in a controlled environment are inherently more reliable than expectations in competitive environments. The fact that people don't understand the key differences in these two environments gives us our strategic leverage point since our expectations for the future are likely to be much more open than those of others (1.9 Competition and Production).

3. To control people's expectations, we must leverage their natural balance between optimism and pessimism. People form their expectations to minimize their confusion while maximizing their happiness. We want to believe the future is predictable, but we hedge our bets because at a gut level we know it is not. A too pessimistic view of the future is depressing, but a too optimistic view is risky and often leads to frustration. Both states of mind undermine our happiness. These opposing states of mind are complementary opposites. The balance between them shifts back and forth depending on character and conditions. To create people's expectations, we must leverage this balance, working to bring the extreme back in balance. (3.2.3 Complementary Opposites).

4. All our words and actions signal our intentions to form others expectations of us. Actions are more costly than words so they are more believable, but we don't have to understand all the details of signaling theory to understand that everything we do tells others about us. Our dress, our manners, what we talk about, and how we talk all give people signals regarding our character and intentions. We can offer honest signals or dishonest ones. We can also offer intentionally confusing signals. People can choose to believe or disbelieve our signals whether those signals are honest or not (2.1.3 Strategic Deception).

5. We shape the expectations of others by offering them a predictive model that conforms with their judgments. Past judgments are the only basis for future expectations. We play into the confirmation bias, people's tendency to search for or interpret information to conform with their viewpoints. One of the advantages of mastering Sun Tzu's principles is that it provides a big, picture model of how the world works that conforms with what people learn from their own experience but never learn to express. We shape their expectations based upon demonstrating that we share **their**

understanding of what is important in a situation by offering a more complete picture of that situations (2.5 The Big Picture).

6. People's pessimism arises from their confusion about competitive chaos. Just as people's plans collide in competitive environments, our expectations also collide. Our expectations can collide with the expectations of others and with our own conflicting expectations. The result is both frustration and confusion, which we seek to avoid by gravitating toward points of view that protect us from frustration but actually do not offer more certainty (7.1 Order from Chaos).

7. People's optimism arises from their desires and their goals. Whether it is realistic or not, we all want others to act the way we want them to. All our expectations are ultimately about our goals and desires. While our expectations can be either optimistic or pessimistic, both directions concern our desire for gain and fear of less. We cannot leverage people's expectations unless our initial contacts with them help us understand those goals and desires (1.6 Mission Values).

8. We improve our certainty in the expectation of others by seeking feedback. We ideally look for confirmation in people's deeds, but words can be useful as well. We want this feedback whether it confirms our success in shaping expectations or not. When our feedback confirms a set of expectations, we are in a much better position to know how to act to satisfy our goals (2.3.3 Likely Reactions).

Illustration:

Let us illustrate these principles by discussing how betting controls the expectations of others in a poker game.

1. Controlling people's expectations is valuable whether or not we expect to confirm them. In poker, everyone is an opponent. We use our betting to establish patterns of behavior that our opponents think they can use to predict our actions in a given situation.

2. People want events or results in an external, competitive environment to be as predictable as those in controlled internal environments. Amateurs understand the role of bluffing and the mathematics well enough to think that people are more predictable than they are. Professionals use these expectations against them, using false tells to set them up for future disappointment.

3. To control people's expectations, we must leverage their natural balance between optimism and pessimism. In a poker game, everyone is shifting back and forth between their greed and fear. We use their greed to encourage them to bet a losing hand. We use their fear to bluff them out of winning hands.

4. All our words and actions signal our intentions to form others expectations of us. In the case of poker, we bet or raise to signal a strong hand. We check or call or fold to signal a weak one. We also have a variety of other behaviors that also provide signals, but those behaviors, like words, are cheap. It is the betting that sends the strongest signals and we establish our patterns of behavior though the course of a game.

5. We shape the expectations of others by offering them a predictive model that conforms with their judgments. Our opponents develop their expectations about us, whether we are a tight player or loose, aggressive or conservative, depending on our signals.

6. People's pessimism arises from their confusion about competitive chaos. When our betting follows no meaningful pattern or violates the patterns that we have established in the past, people are confused about what we hold. In those situations, they are more likely to be cautious.

7. People's optimism arises from their desires and their goals. When our betting follows a certain pattern and others think they know whether or not our hand is strong or weak, people grow more optimistic about making the right decisions.

8. We improve our certainty in the expectation of others by seeking feedback. When we seek to encourage their betting and they bet, we confirm our model of their expectations. When we seek to discourage their betting and they do not bet, we also confirm our understanding of how we have shaped their expectations.

7.3.0 Strategic Innovation

Sun Tzu's six key methods defining a simple system for innovation.

"There are only a few basic colors.
Yet you can always mix them.
You can never see all the shades of victory."
Sun Tzu's The Art of War 5:2:14-16

"Innovation is not the product of logical thought,
although the result is tied to logical structure."
Albert Einstein

General Principle: Systematic strategic innovation comes from working on the smallest possible parts of a process.

Situation:

The creativity of surprise is vital to every aspect of good competitive strategy, but most of us do not understand what strategic innovation is and how we accomplish it. We are taught two ideas about invention that work against the everyday creativity that we need in strategy.

- First, we think innovation is a flash of inspiration, a "great idea" that just pops into our mind.
- Next, we think that these great ideas are the realm of special geniuses who are far out of the mainstream of regular thought.

This view of creativity is useless for the purpose of strategy. First, we cannot wait for ideas to pop into our heads because we need ideas every day. Second, strategy requires small dashes of creativity based on a firm foundation of practical knowledge. We all have a million ideas, and very few of them are great, but that doesn't matter. More to the point, they are irrelevant to the need at hand. If anything, great ideas are a distraction because, though they seem great when we have them. Very, very few prove to be valuable at all to the situation at hand.

Opportunity:

People think inventiveness is difficult, depending on an inborn ability. In school, we are taught to think of inventors as rare, exotic creatures. The truth is that strategic innovation is easy and almost automatic once we master its perspective. Few recognize this possibility.

In a world in which people are trained simply to follow instructions, most of us simply overlook creative approaches that are right in front of us. Strategically, innovation is not a matter of creating something that is completely new. New ideas have a low-probability of success. If we want a high-probability of success, our creativity must be based on what has been proven to work in the past (7.2 Standards First). Our opportunity is in mastering a method that allows us to create something new whenever we have the need.

Key Methods:

Sun Tzu's mental model for understanding how to successfully innovate in a consistent way requires mastering six simple methods.

1. Strategic innovation requires decisions about parts rather than wholes. Up to this point, we have been making competitive decisions based on the situation as a whole. Innovation and surprise focus our decisions on the smallest possible pieces of the whole. Situation awareness is a matter of putting together a big picture from little pieces of information. Strategic creativity reverses that process, breaking things down into smaller pieces to identify specific targets for innovation. (3.2.4 Emptiness and Fullness).

2. Proven methods must be broken into their component parts. This process starts by breaking down things into their separate components. Everything developed by the human mind is made up of smaller components. Machines are made of parts. Processes are a series of steps. Recipes are a number of ingredients. Sun Tzu's strategy offers a systematic method for identifying these parts. This process of breaking components down can go on indefinitely, since each component can itself be broken down into finer components (7.3.1 Expected Elements).

3. Everyday innovation simply rearranges existing parts. This is the most common and easiest form of innovation. When we have a comprehensive process for breaking anything into its components, that same system tells us how they can be arranged. It requires no new ingredients or components. The existing order of steps or components creates a certain set of expectations. Any change in order creates an innovation that upset expectations and creates surprise. We examine how these components work together and ask ourselves if they will still work if we simply rearrange them to create something unexpected (7.3.2 Elemental Rearrangement).

4. Deeper innovation requires eliminating an existing part and possibly replacing it with a new one. This is the less common and more challenging form of innovation. It requires a process to work differently, without an existing component or with a replacement component. One advantage of this approach is that the existing order of steps or components can be otherwise maintained. We examine how these components work together and ask ourselves if they will still work if we simply eliminate a part or replace it (7.3.3 Creative Innovation).

5. The change to proven methods should be made in as small an increment as possible. This approach minimizes mistakes and reduces potential wasted efforts (5.4 Minimizing Action).

6. Innovations that are too small to create surprise must be combined for impact. One of the principles for creating surprise is that the change must be large enough to force attention. When we improve in small increments, individual changes lack the impact needed to get attention. In these situations, small changes can be made in secret and unveiled together to generate the desired result (7.1.1 Creating Surprise).

Illustration:

Let us illustrate how these key methods are used in business by examining the success of Starbucks in changing the model for selling cups of coffee.

1. Strategic innovation requires decisions about parts rather than wholes. In the end, we still go into a retail store and get a cup of coffee with milk just like we did before Starbucks. What Starbucks changed was parts of the process.

2. Proven methods must be broken into their component parts. In the original process, beans were ground ahead of time. Coffee was brewed ahead of time. A customer then ordered a cup of coffee. The brewed coffee was poured. Then the customer added their own milk or cream. The coffee shop environment provided was cold and sparse.

3. Everyday innovation simply rearranges existing parts. Starbucks used the same key components were the same, but the order was changed. The order is taken. The coffee is then ground fresh. The coffee is then brewed instantly. The milk is added warm so as not to cool the coffee. Then the drink is served. The environment was warm, inviting people to linger.

*4. **Deeper innovation requires eliminating an existing part and possibly replacing it with a new one**.* Starbucks replaced drip brewing with the steam brewing used in Europe, which required a darker roast of bean.

*5. **The change to proven methods should be made in as small an increment as possible**.* Nothing here was revolutionary. All of these methods had long been used and proven in Europe.

*6. **Innovations that are too small to create surprise must be combined for impact**.* Many of the changes Startbucks instituted appeared before, but in isolation, they were not enough to make an impression.

7.3.1 Expected Elements

Sun Tzu's seven key methods on dividing processes and systems into components.

"There are only a few notes in the scale.
Yet you can always rearrange them.
You can never hear every song of victory."
Sun Tzu's The Art of War 5:2:11-13

"Both traditions want people to think. They want people
who are problem solvers and can take apart a problem
and put it back together again."
Marlene Barron

General Principle: Creativity starts by separating components in terms of space, time, formula, and purpose.

Situation:

Linear thinking [2] requires using pre-planned processes, working with systems and machines. We are trained to use these systems without understanding them. We can start to think that we need not and cannot understand how systems work, but even things that can be hard to make can be easy to understand. We are not taught a comprehensive method for taking existing things apart to see how they are made to work. We take the existing components for granted. When we use products, machines, and processes, we are not aware of the parts. The human mind filters out what is expected and taken for granted.

Opportunity:

Sun Tzu teaches that opportunities are hidden (3.2.2 Opportunity Invisibility [3]). As we lose sight of the components of which things are made, an opening is created. We want to identify overlooked components that we can exploit. Those who take the time to break things into their parts can use this understanding to their strategic advantage.

Key Methods:

The following seven key methods describe Sun Tzu's systematic process for identifying the elements that can be rearranged or replaced to create surprise.

1. Everything that people put together can be taken apart. Unlike the complexity that arises in complex, adaptive systems, which is beyond our understanding, human constructions can be broken down into smaller pieces. Machines are made of parts. Processes are a series of steps. Recipes consist of ingredients. When any of these are taken apart, we better understood it. Every created object and every intentional action is made of small components (7.2.1 Proven Methods [4]).

2. Steps in a process are events arranged in time. Arrangements in time describe steps in a process, each having a length of time, a place in the sequence, and a frequency of repetition (1.8.3 Cycle Time [5]).

3. Parts are arranged in a physical relationship to each other to create organization in space. Arrangements in space describes how parts are put together in a machine or a picture, having shape, relative size, and attributes of interaction (4.4 Strategic Distance [6]).

4. The relative portions of ingredients in a recipe are the qualitative parts of the formula. Portions in a formula are based on relative, measurable quantities. Formulas describe how ingredients are put together where those ingredients have different characteristics and interact with each other. The relative quantity of each of those components is the key to the recipe (2.2.2 Mental Models [7]).

5. Every step, part, or ingredient in a system fills a specific need, and all needs are potential openings. Systems, relationships, and processes satisfy people's needs. Whether people recognize it or not, each part, each step, each ingredient satisfies a piece of that need, filling a small opening. To understand the component, we must understand its value, meaning, and purpose as part of the whole (2.4.5 Mission Perspective [8]).

6. Every step, part, or ingredient of a system creates a specific expectation. Just as we take the expected for granted, our brains are geared to recognize the abnormal, the things that are out of place. By shifting from what is normal, we have the opportunity to get people's attention and create surprise (7.2.2 Preparing Expectations [9]).

7. Rearranging parts may or may not improve efficiency, but it always creates surprise. When we focus on internal production, efficiency is most important, but when we focus on external competition, the surprise is most important. From the surprise, we seize initiative, creating momentum. To create surprise, we don't have to improve the process. All we have to do is violate expectations (1.9 Competition and Production [10]).

Illustration:

Sun Tzu describes this method for understanding in terms of sound, sight, and flavor. Let us combine his description with a description of the system, the computer, that I am using to write this.

1. Everything that people put together can be taken apart. We can take apart computers. We can see how their pieces fit together. Those who are in the computer business must take them apart in order to improve them.

2. Steps in a process are events arranged in time. Using a computer is a process. Activities follow in a certain sequence, requiring a certain amount of time. I must turn it on, select a program to run, choose what documents I want to work on, start working, save my work, and so on.

3. Parts are arranged in a physical relationship to each other to create organization in space. As a machine, it has physical components organized in space. I expect the keyboard to be below the screen, the keys to be arranged on it in a certain way, the touch pad to be in front of the keyboard, and the touch pad buttons in front of it.

4. The relative portions of ingredients in a recipe are the qualitative parts of the formula. In a computer, the quantitative elements are the size of its memory, its screen, its disk-drive and so on. Software depends on certain minimum quantities in order to function.

5. Every step, part, or ingredient in a system fills a specific need, and all needs are potential openings. We need a keyboard to get data into the system. That need can be fulfilled by other forms of data entry than typing. We need a screen for data output. Other forms of data output can satisfy that need.

6. Every step, part, or ingredient of a system creates a specific expectation. I have certain expectations for how the software will work because I know the steps that have worked in the past to perform a certain function. The same is true of the physical parts, such as the layout of the keyboard. For certain computer parts--the power button, the volume control, etc. I have no expectation because there is no standard design or location, so those components have no affect on expectations.

7. Rearranging parts may or may not improve efficiency, but it always creates surprise. To create surprise, we must change the order of events or elements. We initially meet expectations by satisfying those expectations, but we surprise by violating them, arranging the component in a novel way. For example in process, computers increasingly skip the "select program" part, loading the appropriate program instantly when we pick the document we want to work on. Small Web-book laptops assume we are going to access the internet and load a browser. In hardware, tablet computers use touch screens as virtual keyboards. This opens the possibility of creating a virtual keyboard that could display programmable keys that display their user-defined functions.

7.3.2 Elemental Rearrangement

Sun Tzu's six key methods for seeing invention as rearranging proven elements.

"There are only a few flavors.
Yet you can always blend them.
You can never taste all the flavors of victory."
                    Sun Tzu's The Art of War 5:2:17-19

"We must always change, renew, rejuvenate ourselves;
otherwise we harden."
                    Johann Wolfgang von Goethe

General Principle: Surprise comes from rearranging components in terms of time, space, and formula.

Situation:

Constructive strategy requires innovating in a minimum of time. To this, we must quickly identify the separate components that shape the situation (7.3.1 Expected Elements). Only then can we see how those elements create certain expectation. However, this knowledge alone doesn't tell us how we can change those elements creatively.

In most of our education, we are trained to use systems, not create new systems. When we use standard systems, we operate within a controlled area (7.2 Standards First). We are comfortable with standards because we know what to expect. However, when we simply operate under standards, we are literally controlled by the system. We are controlled by those who developed those systems for their own \purposes, even though we use those systems for our own benefit.

Opportunity:

If we want to get more control over our lives, we must develop systems that we control. Whenever we operate in any competitive arena, we work outside of the limits of existing control. We have the opportunity to create new areas of control, but we can only do this by creating our own systems, procedures, and formulas. Controlling our own behavior is a good start, but real power comes from understanding the effect of our systems on others (2.3.1 Action and Reaction).

Developing new methods from scratch is both risky and difficult (7.2.1 Proven Methods). Existing systems influence our expectations by making us think that we cannot step outside of them (7.2.2 Preparing Expectations). We are taught to treat existing processes as sacred. They are not sacred. They are simply productive. In competition, the value of innovating systems is that they create surprise and change momentum.

Key Methods:

The following key methods explain the process for reordering elements for strategic advantage.

1. All changes to existing systems that violate expectations are strategically useful. The primary goal of strategy is to surprise. While changes that make systems more productive are useful, we start with a much simpler goal of creating what interrupts the normal flow of events (5.4 Minimizing Action).

2. We must identify the components parts in the situation by dividing it in time, space, and formula. Time components arrange tasks in a certain sequence. Space components are arranged in physical and psychological space. Formula components have different proportions creating a formula. At this level of innovation, we are not changing the components. We are using the existing proven methods. Because the end result is made of all the parts of the original system, the new version will "work," at least in some sense of the word. It will, however, work differently (7.2 Standards First).

3. We must identify the expectations these components create. We normally see components in terms of their function. Each part of a system or each step in a process does something specific. We must take that recognition one step further. That function creates an expectation. We need to see each of these components in terms of the specific expectations that they create (7.2.2 Preparing Expectations).

4. We must consider reshuffling or reordering components in time, space, and formula to confound expectations. These three are a) reordering components in time, performing tasks in a different sequence, b) rearranging components in physical and psychological space, setting up different interactions, c) changing proportions in the formula, adjusting their relative quantities in small ways (7.3.1 Expected Elements).

5. We must pick the quickest and easiest method that interrupts expectations. This reshuffling is best if done quickly. Slight changes in order, arrangement, and proportion can dramatically affect the expected situation (7.1.1 Creating Surprise).

6. Some changes will create long-term improvements as well as simple surprises. This happens through trial and error. Because change creates a surprise, every change at the right time is valuable. However, our strategic need to make constant changes leads naturally to deeper exploration of the system. Eventually we find improved arrangements that are permanent improvements (1.2.2 Exploiting Exploration).

Illustration:

Since innovation happens much more quickly in high-tech, let us use innovation in that arena to demonstrate some of these basic ideas.

1. All changes to existing systems that violate expectations are strategically useful. For example, it is too early to know if the Apple iPad will be a success in terms of innovation, but it is a strategic success because it focuses consumers on the Apple brand and developers on the platform.

2. We must identify the components parts in the situation by dividing it in time, space, and formula. Ordering in time: People pay for a product before using it. Arrangement in space: Computer applications on the mobile device, desktop, or the server. Re-proportioning the formula: making an iPod bigger, changing it into a tablet.

3. We must identify the expectations these components create. Ordering in time: People expect to have to decide about the value of a product before buying it. Arrangement in space: People expect to have a mobile device, desktop, or server access before using the applications that run on them. Reproportioning the formula: people expect a certain device size.

4. We must consider reshuffling or reordering components in time, space, and formula to confound expectations. Re-ordering in time: The concept of freeware and free software demonstrations reverses the expectation to pay for a product before using it. Rearrangement in space: Google Apps is a spacial change giving people access to desktop apps from a server environment. Re-proportioning the formula: the iPad changes the expectation of limited screen space in a mobile app.

5. We must pick the quickest and easiest method that interrupts expectations. All of these changes were easy for the company making them.

6. Some changes will create long-term improvements as well as simple surprises. In the end, all applications may be offered initially as freeware and all may be available on servers. Of course, the iPad tablet's success will create a new direction for future innovation.

7.3.3 Creative Innovation

Sun Tzu's seven key methods on the more advanced methods for innovation.

> *"Surprise and direct action give birth to each other.*
> *They are like a circle without end.*
> *You cannot exhaust all their possible combinations!"*
> Sun Tzu's The Art of War 5:2:24-26

> *"If necessity is the mother of invention, discontent is the father of progress."*
> David Rockefeller

General Principle: Deeper invention requires subtracting, adding, or replacing components.

Situation:

We see the nature of the world as limited. We look at our limited knowledge of our current situation and envision running out of resources. While our regular method of innovation by rearranging elements is quick and easy, we will eventually come up against its limits (7.3.2 Elemental Rearrangement). Since there are limited number of elements in systems, there are also limits on how they can be rearranged. While all arrangements may surprise, only a few rearrangements will be actual improvements. For 2,500 years, the philosophy of limits has been championed by those in power to justify taking more power in an attempt to stop change. In China, the aristocracy suppressed Sun Tzu's philosophy for just this reason.

Opportunity:

Sun Tzu's strategy is diametrically opposed to this point of view of limited resources because those limits are based on our limited knowledge (2.1.1 Information Limits). While our knowledge is always limited, it also grows over time (2.6 Knowledge Leverage). From its beginning 2,500 years ago, Sun Tzu taught that our undiscovered resources were infinite. Time has proven his astounding prediction correct. If we regularly practice using "regular" innovation, we will also eventually discover opportunities for more powerful forms of invention. These methods for creating "special" innovations are never as quick or as certain as simple rearrangement, but they can provide the infinite number of possibilities that our progress demands.

Key Methods:

Sun Tzu offers seven principles of creating innovations with persistent value.

1. Innovation starts as a thought experiment so that we can quickly test the new envisioned system mentally. Unlike rearranging components, more advanced methods of innovation open up many more possibilities. We do not have time to explore them all.

Their result will always have to be tested in the real world. This takes times and resources, which are costly. In using thought experiments, we can work through many possibilities to find the best one very quickly (2.2.2 Mental Models).

2. We must identify the components parts in the situation by dividing it in time, space, and formula. Time components arrange tasks in a certain sequence. Space components are arranged in physical and psychological space. Formula components have different proportions creating a formula. At this level of innovation, we are not changing the components. We are using the existing proven methods. Because the end result is made of all the parts of the original system, the new version will "work," at least in some sense of the word. It will, however, work differently (7.2 Standards First).

3. We attempt to identify components that can be eliminated entirely. We look for ways to eliminate steps in the sequence, the number of components, or the volume of ingredients. This is the easiest method to innovate a process. By definition, simpler systems are better systems. They have fewer costs, are less prone to break, and, when they do break, they are easier to fix. Any innovation that eliminates a component is valuable (4.2 Choosing Non-Action).

4. We attempt to identify components that are proven to work in a similar situation or function. We look for analogous processes, systems, and procedures that have similar steps, components, or ingredients. Seeing analogous parallels gets easier as we are trained in Sun Tzu's system because its strategic system is built on finding parallels in unique situations. The classical Chinese framework of science of the five Chinese classical elements is a system of parallel analogies. We use the key elements in strategic analysis to train the mind to see parallels in situations. Analogous elements can replace each other in innovative arrangements (1.3 Elemental Analysis).

5. We attempt to replace one existing element with an analogous alternative. We look for ways to replace one step in the sequence with a different step. We replace one component or ingredient for a different component or ingredient. Using this method, we try to keep all the other components the same. We are looking for a element that is better in some tangible way or less expensive than the one it replaces (3.1.2 Strategic Profitability).

6. We attempt to add one new element to fill an opening in the existing system. Conceptually, this is very similar to identifying the openings that create opportunities. We use our understanding of similar systems to identify new elements that might work. We look for a place to add one step in the sequence to improve the result. We look for a new component that will make the system better. We look for a new ingredient that will make the formula stronger. Using this method, we try to keep all the other components the same (3.0 Identifying Opportunities).

7. Test the resulting changes to see what the effect is on the whole system. Unlike a rearrangement, that just needs to create surprise, the change here is less likely to work. This means it requires more testing. Until it is tested, we can get no advantage from the surprise it may create because we are as likely to be surprised by the result as our opponents. This final step is critical to the success of any innovation at this level (5.4.1 Testing Value).

Illustration:

Let us these methods to explain simply the evolution of software and word-processing systems.

1. Innovation starts as a thought experiment so that we can quickly test the new envisioned system mentally. We do not try to work out every idea in a word-processing program. We have to think through and model it first.

2. We must identify the components parts in the situation by dividing it in time, space, and formula. We think about the software program and its sequences of commands, the arrangement on its screen, and its balance of functionality. The original designs of word-processing programs were much different than those we see today because of the force of innovation.

3. We attempt to identify components that can be eliminated entirely. Early word-processing programs required a "return" press at the end of each line like a typewriter. It was eventually realized that it was unnecessary and removed. As software programs advance by adding new features, they grow bigger, slower, and more complex to use. Over time, this creates an opportunity to eliminate the least valuable of those features and offer a product that is smaller, quicker, and simpler.

4. We attempt to identify components that are proven to work in a similar situation or function. We look at competing and other popular software products to see how they are sequenced, arranged, and balanced to get new ideas for our own.

5. We attempt to replace one existing element with an analogous alternative. While wordprocessing programs don't normally need mathematical spreadsheets in them, they do require something similar, textual information in rows and columns. In word-processing, this was originally done through complicated tabbing. These procedures are best replaced by the row and column framework on a spreadsheet.

6. We attempt to add one new element to fill an opening in the existing system. Word processing and spreadsheets were once very separate programs, but as people began to need to insert spreadsheets in their written documents, features were added to link the two.

7. Test the resulting changes to see what the effect is on the whole system. In software, we actually want to test our models by running them past users before we do the actual programming. After the programming, we have to test usability again.

7.4.0 Competitive Timing

Sun Tzu's six key methods on the role of timing in creating momentum.

A hawk suddenly strikes a bird.
Its contact alone kills the prey.
This is timing."

Sun Tzu's The Art of War 5:3:4-6

"You win battles by knowing the enemy's timing, and
using a timing which the enemy does not expect."

Miyamoto Musashi

General Principle: Surprises should be revealed at the height of expectations or the height of chaos.

Situation:

The world of competition is chaotic and confusing. We uses standard methods to create expectations to give others the sense that they are in control. We unleash surprises to take away that sense of control and replace it with alternatives that we control. Since we are more prepared for the surprise than others, especially our rivals, we have more objective control. This little bit of objective control is magnified subjectively, as people compare us to our potential rivals.

We use the constant tiny shifts in our methods between standards and innovation to build up our momentum. Released gradually into our environment, those little bursts of momentum are quickly dissipated. The competitive environment is large and, on a day-to-day basis, we cannot have any real impact upon it. Our small innovations are quickly copied by others. We need something more.

Opportunity:

For potential supporters, we want to use the excitement of surprise to give them the emotional impetus that they need to make a decision in our favor. For our competitors, we want to demonstrate our momentum at the right time. This increases their confusion and decreases their confidence. Even though our momentum will always be small in the larger world, the difference between that momentum and others' expectations can be enough to tip the balance if it is introduced at the right time.

We use standard methods to navigate challenges, but we must get creative to establish new positions. Too many people defuse the power of momentum through poor timing. By introducing innovations at the wrong time or in the wrong way, we can strengthen or kill any momentum we have. We cannot release changes too soon, but we also cannot go too long without releasing them. When we release them, we must be ready to claim our position, the final step in the Listen>Aim>Move>Claim cycle. One step must follow another quickly. Momentum used correctly can wash away any obstacles that we face in establishing a position.

Key Methods:

The following six key methods describe the basic elements of good strategic timing.

1. Timing is the difference between strong moves and weak ones. The same move doesn't have the same power at different times. While surprise and innovation are always useful, their utility is magnified by having the right conditions in the environment. We use timing to leverage the chaos, complexity, and resulting confusion that defines competitive environments (3.2.1 Environmental Dominance).

2. Timing switches from standard practices to innovation and back again at the most productive times. Because the impact of surprise is only temporary, we must use it wisely. Momentum requires both standards and innovation. Just as the impact of innovation must be setup by creating expectations through standards, the gains won from innovation must be maintained by standards after the fact (7.1.3 Standards and Innovation).

3. We prepared our surprises and innovations in advance, keeping them secret. Instead of dissipating our momentum potential at the wrong time, we keep our innovations secret, hidden from the larger environment. We accumulate potential surprises over time until the time is right to use them. (2.7 Information Secrecy).

4. We wait until the right psychological moment, when confusion and chaos peak or when our opponents respond to our expected action. Either of these two situations offers us the psychology we need to leverage our surprise. When chaos and confusion dominates and reaches its height, people are psychologically vulnerable to surprise. When our opponents think they have a response prepared for our expected actions, their confidence also create a vulnerable psychological state (7.1.2 Momentum Psychology).

5. We then release our surprises in an instant. At the right moment, the faster we can make people aware of our surprise, the better. We want to focus this initial surprise on the smallest possible moment in time to create the maximum of confusions (5.5 Focused Power

6. We wait long enough for others to react, then we followup with another surprise. This is one reason we accumulate potential surprises. A single surprise only sets the table. The followup surprise wins the day. Since we know the surprise we plan, we can anticipate the reaction. We can choose our followup surprise to further undermine that reaction, completely taking control of the situation at least for that moment (7.2.2 Preparing Expectations).

Illustration:

Let us illustrate these ideas with the typical "October Surprise " used in politics, specifically in the 2008 election between Obama and McCain and the 1972 contest between Nixon and McGovern.

1. Timing is the difference between strong moves and weak ones. As every close Presidential election, an unexpected event will arise that is called an October surprise whether it is planned or not. In the last election, it was the financial crisis from Fanny, Freddy, and Goldman Sachs packaging "affordable mortgages" as high-grade investments. In 1972, it was Kissinger's announcement of "peace is at hand" in Vietnam.

2. Timing switches from standard practices to innovation and back again at the most productive time. Both in before the surprise and in reacting to it, the politician must demonstrate his standard abilities. The candidate that makes the fewest mistakes in their standard response to the surprise succeeds. In 2008, Obama handled the timing right by using it to return to his well-established "blame Bush/Republicans" theme but McCain broke down, reacting in a non-standard way, "halting" his campaign. In Nixon's case, the controlled surprise occurred after a campaign that had already given him a substantial lead. The surprise itself was designed around the central theme of Nixon's opponent, McGovern, ending an unpopular war.

3. We prepared our surprises and innovations in advance, keeping them secret. Since politicians are poor strategists, they are more often the victims of surprise than its controllers. That was certainly true in the last election. However, the first October Surprise was on October 26, 1972, when Henry Kissinger announced a breakthrough in negotiations with the N. Vietnamese on the eve of the election vote between Nixon and McGovern.

4. We wait until the right psychological moment, when confusion and chaos peak or when our opponents respond to our expected action. While the financial crisis wasn't planned, it certainly came at the right moment, when McCain was closing with Obama in the polls. In 1972, the surprise gave Nixon the momentum necessary to win by 20%.

5. We then release our surprises in an instant. In both cases, the news was unexpected and sudden.

6. We wait long enough for others to react, then we followup with another surprise. Politicians, being poor strategists, seldom have a series of surprises planned to seize the momentum at that point. In 2008, neither politician was in control and neither knew how to prepare a surprise, much less a followup. In 1972, it was simply unnecessary. Since McGovern's campaign was primarily a protest to the war in Vietnam, the "peace is at hand" announcement was the final nail in the coffin, costing him every state except Massachusetts.

7.4.1 Timing Methods

Sun Tzu's four key methods about the three simplest methods of controlling timing.

"When you fall behind, you must catch up.
When you get ahead, you must wait.
You must know the detour that most directly
accomplishes your plan."

Sun Tzu's The Art of War 7:1:11-3

"We look smarter than we probably really are, but it was good timing."

Victor Campbell

General Principle: Control people's emotions by speeding up, slowing down, or switching the timing of expected events.

Situation:

Controlled environments consist of a series of scheduled events, but most events in competitive environments occur unexpectedly. Key conditions, such as opportunities, arise out of complex inter- actions that cannot be predicted. Decision-making in controlled environments is easy because we know what to expect, and, more importantly, when to expect it. Decisions about timing in competi- tive environments are much more uncertain. We respond to the unknown emotionally. The time pressure in competitive environ- ments naturally results in frustration, tension, and fear.

Opportunity:

Though we cannot predict the flow of competitive events, we do control the timing of our own competitive actions and responses. We can use this control to impact people's emotions positively or negatively, as we choose. We know where their information is limited (2.1.1 Information Limits). Our opportunity is to work on this emotional gap. To the extent that we can influence the timing of events, we can either increase or decrease people's sense of cer- tainty and control. We use timing to give ourselves a competitive edge. In areas where others have a natural advantage because they control most of what happens in that environment, we can use the timing of responses to disrupt that advantage.

Key Methods:

The following key methods describe the goal and major methods for controlling timing in competitive environments.

1. The use of timing is primarily psychological. Our goal is to increase or decrease people's feelings of confidence and control. We use our control of timing intentionally to create a certain mental state in others that gives us more control over the situation. No matter which timing methods we use, our goal should be to positively affect our supporter and negatively impact our opponents. Unexpected timing creates a predetermined emotional reaction where the expected event creates no reaction at all (7.1.2 Momentum Psychology).

2. We can delay our actions to slowing down expected events. Slowing things down is the easiest method to affect timing. Done correctly, slowing down events can decrease our costs while increasing both the cost and frustration of opponents. We can use it intentionally to increase the tension in a situation so that we frustrate people's expectations. This creates the opportunity to relieve that tension with a surprise (4.2 Choosing Non-Action).

3. We can use our resources to speed up expected events. Speeding things up is generally harder than slowing them down, but it is a powerful tool. By speeding up events we can catch people offguard. The emotional effect can be either positive of negative. We can speed up expected events to better satisfy supporters who expect to wait. We can also speed up expected events to increase the pressure on opponents (5.3.1 Speed and Quickness).

4. We can replace an expected event with an unexpected one. Changing the expected into the unexpected demands the most creativity, but it can also be the most rewarding. Thinking ahead, we set up the expected event with the purpose of changing it at the time of our choice. We can also let others set up the expectations and then invent a way to transform the expected event into something. This works both to please those who support we want and to frustrate those who are opposing us. We come up with ideas for replacement using the normal methods of strategic creativity (7.3 Strategic Innovation).

Illustration:

Let us think about how a lawyer might use these methods to frustrate an opponent in a civil lawsuit.

1. The use of timing is primarily psychological. The purpose of controlling timing is simply to create frustration and increase legal expenses for opponents, not to win the case.

2. We can delay our actions to slowing down expected events. We can set a court date with the advanced intention of canceling it the last moment. We let our opponents prepare for that date, then at the last minute, we can call the judge and ask for the date to be moved because we came down with the flu.

3. We can use our resources to speed up expected events. We can plan a distant court date, say six months ahead of time, with the intention of changing it. While our opponents take their time getting ready, we do all the work necessary to have our case ready in three months. We then ask the court to move up the court due to a later conflict in our calendar. We can tell the judge that the opposition has already had three months to get ready.

4. We can replace an expected event with an unexpected one. We set up a deposition for one person. Then, at the last minute, that person has "unexpected" scheduling conflicts. Rather than completely cancel the deposition date, we arrange to be in another place to be deposed.

7.4.2 Momentum Timing

Sun Tzu's five key methods on the relative value of momentum at various times in a campaign.

"Your momentum is like the tension of a bent crossbow. Your timing is like the pulling of a trigger."
Sun Tzu's The Art of War 5:3:12-13

"If your position is everywhere, your momentum is zero."
Douglas Hostadter

General Principle: Momentum is more valuable at the end of a move or campaign than the beginning.

Situation:

Inertia can a) prevent us from getting going, b) slow our progress, and c) prevent us from completing a move. The momentum created by surprise is needed to overcome inertia, but that momentum fades quickly. Momentum tends to shift from one side to another. If we do not choose the right moment to try to create momentum, this work can be largely wasted. Basic methods of controlling timing are easy to use frequently, but timing surprises to change momentum is more challenging (7.4.1 Timing Methods).

Opportunity:

There are important pressure points at which momentum is most valuable. These pressure points are determined by the specific conditions of our situation. The longer a move or campaign continues, the more everyone expects it to continue along the same path, the greater its apparent inertia (7.2.2 Preparing Expectations). The better we understand the direction of that inertia, the easier it is for us to know the point at which releasing a surprise is the most valuable. The direction of inertia can only be changed by the application of a shift in momentum.

Key Methods:

The following five key methods explain the relative value of momentum at various times in a campaign.

1. The momentum needed to overcome inertia only comes from combining strategy practices with an innovation. All appropriate responses are amplified by the use of innovation creating surprise. We must use both the standard methods of strategy and know how to innovate in all those situations (7.1.3 Standards and Innovation).

2. Momentum is more valuable at the end of a move or campaign than the beginning. There are three points at which we can use momentum, the beginning, middle, or end. All of these points are not created equal. The most valuable is the momentum that gives us victory at the end. The least valuable is the momentum that gets us started in the beginning. The surprise that keeps us going in the middle is simply a necessity (6.3 Campaign Patterns).

3. If inertia prevents us from getting started, we can start our move or campaign with a surprise. This is valuable in a situation where we need to get some type of foothold to get started. However, surprises that get initial attention create the least valuable form of momentum, or, more accurately, the most over-rated. In today's world, the attempt to introduce new organizations via an attentiongetting "surprise" has become common. Unfortunately, these attempts seldom work. When such an attempt does get attention, it can get a lot of attention, which makes this method seem like a better strategy than it really is. Its weakness arises from its failure to start with standards (7.2 Standards First).

4. If inertia is slowing us, we can use surprise to make faster progress. Momentum is more valuable to get us unstuck in the middle of a campaign. We can use it to lock in our progress thus far and create more optimism about our potential success. Applied at the proper time, it can help us avoid the later, most difficult stages of a campaign (7.1.2 Momentum Psychology).

5. We use surprise toward the end of a move or campaign to overcome the final barriers that stand between us and success. Momentum that gives us victory is the most valuable because it decides the issue, getting us to the new position where our efforts can pay off. At this stage, we also have had the most time to prepare the situation, creating the expectations that in turn create the most momentum (7.2.2 Preparing Expectations).

Illustration:

Let us illustrate these key methods for the art of sales.

1. The momentum needed to overcome inertia only comes from combining strategy practices with an innovation. A sales presentation that is completely routine is completely forgettable. It might inform buyers, but it will not motivate them to decide.

2. Momentum is more valuable at the end of a move or campaign than the beginning. The goal of every sale call is to move the sale process forward, but the goal of the process is to get a decision in our favor from the buyer.

3. If inertia prevents us from getting started, we can start our move or campaign with a surprise. If, for example, we cannot even get into see the buyer, we may have to get innovative to get the appointment.

4. If inertia is slowing us, we can use surprise to make faster progress. If the sales process bogs down, prospects can easily lose interest. We can use surprise and innovation to recapture interest and create emotion to keep it moving.

5. We use surprise toward the end of a move or campaign to overcome the final barriers that stand between us and success. Emotion is required to commit to a buying decision. This means that the emotion created by a change of emotion is the most valuable at the close. The surprise should not be so disconcerting that the buyer must rethink everything, but surprising enough to create excitement.

7.4.3 Interrupting Patterns

Six key methods regarding how repetition creates patterns for surprise.

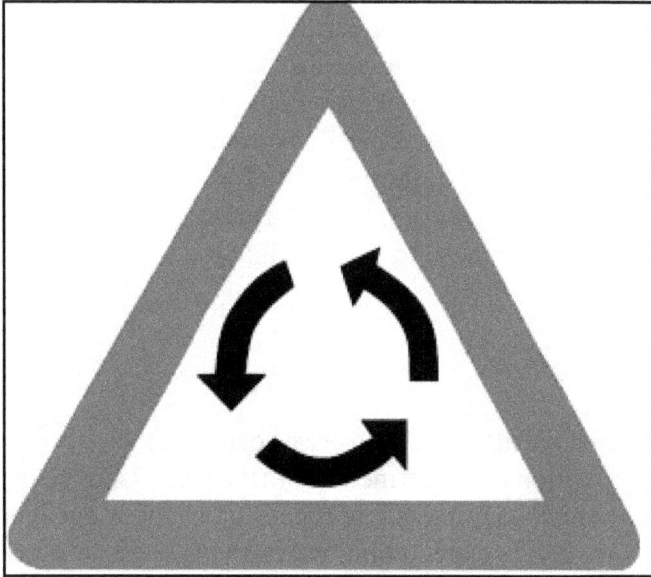

"You must force the enemy to move to your advantage. Use your position."

Sun Tzu's The Art of War 5:4:16-17

"Repetition of the same thought or physical action develops into a habit which, repeated frequently enough, becomes an automatic reflex."

Norman Vincent Peale

General Principle: Good timing requires creating and interrupting patterns of repetition.

Situation:

While a single surprising event can determine success in a given meeting over the length of a competitive campaign requires multiple surprises. The problem is that when repeated, a surprise ceases to be surprising. Because we are human, we gravitate toward patterns of behavior. We repeat what has worked in the past. We use regular cycles of specific actions at certain times in a particular order. People fall into these patterns because they are comfortable and make life easier because fewer decisions are required. People fall into these formulaic patterns even when they attempt to surprise people. Everyone who regularly watches horror movies is familiar how the "cat jumping out of closet" surprise is set-up but movie makers still use it because they know that it has worked well in the past.

Opportunity:

While repeated attempted surprises can lose their ability to create emotion, repetition can also increase the surprise if done correctly. What we are really saying is that repetition changes expectation. Whenever we create expectation, we can violate those expectations to create surprise.

These patterns of behavior make people predictable.

Key Methods:

There are six key methods for using patterns to create surprise and to build momentum.

1. The secret of timing interruptions is building pressure and releasing it at the right time and place. The breaking of a regular pattern to surprise must have an impact. We must time our surprises precisely. Released at the appropriate time, our built up momentum introduces a critical amount of control into the chaos of competition. For a period of time, it becomes a force with which we control and others must cope. It is this control that has the most to impact on others' attitudes about our position (7.4 Competitive Timing).

2. The repetition of similar events in a regular pattern is comforting because it creates expectations. By being dependable and seemingly predictable in our patterns, we win people's trust by ***not*** exciting them. It is that trust that moves people into position to be surprised. A regular cycle of behavior makes this easier. People move forward when they think that they know what to expect. We use patterns to make people comfortable so they can stay with us in the process and so we don't lose them. We must innovate continually but secretly. While we innovate, we uses standards to shape people's expectations so that they are not expecting anything novel or shocking (7.2.2 Preparing Expectations).

3. The repetition of contradictory events at seemingly random times creates surprise and excitement. We must time our surprises to break the pattern. Whether we have set up expectations through our patterns or they have set their own expectations through their habits, we can create a reason to interrupt that pattern. Momentum is wasted if it is released before people are ready. We prepare our surprises in advance but keep them a secret (7.1.2 Momentum Psychology).

4. Interruptions in patterns should appear random, but they should be designed to create decisions. Since people use habits to avoid making decisions, we interrupt those patterns to force decisions on them. People's decisions take place in an instant. We must make our impact at the point of decision. We must time our surprise so we release that tension in the direction that we want (6.8 Competitive Psychology).

5. We must invest only in efforts that win supporters or frustrate opponents to build our positions. We want to confuse people only in a way that gives us control. We only want to create confusion and chaos at the point at which we are ready to provide direction in the situation. A sudden shift from what is expected creates tension. We want to use that tension as the basis for building our position not increasing chaos (7.1 Order from Chaos).

6. We use surprise to encourage others to think or act in a new way. We use momentum to give us a brief moment when we control others. We use control of our supporters to control our competitors. We want to shape the process so both supporters and competitors rush forward without stopping, going where we want them to go. We release them only at the right time to get the decisions that we want. This requires thinking about timing and knowing exactly where we are in our moves (2.3.1 Action and Reaction).

Illustration:

Let us illustrate these key methods in the context of making a presentation.

1. The secret of timing interruptions is building pressure and releasing it at the right time and place. Most presentations are boring, predictable, and forgettable. We can use patterns and inter-ruptions to create more impact in our presentations.

2. The repetition of similar events in a regular pattern is comforting because it creates expectations. At the beginning of a speech, we can set out the pattern, the topics to be covered and the pattern in which they are covered.

3. The repetition of contradictory events at seemingly random times creates surprise and excitement. After establishing a fairly boring pattern, say by showing a series of slides, we can interrupt that pattern, say by showing a slide upside down and standing on our head to give it.

4. Interruptions in patterns should appear random, but they should be designed to create decisions. The upside down slides should make a point, create a pattern of their own, and illustrate a decision that has to be made. For example, they could illustrate how people go out of their way to make things difficult rather than make a decision.

5. We must invest only in efforts that win supporters or frustrate opponents to build our positions. We should use this technique only to the point it is valuable for making its point and entertaining the audience, past a certain point, like any repeated device, it becomes boring and annoying.

6. We use surprise to encourage others to think or act in a new way. It isn't enough to simply have the presentation be memorable, we want it to be effective at getting the decision that we want. The point of the surprise is completing the move.

7.5.0 Momentum Limitations

Sun Tzu's six key methods on the implications of momentum's temporary nature.

"Surging water flows together rapidly.
Its pressure washes away boulders.
This is momentum."
Sun Tzu's The Art of War 5:3:1-3

"If you're coasting, you're either losing momentum or else you're headed downhill."
Joan Welsh

General Principle: We must translate a temporary advantage in momentum into a permanent advantage in position.

Situation:

While it takes time for positions to erode, the momentum from surprise is lost almost immediately. In Sun Tzu's division of the elements of a position, it is a temporary environmental component of a position, not a persistent one (1.4 The External Environment]). As such, momentum is never controlled by one party for very long. By definition, surprise cannot last. It quickly becomes part of the new status quo. It can not be gained and only lost by the party that has it. As with all complementary opposites, we can leverage this natural balancing of temporary and persistent elements to our advantage, but only if we understand how.

Opportunity:

Whether we have just won momentum or just lost it, we have an opportunity. Those two opportunities are very different. If an opponent currently has momentum, we have the opportunity to seize that momentum for ourselves, ideally at just the right time (7.4.2 Momentum Timing). If we currently have momentum ourselves, our job is the more complicated task of translating that temporary advantage into a more permanent aspect of our position.

Key Methods:

The following six key methods describe how we must deal with momentum's limitations in advancing our position.

1. We must react immediately to shifts of momentum. One of the foundations of strategy is the idea that all strategic positions are temporary. The temporary nature of momentum forces us to think one step ahead of the curve. We always have to be thinking about the next move in the game. Since innovation plays a role in every situation, a major part of good strategy is working these swings of momentum correctly (1.1.1 Position Dynamics).

2. When we lose momentum to an opponent, we must prepare for getting it back. Momentum switches back and forth. Only the competitor that has momentum at any given time is in a position to lose it. The most productive way to think about the loss of momentum is to see it as an opportunity to frustrate opponents by stealing their new found momentum away again (7.3.1 Expected Elements).

3. We stop opponents from converting their momentum into blocking their advance. This is only important when any advance in their position blocks us. When it does, we must stop them from making successful claims based upon their momentum. This requires knowing the specific components necessary for making a claim (8.2 Making Claims).

4. When we gain momentum in a contest, we use it to get in position to make a claim. When we have momentum, we must translate its energy into a permanent improvement in our position. In Sun Tzu's terms, this must mean we must shift from the "Move" step to the "Claim" step of the adaptive loop (1.8 Progress Cycle).

5. Translating momentum into persistent position requires gaining control of additional resources. This requires either taking control of new resources physically or subjectively leveraging the new subjective opinions of others regarding our capacities (7.5.1 Momentum Conversion).

6. When innovation is translated from momentum into position, its ability to create new momentum diminishes. This is the process by which the spread of innovation creates new standards. These new standards become part of the expectations by which comparisons are made (7.5.2 The Spread of Innovation).

Illustration:

These principles can be illustrated in any competitive arena. Let's look at some examples in sports, business, and politics.

1. We must react immediately to shifts of momentum. In any type of sporting, business, or political contest, as long as both "teams" use the expected game plan, the historically stronger team has the advantage. These expectations are destroyed when the underdog does something surprising to seize the initiative. On the field, we can actually see the psychological effects of momentum.

The team that has the momentum plays more confidently. Seizing the initiative improves their execution in tangible ways.

2. When we lose momentum to an opponent, we must prepare for getting it back. But that burst of energy and inspiration cannot last. With momentum on their side, the opponent plays with more confidence and focus, but their momentum only lasts until the opposing team is able to undermine that sense of superiority, seizing back the initiative with their own surprise.

3. We stop opponents from converting their momentum into blocking their advance. When a team loses momentum, they must focus on not making any mistakes and instead focus on technique for slowing down the play. When a company loses momentum to a competitor's announcement, they must immediately work to confuse the market by countering with their own announcements so that customers will wait to see what happens before buying. When a politician loses momentum by losing a primary in a surprising manner, he or she must avoid overreacting and further alienating voters. Instead, he or she must create a new surprise by congratulating the opponent and honestly recognizing what the opponent did better and he or she did wrong.

4. When we gain momentum in a contest, we use it to get in position to make a claim. When a team seizes momentum by making a surprising play, they must immediately do their best to score. When a company seizes the momentum by making a surprising announcement, they must immediately work on translating that announcement into sales or commitments for sales. In a political battle, the surprise, such as a win in a primary in a U.S. presidential race, should immediately be converted into broader endorsements.

5. Translating momentum into persistent position requires controlling additional resources. In a sports contest, it must be converted into a score. In business, it must be converted into sales. In politics, it must be converted into votes.

6. When innovation is translated from momentum in position, its ability to create new momentum diminishes. They create a new set of expectations about which contestant is the strongest. This brings us back to step one in this process.

7.5.1 Momentum Conversion

Sun Tzu's six key methods on converting momentum into positions with more value.

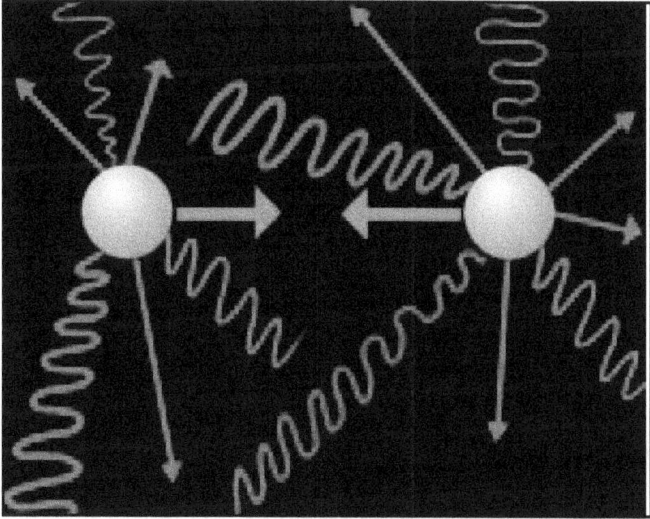

"You make your men powerful in battle with momentum.
This should be like rolling round stones down over a high, steep cliff.
Momentum is critical."

Sun Tzu's The Art of War 5:5:13-15

"Creativity is not the finding of a thing, but the making something out of it after it is found."

James Russell Lowell

General Principle: Momentum permanently affects a position by making our claims more successful and profitable.

Situation:

Many people don't get any benefit from their creativity. Sun Tzu sees momentum as potential energy. It needs to be converted into movement. His analogy is converting an object's potential energy into movement by rolling it downhill. People fail to see how creativity must be used as a part of the larger process. In school, many of us are taught to confuse creativity with self-expression, which is an end in itself. The solution to this confusion is creativity. Both creativity and the momentum that it can produce are only means to an end.

Opportunity:

In Sun Tzu's system, our creative opportunity is part of the larger process. Sun Tzu's strategy is a method for making decisions about changing conditions to improve positions. We use creativity to create surprise, surprise to create momentum, momentum to complete a move, and a move advances our position in a way that pays. Our opportunity is to combine innovation with standards to create surprise (7.1.3 Standards and Innovation). We combine surprise with timing to create momentum (7.4 Competitive Timing). We combine momentum with our current position to complete a move. We combine this move with economics to make our position pay.

Key Methods:

The following six key methods look at how momentum not only completes a move but makes it pay.

1. In competition, our physical positions arise from other peoples support of our position. All of our assets come from our position--the paycheck from our job, the good will in our business, social, and personal relationships, and our property and other assets. That position depends on others recognizing our rights of ownership. Without that support, we lose those assets (2.3 Personal Interactions).

2. Temporary momentum changes people's subjective view of our position. The momentum itself may fade, but the fact that we have been creative and surprising becomes part of our position's history. People's persistent attitudes about us factor in these abilities made visible by a momentum shift (1.2 Subobjective Positions).

3. The momentum from surprise completes the move to setup claiming rewards. Just like standard responses set up the expectations that surprise changes to create momentum, that momentum sets up the expectations that lead to the next element of getting rewarded, making a claim (8.2 Making Claims).

4. Making a claim require others to make decisions about us. This is the topic of the next section, but the basic concept is simple: we must ask for rewards in order to get them. Claims take advantage of the momentum we have created. When we complete our moves after getting momentum, other people have a different mindset about us when they make these decisions. They are much more likely to make decisions in our favor because of the new perspective created by momentum (2.3.1 Action and Reaction).

5. This change in perception reduces our costs and amplifies our rewards for a move. A lot goes into a making a move in Sun Tzu's system, from picking the right opportunities to knowing the right responses to the conditions we find, to creating momentum, to making claims. But the end goal is always the profitability of our move. We can use momentum to make our moves pay better than they would otherwise (3.1.2 Strategic Profitability).

6. These rewards remain long after momentum is lost. Despite the temporary and limited nature of momentum, the rewards that it wins are long-lasting. When we ask supporters for their support with momentum, they will give it. After people have given their support, they do not take it away unless we give them a reason to do so. In the future, opponents will treat our moves with more caution, expecting us to turn around challenges in surprising ways. The rewards we have won verifies our abilities. Others who did not witness our moves or momentum can see their effects embodied in our position (7.5 Momentum Limitations).

Illustration:

Let us illustrate these ideas by looking at how Apple leverages their innovations into sales.

1. In competition, our physical positions arise from other peoples support of our position. Apple has developed a reputation for innovation that leads others to follow it instead of attack it.

2. Temporary momentum changes people's subjective view of our position. Introduction of novel products has shaped people's perceptions of Apple. Even when their ideas are less than successful, think back to the Newton, every new innovation adds to this reputation because it has become a permanent aspect of their market position.

3. The momentum from surprise completes the move to setup claiming rewards. The recent introduction of the iPad was introduced as a market innovation that gives Apple momentum in a new segment of the market, competing with devices such as Amazon's Kindle.

4. Making a claim require others to make decisions about us. In the case of the iPad, these claims will either succeed or fail when the new device goes on sale next month. iPhone and iPod Touch users will have to decide if the new idea is valuable.

5. This change in perception reduces our costs and amplifies our rewards for a move. Because the device is creative, it gets a lot of free publicity, reducing Apple's costs of advertising, and Apple is able to charge a premium for it, increasing their rewards.

6. These rewards remain long after momentum is lost. If successful, a year of two from now the iPad will lead a new segment and as the leader reap the majority of market profits. However, even if the product fails like the Newton, it will still enhance Apple's reputation as an innovator. This brings us back to step one that made the move possible.

7.5.2 The Spread of Innovation

Sun Tzu's four key methods for using the spread of innovation to advance our position.

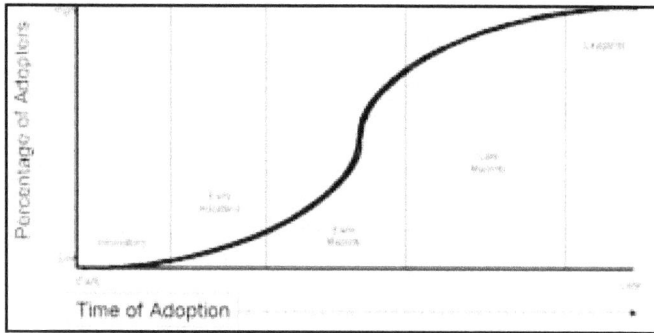

Sun Tzu's The Art of War 5:4:16-20

Daisaku Ikeda

General Principle: Innovation spreads in a pattern that favors early adopters not inventors.

Situation:

The problem is that the competitive landscape is constantly changing in ways that most people fail to predict. While momentum from creative surprise evaporates more quickly than we expect, successful innovations spread throughout the competitive landscape much slower than we expect. Worse, that spread is not smooth and constant, but lumpy and variable. The new landscape arises gradually, not from the actions of any one player, but by the decisions by different groups of people at different times. This means that as an innovation spreads, the landscape is broken by different sets of standards at different places that are distributed in unpredictable ways.

Opportunity:

The opportunity is that, despite most people's failure to predict changes in the competitive landscape, those changes are predictable in a more general way. As Sun Tzu puts it, as people change their position, abandoning old positions, others are forced to change their positions as well. One group may adopt a position that others are abandoning, but there is an overall pattern to the march of progress that we can understand in assembling our big picture of what is happening (2.5 The Big Picture). Today, we know that innovations are adopted in a pattern that is called the S-Curve. This curve starts with a small number of innovators, then a slightly larger number of early adopters, followed by a jump up to a big number of early majority, followed by the late majority, which is followed by dwindling number of laggards.

Key Methods:

The following four key methods describe how we use the spread of innovation to advance our position.

1. Most of us perceive that new methods are adopted rapidly, but this is wrong. This viewpoint reflects the perspective of the early and late majority to which most of us belong. The *early* spread of a new method, from innovator to early adopter occurs beneath the radar. Studies show that it takes from eight to twenty years for a new method to reach critical mass and take off. After reaching critical mass, the new method seems suddenly to become common knowledge, rapidly expanding in use (1.8.3 Cycle Time).

2. In this adoption curve, the opportunity resides only in the "early adopter stage." The earlier, innovator stage is a low probability point in the curve because the vast majority of innovations are never proven to have a broader utility. The early adopter stage is proves the broader value of the innovation. Once we understand the pattern by which innovation spreads, we realize that invention itself is not as valuable as the spread of innovation made possible by the proof provided by early adopters (3.0 Identifying Opportunities).

3. We position ourselves to "ride the curve upward." We use our own creativity primarily for surprise. We cannot expect to create trends that move through society. Instead, we attempt to discover new methods after they have been proven but before they have become popular. We work to find innovation in the "early adopter" stage dramatically increasing our chances of success and leveraging the larger trend toward new methods (4.0 Leveraging Probability).

4. We gradually develop expertise in the new methods that will eventually become valuable to others. We explore new methods adopting them gradually. Given the long adoption cycle, we need not rush. We practice these new methods so that their use becomes routine. Over time, we understand these methods well just as the majority begin to adopt them. This makes us an expert in the new system just as the opening is being recognized by more and more people. This positions us on the new battlefield long before others (3.1.4 Openings).

Illustration:

Every era is ripe with examples of how the people who are the most successful are not those who develop an innovation, but the early adopters who are in the right place as the innovation reaches its broader market. Henry Ford didn't invent the automobile, interchangeable parts, nor the assembly line. He was merely the early adopter of these ideas and the first applying them to car manufacturing. Bill Gates invented neither a computer language nor an operating systems, but he was an early adopter, adapting an existing language, Basic, to a new generation of microprocessors, and, after that, an early operating systems to a new generation of personal computers. After that, he simply adapted other software products--word processing, spreadsheets, email--before they had reached their mainstream audiences.

1. Most of us perceive that new methods are adopted rapidly, but this is wrong. The first cars powered by internal combustion engines appeared in 1806. The Ford Motor Company didn't appear until almost 100 years later, 1903. The first computer was introduced in 1936. Bill Gates and the personal computer arose almost fifty years, later, in the 1980s.

2. In this adoption curve, the opportunity resides only in the "early adopter stage." For car, this stage lasted for 100 years. For computers, there were several adoption cycles: mainframes, minis, and PCs.

3. We position ourselves to "ride the curve upward." Both Ford and Gates positioned themselves by bringing mass production and mass distribution to their respective fields.

4. We gradually develop expertise in the new methods that will eventually become valuable to others. While their early leads were important, early Ford and early Microsoft made themselves valuable to customers by bringing ideas introduced by others to the mainstream market by commercializing them.

7.6.0 Productive Competition

Sun Tzu's eight key methods for using momentum to produce more resources.

"There is no limit to the ways you can win."
Sun Tzu's The Art of War 5:2:23

"Price is what you pay. Value is what you get."
Warren Buffett

General Principle: Productive competition is not a zero-sum contest because innovation creates value.

Situation:

Most people don't understand how competition produces more value. One of the most common and destructive strategic mistakes is thinking that we can only win by taking from others. Contests where the winner succeeds only at the expense of the loser are called zero-sum games. While zero-sum contests like chess exist, even in real life competition, if all competition was zero-sum, progress would be impossible. The very idea of a zero-sum world is at the root of most human suffering and individual failure. It is a worldview built on a basic misunderstanding about the nature of competition, success, and human creativity.

Opportunity:

Our opportunities come from understanding how competition produces value. What we perceive as wealth and value comes from our knowledge. If our knowledge was limited and fixed, wealth and value would also be fixed as well (1.2.1 Competitive Landscapes). Since our knowledge grows, however, it creates new forms of value. Competition, rather than destroying value, is necessary to proving value. Without competition, we cannot compare one set of ideas against another to find out which is more valuable (1.3.1 Competitive Comparison). Competition tests our mental models and out of that test, we develop better models and more wealth in the competitive landscape (2.2.2 Mental Models).

Key Methods:

These are the key methods describing how competitive innovation makes the world more productive.

1. Only our knowledge makes resources valuable. When our knowledge was limited to hunting and gathering, resources were scarce. As our knowledge has expanded, resources that were once useless have become valuable. The difference between poor countries and rich is not in their natural resources It is in the knowledge of their people in knowing which methods work best (2.1 Information Value).

2. Control of resources goes to those who can use them most productively. Stone-age people fought over their hunting grounds because their knowledge was limited, which limited their resources. Those who fought over limited resources did not inherit the earth. The world went to those who mastered new skills to create more value from new resources. Our increasing knowledge opens up new forms of value. Old knowledge is replaced over time by more productive knowledge. Individuals may cling to cherished ideas of what works, but over time, we all eventually move from what works to what works better (1.8.1 Creation and Destruction).

3. Destructive competition does not determine the control of resources over the long-term. Conflict seeks to destroy opponents' positions. This does not create more value. It is costly to both winner and loser. Greater knowledge about how to a destroy an opponent give an advantage to pure destroyers over pure producers. However, pure destroyers lose to those who combine knowledge of both production and competition. Over the long-term, the real winners are those who have more knowledge about how to use resources productively because they can apply more resources to defense, which is always less expensive than any form of direct attack (1.1.2 Defending Positions).

4. Productive competition depends on exploring new opportunities that expand our knowledge. To avoid conflict, Sun Tzu's methods required us to look for openings, that is, resources that might offer advantages that others overlooked. We explore those openings to learn their value as a way of building up our position. Exploration exposes us to new resources. The exposure gives us new ideas about how to exploit those resources. Through this process, our knowledge about what resources are available and how to use them grows throughout our lives. That knowledge has grown from generation to generation throughout human history (7.6.1 Resource Discovery).

5. Only productive competition can determine the most productive use of resources. Productive competition is different from destructive conflict. Sun Tzu's productive competition is based on the idea of building up positions, which requires getting the most value out of resources. Competition does and must create more knowledge since it compares two alternative positions through outcomes. Only such comparisons can separate the good idea from the better one. By creating new knowledge, competition creates new ways of making resources more valuable (1.3.1 Competitive Comparison).

6. Since competition requires innovation, it leverages more value from the existing resources. We all take what we have and do the most we can with it. In competition, we focus our creativity on creating new methods via surprise. Surprise requires first mastering best practices and then going beyond them. That innovation has the by-product of discovering new, more powerful methods of using resources. Since competition exists in a more dynamic environment than production, it results necessarily in more new ideas and separates the good ideas from the bad and the better. Creative techniques are not only critical to success in competition, but they must inevitably result in more knowledge (7.3 Strategic Innovation).

7. Both exploration and innovation expand our knowledge of what works. Exploring new opportunities discovers untapped natural resources. Exploring new methods gives us the tools that we need to better use those new resources. This knowledge is the basis of good decisions and responses to our immediate situation, but it is more than that. This new knowledge is the basis on which competitive positions are continually created and destroyed (2.1 Information Value).

8. The process of productive competition continually creates entirely new forms of ground. Hunters and gathers learn agriculture become farmers. Farmers become manufacturers. Manufacturers of a few products become manufacturers of more and better products at lower prices. At every step of this process, we discover ways to turn resources that were once useless and make them valuable. The most powerful devices that we have ever created are computers based on integrated circuits. These chips are made of silicon, common, ordinary sand. The expansion of human knowledge can actually create new forms of ground as the basis of competition Today's internet is a great example since, without it, you would not be reading this (7.6.2 Ground Creation).

Illustration:

Let us apply these key methods very simply to a person's professional sales career.

1. Only our knowledge makes resources valuable. The sales skills we have, the more valuable we are to employers because the more we can do for them.

2. Control of resources goes to those who can use them most productively. As we prove our skills by generating sales for our company, we alternatively 1) get a better sales territory from our existing employer, 2) move to a new employer who will reward us better for our sales skills, or 3) start our own organization to benefit from our sales skills more directly.

3. Destructive competition does not determine the control of resources over the long-term. While we might win a sale or two by damaging the reputations of our competitors, over the long-term, such tactics will isolate us within our industry. We will eventually be overshadowed by those who can produce sales without being seen as a threat.

4. Productive competition depends on exploring new opportunities that expand our knowledge. Ten years of sales experience is different than one year of sales experience repeated ten times. If we don't explore new areas of sales responsibility or new positions at different organizations, we cannot expand our knowledge.

5. Only productive competition can determine the most productive use of resources. We learn which sales methods work and seeing who wins which sales. We learn better techniques whether we win the sale or lose it. If we win the sale, we know our methods were better in that situation. If we lose the sale, we know that our competitors techniques were better and can copy those techniques.

6. Since competition requires innovation, it leverages more value from the existing resources. Each sales situation is unique, requiring some innovation on our part. The more we learn to personalize each sale, bringing in unique aspects of the customer's situation, the more successful we are.

7. Both exploration and innovation expand our knowledge of what works. As we get more experience, we will blend the best of our current standard sales techniques with the new sales methods that we use and those that we encounter.

8. *The process of productive competition continually creates entirely new forms of ground*. The best salespeople discover new markets and create new products to address the needs in them.

7.6.1 Resource Discovery

Sun Tzu's six rules for using innovation to create value from seemingly worthless resources.

"Manage your military position like water. Water takes every shape.
It avoids the high and moves to the low.
Your war can take any shape.
It must avoid the full and strike the empty."
Sun Tzu's The Art of War 6:8:1-5

"Things only have the value that we give them."

Moliere

General Rule: The value of resource and their limits are discovered by filling pools of needs.

Situation:

Foolish nations, organization, and businesses will continue to fight costly battles over resources that grow less and less valuable over time. "Valuable" resources are always becoming less valuable as human knowledge increases. The misconception is that wealth comes from our resources rather than our knowledge. If the only real resource is the human mind, an increasing population cannot make the world tpoorer but richer because we have more minds. This is why places like Hong Kong, with virtually no natural resources other than trained minds, are much richer per person than places such as Africa where there are many more resources but few trained minds.

Opportunity:

Everyone of us has the potential to discover valuable resources. The value of resources arises from our complex interactions with each other and our environment. Our network of minds has more knowledge, ability, and resources than any individual, so we work with one another to create value from our resources. The same vast human network also forms a complex topology of needs. We employ our resources as part of a value chain transforming our resources into products that meet those needs. That complex, adaptable chain is constantly forming and reforming itself as we find new ways to introduce new resources to generate more types of value. Since the network is infinitely complex, drawing resources from everyone in the world that flows out to everyone in the world, it contains innumerable points at which we can create more value (7.6 Productive Competition).

Sun Tzu's Rules:

These are the rules defining how new resources are discovered.

1. The endless flow of our resources fills the infinite voids of our needs. This is what Sun Tzu describes as the eternal balance of fullness and emptiness. We fill our needs with limited resources, starting with our own limited time, physical and mental capabilities. When one set of needs are filled, we become aware of a new set of needs. Those who use their resources the most wisely can generate additional resources to fill more needs. Our decisions both consume or generate value (3.2.4 Emptiness and Fullness).

2. We must attempt to conserve resources by substituting less valuable resources for more costly ones. Our incentive is to consume less expensive resources satisfying one set of needs so we can have more resources to satisfy other needs. Many of these substitutions do not work except to create surprise, but by the process of continually substituting undervalued resources for more valuable ones, we eventually discover new resources that can fill our endless pools of need (7.3.3 Creative Innovation).

3. To avoid competing for valuable resources, we must explore new areas for potential value. Competing for resources makes them more expensive so we look for areas where the value of resources are overlooked. Human knowledge is always limited. Our individual ignorance represents one boundary of human knowledge. We all can explore at the boundaries of our knowledge with the potential to make a discovery of something that will work better given our unique position (2.1.1 Information Limits).

4. Our use of undervalued resources spreads to more applications. We chart the topology of human needs by filling them like water fills a series of pools. When new resources are discovered, the flow out from them fills unforeseen shapes of needs. We copy our own success. We copy each others' success. One discovery about how to utilize an undervalued resource leads to another. Success in one area inspires new ideas in another. Knowledge is easily duplicated and enhanced by its application to new areas. Different pools of need are filled with the new resources (7.5.2 The Spread of Innovation).

5. As the use of undervalued resources spreads, its cost rises with its value. As we fill those pools of need, we discover limits of value through competition. We expand our limited knowledge by identifying new resources. As the use of those resources becomes more popular, their limitation of supply become more apparent. People start competing for them, raising their price. What was once a limitation in knowledge is magically transformed into a new resource limitation (3.1.1 Resource Limitations).

6. These now more costly resources channel our search for advantage in a new direction. The pools of need are still there when the limits of any given resource are reached. We go back to looking again for undervalued resources, starting the cycle again (1.8 Progress Cycle).

Illustration:

Let us illustrate these principles by charting the discovery of value in the internet.

1. The endless flow of our resources fills the infinite voids of our needs. Everyday, we discover new resources on the internet for filling new types of needs.

2. We must attempt to conserve resources by substituting less valuable resources for more costly ones. Each of us is looking for easier ways to address all of our needs. The Internet offers a new and seemingly endless source of new resources. We can find information, download products, and make connections with a fraction of the effort such tasks once took.

3. To avoid competing for valuable resources, we must explore new areas for potential value. While the vast majority of companies fail to find new pools of value, Amazon, eBay, Google, Facebook, and many others have found them.

*4. **Our use of undervalued resources spreads to more applications**.* As one of these pools is discovered, others try to add on and expand it for their own benefit. We get Amazon partners, eBay reseller, Google advertisers, Facebook applications, and on and on.

*5. **As the use of undervalued resources spreads, its cost rises with its value**.* Eventually, these areas become more competitive and less profitable. ***These now more costly resource channels our search for advantage in a new direction***. People go on to look for the next big thing, mobile applications, video-on-demand.

7.6.2 Ground Creation

Sun Tzu's six key methods describing how we use the creation of new competitive ground to be successful.

"Water follows the shape of the land that directs its flow. Your forces follow the enemy who determines how you win."

Sun Tzu's The Art of War 6:1:1

"New discoveries in science will continue to create a thousand new frontiers for those who still would adventure."

Herbert Hoover

General Principle: Breakout innovation opens up new profitable ground for exploitation with the Progress Cycle.

Situation:

The direction of innovation flow is impossible to predict. Its opportunities are determined by shape of the landscape, but unlike the physical landscape, the competitive landscape is constantly reforming as we all constantly adjust our positions. We do not know what the innovation ultimately makes possible. We also do not know how people will react to these innovations. We also cannot see the "low spots" on the periphery of the landscape that define the potential areas where standard methods can break out in the next innovation. New competitive areas are created by the joining of two characteristics that are invisible until they meet: unfulfilled need, Sun Tzu's emptiness, and innovations potential, Sun Tzu's fullness. When these areas form, we can channel our efforts and resources into an entirely new form of opportunity.

Opportunity:

The production mindset tries to plug the holes to control the existing landscape, making it more stable. The competitive mindset uses openings to explore new competitive terrain (3.1.4 Openings). Competitive strategy destabilizes existing terrain through the use of innovation to create surprise and momentum. The flow of competitive innovation destroys the original pool from which it springs, but everyone benefits over the long run (1.8 Progress Cycle). The rules of ground creation leverage our creative momentum to take us to new positions.

Key Methods:

The following key methods describe the way in which we use the creation of new ground to create value.

1. We cannot predict the direction in which new ground will be created from breakout innovations. New ground means a new competitive arena that offers new forms of rewards. This critical limitation on our knowledge means that the direction of competition will constantly change in chaotic ways (2.1.1 Information Limits).

2. *We must discover and adapt more quickly to new terrain than our competition*. Since we cannot know the direction or potential of these breakouts, we must be prepared to adapt to these changes if we wish to benefit from them. If we are to be successful utilizing these changes, we must use the Progress Cycle of Listen->Aim->Move->Claim more quickly than others (1.8 Progress Cycle).

3. *We must listen to be the first to discover breakout innovations opening new landscapes*. We look for openings in the landscape to use them as passages to new areas of opportunity. The competitive mindset is exactly opposite of the production mindset, which seeks to plug those openings in defense of existing positions. Psychologically, the fear of loss outweighs the hope for gain, which keeps most people locked into their positions. Those with dominant positions find it especially difficult to move from them. Sun Tzu's strategy is always a philosophy of expansion that looks for new areas before our potential competitors find them (3.0 Identifying Opportunities).

4. *We select opportunities that aim at breakout innovations that fit our capabilities*. Not all breakout innovations have a universal impact. The world only rarely creates an internet-scale revolution that changes everything. Since a more competitive world creates an increasing wealth of novel ideas, we must know how to be selective about which breakout innovations that we pursue. The most important rule in this regard is making sure that we can get to the breakout area by traveling a minimum of distance from our current position and that its shape fits our capabilities (5.0 Minimizing Mistakes).

5. *We must move to win an early position in those areas*. Since these are new areas, there will be a wealth of challenges to overcome. In all new areas, we must climb the learning curve. This requires knowing how to adapt standard methods to the novel conditions in new competitive arenas (7.0 Creating Momentum).

6. *We must establish visible claims in the new area and have our position attached to it*. Only by claiming positions that created rewards can we sustain positions in new areas. We must initially stake small claims that are easily supported. Those positions become larger and more profitable over time as the early and late majorities discover the new area. The expansion of spac e in these new competitive areas grows our position and their rewards with a minimum of effort (8.0 Winning Rewards

Illustration:

To illustrate these principles, let us look at the series of breakout innovations that flowed from the invention of the microprocessor in 1971.

*1. We cannot predict the direction in which new ground will be created from breakout innovation*s. No one could foresee where the microprocessor would lead when it was invented in 1971. Most people saw it only as applying to a new generation of calculators. Instead, it created a series of innovations in desktop computers, software, worldwide networking, and now mobile devices. Each of these successes laid the foundation for the following innovation. Microprocessors created for calculators, opened up the new area for personal, desktop computers. Those small computers opened up consumer software business. Software opened up the potential for computer networks. Networks opened up the potential for the internet. The internet opens up a million new areas of including on-line training from organizations such as that of the Science of Strategy Institute.

2. We must discover and adapt more quickly to new terrain than our competition. The initial pioneers got to these areas very early. Microsoft and Apple were there at the beginning of the microprocessor and have ridden each successful wave, though their timing hasn't always. Each of these pools of innovation spread from the initial breakthrough and took from eight to twenty years to move from innovation to maturity.

3. We must listen to be the first to discover breakout innovations opening new landscapes. Some of these areas proved to be large pools, opening up vast, new worlds of competition, but many may remain small for a long time. Despite companies such as Yahoo being around for a long time, neither Microsoft or Apple were very interested in Internet searches, for example, until others found the profitable point in the landscape.

4. We select opportunities that aim at breakout innovations that fit our capabilities. The founders of Microsoft and Apple were both hobbyists already involved with computers at the college level but without established positions to defend in the computer business. We see this pattern duplicated over and over. Google was started by Larry Page and Sergey Brin while the two were attending Stanford University as Ph.D. candidates. They were researching search logarithms.

5. We must move to win an early position in those areas. The companies that were successful in each new wave of invention were those that were committed to the arena before it was seen by others to be profitable. Google was first incorporated as a privately held company on September 4, 1998, with its initial public offering to follow on August 19, 2004. Today, it is the most successful company in terms of sales and stock value in the Internet arena.

6. We must establish visible claims in the new area and have our position attached to it. In all these areas of technology, there were other also-rans who had comparable technology, but none of them established the visibility and thereby the acceptance of the eventual market winners. By virtue of their visibility, they were able to create the markets that they came to dominate.

Sun Tzu's Playbook

Volume 8:
Rewards

About Winning Rewards

The seven previous volumes of principles explain the principles put you in the position to win success. The focus of the methods in this volume of Sun Tzu's Playbook is proving that your new position succeeds by using it to win rewards.

Positioning for the Payoff

Sun Tzu's strategy deals with the comparisons inherent in competition. The strategic process positions you to be at the right place at the right time. At every step, you learn more about the potential rewards of a situation. The knowledge you acquire is necessary to making a position pay off. However, the process is not yet complete. Without asking for rewards, all your work is wasted. The sad truth is that people are rewarded for providing value to others but only if they claim those rewards. They are rewarded for positioning themselves so that they can win rewards, but the actually winning of awards is its own sub-process.

All competitive positions must generate rewards. Only those rewards give you more resources. Moving to a new position requires using your existing resources. If that move doesn't produce more rewards than it consumes, it isn't profitable. This concept of strategic profit is an innate part of every aspect of Sun Tzu's system.

In a sense, every successful person is a salesperson. Winning rewards is closing the sale. You must sell others on rewarding you. Supporters are always free to choose whether to reward you or not. They choose to reward you for their own reasons. You are at their mercy. In every such competitive choice regarding rewards, their desire for gain battles against their fear of loss. They want to reward you if it helps them. They do not want to reward you if it doesn't help them.

The core of being rewarded is making claims. The ability to make claims connects the value of your position to the needs of others. The claims you make cannot be totally selfish and get rewarded. All claims are based on the Golden Rule—doing for others so that they will do for you. Your values connect you to your supporters. Happy supporters are absolutely necessary for making a position rewarding over the long term.

All rewards, including money, are a by-product of the personal relationships. You follow the other person's lead to win rewards. Winning rewards is like a dance. You must stay in sync with what others are thinking and feeling during the process. When they get ahead of you, you must catch up. When you get ahead of them, you must slow down. You must know how to control the contact without seeming to be in control.

Learn What Specific People Want

You position yourself to win rewards among groups of people. However, Sun Tzu teaches that groups do not make decisions. Only individuals make decisions. You position yourself to influence a group of individuals who can reward you in your competitive arena, but you must win each individual to get the group's support.

Every individual is different. You must learn quickly what individuals care about, that is, what they will reward you for. You must have an interest about their individual desires. You must demonstrate that you care. People don't care about you if you don't first care about them. The faster you learn what individuals need, the faster you can help them decide to reward you.

In making claims, you must become a partner in the process of getting rewarded. You must make it easy for others to reward you. You must know where their interests and desires are. You must avoid getting bogged down in trivialities. You must be knowledgeable about what you offer that deserves rewards, but the real challenge is connecting with people. To do so, you must take advantage of the way they think.

Other people will never believe it if you claim to care about them more than you care about yourself. Nor should you ever believe that people don't care about their own interests. However, you can share goals with others, going back to the ideal of a "shared mission" explored in the first volume of Sun Tzu's Playbook.

Potential supporters *can* believe that you put your long-term goals above your more immediate self-interest. People can also believe that by rewarding you, they can help themselves. Your concern about their individual needs signals whether or not you believe winning their supported by supporting them.

People into Relationships

At first, Sun Tzu's methods for winning rewards can seem contradictory. To win rewards, you must, at some level, forget your desire to win rewards. If people think you are using them, they will abuse you. If people think that you are pushing them, they will push against you. You don't want them to fight you.

To make claims, you must get attention from others, but to get rewarded, you must also pay attention to the people who can reward you. Your claims must communicate with them. Your claims must sometimes be forthright and determined. You must stand up for your belief in the value of what you offer. You must suggest a good process for offering rewards. You must also sometimes be quiet and patient. You must sometimes keep your personal goals to yourself and let others dictate the pace of the process.

If providing value for others is the basis of winning rewards, you can avoid the most common mistakes in making claims. Short-term thinking exaggerates the conflicts inherent among individuals. Long-term thinking allows you to find common ground. Your opportunities come from viewing problems through the eyes of others.

You must also be brave enough to ask for a reward when the time is right. In the end, potential supporters need your help to make a decision. This is another way that you serve yourself by serving them. If you don't make it clear that they have to decide, they won't decide. You leverage the situation by giving them a good reason to decide on rewarding you sooner rather than later.

Your job is to get them excited enough so that addressing your claims is easy. You can approach different people from different directions.

Open-minded people like to hear a variety of reasons to reward you. Get them to agree with any of a list of reasons. Then you can ask them to decide.

For narrow-minded people, you need to find a new reason to reward you. Dangle a novel idea in front of them like bait on a hook. Ask them to reward you based upon seeing the situation from a new angle. This is how you are successful in getting rewarded by narrow-minded customers.

Use Showmanship

You don't claim rewards simple by using words. You talk as little as possible until you understand what people care about. Then, words alone are not enough to get others to see your point. You need pictures, props, and gimmicks.

Demonstrating your value is not nearly enough. Use illustrations and charts. Use showmanship and magic. Use your knowledge to entertain and surprise them. Use the ideas for creating momentum discussed in the previous chapter. You must develop pictures, props, and gimmicks to get people's attention. Make sure customers have the time for you to go through your routine.

You must get your other people's attention. During contact with them, you must use emotion. People only reward others because they feel like rewarding them. The purpose of showmanship is to stimulate their feelings.

People are easily confused about what you want. Keep your presentations asking for recognition short and clear so that they don't frustrate listeners. Make sure that you really understand what their needs and concerns are so that they can understand you needs and concerns. This is how you make people comfortable when you ask them for rewards.

When you ask for a reward, wait for a response. Stay friendly no matter what the answer. Others must offer objections to test the strength of your beliefs. Friendliness, enthusiasm, and patience wear down the people's resistance to rewarding you. It is the same process whether you are asking for a raise or asking for a first kiss. You will be successful if you serve the needs of others. This is how you master persuasion.

Gauging the Value of a Position

If you follow the principles in the first seven volumes of this Playbook, you can put you in a strong position. If you avoid some simple mistakes in acquiring rewards, that position can prove wether or not it is valuable.

First, avoid long drawn-out reward cycles. Like every other part of the campaign, your first rewards should be quick, small, and local. As positions are established, you can build up to larger rewards and longer reward cycles. First, you must prove that your competitive position is valuable winning rewards from others. If you cannot get rewarded, you have chosen the wrong position.

If the initial process is easy and quick and creates happy relationships, your new position will be valuable. Happy relationships lead to more happy relationships and to even more quicker, easier, and more successful rewards. Successful initial claims provide the basis for future claims. Start fast to get rewarded. Take advantage of people's desire to follow others and build on your success. If you generate rewards quickly from new positions, those rewards can quickly pay for the next round of growth and expansion.

The ability to get rewarded arises naturally from good positions if you do nothing to undermine them. Use common sense and do not do anything to create conscious resistance. Do not say anything to threaten firmly held beliefs. Reflect your supporters' interests in everything you do.

Winning rewards is the same both in your business and personal life. It all comes down to creating rewarding relationships from your position. Do not continue to ask for rewards from those who have already agreed to reward you. Do not press the potential supporters too hard for a decision. You must use timing. Avoid asking for attention and decisions when people's minds are busy. Ask for rewards when resistance fades and people want to clarify the relationship so that they can relax and move on. These are the simple principles of customer contact.

How you ask for rewards is the final part, necessary part of your strategy. If you have understood your strengths and weaknesses, chosen the right opportunities, and positioned yourself correctly, you are ready to be rewards. You must know how to ask for rewards at that point. If you think long-term and use showmanship, your rewards are assured.

Some Final Thoughts

You will not be rewarded according to what you deserve. You are rewarded based what you can claim. This means understanding why people reward some claims and not others.

As you read the principles about winning rewards, remember that your goal is to eliminate conflict from the \process. This can seem like a contradiction: you must take a long-term perspective to winning rewards while being rewarded as quickly as possible.

Claiming any rewards—a pay raise, a promotion, a personal favor, or a kiss—is an emotionally demanding process. You must have the right attitude. You must understand the basics of the psychology of persuasion. You must use all the tools of communication and entertainment to make the process emotionally satisfying for your those who you want to reward you.

8.0.0 Winning Rewards

Sun Tzu's seven key methods on how we harvest the rewards of a new position.

"Make victory in war pay for itself."
Sun Tzu's The Art of War 2:5:1

"People often resist change for reasons that make good sense to them, even if those reasons don't correspond to organizational goals. So it is crucial to recognize, reward, and celebrate accomplishments."
Rosabeth Moss Kanter

General Principle: Moving to a new position must generate more resources than it consumes.

Situation:

"Advancing a position"doesn't mean simply changing a position. We can easily confuse motion with progress. A sports team can move the ball down the field but unless they score, they don't make progress. Movement isn't progress unless it gets us closer to our goals in a meaningful way. We have a tendency to place too much value in a new position simply because we work to get there. We also have a tendency to continue to invest in non-rewarding positions hoping to turn them around. Sun Tzu's strategy defines success as making victory pay. Winning a new position alone is not success. We must know the methods for turning advances into rewards.

Opportunity:

Our opportunity at this point in the process is to discover the real value of a move. We describe all moves as experiments because we cannot know exactly either the cost or benefits of a new position before attaining it. In the aim step, we select the highest probability opportunities, but a high probability of getting rewarded is far from a guarantee (4.0 Leveraging Probability). After winning a new position, we are in a position to discover what it is worth. If it isn't worth maintaining, it is not worth claiming.

Key Methods:

The following key methods describe how competitive rewards are won.

1. A new position isn't successful unless it gives us additional, tangible resources. We need tangible validation from other people because we have the tendency to overvalue positions. We also have a tendency, called false consensus effect , to over-estimate how much people agree with our assessment. We need other people to give us valuable resources on the basis of our new position to prove its value (8.1 Successful Positions).

2. We must make claims on others in order to get rewards. Positions exist both as facts and opinions. We can do the work necessary to win a new position and create value, but we cannot get rewarded for that work unless we ask others for those rewards. People take conditions for granted. Unless we ask, people may not recognize our work nor think about rewarding us. Only by asking can we start to change the subjective perception of our position (8.2 Making Claims).

3. *To maximize our rewards, we need a clear process that increases our value as perceived by others.* We see and understand the value of our new position, but others are not automatically aware of it, even if its reality is right in front of them. We must know how to gauge, package, engage, and manage that perception of value (8.3 Securing Rewards).

4. *All claims are built on a foundation of individual contact.* Though claims can be made to larger groups, in the end rewards are given by individuals. Individual decisions are affected by the group, but choices are made only by individual. This means that we get rewarded by understanding and following the principles for successful individual contact. Mismanaging contact dramatically decreases our chances of making successful claims (8.4 Individual Support).

5. *To assure action on our rewards, we must know how to leverage people's emotions.* People only take action when they are motivated to do so. That motivation is largely emotional, especially when it comes to winning rewards. The less emotion we generate, the longer it will take to get rewarded. The faster a new position produces tangible rewards, the less our risk and the greater its long-term value is likely to be. The longer a position requires to show its value, the lesser that value is likely to be. It is usually less costly to find a better position than it is to continue to invest in a losing position. Unless we understand and know how to use emotions in our claims, we will never get as much as our position deserves (8.5 Leveraging Emotions).

6. *To claim rewards, we must know how to claim people's attention.* In today's increasingly crowded environment, more and more people are competing for our attention. The chaos of crowded, dynamic environments creates the desire for clarity and simplicity in making claims. We must know how to contrast our claims with the claims of others in order to get attention (8.6 Winning Attention).

7. We must get rewarded in a way that makes future rewards more likely. The "rules of the ground" dictate how claims must be made. Each competitive arena has its own rules. We must know the rules of the ground regarding getting rewarded before we advance to a new position. Learning the rules of the ground is part of the listening stage of strategy, but we set up future rewards by the way we claim our current rewards. At the claim stages, we must conform to those rules to make our new position pay (8.7 Productivity Improvement).

Illustration:

We often compare this process to a prospector staking a claim on a gold mine.

1. A new position isn't successful unless is gives us additional, tangible resources. The process of searching and finding gold isn't enough to get rewarded. A miner who finds gold and doesn't stake and develop his claim correctly has wasted his time.

2. We must make claims on others in order to get rewards. Others must verify that our claim is recorded legally and that the gold is valuable by being willing to buy it.

3. To maximize our rewards, we need a clear process that increases our value as perceived by others. In gold mining, the process is standardized to essaying the gold, staking the claim, filing the claim, and working the mine. Without the process, no formal claim can be made.

4. All claims are built on a foundation of individual contact. We must have others test our goal and legally verify our claim. The testing step is getting the newly discovered ore assayed to see if it is worth mining. The visible claiming step is the same as filing the claim with the government.

5. To maximize our rewards, we must know how to leverage people's emotions. The more excited people about the value of gold, the more likely we are to find investors to help us set up the mine and buyers willing to pay us for the gold.

6. *We must often get the attention of others to get the rewards we deserve.* Gold is a well recognized form of value. Some may not be impressed by it, but most are if we simply make our possession of gold known.

7. *We must get rewarded in a way that makes future rewards more likely.* There are many ways to get rewarded from a gold mine. We could mine it ourselves and sell the gold or we could sell the claim. We must choose the methods that are mostly likely to maximize our return over time. **PDF Download :** Article PDF: 8.0 Winning Rewards

8.1.0 Successful Positions

Sun Tzu's seven key methods on how we harvest the rewards of a new position.

"Make victory in war pay for itself."
Sun Tzu's The Art of War 2:5:1

"People often resist change for reasons that make good sense to them, even if those reasons don't correspond to organizational goals. So it is crucial to recognize, reward, and celebrate accomplishments."
Rosabeth Moss Kanter

General Principle: Moving to a new position must generate more resources than it consumes.

Situation:

"Advancing a position"doesn't mean simply changing a position. We can easily confuse motion with progress. A sports team can move the ball down the field but unless they score, they don't make progress. Movement isn't progress unless it gets us closer to our goals in a meaningful way. We have a tendency to place too much value in a new position simply because we work to get there. We also have a tendency to continue to invest in non-rewarding positions hoping to turn them around. Sun Tzu's strategy defines success as making victory pay. Winning a new position alone is not success. We must know the principles for turning advances into rewards.

Opportunity:

Our opportunity at this point in the process is to discover the real value of a move. We describe all moves as experiments because we cannot know exactly either the cost or benefits of a new position before attaining it. In the aim step, we select the highest probability opportunities, but a high probability of getting rewarded is far from a guarantee (4.0 Leveraging Probability). After winning a new position, we are in a position to discover what it is worth. If it isn't worth maintaining, it is not worth claiming.

Key Methods:

The following key methods describe how competitive rewards are won.

1. A new position isn't successful unless it gives us additional, tangible resources. We need tangible validation from other people because we have the tendency to overvalue positions. We also have a tendency, called false consensus effect , to over-estimate how much people agree with our assessment. We need other people to give us valuable resources on the basis of our new position to prove its value (8.1 Successful Positions).

2. We must make claims on others in order to get rewards. Positions exist both as facts and opinions. We can do the work necessary to win a new position and create value, but we cannot get rewarded for that work unless we ask others for those rewards. People take conditions for granted. Unless we ask, people may not recognize our work nor think about rewarding us. Only by asking can we start to change the subjective perception of our position (8.2 Making Claims).

3. *To maximize our rewards, we need a clear process that increases our value as perceived by others.* We see and understand the value of our new position, but others are not automatically aware of it, even if its reality is right in front of them. We must know how to gauge, package, engage, and manage that perception of value (8.3 Securing Rewards).

4. *All claims are built on a foundation of individual contact.* Though claims can be made to larger groups, in the end rewards are given by individuals. Individual decisions are affected by the group, but choices are made only by individual. This means that we get rewarded by understanding and following the methods for successful individual contact. Mismanaging contact dramatically decreases our chances of making successful claims (8.4 Individual Support).

5. *To assure action on our rewards, we must know how to leverage people's emotions.* People only take action when they are motivated to do so. That motivation is largely emotional, especially when it comes to winning rewards. The less emotion we generate, the longer it will take to get rewarded. The faster a new position produces tangible rewards, the less our risk and the greater its long-term value is likely to be. The longer a position requires to show its value, the lesser that value is likely to be. It is usually less costly to find a better position than it is to continue to invest in a losing position. Unless we understand and know how to use emotions in our claims, we will never get as much as our position deserves (8.5 Leveraging Emotions).

6. *To claim rewards, we must know how to claim people's attention.* In today's increasingly crowded environment, more and more people are competing for our attention. The chaos of crowded, dynamic environments creates the desire for clarity and simplicity in making claims. We must know how to contrast our claims with the claims of others in order to get attention (8.6 Winning Attention).

7. We must get rewarded in a way that makes future rewards more likely. The"rules of the ground"dictate how claims must be made. Each competitive arena has its own rules. We must know the rules of the ground regarding getting rewarded before we advance to a new position. Learning the rules of the ground is part of the listening stage of strategy, but we set up future rewards by the way we claim our current rewards. At the claim stages, we must conform to those rules to make our new position pay (8.7 Productivity Improvement).

Illustration:

We often compare this process to a prospector staking a claim on a gold mine.

1. A new position isn't successful unless is gives us additional, tangible resources. The process of searching and finding gold isn't enough to get rewarded. A miner who finds gold and doesn't stake and develop his claim correctly has wasted his time.

2. We must make claims on others in order to get rewards. Others must verify that our claim is recorded legally and that the gold is valuable by being willing to buy it.

3. To maximize our rewards, we need a clear process that increases our value as perceived by others. In gold mining, the process is standardized to essaying the gold, staking the claim, filing the claim, and working the mine. Without the process, no formal claim can be made.

4. All claims are built on a foundation of individual contact. We must have others test our goal and legally verify our claim. The testing step is getting the newly discovered ore assayed to see if it is worth mining. The visible claiming step is the same as filing the claim with the government.

5. To maximize our rewards, we must know how to leverage people's emotions. The more excited people about the value of gold, the more likely we are to find investors to help us set up the mine and buyers willing to pay us for the gold.

6. *We must often get the attention of others to get the rewards we deserve*. Gold is a well recognized form of value. Some may not be impressed by it, but most are if we simply make our possession of gold known.

7. *We must get rewarded in a way that makes future rewards more likely*. There are many ways to get rewarded from a gold mine. We could mine it ourselves and sell the gold or we could sell the claim. We must choose the methods that are mostly likely to maximize our return over time. **PDF Download :** Article PDF: 8.0 Winning Rewards

8.1.1 Transforming Resources

Sun Tzu's six key methods for converting the intangible value of positions to the resources we need.

"Victory comes from everyone sharing the same goals.
Victory comes from finding opportunities in problems."
Sun Tzu's The Art of War 3:5:4-5

"The major reason for setting a goal is for what it makes
of you to accomplish it. What it makes of you will always
be the far greater value than what you get."
Jim Rohn

General Principle: We must convert positions into needed resources by asking those with whom we share values.

Situation:

Our problem is the wide range of goals and values at work within competition. Value comes from our mission but missions can define many different types of value (1.6.2 Types of Motivations).

These values range from the very physical and concrete to the very abstract and idealistic. However, our world is constructed so that our physical, concrete needs must be met if we are to survive to address abstract and idealistic goals. Sun Tzu's strategy is a process that we can use as long as we have the resources to do so. If we run out of those physical resources, the contest is over.

Opportunity:

Fortunately, even extremely abstract forms of value can be translated into concrete resources as long as those values are shared by others (1.6.1 Shared Mission). When free to do so, people readily exchange resources that they have in abundance for things that they value but cannot get directly, even when those values are quite abstract.

Key Methods:

The key methods for converting the resources that we win into the resources we need are:

1. We must eventually convert advances into tangible resources. We need resources to continue advancing our position. We spend our limited time, effort, and other resources to improve our position. To make our investments worthwhile, our advance must return more resources than it costs. In practical terms, this means that we must know how to convert the value a new or expanded position into more immediately and generally useful forms of value such as money (3.1.2 Strategic Profitability).

2. We translated less tangible resources into more tangible resources through shared missions. Positions that serve completely selfish motives cannot be converted into more fungible forms of value. Others do not reward us for gratifying our selfish desires and emotions. Even beggars have to go to the trouble of making public spectacles of themselves in order to give others the gratification of feeling generous and sensitive by giving to them (1.6.1 Shared Mission).

3. The general rule is that we convert resources by exchanging our less tangible resources for the more tangible resources of others. This is possible because people need both tangible and intangible things. This exchange worked according to the principles of complementary opposites. Give us access to resources that are relatively rare, we must translate those resources into those that are more plentiful. We must see how our strengths and abundances can compliment the weaknesses and needs of others. There are many forms of these conversions (3.5 Strength and Weakness).

4. We must identify and connect with those who share our values, lack our resources, but have the resources that we need. This rule simply combines the previous two in a simple action. This connection creates the potential for an exchange to takes place (1.6.1 Shared Mission).

5. We must communicate the value of the exchange. Those with whom we make contact must understand how what we offer serves our shared mission. This doesn't happen automatically. It must be communicated in terms of a shared mission and the emotion that it generates (8.5 Leveraging Emotions).

6. We must ask for the exchange to take place. Unless we ask, the exchange will not occur. The two previous methods set up the potential and motivation for action, but only our action of asking can trigger the required response (2.3.1 Action and Reaction).

Illustration:

Let us illustrate this idea with an extreme example: how do we convert a very idealistic position, say as a missionary, into tangible rewards?

1. We must eventually convert advances into tangible resources. Mother Teresa could not have continued her mission in India without physical support of others.

2. We translated less tangible resources into more tangible resources through shared missions. Her basis for doing this was the fact that others shared her ideas. If they did not, she could not have converted her position in India into anything.

3. The general rule is that we convert resources by exchanging our less tangible resources for the more tangible resources of others. In this case, she exchanged the highest mission values—-those philosophical values that make the world a better place over the long-term for the lowest mission values—the need for money and other tangible supplies such as medicine.

4. We must identify and connect with those who share our values, lack our resources, but have the resources that we need. Mother Teresa was able to indentify people who shared her values and contact them, first in personal meetings, later through larger meetings, and finally through large campaigns.

5. We must communicate the value of the exchange. Mother Teresa communicate the concept of her work, helping people die with dignity, and its value to the world to those who were most likely to here and appreciate that message.

6. We must ask for the exchange to take place. Mother Teresa asked people to help according to the basic principles of"ask and you shall receive"and she was not disappointed. People not only gave the physical resources she needed, but gave of themselves, joining her mission.

8.1.2 Reward Boundaries

Sun Tzu's six key methods defining the limits of our control over a position and its rewards.

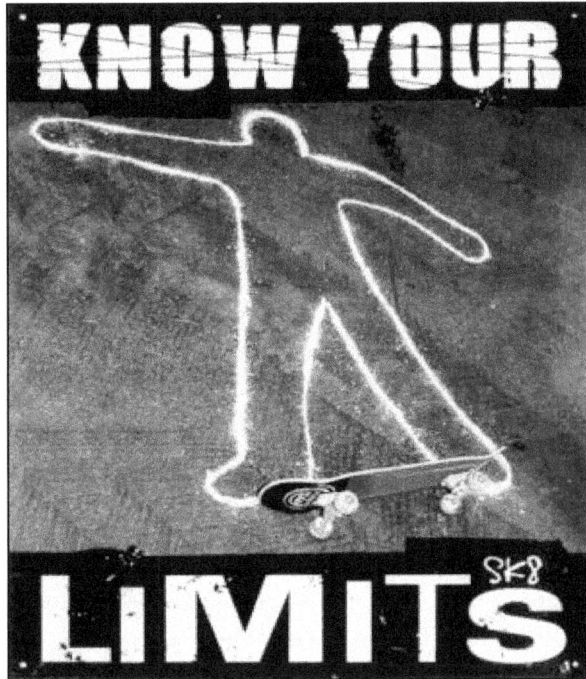

"You can fail to understand your position and meet opponents.
Then you will fail."

Sun Tzu's The Art of War 10:3:8

"Well, everyone will come to that conclusion sooner or later; for there is a limit to the capacity of man to control events. You may call it Destiny. Another may call it Providence; and a third, God. Names do not matter. It

is the humility that matters; the wonder and the sense of awe that matters."

Atharva Veda

General Principle: Each new advance requires us to discover a new sets of boundaries.

Situation:

Successful moves often lead to tragedy instead of rewards. Since we naturally compare a new position to other positions, especially our past position, the most successful our advance, the more difficulty we have in understanding those limits (1.3.1 Competitive Comparison). The further we come in a short period of time, the more likely we are to misunderstand the boundaries on any strategic position. Political and military history consists of many examples of this problem, called hubris by the ancient Greeks. Modern popstars and especially lottery winners also provide a wealth cautionary examples.

Opportunity:

The boundary conditions on any position represents our span of control. A good understanding of the basic principles of strategy force us to realize that, no matter how great our resources, they are always limited (3.1.1 Resource Limitations). The most critical strategic resource is always information. Despite a flood of information, our information too is always limited (2.1.1 Information Limits). Just as the wealth of information in the modern world has the "haystack effect" of making critical information harder to find, a wealth of resources of all kinds can be finding our limits more difficult. The challenge of too much information in a world flooded with communicationis is so serious that the Institute offers a whole series of free, public articles about it.

Key Methods:

The following key methods explain how we must respect our limits in order to get rewarded.

1. All positions are defined primarily by their limits. It doesn't matter how far we advance our position. It doesn't matter how high we rise within an organization. It doesn't matter how much better our position is relative to the position of others around us. Our span of control is always limited (1.9.2 Span of Control).

2. When one limit is removed, another previously hidden limit takes its place. We advance our position to remove a limit, but when one constraint is removed, there is always another. Influence and control flows through our position like water through a series of pipes with different capacities. When we expand the most constrained point, there is still a constraint somewhere in the system. That constraint only appears after the greater restraint is removed, so the destruction of one limit naturally seems to create another in its place (1.8.1 Creation and Destruction).

3. As we complete a move, we must gather information to quickly assess our limits. Understanding we have limits is different from know what those limits are. We can make mistakes both ways by either missing real limits or imagining false ones. The larger our advance, the less we know about our limits and the harder we must work at understanding those limits (2.2 Information Gathering).

4. Learning about limits requires extending our contact network. All aspects of Sun Tzu's system are loops. In this case, the final claiming step of the Progress Cycle require us to go back to the first step. We need to turn to others to get perspective on our limits. In new positions, we must contact others who are more familiar with the territory than we are. New positions often required building entirely new networks (2.4 Contact Networks).

5. It is safer to underestimate rather than over estimate our control. Underestimating our control means we cannot maximize our rewards, but overestimating our control can result in losing control. No matter how plentiful our resources seem, we are always relatively powerless compared to the large environment. When we rise to positions of "power," others may think that we control conditions, but we do not. We are usually better off limiting our own and other people's expectations about what we can control (5.0 Minimizing Mistakes).

6. Increasing our control in one area often descreases our control in another. This is a natural result of our position existing at a balancing point of complementary opposites. We must adapt to the shift of these forces as we enter a new position, which will offer us a new set of opportunities and a new set of problems (3.2.3 Complementary Opposites).

Illustration:

Whenever we get our heart's desire, we discover that it comes with a new set of limits, but let us illistrate with getting promoted to take over our bosses job.

1. All positions are defined primarily by their limits. Before our promotion, we likely over-estimated what our boss could and couldn't decide, such as how much employees are paid.

2. When one limit is removed, another previously hidden limit takes its place. As boss, we can theoretically set any pay we want for our people, but we are constrained by the need to be profitable. If we lose money, we won't keep our job. If we raise the pay of one person, we likely have to adjust the pay of everyone. We do not discover all these complications until we take over the job.

3. As we complete a move, we must gather information to quickly assess our limits. As a new boss, we cannot exceed our authority but must live up to our responsibilities. We cannot afford to make decisions outside of our span of control because such decisions cannot be executed and we end up stepping on others' toes. However, we must make the ones we are responsible for making.

4. Learning about limits requires extending our contact network. We should ask both our former boss and new superiors about our limits to our responsibilty and authority. However, as Sun Tzu teaches, this isn't enough. We must learn about our authority and responsibility for a broad array of people who see our situation from a perspective that our superiors cannot.

5. *It is safer to underestimate rather than over estimate our control.* As a boss, when we violate our boundaries of authority, the effects in damaging relationships are going to be more damaging and long-lasting that failing to initially recognize all our responsibilities.

6. *Increasing our control in one area often descreases our control in another.* As a boss, we have more ability to give other people orders, but we usually get less accurate and timely information as our employees tend to filter the information that gets to us.

8.1.3 Reward Timing

Sun Tzu's six key methods for identifying rewarding positions based upon timing.

"Mastering speed is the essence of war."
Sun Tzu's The Art of War 11:2:16

"Being rich is having money; being wealthy is having time."
Margaret Bonnano

General Principle: The benefits of a position are judged by the relative frequency and consistency of positive events.

Situation:

The advantages of new positions come in a variety of flavors. The problem is that we can only judge the value of new positions once we have moved into them, not before (3.1.5 Unpredictable Value). We cannot know if we have actually improved our position until it proves to be more rewarding than our previous position (1.3.1 Competitive Comparison). Some forms of rewards, especially financial rewards, are quantifiable and theoretically easy to compare, but most of us don't keep detailed ledgers. We keep mental ledgers that record a wide variety of things. Other forms of rewards, such as our level of pleasure, are difficult to compare because they are measure in quality of the experience rather than a comparable quantity. Most situations are a trade-off between quantitative and qualitative values.

Opportunity:

People actually do keep a mental ledger balancing the costs and benefits of things. This quantitative measure works generically for all types of value. It affects every form of advantage and benefit generated by a new position. It is the relative frequency of positive and negative events. This positive and negative feedback is what registers on our mental ledger and it measures in terms of speed and timing. Time passes at a regular, measurable rate for every type and form of position. While rewards must be compared in other ways as well, the consistency of time offers a standard yardstick for comparing the value of any new position to any old position (8.1.1 Transforming Resources).

Key Methods:

Six key methods for evaluating the profitability of a position based on speed and quickness.

1. The key to using time to evaluating new positions is thinking about events. Events can be either positive, negative, or neutral. In using time, we can think about the"reward"as any positive event and the"cost"as the number of other events it takes to get to that positive event (5.1.1 Event Pressure).

2. *Profitability must always be tied to a time period*. New positions are more advantageous if they are more profitable than old positions. While time represents just one dimension, it affects the profitability of a position in a variety of ways. We can think generically about the balance of positive events against negative ones as the *profitability* of a position (3.1.2 Strategic Profitability),

3. *More profitable positions create positive events more quickly after our investment than less profitable positions*. This is an issue of quickness in an environment in which opportunity windows close quickly. A new position is more advantageous than a previous position only if its positive events occur more closely to our investments creating those events (5.3.2 Opportunity Window).

4. *More profitable positions create positive events at a faster rate than less profitable positions*. This is simply a matter of the volume of positive results a new position creates. A new position is more advantageous than a previous position only if it generates more positive events in the same amount of time (5.3.1 Speed and Quickness).

5. *More profitable positions create positive events with a greater frequency relative to negative events than less profitable positions*. All positions have both costs and benefits. A position can produce more positive events but also produce more negative ones as well. The issue is the balance between the two. A new position is more advantageous than a previous position only if generates a more positive balance of rewarding and costly events (8.1 Successful Positions).

6. *More profitable positions create positive events more regularly and consistently than less profitable positions*. Consistency creates expectations that people can depend upon. Inconsistent rewards are less valuable than more dependable ones. A new position is more advantageous than a previous position only if its generates positive events more predictably ([7.2.2 Preparing Expectations](#)).

Illustration:

The point of these very generic principles is that they work for a wide variety of competitive situations, where the focus on specific types of rewards do not.

1. The key to using time to evaluating new positions is thinking about events. The value of this system is that a"positive event"can apply to virtually every type of position and every type of value, even when that value is not quantifiable in other ways. It doesn't matter if we are talking about a romantic relationship, a sales call, or a shopping trip, we can say whether the event was positive or not.

2. Profitability must always be tied to a time period. As my Inc. 500 software company grew, we needed a guideline for evaluating new software development projects. We developed the goal of making the new product salable within 90 days. I notice that a similar yardstick is now used by the [YCombinator](#) , a seed-stage fund for software start-ups.

3. More profitable positions create positive events more quickly after our investment than less profitable positions. In many situations, there is gap in a time between the investment event and any positive result. For example, we can try to contact someone a long time before actually getting in touch with them. The closer these two events are in time, the better our position. For example, people call back their bosses faster than they call back their subordinates.

4. More profitable positions create positive events at a faster rate than less profitable positions. In making sales calls, contacts can have a positive result in terms of moving the sale forward even when it doesn't generate a sale. We have improved our position if we improve our contact to positive result ratio.

5. *More profitable positions create positive events with a greater frequency relative to negative events than less profitable positions.* A store can offer the best prices more frequently, but those prices can be negated if shopping trips fail to find the products we want, involve poor service, and where policies such as the ability to get refunds add additional costs. Though we cannot keep track of the dollars involved, we can keep track of the balance of events.

6. *More profitable positions create positive events more regularly and consistently than less profitable positions.* In a romantic relationship, contacts that are more consistently and predictably positive represent an advance in the relationship.

8.2.0 Making Claims

Sun Tzu's five key methods for claiming rewards after winning positions.

"Take the enemy's strength from him by stealing away his money."

Sun Tzu's The Art of War 2:4:7

"You are important enough to ask and you are blessed enough to receive back."

Wayne Dyer

General Principle: We must make our claims legitimately to get rewards.

Situation:

Many hard -working, creative, productive people never get rewarded because they fail to make appropriate claims. Some people are rewarded more for their efforts than others. This is not because the people with whom they deal are evil. It is only because the people with whom they deal are human. Benefits and rewards do not naturally flow from even the most advantageous position. If we want to get rewarded, we must understand what a claim is and why it is required to make claims in order to get rewarded.

Opportunity:

In life, we don't get what we deserve. We get what we can successfully claim. What are we really positioning ourselves for through the use of strategy? We are positioning ourselves for making a successful claim. As a psychological and practical matter, we must make claims in order to get rewarded. Rewards are the only proof that what we are doing has value, and we will only get those rewards if we make claims.

Claiming is a responsibility that we only learn as adults. As children, we do not have to make claims. As babies, we cry to get attention. When we are children, our parents pay attention to us because it is their responsibility to do so. It is up to our parents to figure out what we need. When we become adults, we can ask for attention but we won't get it without a reason. It is no one's responsibility to figure out what we need. As children, our parents take care of us. As adults, those with authority over us do not take care of us without giving them a reason. As children, our audience always applauds when we take a bow. As adults, there is always a risk in taking a bow: the silence can be deafening.

Key Methods:

Five key methods describe why claims must be made and what they accomplish in terms of positions.

1. A claim is an outward, visible sign that gains us a benefit or reward from changing our position. Claiming is required both to get our position recognized and to win rewards from a position. Staking a claim is a process, requiring several components (8.3 Securing Rewards).

2. We can only make a claim based upon an external comparison of our position with others. Competition is about being compared to others by others. Like all strategic measures, this is a relative comparison. We must set up comparisons that give us an advantage rather than set us up for failure. We choose our battles, setting up the basis for comparison. This means that we must pick the right group of people with whom we wish to compare ourselves in order to justify our claims. We obviously must pick a group with which we compare relatively well, but it is surprising how often people do the opposite, at least in their minds, making claims impossible (1.3.1 Competitive Comparison).

3. The most important aspect of this process is internal. We must believe our position as valuable to others. We cannot confuse our position with our personality or our ego. Strategically, we think only about position so we can distance our emotional issues from the strategic situation. We must believe that our position deserves a reward before we can claim a reward. (1.0 Strategic Positioning).

4. An objective move to a new position has no meaning until it is subjectively recognized by others. While this process starts from the inside, it is only completed by outside recognition of the value of our position. We must see our position as worthy of rewards from the perspective of others before making a claim. If we have an inflated view of ourselves, our claims are doomed. If we cannot measure up to the judgments of others, our claim will fail. Other must look at our position, compare how it has improved relatively to the position of others and see our advance both objectively and subjectively (1.2 Subobjective Positions).

5. We must actively communicate that perception of our position to those who can reward us. Claims are a matter of communication. If our claims are not communicated, there is no claim at all (8.4 Individual Support)

Illustration:

A more subtle example is advancing our position by losing weight.

1. A claim is an outward, visible sign that gains us a benefit or reward from changing our position. Many people struggle with weight loss because they don't approach it as strategic positioning. Even if they physically lose the weight, they fail to make the appropriate claims on their new position. Too often this means that they fall back to their old position, putting the weight back on.

2. We can only make a claim based upon an external comparison of our position with others. No one is ever happy with their weight, mostly because they compare themselves to the wrong people. Teenage girls who weigh 120 pounds compare themselves to skinny models that weigh 90 pounds. Older women compare themselves to teenagers. By comparing themselves to the wrong groups, people set themselves up for a downhill slide. Even if we weigh 400 pounds, we can make progress if we compare our changing position to those of other 400 pound people. Setting the right gauge allows us to feel our progress rather than be frustrated by it.

3. The most important aspect of this process is internal. After, we lose weight, we will still think we are fat unless we *internally* claim a our new position as a thin person, for example, by buying new clothes. If we want to lose weight and keep it off, we must see ourselves differently. We must see ourselves as a person that can control our weight rather as a person who is the victim of it.

4. An objective move to a new position has no meaning until it is subjectively recognized by others. We will continue to think of ourselves as fat if no one recognizes that we have lost weight. Our mental image of ourselves is formed by our encounters with others. We must claim our position. If we demand recognition from others by making an issue about getting complements, we are more committed to maintaining our new position.

5. We must actively communicate that perception of our position to those who can reward us. If we wear clothes that hide our body, we cannot communicate our weight loss. If we don't commit ourselves to keeping the weight off, we will not keep it off.

8.3.0 Securing Rewards

Sun Tzu's five key methods on maximizing the rewards from a position.

"Some military commanders do not know how to adjust their methods.
They can find an advantageous position.
Still, they cannot use their men effectively."
Sun Tzu's The Art of War 8:1:19-21

"Men are rich only as they give. He who gives great service gets great rewards."
Elbert Hubbard

General Principle: There are four components to getting the most value out of a position.

Situation:

To be successful, we must maximize the benefits we get out of every move. Unfortunately, most people do not have any framework for thinking about the process by which we secure rewards. The problem is that the advantages of a new position are not realized simply by occupying it. Understanding that we must claim rewards is not enough. If we do not know how to use our new position in a process of securing rewards, occupying a position can actually be dangerous. Sometimes, the way in which we get the benefits out of our new position are obvious, but the process by which we maximize rewards is often overlooked.

Opportunity:

The Progress Cycle are not only the four ingredients for advancing a position (1.8 Progress Cycle). The adaptive loop of Listen>Aim>Move>Claim is scale-free and self-similar. This means that it is duplicate in each individual part of the process as well as the process as a whole. At each level, it can be repeated again in a similar, but not identical, way. In the case of the claiming process, we have developed a specific set of terms for these four steps to help us remember them, but beneath this special terminology, we can see the LAMC loop at work. We sometimes describe these four components as four spans in a bridge that takes us from where we are to where we want to go. Just a bridge doesn't take us anywhere unless every span is in place, without the claiming process, our progress often fails.

Key Methods:

There are key methods for using the adaptive loop to maximize our rewards.

1. We must gauge the value of our new position. We must recognize that our perspective is different from those whose support we are hoping to gain. We need a comprehensive method for gauging the value of our position from their perspective so we can claim the appropriate benefits (8.3.1 Gauging Value).

2. We must __package__ the value to clarify its perception. We leverage the boundaries of our position to maximize the perception of its value. Objectively a fact is a fact, but subjectively facts are only important in how others related to them. Fuzzy positions are like an unfocused picture. People cannot see the value (8.3.2 Distinctive Packaging).

3. We must __engage__ others to recognize that value. We must communicate value in a way that demands recognition. This take courage. Good packaging make this easier, but in the end, we must demand others to make a decision about the value of our new position. Engagement requires confronting people with the choice and insisting that they make it (8.3.3 Rules of Engagement).

4. We must __manage__ the value to produce needed resources. Finally, we must manage the position to deliver on the expectations that we have created. When people reward us, we live up to our responsibilities by leveraging the value of the position in the ways that we have promised them(8.3.4 Position Production).

5. We must repeat this cycle in small increments to maximize our rewards. Large initial claims are more likely to fail. How much we get in the long-term is often determined by how often we go through this loop. In each cycle, we must balance our fear of loss with our greed for more. As with all adaptive loops, each cycle brings us closer to our goals of maximizing value (5.4 Minimizing Action).

Illustration:

We often use the analogy of a prospector filing a claim on a gold mine to illustrate these concepts very simply.

1. We must __gauge__ the value of our new position. We must get the gold ore assayed to see its true value,

2. We must __package__ the value to clarify its perception. We must get the right location, especially the borders, for our claim.

*3. **We must <u>engage</u> others to recognize that value**. We must file the claim with the appropriate officials.

*4. **We must <u>manage</u> the value to produce needed resources**. We must make the decision of either choosing to sell the claim or operate the gold mine ourselves.

*5. **We must repeat this cycle in small increments to maximize our rewards**. If we choose to sell or mine ourselves, we must go through this process again to maximize the results of our decision.

8.3.1 Gauging Value

Sun Tzu's five key methods on the methods for correctly measuring a position's value.

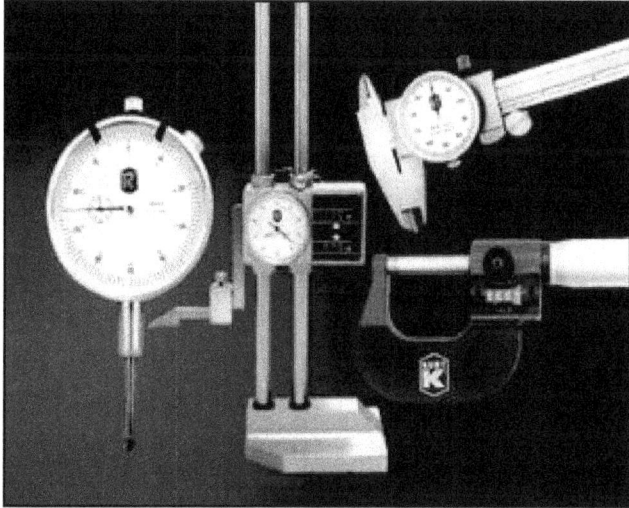

General Principle: There are two key perspectives and five key components in gauging a position's value.

Situation:

To get rewarded, others must recognize the value in supporting us. Their alternatives are either ignoring us or challenging us. We will not get this recognition without the properly gauging the value of our position (8.2 Making Claims). In making claims, we run into two opposite problems with gauging value: the problem of an ego and the problem of insecurity. Our ego tempts us into inflated claims. Our insecurity frightens us away from making any claims. Most people know neither the key elements that make a position valuable nor the role of perspective in gauging the value of a position.

Opportunity:

Gauging the value of a new position involves both objective (physical) and subjective (people's opinions) components of a strategic position (1.2 Subobjective Positions). Our opportunity depends heavily on leveraging what people think, the subjective aspect of this equation (3.6 Leveraging Subjectivity). This is an economic issue. It is less costly to change people's subjective impressions than our physical situation (3.1.2 Strategic Profitability). Even if we physically control a gold mine, its value requires a subjective judgment: the perception of our ownership.

Key Methods:

The following five key methods describe the methods by which we gauge the value of our position to make a claim.

1. Our claims must be both believable and relevant to others. If we make claims that others find unbelievable, they offer us no advantage. If we make claims that no one cares about, we cannot be rewarded. Without making claims from the proper perspective, our claims can hurt us more than they help us. We must test all our claims by both their believability and their relevance (2.3.1 Action and Reaction).

2. We enter the claim stage with most of what we need to know to properly gauge our claims. We learn what we need to know from aiming at an opportunity and completing our moves. During this process, we are continuously gathering information. This information covers all five elements that define our position. The challenge is pulling that information together, filtering it, identifying and highlighting the key points of value (2.5 The Big Picture).

3. We must use our unique,"close up"understanding of the resources and advantages our position offers. We know our position better than anyone else. To make sure that we don't overlook any aspect of value, we must think about all five dimensions that define a position, 1) mission, 2) climate, 3) ground, 4) character, and 5) methods (1.3 Elemental Analysis).

4. We translate our close-up view of value into a perspective that is relevant to those who can reward us. Our potential supporters can be customers, a boss, or even an opponent who we wish to intimidate. What defines them as potential supporters is that we want something from them. This translation process is exactly that: putting one view of value into the terms of another (2.0 Developing Perspective).

5. This translation requires asking five questions about the value of our position to others. 1) How do others share the value of what we see as our mission? 2) How do the changes that concern them increase the value of our position over time? 3) How do the resources from the ground we control benefit others? 4) How do aspects of our character complement their weaknesses and strengths of their character? 5) How do our skills and systems increase the value of their skills and systems? (2.3.4 Using Questions).

Illustration:

Let us look at the challenge of gauging value in getting rewarded for the value of expanding our responsibilities at work.

1. Our claims must be both believable and relevant to others. If we want to get rewarded for the work we are doing, we must make a claim, but that claim cannot be based on our perspective, the effort we put into the work, but from the perspective of our boss and what he rewards people for doing.

2. We enter the claim stage with most of what we need to know to properly gauge our claims. As our responsibilities at work expand, we know what we are doing. We also know our boss and what he cares about.

3. We must use our unique,"close up"understanding of the resources and advantages our position offers. We are close to our jobs, so we know what we are doing and how our role has expanded over time. The person who controls our paycheck never has the same information.

4. We translate our close-up view of value into a perspective that is relevant to those who can reward us. We must put that value into terms that our boss will accept and care about. Sometimes, how he rewards people is a matter of company policy not personal choice. Before making our claim, we must translate what we do into terms of value that our boss can relate to and for which he can compensate us.

5. This translation requires asking five questions about the value of our position to others. How does the additional work we are doing 1) produce more value related to our organization's and boss's goals? 2) affect the changing business conditions that create challenges and opportunities for our organization and boss? 3) generate more resources (income, customers, products, etc.) for the organization? 5) depend on our particular strengths character (creativity, leadership, courage, etc) lacking elsewhere in the organization? and 6) depend on our particular skills (knowledge, experience, contacts, etc) lacking elsewhere in the organization?

8.3.2 Distinctive Packaging

Sun Tzu's nine key methods for creating the perception of value.

*"You must master gongs, drums, banners, and flags.
Place people as a single unit where they can all see and
hear."*

Sun Tzu's The Art of War7:4:6-7

*"The most important persuasion tool you have in your
entire arsenal is integrity."*

Zig Ziglar

General Principle: We must package the advantages of our
position to maximize the perception of value.

Situation:

Strategically, perception is not reality, but it is a key component
of reality (1.2 Subobjective Positions). Our challenge is having

people recognize the greatest value of our position. Just because we understand the value of our position doesn't mean that others will. This is particularly a problem when we have recently advanced our position--taken on new responsibilities at work, brought out new products, become more committed to a relationship, etc. The problem is that others always tend to continue to think of us in terms of where we were rather than where we are today.

Opportunity:

When perception and reality separate, reality provides the anchor, and perception provides the energy. As complementary opposites , they create one another in a constant cycle (3.2.3 Complementary Opposites). This means there are real limits to how far apart reality and perception can drift apart. In packaging a new position, we have an opportunity to sharply define the value of our new position from either reality or perception. All four methods for winning rewards from our position requires understanding psychology, but packaging methods use the deepest psychology (8.3 Securing Rewards).

Key Methods:

We use the following nine key methods to sharpen people's perception of the value of our position relying heavily on psychological research.

1. A package must clarify the new boundaries of our position. A fuzzy position is as difficult to appreciate as a fuzzy picture and less valuable. The job of packaging is to bring our position, especially how our limited resources are being better used, into sharp focus (3.1.2 Strategic Profitability).

2. A package must clarify the position's value to others. We want to focus the value of our position from the perspective of the specific people whose estimation determines the rewards of that position. This perspective can only be understood in terms of their values, not ours (3.6 Leveraging Subjectivity).

3. *A package must clarify h*ow *our position has grown in value*. In clarifying our position, we should show how our boundaries have changed and grown to encompass more value. Strategic comparisons are all relative: comparing one position to another (1.3.1 Competitive Comparison).

4. *The resulting package must not only persuade but correctly set expectations*. If the package, that is, the perception, oversells the position, it creates disappointment in the reality. Thinking longer term, we don't want people to be unhappy after they open the package. Packaging is preparation and practice for the next step, engaging people to recognize and reward the value of our position (7.2.2 Preparing Expectations).

5. *We want to package the value of our new position to others as an agreement*. People want to honor commitment, even if the original incentive or motivation is subsequently removed. The Asch conformity experiments demonstrate that people will act. We should package our new position as honoring our half of an agreement (1.6 Mission Values).

6. *We want to package the value of our new position to others as a Trend*. People will do things that they see other people are doing. We want to package the value of our position with"social proof"of recognition by others. (1.3.1 Competitive Comparison)

7. *We want to package the value of our new position to others as a Rarity*, Scarcity generates demand. We need to highlight the elements of our position that are difficult to find (1.3.2 Element Scalability).

8. *We want to package the value of our new position to others as a Command*. People want to obey authority figures. Milgram experiments in the early 1960s and the My Lai massacre.We should package in any evidence that those in authority have ordered such rewards. (1.5.1 Command Leadership)

9. *We want to package the value of our new position to others as a Favor*. People tend to return favors out of reciprocity but respond poorly to demands. We should package our new position as giving a gift that has not been returned (1.5.2. Group Methods.

Illustration:

Extending the example we used in the article gauging a position's value, packaging for getting rewarded for extending our responsibilities at work (8.3.1 Gauging Value).

1. A package must clarify the new boundaries of our position. We specifically identify the new responsibilities that we have undertaken, when and why we took those responsibilities.

2. A package must clarify the position's value to others. We translate these responsibilities from the tasks involved to the value that those tasks generate both for our organization and for the specific person with who we are dealing.

*3. A package must clarify h*ow *our position has grown in value.* To sharpen the value of our position, we should specifically contrast what we were doing, what we stopped doing, and how what we are doing now is more valuable.

4. The resulting package must not only persuade but correctly set expectations. We want to package our position in a way that doesn't set expectations that we cannot live up to.

5. We want to package the value of our new position to others as an agreement. We can connect our extension of responsibilities to a pay-raise as part of previous agreement.

6. We want to package the value of our new position to others as a trend. We can demonstrate that others with similar extensions of responsibilities have been similarly rewarded.

7. We want to package the value of our new position to others as a rarity. We can make it clear that those who show such initiative are rare.

8. We want to package the value of our new position to others as a command. We can maintain that rewarding behavior like ours has long been part of company policy.

9. *We want to package the value of our new position to others as a _favor_.* We can package the work that we have done as a favor that has helped our boss and his position.

8.3.3 Rules of Engagement

Sun Tzu's nine key methods outlining the do's and don't of making claims.

"Victory goes to those who make winning easy. A good battle is one that you will obviously win."
Sun Tzu's The Art of War 4:3:13-14

"The modern nose, like the modern eye, has developed a sort of microscopic, inter-cellular intensity which makes our human contacts painful and revolting."
Marshall McLuhan

General Principle: We must know how to engage people to win recognition of our value.

Situation:

Sun Tzu's strategy requires us to retrain our instincts about how to make decisions about conditions. Our only inborn"strategic"reactions to others are the"flight or fight"response (2.3.3 Range of Reactions). Needless to say, in a society where we can only get rewarded through our contact with other people, these reactions are not very useful.

The problem is that we are increasingly isolated by modern forms of communication. This isolation is a major strategic problem because we cannot get rewarded for advancing our position without engaging \others (8.2 Making Claims), leveraging our position into rewards. Modern communication tools such as Twitter can increase our isolation in an increasingly crowded world when they are used to disengage us from meaningful contact with others.

Opportunity:

Direct human contact is the primary source of all strategic rewards. If we go back a hundred years, its was also the source of all entertainment and diversion. People didn't have to be trained in human contact because their lives revolved around it. The opportunity today is that most of us our relatively unskilled and uncertain in our direct contact with others.

In a sense, all the principles of Sun Tzu teach us how to better conduct human contact. Because so few of us develop the skills of human contact, certain professions--salespeople, politicians, people in the media-enjoy a huge advantage because they have an opportunity to develop these atrophied skills. Skill at contact begins with understanding why we must seek it our in order to be rewarded.

Key Methods:

The following nine key methods explain the best ways to engage others while making a claim.

1. The rules of engaging others apply to every type of contact. The general do's and don'ts for engaging others to claim rewards apply to every kind of meeting from one-to-one meetings, to group meetings, to making public appearances, to sending out emails, and so on. Other Playbook articles deal with the specific methods of working with individuals one-on-one (8.4 Individual Contact).

2. These generic principles of claiming are always trumped by"the rules of the ground". Different competitive arenas--selling a product, proposing marriage, constructing an alliance, winning a football game and so--require that the specific rules of the game be followed. We don't score in a relationship the same way we do in a football game. (2.4.1 Ground Perspective).

3. Do make more frequent and broader contact increase our probability of rewards. We engage people to that, even if they don't reward immediately, we set up another contact where they can (4.0 Leveraging Probability).

4. We must be prepared for personal encounters where we make a claim. Making a claim is a delicate matter and without the proper preparation, it leads only to disaster. If the opportunity for a meeting suddenly appears, we cannot take it unless we know exactly what will work. Making a claim is a delicate matter and without the proper preparation, it leads only to disaster (5.0 Minimizing Mistakes).

5. We should set up special claim encounters outside of the regular course of events. On occasions where people expect claims to be made, claims are also normally rejected. Claim engagement must involve at least an element of surprise and creativity (7.0 Creating Momentum).

6. Our contacts must reinforce the firmly held beliefs of others and the advantages of their position. We cannot use our claim directly challenge the legitimate position of another. Our claims should be consistent with what people believe, especially about their own position (3.1.3 Conflict Cost).

7. *Rewarding contacts move quickly and lightly rather than slowly and heavily.* A series of quick, small, successful claims is more certain than pushing for a large, significant award (5.4 Minimizing Action).

8. *We must work hard to be heard and understood.* Others do not necessarily hear what we say. In claim situations, it is totally our job to make sure that we are heard and understood (2.3 Personal Interactions).

9. *Our focus must always be on creating a common cause with others.* While we look for awards to satisfy our needs, they are only given if we satisfy the needs of others (1.6.1 Shared Mission)

Illustration:

Let us illustrate these ideas with examples from selling.

1. *The rules of engaging others apply to every type of contact.* When we are selling, we are always selling whether we are making a sales call or making a presentation to the Rotary.

2. *Generic principles of rewarding contact are always trumped by"the rules of the ground".* Jet planes are not sold in the same way that vacuum cleaners, even if they have many things in common.

3. *More frequent and longer contacts increase our probability of rewards.* If we want to sell a product or service, the more people that we can contact more often, the more we will sales.

4. *We must be prepared for personal encounters where we make a claim.* If we run into our prospect when we are unprepared, we should take the opportunity to build the relationship rather than trying to close the sale.

5. *We should set up special claim encounters outside of the regular course of events.* More sales are closed on the golf course than the board room.

6. Our contacts must reinforce the firmly held beliefs of others and the advantages of their position. If we want to close a sale, the least successful method is to pressure people into an immediate decision. Even if it works, it never creates a satisfied, repeat customer.

7. Rewarding contacts move quickly and lightly rather than slowly and heavily. For a salesperson, it is always better to make a small sale now that can lead to a sale in the future than try to get a large sale immediately.

8. We must work hard to be heard and understood. After we make a statement about the value of a product, it is always best to ask the other prospect for a confirmation of that value in their own words.

9. Our focus must always be on creating a common cause with others. In sales, we teach that getting rewarded is not about how great our product is, but how great the product can make our customers.

8.3.4 Position Production

Sun Tzu's seven key methods describing the shift from profitable competition to profitable production.

"This is how you serve your country.
This is how you reward your nation."\
Sun Tzu's The Art of War 10:3:20-21

"I feel that the greatest reward for doing is the opportunity to do more."

Jonas Salk

General Principle: We must use organizational skills to produce the most value of our position to satisfy expectations.

Situation:

Our success in competition takes us from the competitive arena into the productive one. We may think that the difficult work is behind us after we get others to recognize the value of our position, but it is simply the start of a new task, one which requires very different skills. The problem is that the strategic skills that win positions are different from the production skills that produce value from those positions over time. We cannot maximize our rewards from competition simply from competitive skills. We need productive skills. Many people cannot make the transition. We see this when people on the front lines of competition are promoted to internal management positions.

Opportunity:

Our opportunity is knowing how to make the switch between the warrior skills of competition and the management skills of production. These two skill sets are mirror images of each other. We can dramatically improve our rewards from competition by shifting from competitive thinking to productive thinking. Since we are all trained in school in the methods of linear planning, many competitors can make the transition rather easily, but only if they understand the transition that is involved.

Key Methods:

The following key methods get the most reward from production within our span of control.

1. We must produce the most possible value from our span of control to exceed expectations. After people reward us, we must reward them by living up to our responsibilities. This means knowing how to produce the most value from the positions which we have been recognized to control (1.9.2 Span of Control).

2. Our skills at production are the complementary opposite of our skills of competition. Our success in generating value from our position depends on recognizing the difference between these two realms and switching back and forth from competition to production as appropriate (3.2.3 Complementary Opposites).

3. A productive mission and goals focus on a well-specified end result rather than a general improvement in position. We seek to produce duplicate, standard products rather than unique, custom solutions (1.6 Mission Values).

4. The controlled climate of production consists of predetermined steps rather than unpredictable events. The steps exist within our span of control so they must be planned in advance. We measure predictability to increase our control. As we increase our control, we minimize waste and effort while maximizing quality (1.4.1 Climate Shift).

5. The controlled ground within our span of control is defined by cooperative action and known resources. This is in contrast with the competitive environments where people compete and resources are undetermined and unattained. Since resources are known and available resources, they can be organized (1.4.2 Ground Features).

6. Productive individual decision-making process requires linear thinking and reductionist problem solving. Reductionism breaks processes into smaller parts to identify the location of problems. A competitive environment requires adaptive thinking and holistic problem solving that fit details into larger picture (1.5.1 Command Leadership).

7. Productive group methods require organizing and designing. These methods seek to control a part of the environment rather than adjust to environment as a whole. This is the opposite of competitive methods that are based on exploring and experimenting (1.5.2. Group Methods).

Illustration:

Below are some general examples of the differences between the skills by which positions are won and the skills by which production from a position is maximized.

1. We must produce the most possible value from our span of control to exceed expectations. In our career, we win a promotion by winning recognition in competition with others, but we justify our promotion by living up to our responsibilities. In business, we win customers by promotion and marketing, but we keep customers by providing excellent service and value. In our relationships, we win affection by positioning ourselves as exciting and interesting, but we keep relationships by proving ourselves dependable and consistent. In sports, when a good assistant coach is promoted to a head coach, he or she must make decisions about planning personnel, pay, and organization as well as about game strategy.

2. Our skills at production are the complementary opposite of our skills of competition. In our career, we must know where competition stops. In business, we must satisfy customer expectations. In our relationships, we must become a team. In sports, a coach must assume complete authority.

3. A productive mission and goals focus on a well-specified end result rather than a general improvement in position. In our career, in business, in our relationships, in sports, we must have clear, specific production goals to be successful.

4. The controlled climate of production consists of predetermined steps rather than unpredictable events. In our career, in business, in our relationships, in sports, we must have clear, well-defined processes and measurement to be successful.

5. The controlled ground within our span of control consists is defined by cooperative action and known resources. In our career, in business, in our relationships, in sports, we must control and organize our resources for maximum benefit.

6. Productive individual decision-making process requires linear thinking and reductionist problem solving. In our career, in business, in our relationships, in sports, we must locate and identify the specific location of problems that are holding us back.

7. Productive group methods require organizing and designing. In our career, in business, in our relationships, in sports, we must work as a team, balancing and respecting our different skills for the maximum benefit.

8.4.0 Individual Support

Sun Tzu's eight key methods describing the general techniques for winning the support of individuals.

*"An organized force is braver than lone individuals.
This is the art of organization."*
Sun Tzu's The Art of War 11:4:18-19

The best way to persuade people is with your ears - by listening to them."
Dean Rusk

General Principle: Our success depends on the individual decisions of others.

Situation:

Rewards usually come down to the decisions of individuals. When a single individual must decide, the average behavior of the crowd no longer matters (1.8.4 Probabilistic Process). Decisions by individuals are different from a group decisions. Individuals are never average. The problem is that strategy teaches us to think in probabilities, but we cannot treat individuals as we do a group. Working with individuals requires its own special methods.

Opportunity:

Working with individuals provides more opportunities to use different strategic methods than working with groups. Both require adapting to the environment, but they differ dramatically in cycle time (1.8.3 Cycle Time). During one-on-one contact, we must adapt from second to second to what the encounter reveals. The more wedded we are to our plans, the less successful we will be. As Sun Tzu indicates in our opening quote, people are naturally afraid to make decisions. If we use the right methods to work with them, we can get the decisions that we want. For this reason, preparation and practice are more important than planning. Quick thinking is more frequently rewarded than well-constructed promotions.

Key Methods:

The following key methods from Sun Tzu regarding individual contact.

1. During individual contact, we must see the situation from the other person's perspective. To get rewarded, we must adapt the special conditions that every individual brings to every decision. Until we know what individuals think, we cannot ask them to make a decision. When making contact with individuals, we must subordinate positioning statements to focus on the specific interests of the individual. We can try to shortcut the contact process. If we do, we will hurt our chances of success (2.0 Developing Perspective).

2. Prepare before the contact but be prepared to adapt during it. When we can know the decision maker before the contact, we must learn all we can about them beforehand but we cannot be surprised if much of what we learn is misleading (2.1.1 Information Limits).

3. Know ***the time and place of meetings but take advantage of unexpected meetings***. The best is when we can control the entire setting to our advantage, but if we happen to get on an elevator with a decision-maker, we should be prepared for contact (2.3.2 Reaction Unpredictability).

4. ***Ask questions and listen without making assumptions***. We must know the conditions before reacting them. Assuming we know a situation because we know the probabilities is always a mistake. Without the proper information, what we say is as likely to hurt our chances of getting a reward as help it. Conditions that dominate the other person's thinking ***are*** the dominant conditions (6.2.1 Campaign Flow).

5. ***Lead the conversation with questions but respond immediately to what is said***. We can lead with questions but not as as a means of controlling it. We must become the decision maker's partner in the process, making it easy for them to reward us. We use questions as a means of discovering an opening. The key information can come only from the other person (2.6 Knowledge Leverage).

6. ***When we want to make a point, we need feedback to get a reaction***. Others do not necessarily hear what we say. In claim situations, it is totally our job to make sure that we are heard and understood by the other person (2.3 Personal Interactions).

7. ***Focus everything on creating a common cause with the individual***. While we look for awards to satisfy our needs, they are only given if we satisfy the needs of others. Decision makers will never believe that we care about them personally more than we care about ourselves. Decision makers ***can*** believe that we are rewarded only by rewarding them (1.6.1 Shared Mission).

8. ***The pressure on the individual must arise from positioning and the situation not from us personally***. We cannot pressure individuals into making the decisions that we want. Transparent pressure aimed at an individual weakens our positioning, creating suspicion and doubt. The subtle jujitsu demonstrated by our ability

to adapt to their needs while asking them to meet our needs is more powerful (<u>5.1.1 Event Pressure</u>).

Illustration:

The science of one-on-one contact has been advanced primarily in selling and negotiations. In business, we draw a distinction between marketing, which applies to groups, and selling, which happens between individuals. In business, this transition from the general to the specific is easy to see. We market our products and position our companies in a general way to groups of people. All our sales, however, are made to individuals and, when we rely on a sales force, but individuals. Marketing looks to create a competitive advantages in positioning, but that advantage must translate into a specific sale to win an award. The Institute's most popular book, *The Art of War for the Sales Warrior* directly applies every strategic lesson from Sun Tzu to the challenge of individual contact.

Let us illustrate these key methods from the perspective of a salesperson:

1. During individual contact, we must see the situation from the other person's perspective. Most salespeople make the mistake of representing the interests of their company. They should be representing the interests of their prospects as addressed by their company.

2. Prepare before the contact but be prepared to adapt during it. When working on large, long term corporate sales, we can research the decision maker before the sale, but in retail sales, we must work with whoever walks through the door so our preparation must focus on knowing the product.

3. Know the time and place of meetings but take advantage of unexpected meetings. If we can get potential customers to visit us, we can control the environment to make the sale more easily but every good salesperson should have an"elevator pitch"prepared for chance encounters.

4. Ask questions and listen without making assumptions. A good salesperson uses the first step in the sales process, the qualification stage, to search for the customer's "hot buttons" that will determine the decision.

5. Lead the conversation with questions but respond immediately to what is said. A good salesperson realizes that it is better to ask than to tell. We prepare questions that lead the conversation in a way that lets the customer tell us they want and what is good about our product.

6. When we want to make a point, we need feedback to get a reaction. A salesperson provides the information that the customer needs to make a decision but must check to make sure that the provided information answers the customer's questions, both asked and unasked.

7. Focus everything on creating a common cause with the individual. The customer knows that the salesperson is trying to make a sale, but the customer can believe that it is good business to create satisfied customers that come back and bring their friends because it is!

8. The pressure on the individual must arise from positioning and the situation not from us personally. Discount deadlines, company policies, limited amount of stock, and so one should provide the pressure to decide. As a salesperson, we should apologize for that pressure while making customers aware of it as a service to them.

8.5.0 Leveraging Emotions

Sun Tzu's eight key methods describing how we use emotion to obtain rewards.

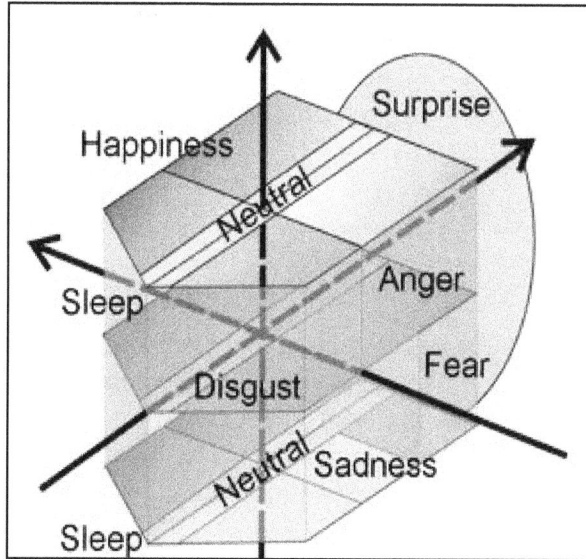

"Offer men safety and they will stay calm.
Endanger them and they will act."

Sun Tzu's The Art of War 5:5:13-14

Let one who wants to move and convince others, first be convinced and moved themselves. If a person speaks with genuine earnestness the thoughts, the emotion and the actual condition of their own heart, others will listen because we all are knit together."

Thomas Carlyle

General Principle: To maximize our rewards, we must leverage the emotion of others.

Situation:

According to Sun Tzu, only emotional energy spurs action. To win rewards, we require action from our supporters. This means that we must trigger emotions in supporters without inflaming the emotions of our opponents. The problem is our own emotions. Uncontrolled, they can either amplify or dampen the emotions of others. Most of us don't think of our emotions as tools to be used. These uncontrolled emotions are as likely to inflame the emotions of our opponents while discouraging the emotions of our supporters. The failure to get rewarded is often the fault of misusing the levers of emotion.

Opportunity:

Our emotions are triggered by actual events and potential events. Actual events trigger happiness or sadness. Potential events trigger hope or fear. Our opportunity to control emotions arises from our understanding of the levers of emotion. These levers include the forces driving change, our control of perceptions, the psychology of groups, and our personal interactions. All of these levers work according to the general principle of complementary opposites. When events go one direction, emotions are amplified or dampened. The perception of potential events is much easier to control than actual events because subjective perceptions of the future are easier to manipulate that physical reality (2.1.2 Leveraging Uncertainty).

Key Methods:

There are eight key methods describing Sun Tzu's principles for using emotion to create action.

1. We must target individuals from whom we want action.
These people are either potential supporters that we want to motivate or opponents who are standing in our way (2.3.1 Action and Reaction)

2. We must identify potential future events that create strong emotions in these people. The most common such emotions are the hope for gain and the fear of loss. Of these two, the fear of loss, known as loss aversion , is stronger (2.4.2 Climate Perspective).

3. Individual emotional appeals can be specific. Emotional appeals to individuals can be focused on very specific actions. They can also be more subtle. They are also effective a higher percentage of the time. However, they require more information on our part (8.4 Individual Support).

4. Group emotional appeals can and should be more aggressive. When dealing with crowds, we can use extreme and broad appeals to emotion. The reaction of the crowd will tend to carry the individual along with it. However, group appeals will be less effective overall and tend to fade quickly. (1.5.2. Group Methods).

5. We must use what is known about the past. The past consists of both trends in a certain direction and of cyclical patterns that repeat themselves. We want to demonstrate a trend that can help or hurt them if they fail to act now (2.6 Knowledge Leverage).

6. We must use what is unknown about the future. The future has many different forms of uncertainty. We must select the ones that work to our advantage to illustrate the dangers of the future. The unknown always creates fear. You want to use the fear of loss if they fail to act (2.1.2 Leveraging Uncertainty).

7. We must take the side of those from whom we want action. We can take the side of both potential supporters and existing opponents. To take their side, we must create an opposing force, an"enemy,"that puts us both on the same side. This enemy can be a person or an impersonal force of nature. Since we are taking their side, we generate emotion by expressing our own emotions (3.2.3 Complementary Opposites).

8. We can argue against the action that we actually prefer. When we take the opposing side, we are using what is known as reverse psychology. Since we are advocating giving us a reward, people know that we are only playing"devil's advocate,"representing the forces that want to deny us a reward. This works because when we push people, they will tend to push back (3.2.5 Dynamic Reversal).

Illustration:

Let us look at how all of these techniques are used to sell the most generic from of value in history, gold. (Full disclosure: as I write this, I have been invested in gold for quite some time, but I recently cut my position in half because of the amount of advertising out there).

1. We must target individuals from whom we want action. If we are running advertisement to sell gold, we run it on stations where people have money (Fox News, talk radio) not the stations where they don't (MTV, teeny-bop radio).

2. We must identify potential future events that create strong emotions in these people. Pitches for gold are based on economic uncertainty, specifically using the fear that people have of another stock market crash and inflation.

3. Individual emotional appeals can be specific. A financial consultant can get into an individual's specific worries based on their history in a way that a television commercial cannot.

4. Group emotional appeals can and should be more aggressive. Television commercials can be much louder, more aggressive, and broader in their claims. A financial consultant would lose credibility if he or she adopted a similar tone in real life.

5. We must use what is known about the past."Gold has tripled in value over the last ten years."

6. We must use what is unknown about the future."Experts predict that we could see it double and double again in the near future."

7. We must take the side of those from whom we want action."I have invested in gold and you should too."

8. We can argue against the action that we actually prefer."Investing in gold is not right for everyone."

On this last point, I am reminded of a good friend and salesperson, Keith Westphal, who would always challenge people about whether or not they could afford to make a given purchase. While qualification is part of the beginning of the sales process, to understand what a customer can afford, he would also use it at the end. When a customer would hesitate to make a decision at the end of the process, he would be sympathetic,"Though we both know this is what you want and need, many customers really cannot afford to make this investment and that is nothing to be embarrassed about."Challenged in this way, people would often make the purchase just to prove him wrong about their finances.

8.6.0 Winning Attention

Sun Tzu's eight key methods describing how to win the attention of others for our claims.

"You can speak, but you will not be heard.
You must use gongs and drums."

Sun Tzu's The Art of War 7:4:2-3

"Every interview is about showmanship. Every person who walks into an interview is operating at a level of showmanship. The only question is whether you are aware of it and whether you follow the principles of good showmanship."

Alan Fox

General Principle: Win the attention of others to get rewarded for claims.

Situation:

In today's increasingly crowded environment, more and more people are competing for attention. We need people to recognize us in order to reward us. We must get people's attention before we can get their support. If people are unaware of us, they cannot support us. People hear only what they want to hear. It requires work to get people to hear our claims. We must compete in an environment full of claims. This makes getting attention when we need it that much more difficult. Getting time with people is hard enough, but making an impression is even harder.

Opportunity:

The chaos of crowded, dynamic environments creates the desire for clarity and simplicity. Our opportunity arises from the nature of complementary opposites. No matter how crowded our environment is, there are always openings because there are always needs (3.1.4 Openings). As conditions change, we must continually adjust our communication to contrast it with conditions. In noisy environments, we speak quietly to get attention. In rooms that are "dead," we speak loudly and ask people to make noise to liven the situation up. In the dark, we use light. In the light, we use shadow. Any method of communication gets old and tired if it goes on too long. We have to change things up to keep it interesting.

Key Methods:

There are eight key methods describing Sun Tzu's principles for getting attention.

1. We win people's attention with change. When our positions are so new that they are unknown, we must excite curiosity and interest in others. If our positions are better known and taken for granted, we must accentuate the changes by making them entertaining. The message must suit changing conditions either by leveraging the change or playing against it (4.8 Climate Support).

2. We win people's attention by stimulating the senses. This means developing pictures, props, and gimmicks to get people's attention. Visual communication is more powerful than words. Movement is more interesting than stability. Strategy often requires a good dose of showmanship and magic. However, we cannot get a decision regarding a reward out of chaos. Showmanship in strategy has its own special principles (2.3.3 Likely Reactions).

3. To get attention, we must first clear people's minds. Our first job is to clear people's minds. People have a lot on their minds. While their minds are cluttered, their resistance to new information is high. We must jolt them strongly enough to draw their attention. Then their resistance fades. People want to be entertained and stimulated but we cannot do this if they are distracted by what is in their heads (2.1.4 Surprise).

4. To get attention, we must give people a focus point for their self interest. We must tailor all messages to individual self-interest. If we want to win people's attention. We must tie our contract together into a single whole. Each idea must lead back to a central point. The central point must address the changing nature of our needs. We must not offer novel concepts alone. We must tie them together with comfortable, familiar ideas. Every reason to make the decision we want must amplify a single, clear message about our shared mission (1.6.1 Shared Mission).

5. To get attention, our focus points must offer simplicity. We must send everyone a consistent message. We must keep any presentation organized so that we don't frustrate our listeners. If people get nervous or frustrated, we hold their attention. We must describe our position simply so everyone can understand and appreciate it. Subtleties are important in education, but when we are asking for a decision, they are confusing. We must offer our ideas and proposals in ways that the decisionmakers enjoy. The work we put into our presentation illustrates our desire to offer something valuable to our supporters (2.1.1 Information Limits).

6. To get attention, we must make systems and processes entertaining and memorable. We must provide mental models and analogies that clarify our ideas while making them entertaining. Memorable communication requires a touch of drama. Most changes in position are not dramatic in themselves. We can dramatize a new position and its value by creating a visual symbol for the change. Pictures, trophies, and other signs of change are remembered (2.2.2 Mental Models).

7. To get attention, we must make balance out the situation. We play it up when we are ignored, and play it down when we are hyped. We surprise people when we can be enthusiastic about the barriers to deciding. Friendliness, enthusiasm, and patience wear down any resistance. We are successful in getting rewarded if we focus on the needs of others (3.2.3 Complementary Opposites).

8. To get attention, we must wait for a response. When we ask for a decision regarding a reward, we must wait for the decision-maker to respond. If the reward is coming to us naturally, we must do nothing that gets in its way.We must stay friendly no matter what their initial answer. Decision-makers must offer objections to test the strength of our position (4.2 Choosing Non-Action).

Illustration:

Here, we should look at the master for getting attention in the media, Apple, especially since this is written on the day before the release of the iPad.

1. We win people's attention with change. Apple has a tradition of releasing only game changing products, products that not only do new things but are new things. Its started with the Apple computer, then the Mac, and continued with the the iPod, followed by the iPhone. Even its failure, like the Newton, attempted to be something new and different.

2. We win people's attention by stimulating the senses. Apple is a design company. It seeks to seduce the eyes and the other senses. It offers far and away the most sensual products, which is why it has done so well.

3. To get attention, we must first clear people's minds. The iPad isn't a new laptop. It seeks to replace the laptop in our thinking. Even before it was announced, the mystery was used to create an open space for something new to appear.

4. To get attention, we must give people a focus point for their self interest. Apple does this in a variety of ways, but the most interesting is the way the product appeals to ego and status. Apple customers gladly pay hundreds more for the first versions of new product simply so they can be the first to get attention from their friends and associates.

5. To get attention, our focus points must offer simplicity. All of Apple's designs are minimalistic, eliminating buttons and controls and, to a large degree, having to think about how things works. Some attack Apple for making simplicity so central to is product design.

6. To get attention, we must make systems and processes entertaining and memorable. Apple's product releases leverage the genius of others to promote its products, garnering appearances on Letterman and Colbert.

7. To get attention, we must make balance out the situation. Apple starts with secrecy, puts out a lot of information, and then goes back to that secrecy as people consume the available information and grow hungry for more. Apple always leaves questions that grow more important over time until it does its next product announcement.

8. To get attention, we must wait for a response. In Apple's case, this response is initially the consumption and growing hunger for more information. This is followed by the product release, which is always less than meets demand. Every step in the promotion cycle is designed to create desire rather than satisfaction.

8.7.0 Productivity Improvement

Sun Tzu's seven key methods for improving internal production to harvest rewards to support external competition.

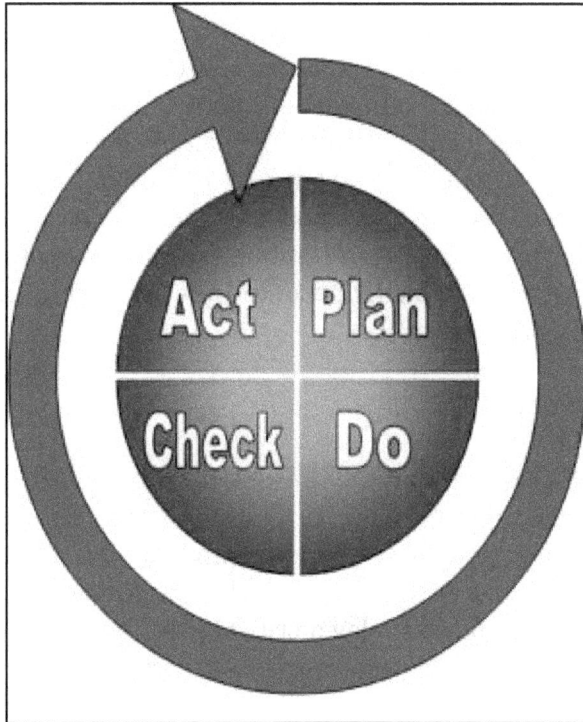

"You must master command.
The nation must support you."

Sun Tzu's The Art of War 3:4:1-2

"Without continual growth and progress, such words as improvement, achievement, and success have no meaning."

Benjamin Franklin

General Principle: We must continuously improve our control over our positions to give us more competitive resources.

Situation:

Our strategic positions have both an inside and an outside. The outside is the surface where our position makes contact with the competitive environment, the realm of strategy. The inside is our span of control, the realm of planning. Through planning and organization, we are able to improve our internal systems and make ourselves more productive within our span of control. The problem is that internal systems take on a life of their own. This problem only gets worse when strategic positions are successful, growing and expanding over time. As a position grows into an organization, its internal systems gradually become more and more isolated from the external environment.

Opportunity:

The easiest way to get more rewards from any existing position is to continually improve our control over it. Planning and organization can dramatically improve the productivity of a position over time. Since our only strategic goal is improving our position, the methods of production play a critical place in good strategy. The practice of continual improvement in particular has much in common with the adaptive loop of strategy (1.8.2 The Adaptive Loop). The differences between the two, however, are critical. Our opportunity is in understanding the differences between these two different loops and, most importantly, the feedback between them.

Key Methods:

The following seven key methods describe the continuous process by which we improve internal productivity.

1. Like competitive progress, productivity improvement is a loop. There are many different forms of the continuous improvement loop but we will discuss the general concept in terms of

Deming's PDCA cycle. This loop was popularized by the quality movement of the 1980's and is one of the best documented versions of the process. The PDCA loop intersects with the Progress Cycle of Listen->Aim->Move->Claim. The beginning and end of its loop start and end with our competitive mission. Its other steps reflect the steps of the Progress Cycle in interesting ways (1.8 Progress Cycle).

2. The productivity loop starts with a design step creating a specification of expected output. In Deming's terms, this is the *plan* stage. In the competitive loop, a general arises from our external mission, which is the core of a the progress cycle. In production, the more specific our goals, the better our internal control (1.9.2 Span of Control).

3. The productivity loop continues with the implementation of the new processes on as small a scale as possible. In Deming's cycle, this is the *do* stage. It is similar to the *move* step in the Progress Cycle and reflects many of its values, including minimizing mistakes by testing ideas in a small way. (5.4 Minimizing Action).

4. The productivity loop then measures the results of new processes against specification. Deming called this the *check* stage. In the process cycle, measurement and comparison comes at the end of the cycle, in the *claim* stage. Both steps compare the previous situation with the new one to determine the success of the change (1.3.1 Competitive Comparison).

5. The productivity loop ends with an analysis to determine any causes for failure. In Deming, this is the *act* stage. Since production processes are linear systems , the causes of problems can be identified by reductionism, breaking a system into its parts. This is the opposite from the way that we loop for opportunities in the *listen* and *aim* stage of the progress cycle, which requires us seeing the big picture (2.5 The Big Picture).

6. By using this productivity loop, we gradually improve the controlled processes through which we create products that we expect to have external value. Through the loop, we learn to eliminate efforts that do not contribute to the process. We learn to do less and less to produce more and more. These process create the additional resources we need in competition with others, since competition is always constrained by resources. (3.1.1 Resource Limitations).

7. The productivity loop relies upon the competitive loop to provide external feedback. In the end, the continuous improvement of production must be measured against external positioning. The PDCA only measures the efficiency of the internal system, but the internal system can only make products. The value of those products can only be measured externally. If we are not guided by external measure, we can fall into the trap of very efficient production that creates no real value. The most efficient internal process in the world are meaningless if their product is not valued outside the system itself (1.4 The External Environment).

Illustration:

We can illustrate these ideas with examples from business, but in all of these examples, we go back to the final rule, connecting internal production to external competition, since this is where this loop goes wrong.

1. Like competitive progress, productivity improvement is a loop. American car companies have all dramatically improved their internal processes over the last twenty years but that hasn't helped them economically. Their internal organization became more and more isolated from the external market. Since they simply improved the systems that produced cars that people didn't want to buy, they ended up going bankrupt.

2. The productivity loop starts with a design step creating a specification of expected output. The product specified must be one people want. Today's leader in retail, Wal-Mart, has developed an extraordinarily efficient distribution system in the pursuit of low prices, low prices alone do not determine value. Retailers have to offer what people want. The previous retail leader in low-prices, KMart, went out of business because nobody wanted what they sold. Retail history is strewn with bankruptcies as leading retailers end up selling the wrong products for the wrong reasons.

3. The productivity loop continues with the implementation of the new processes on as small a scale as possible. You can see the difference in the scale of internal testing by comparing manufacturing cars with selling retail products. Test of distribution for any product can be performed on a very small, affordable scale. In manufactuing, we can safely make small changes to improve the production of an existing car, but the creation of a new car requires a substantial investment even at the smallest scale. Yet it is the new car rather than the existing one that requires external testing to verify its value.

4. The productivity loop then measures the results of new processes against specification. Whether you are manufacturing a car or selling retail products, there is a difference between an internal test of process and an external test of value. A manufacturing or distribution test, only tests the internal efficiency of the process.

5. The productivity loop ends with an analysis to determine any causes for failure. Plans for manufacturing and distribution that work on paper often do not work in reality. This is true even for the controlled environment of the factory or the distribution system. However, because information is both more available and less dynamic in a controlled environment, we can get a fix on causes and control them.

6. The productivity loop relies upon the competitive loop to provide external feedback. In business, the control of the internal by the external is called"market discipline."Continuous improvement has dramatically improve the quality of products and the efficiency of production processes for everyone as more people master these methods. But while more efficient production makes us more competitive, competitive success requires more than improving production methods.

7. By using this productivity loop, we gradually improve the controlled processes through which we create products that we expect to have external value. Let us end with an illustration that is not from business, but from our personal relationships. We can continually improve our relationships by working on improving ourselves through this productivity loop. For example, we can work at eliminating our bad habits. However, the more we focus on ourselves in our relationships, the less happy the relationship as a whole can be. Relationships produce value but unlike making products, there is no such thing as a more efficient personal relationship.

8.7.1 Position Erosion

Sun Tzu's eight key methods for gauging the erosion of our current positions.

"Positions turn around.
Nevertheless, you must never be defeated."

Sun Tzu's The Art of War 5:4:5-6

"I know of no more encouraging fact than the
unquestioning ability of man to evaluate his life by a
conscious endeavor."

Henry David Thoreau

General Principle: We must continuously improve our control over our positions to give us more competitive resources.

Situation:

Positions erode slowly. It is easy to take our positions for granted. We tend to over-value exiting positions as they decline over time. We base our judgments upon the past. We find it difficult to see a gradual decline. We defend an existing position simply because it is ours. As a position declines, we continue to investing in its maintenance even when it is no longer returning meaningful rewards. Past success doesn't mean future success, but the more successful a position has been in the past, the more we tend to invest in it whether those investment pay off or not.

Opportunity:

We must always have new goals. No matter how far we progress in life, we can envision a better position. Few of us are so comfortable that we do not desire more. At the very least, all of us desire to hold onto what we have. Positions can improve automatically if the climate improves even if the tendency is for them to degrade over time. All positions have advantages and disadvantages. We use the advantages of our position to reap its rewards. Our current balance of costs and rewards provides a valuable tool for evaluating whether we can maintain our position or if we must advance it.

Key Methods:

The following eight key methods explain how we recognize when our position is eroding.

*1. If we do nothing to improve our position, we should expect it to degrade over tim*e. Though improving conditions can automatically improve our position, the typical situation is that a static position is increasingly inappropriate to conditions (1.1.1 Position Dynamics).

2. If our position seems static, we should assume it is declining. Many changes in conditions that erode a position happen below the surface. A situation that looks static is probably declining without our seeing it (1.1.2 Defending Positions).

3. All progress in developing an existing position reaches a point of diminishing returns. When we work to continuously improve our existing position, we will reap more rewards. This means that we have to continually re-evaluate every part of our position (8.7 Productivity Improvement).

4. To evaluate the erosion of our position, we must use an objective form of measurement. If easily measured rewards (such as money) are not available, use the positive event/investment event measurement system (8.3.1 Gauging Value).

5. To evaluate the erosion of our position, we must track investments in maintaining or improving it over time. Physically recorded measurements are more reliable than mentally recorded ones, but not always practical. Minimally, we should have an idea of frequency of investment (1.8.3 Cycle Time).

6. To evaluate the erosion of our position, we must track its rewards over time. Physical measurements are better but the frequency of rewards is an easier and more universal measure (8.1.3 Reward Timing).

7. To evaluate the erosion of our position, we must know the trend of an existing position. If our position is improving or declining, we should know it. We should also have a sense for how quickly it is improving and declining and the change in relationship between investment and rewards (1.3.1 Competitive Comparison).

8. As our position is declining, the urgency of advancing it increases. We need to work to find new opportunities to change the trend. (3.0 Identifying Opportunities.

Illustration:

These key methods are interesting because they apply to every aspect of our lives.

1. If we do nothing to improve our position, we should expect it to degrade over time. Our lives are made of many different positions: positions in relationships, positions at our work, positions in our health, etc.

2. If our position seems static, we should assume it is declining. If our careers, our romantic relationships, oru health, and so on seem static, they are really getting worse without our recognizing it.

3. All progress in developing an existing position reaches a point of diminishing returns. In selling, we should known if we are making progress or losing ground with each prospect, even before there are sales to record. We should track our positive calls versus no progress calls both for each prospect and for our sales day as a whole. A positive increase in this trend shows we are improving our position when we have no other measure.

4. To evaluate the erosion of our position, we must use an objective form of measurement. Perhaps the hardest positions to evaluate are our personal ones. In our relationships, we should known if we are making progress or losing ground in each of our important sales relationships. We should have a sense of our number of enjoyable shared experiences over time so we know when our relationships are being kept alive or not. A positive increase in this trend shows we are improving our relationships.

5. To evaluate the erosion of our position, we must track investments in maintaining or improving it over time. In our health, we should known if we are making progress or losing ground in our investment in our physical condition. When we are younger, we take our health for granted,

6. maintaining it without seeming to have to make an investment. Our weight is a useful generic measure of health, but the frequency and length of our exercise is important. As we gradually become less physically active in our daily lives, we must replace that activity with purposeful exercise, increasing it rather than decreasing it as we get older.

7. To evaluate the erosion of our position, we must track its rewards over time. We should have an idea of the direction of all of these positions over time. Reward in business or selling are easily measured in dollars. Rewards in relationships and health are harder to track but even more real. Even as we age, our health can become more robust if we stop taking health for granted and start working on our health daily. Our relationships can grow deeper over time, but again, only if we work at them.

8. *To evaluate the erosion of our position, we must know the trend of an existing position*. All well-run businesses have income statements that compare their current sales and expenses to the past so they can see the trend. This idea simply expands this same concept of accounting to a wider variety of situations.

9. *As our position is declining, the urgency of advancing it increases*. When we grow stagnant, we must look more intensely for new areas in which to advance in both our professional and personal lives.

8.7.2 Abandoning Positions

Sun Tzu's six key methods describing how we abandon a losing position safely.

*"If you are defeated, you can recover.
You must use the four seasons correctly."*
Sun Tzu's The Art of War 5:2:9-10

"Come on, come on and there'll be no turning back. You were only killing time and it'll kill you right back."
Jim Steinem's"Out Of The Frying Pan (And Into The Fire)"

General Principle: We must establish new positions quickly but leave existing position as slowly as possible.

Situation:

More frequently than we would like, we must abandon a losing position. Abadoning a position is difficult because our strategic position gives us all our resources. A losing position is not just a position that costs more to win than it is worth. It is any position that costs more to maintain that it is worth. It must be abandoned, but, as is so often the case, the biggest danger in abandoning a losing position is overreacting. A bad situation can always be made worse by not handling it correctly. When we are in a losing position, it is all too easy to jump out of the frying pan and into the fire.

Opportunity:

The need to abandon a bad position must be viewed as an opportunity. The worse a position is, the more easily it can be improved. When we hit bottom, every direction is up. Though we cannot magically turn a bad position into a great position overnight, we can safely abandon losing positions for better ones if we know the secrets. We must minimize our mistakes (5.0 Minimizing Mistakes). We can then find a way out by using the uncertainty of the environment (5.2.1 Choosing Adaptability), the inevitable up and down cycles of conditions (1.4.1 Climate Shift) and the natural balance of strength and weakness (3.5 Strength and Weakness).

Key Methods:

The following six key methods describe what we must do to abandon a failing position safely.

1. To abandon a losing position, we must first focus on the big picture. We must understand the conditions surrounding our position. We must understand the surrounding conditions to find the direction in which we can move the most safely (2.5 The Big Picture).

2. To abandon a losing position, we must keep our move a secret by avoiding meeting opponents. We never want to meet opposition when we are in a losing position. If opponents know we are in a losing position, they will come after us, so we must keep our situation a secret, even from our contact network (2.7 Information Secrecy).

3. To abandon a losing position, we must consider its holding power. Even a losing situation can temporarily be better than the alternatives. Moving from a position has its own costs. These costs are associated by what we call the"holding power"of the position. The extremes of holding power are"sticky"and"slippery"positions. Sticky positions cannot be abandoned without preparing to pass through an even worse position. Slippery one positions are disastrous if we leave them in the wrong direction. Before we move, we must know how to handle these problems of holding power correctly (4.5.3 Surface Holding Power).

4. To abandon a losing position, we must determine the nature of climate shift. There is a difference between being in the down part of a cycle and in a long-term downward trend. A cycle will return, at least temporarily. If we are in a cycle, we should move when the cycle improves, temporarily giving us more resources. If we are in a trend, we must find a way to get on the opposite side of that trend as quickly as possible, using the methods of reversal (3.2.5 Dynamic Reversal).

5. To abandon a losing position, we must find what is the most valuable in our knowledge about our position. The issue is always how we can get the most value out of a position. The primary value of every position is the knowledge that it gives us. Our position's unique perspective can give us insight that can be valuable to others. Experience from a losing position can create value simply by helping others avoid similar mistakes (1.6.1 Shared Mission).

6. To abandon a losing position, we must establish alternative positions quickly but leave the existing position as slowly as we can afford. The general rule is that it is best to take new positions quickly but leave existing position slowly. We cannot afford to panic in any case, but the speed with which we move must be determined by whether position is suffering from a slow bleed or from a gushing artery. (5.6 Defensive Advances)

Illustration:

Let us illustrate these principles drawing from many different competitive arenas

1. To abandon a losing position, we must first focus on the big picture. If we are having problems in our career, we must determine whether the source of the problem is our company, our industry, our profession, or in ourselves.

2. To abandon a losing position, we must keep our move a secret by avoiding meeting opponents. If we find out our company is on the verge of laying people off, we must keep that a secret from everyone else at work or else we will compete with them in our job search.

3. To abandon a losing position, we must consider its holding power. A marketing agreement can prove to be costly, but abandoning that agreement can even be more costly if it generates lawsuits and makes future marketing agreement with anyone less likely.

4. To abandon a losing position, we must determine the nature of climate shift. If we are out of work as a computer programmer in today's market, we do not have to find a new career. If we are out of work as a assembly line worker, we do.

5. To abandon a losing position, we must find what is the most valuable in our knowledge about our position. If we get into trouble borrowing money, there is value in our knowledge in helping others avoid that problem.

6. To abandon a losing position, we must establish alternative positions quickly but leave the existing position as slowly as we can afford. Like rock climbing, we cling to our current hold until we are certain of our next hold, but if our current hold is crumbling , we may have to trust to fate and jump.

Sun Tzu's Playbook

Volume 9:
Vulnerabilities

About Vulnerabilities

After you have proven that your advanced position pays, you need to defend that position. Until you secure its safety, you have not finished advancing your position. New positions are fragile. Competitors are quick to copy successes. You must protect the key resources on which your new position depends. This is the topic of this final volume of Sun Tzu's Playbook.

Sun Tzu's principles concerning the vulnerabilities covered in this volume are ambiguous. They can be read as a guide to protecting a position or attacking it. To Sun Tzu, attacking and defending are two sides of the same process. You cannot do one without understanding the other.

In this volume, we look at these issues mostly from the point of view of defense, simply because so many other parts of Sun Tzu's methods focus on advancing a position. The perspective teaches you to recognize when you are vulnerable. It teaches you to prepare for the most common forms of attack. When you have a dominant position, you cannot leave openings through which opponents can undermine you. Most attacks are harmless if you respond appropriately, and that is why you must master this final formula.

The final line of defense is protecting yourself from direct attacks that are invited by your areas of vulnerability, the focus of this chapter. These vulnerabilities arise out of the fact that the climate is always changing, creating potential openings for rivals. We can categorize these types of vulnerabilities as *climate vulnerabilities* because they arise from changes in the environment. Those who might use these vulnerabilities against us are called *climate rivals.* We refer to the use of these vulnerabilities against us as *climate attacks.*

Success Is Always a Target

You must defend any new, successful position against competitors. Success invites competition. Success invites imitation. Success invites attack. All these principles factor in this fact of human nature.

Fortunately, it is easier to defend an established position than it is to build it. As long as you don't take your new position for granted, the techniques of defending a position are relatively easy. Defense is easier and more certain than advance.

Your first line of defense is pursuing opportunities that are easy to defend. This is the focus of Volume Four of the Playbook. Your second line of defense is responding to competitive situations correctly. This is the focus of Volume Six.

The Five Targets

The first principles discussed in this volume relate to defending the resources on which your current position depends. Sun Tzu teaches the positions depend on five resources: individual supports, short-term assets, logistical resources, long-term assets, and organizational relationships. There are five targets in a changing environment that competitors will target as vulnerabilities.

1. First, they will try to win away your supporters. These are personnel risks.

2. Second, they will try to win away the resources you need for short-term survival. These are immediate resource risks.

3. Third, they will try to disrupt your systems of transportation and communication. These are logistical risks.

4. Fourth, they will try to devalue the long-term investments that you have made. These are your asset risks.

5. Finally, they will try to undermine your working relationships with others. These are your organizational risks.

You have to defend all five targets. For these attacks to succeed, you must leave opponents an opening. If you fill the opening opponents target, you can block their duplication of the work you have pioneered.

It takes time for rivals to target these vulnerabilities. You must be standing still for them to catch you. Your first defense is to stay ahead of others, upgrading these assets and systems before they can be used against you.

The environment must make targeting your different types of resources easy for them. When the environment is changing quickly, you cannot always adapt as swiftly as you need to. This offers competitors a target. Do not invest in moving to new positions unless the resources on which your current position depends are secure.

You also need to keep an eye on how change is affecting your rivals. If change is making their current position untenable, they may attempt desperate measures to undermine you position. You must make sure that none of your resources offer a tempting target.

You can know when you are susceptible to climate attacks by studying the signs in your environment. You must act to cut off these attacks before they get started. If you do nothing, you are inviting these attacks.

Protect Your Relationships

The next few principles in this chapter relate to protecting relationships during times of crisis. During a climate that encourage attacks, your relationships with others are the key to meeting these attacks. You must make it difficult for competitors to undermine your key relationships. Using changing conditions to shift allegiance is the quickest way for competitors to undermine your success. The easiest way to defeat this threat is to use your relationships well.

You must win the support of others. Do not overburden these relationships. People maintain their past relationships unless given a reason to change. If you care about your relationships and keep the working with you enjoyable, people will want to stay with you if they possibly can.

Keep engaged in your relationships. You don't want lose valuable connections because they are taken for granted. Share the challenges you face with others and ask for their advice. Ask how you can work together more closely. Treat the people with whom you work like a family and treat your family better in the future than you have in the past. Your people must see that you are committed to your relationships. People judge how you will treat them by how they see you treat others.

In good times, share your success with others. Everyone should benefit from their connections with you.

In bad times, people should know that they can depend on you. They should see that you honor your commitments, even when difficulties arise.

People get nervous in times of change. You must demonstrate your confidence in the future. Supporters must respect your expertise as a leader. Sometimes, this requires confidence and detachment. You must care about your relationships, but you must not turn any relationship into a burden.

You must control what your supporters see and hear. They must believe in you without your explaining your reasoning. You can reinvent your relationships. You must be able change the enterprise's direction.

Five Forms of Attack Defense

Next, this volume looks at various forms of climate attack and how we defend against them. During times of change, everyone tries to think more competitively, that is, they start comparing their alternatives. You must prepare for five different types of competitive challenges. You must know how to adapt to them to secure your current position.

First, competitors will try a direct attack. They will want to undermine your mission at the core of your position. This requires a defense against division.

Second, competitors will an indirect attack, trying to panic those who support you. They may launch this attack through the media or through the court system. This requires a panic defense that requires that you remain calm and avoid overreaction.

Third, competitors will try an attack using openings you create. You will make mistakes. They will try to use them to undermine your position. These requires knowing how to defend openings and make things right when situations go wrong.

Fourth, competitors will try an attack to win your partners. This requires knowing how to defend alliances.

Finally, your competitors will find a tipping point to undermine your position's dynamics. This requires knowing how to defend your position's balance.

You must recognize these five forms of competitive attack. You must actively protect your positions against them. You must recognize and respond to them immediately as you do to different campaign situations.

Climate attacks are more dangerous than normal changes in the climate. Changes in the climate can undermine your position. Changes in the climate can force you to adjust your relationships. Climate attacks are different. These attacks can destroy your position completely if you do not understand the principles for response.

Do Not Overreact

The final principles in this chapter balance the dangers of climate vulnerabilities against their benefits. As we said in the beginning, these vulnerabilities are a double-edged sword. Yes, they can be used against you, but you can also use them against your opponents. To do so, however, you must understand the dangers.

Climate is the elements of emotion. During times of change, emotions run high. To balance this, these are the times when it is most important to maintain a cool head. You must not overreact to climate shifts or the attacks they make possible. Avoid letting change become an emotional issue. Your feelings about your competitors must not confuse you. Stay focused on your position.

You must respond to the situation, not to the emotion. You must defend your position, not hurt your competitors. In the long run, you beat the competition by finding new openings to advance your position. When your position is secure, you must focus on the next opportunity. Your success demands continual progress. You want to devote your mind to improving your business, not to hurting competitors. Your best defense against competitors is utilizing every opening they give you.

To be successful, you must not change your position simply to create problems for competitors. Make problems for rivals only when it helps you to do so. If there is no profit in hurting your opponents, you cannot afford to act against them. One of Sun Tzu's most basic principlesis tht you can destroy your own position in fighting your opponents.

No matter how many competitors you destroy, you will always have new competitors. If you weaken your business destroying a competitor, it is just a matter of time until the next competitor destroys you. You want to hurt competitors only when it pays to do so. You want to weaken them only when that action makes you stronger in the market as a whole. You must avoid taking actions that weaken you along with your competitors.

Any attack can be a problem, but it can also be an opportunity. You must look at every attack dispassionately, seeing whether you can turn it to your advantage. For every attack that hurts you, there will be another attack that helps you. Only your competitors can create opportunities for you.

Final Thoughts on Defending Vulnerabilities

Truly dominating positions make attacks extremely difficult. If you pick the right opportunities and build up the right positions, you can prevent competitors from even thinking about challenging you.

Competitors follow the path of least resistance. If you make what you do look difficult, they will be much less likely to copy you. It is worth the time to control appearances.

It is always easier to defend than attack. If you establish a position first, it will always be more profitable for you to defend it than it will be for competitors to attack it.

9.0.0 Understanding Vulnerability

Sun Tu's six key methods regarding the use of common environmental attacks.

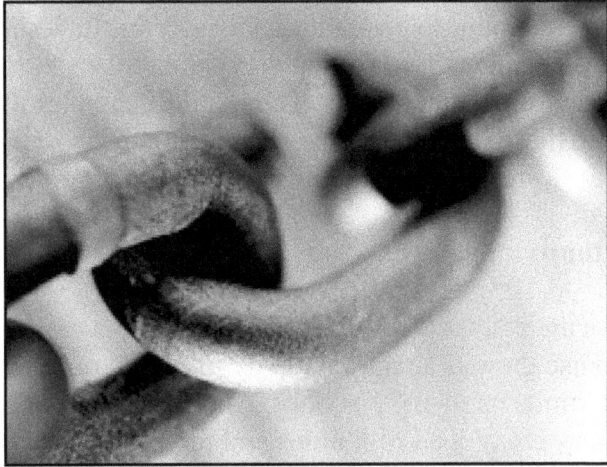

"Everyone attacks with fire."
Sun Tzu's The Art of War 13:2:1

*"There can be no vulnerability without risk; there can
be no community without vulnerability; there can be no
peace, and ultimately no life, without community."*
M. Scott Peck

General Principle: We must know the five targets and five types of environmental attacks.

Situation:

This article introduces the ninth and final section of The Playbook. It covers vulnerability to environmental crises that Sun Tzu called "fire attacks." Established positions have a degree of natural security from opponents, but positions are always vulnerable to conditions in the environment. When conditions are right, opponents can use the environment as a weapon against us. In Sun Tzu's The Art of War, fire attacks were a loophole in the rule that damaging opponents is too costly to long-term success. These environmental attacks damage opponents without the risks or costs of direct conflict. In our modern world, rivals use the government, the media, or special interest groups to create these fire storms. Law suits, government investigations, and bad publicity are today's form of fire attacks or environmental attacks. Though the examples we see on the news are those directed at large organizations, most environmental attacks are directed at individuals and small organizations.

Opportunity:

Once we understand the principles of environmental vulnerability, we can use these principles not only to defend our own position, but to undermine opposing positions. All environmental attacks are attacks by proxy. The conditions and forces in the environment do the work. An opponent's role is limited only to sparking that attack, usually in a hidden way working behind the scenes. Our first concern is with defending our position against these vulnerabilities (5.6.1 Defense Priority). This knowledge also has its offensive use. The general rule here is that we must do so only to advance our own position, not simply destroy the position of another.

Key Methods:

To use the environment against an opponent, the conditions must be right.

1. The conditions for these environmental attacks depend on changes in climate to create needed fuel. This fuel in the environment is consumed to power these attacks. If we are not using environmental forces for destructive attacks, we are in a war of attrition, which means we are using our own resources and not those in the environment. This is costly and must be avoided. We cannot create these environment conditions only trigger and use them when they exist Attacks-by-proxy are not always possible. Positions must be susceptible to them. This is largely a matter of climate. Popular figures are impossible to attack. Unpopular figures are easily attacked. These attacks some times work best as attacks against individuals, other times, against faceless organizations, and still at other times, against new projects (9.1 Climate Vulnerability).

2. There are five points at which a position is vulnerable to environmental attacks. If we recognize these five targets, we can see when they are vulnerable. This recognition can be used to either defend our own position or attack our opponents (9.2 Points of Vulnerability).

3. Environmental attacks are primarily a test of leadership skills. Defense against these attacks are the single greatest test of leadership. One constant rule for defense is that we cannot panic. Overreaction usually causes more damage than the attack itself. Our decisions and reactions in these situations determine whether we maintain support for our position or create openings for our opponents *(9.3 Crisis Leadership)*.

4. We must know how to defend against five types of environmental attacks. Their nature determines how we must defend against them. These details will be the topics of future articles. Different types of environmental attacks follow different courses of events, but these attacks can all be defended. Some of these attacks can even be turned against opponents that instigate them (9.4 Crisis Defense).

5. We can use environmental attacks against others only if we understand the techniques and their dangers. We must not use these opportunities to damage the positions of others simply because we can. The goal of strategy is always to improve our own position. Simply hurting others is a waste of resources. Environmental attacks can be a dangerous two-edge sword. They can be turned against us. Most importantly, today's rivals can be tomorrow's allies (9.5 Crisis Exploitation).

6. Defending a position requires constantly monitoring our environment for vulnerabilities. Though the world is constantly changing, we are often blind to change. Both opportunities and vulnerabilities can be difficult to see. The direction of our position is much easier to see if we continually compare it to the past using the right yardsticks (9.6 t Vigilance).

Illustration:

These attacks are growing more common in today's world. Politicians, lawyers, media people, and grievance hustlers of all types have promoted this form of competitive attack. Though these groups and people are working to advance their own positions, their self-interest must be hidden. For the modern attack-by-proxy to work, the attack must be positioned for the good of society and the public. Let us look at how these attacks are used against businesses by their competitors.

1. The conditions for these environmental attacks depend on changes in climate to create the needed fuel. There is only so much public outrage. The public eventually gets bored with an issue such as global warming and moves on to some fresh outrage. Once the public moves on, the politicians, lawyers, and the rest do was well. In an anti-business climate, businesses become susceptible. In an anti-military climate, the military becomes susceptible. In a anti-politician climate, politicians are susceptible. The first rule of defense against attacks-by-proxy is keeping in touch with the social climate.

2. There are five points at which a position is vulnerable to environmental attacks. Sometimes, these attacks work against individuals, other times, against large organizations, and still at other times, against new projects whose forms of change can be made to seem threatening.

3. Environmental attacks are primarily a test of leadership skills. In the modern era, the phrase, "it wasn't the crime but the cover-up," is a common form of over-reaction.

4. We must know how to defend against five types of environmental attacks. A direct attack on core values, such as an attack on the profit incentive for large corporations, must defended differently than an attack that demonizes an individual.

5. We can use environmental attacks against others only if we understand the dangers. Sun Microsystems instigated a series of antitrust actions against Microsoft via California politicians, but they forced Microsoft to get more involved in politics and, in the end, it was Sun that was acquired by a software company, Oracle systems.

6. Defending a position requires constantly monitoring our environment for vulnerabilities. In business, we must constantly be aware of how the motivations of others in the environment are changing. Politicians, lawyers, and the media constantly need fresh meat for their grinders. We must constantly shift our position to avoid becoming their targets.

9.1.0 Fire Storm Vulnerability

Sun Tzu's seven key methods describing our vulnerability to environmental crises.

"To attack with fire, you must be in the right season. To start a fire, you must have the time."
Sun Tzu's The Art of War 13:2:1

"When we were children, we used to think that when we were grown-up we would no longer be vulnerable. But to grow up is to accept vulnerability... To be alive is to be vulnerable."
Madeleine L'Engle

General Principle: Changes in climate create vulnerability to a crisis.

Situation:

Vulnerability describes an opening created by the climate, the temporary conditions in our environment that endanger our position. Vulnerability arises specifically from our position's dependence on our environment. We depend on our environment for our resources. Vulnerabilities weaken our ability to control our resources. Just as our environment contains resources, it also contains threats to those resources. These threats are the potential fuel for the problems, called fire storms, that can erupt and endanger our position. We use the term *fire storm* to connect to connect the concept of a climate crisis to Sun Tzu's original discussions of fire as a weapon.

Opportunity:

Temporary conditions are always changing. Some of these changes create the conditions in which fire storms can erupt (1.3.1 Competitive Comparison. Our opportunity is in seeing when changing climate creates the fuel for fire storms. Those who see where positions are vulnerable can know how to use conditions for defense or attack (9.1 Climate Vulnerability). If we know where these vulnerabilities lie, we lessen our risk to such threats and can leverage them against our opponents.

Key Methods:

The following key methods explain how fire storms arise and create vulnerability.

1. A fire storm requires a spark. Changes in climate create the conditions that fuel environmental vulnerability, but the presence of fuel alone doesn't start a fire. An event must trigger the crisis. While the spark can arise from natural causes, more often than not the source of that spark is created by the actions that people take or fail to take (2.3.1 Action and Reaction).

2. Some fire storms are self-inflicted wounds. These environmental crises are unintentional triggered by people who fail to understand conditions. Self-inflicted wounds arise from a failure to recognize potentially dangerous conditions and undertaking actions that trigger the danger inherent in those threats (2.5 The Big Picture).

3. Other fire storms are attacks-by-proxy. These are intentional triggered by opponents who understand conditions. Attacks-by-proxy arise from the desire to weaken a position that cannot be attacked directly (9.0 Understanding Vulnerability).

4. We maintain the safety of our position by studying the changes in our environment. If we recognize potentially dangerous conditions in the environment, we do not undertake actions that can potentially trigger the danger inherent in the situation. The best time to act to protect ourselves is before competitors can get started. If we do nothing, we make eventual problems from conditions in the environment much more likely and perhaps unavoidable (5.6.1 Defense Priority).

5. A failure to recognize dangerous conditions is often a failure of perspective. If we have a wellrounded contact network, we should get an early warning from others as these conditions develop. This is one reason why we need people in our network that see situations with fresh eyes (2.4.2 Climate Perspective).

6. A change in climate can create new opponents. We are never safe simply because we have tried to avoid creating enemies. The environment can create opponents for us. One of the ways that we are blindsided by fire storms is when we fail to see how change creates new opponents (9.1.1 Climate Rivals).

7. There are standard processes by which threats emerge. If we recognize the process by which threatening conditions normally arise, we can forecast firestorms and more frequently use them to our benefit (9.1.2 Threat Development).

Illustration:

Real life provides us many examples of people missing environment threats, both those that should be obvious and those that are much harder to foresee. Both self-inflicted wounds and attacks-by-proxy are common. Let us look at these principles from the perspective of political developments in the 2008-2012 period.

1. A fire storm requires a spark. Both Obama and then the Tea Party movement seem to have arisen almost overnight, the conditions of government over-reach and over-spending have been going on for a decade to prepare the way for it. However, it was the spark of the bail-out bills and other huge increases in spending during an economic downturn that sparked it.

2. Some fire storms are self-inflicted wounds. Politicians who fail to recognize changes in political climate often create fire storms by pushing through legislation that enrages the public. After unpopular bailout and stimulus bills, the climate and health care bills are self-inflicted wounds, triggering outrage.

3. Other fire storms are attacks-by-proxy. New laws often make novel attacks that are impossible to foresee. For example, the Endangered Species Act enabled radical environmentalists to hobble both new development and traditional economic activity such as farming and logging by pressing the government into protecting little known species like the spotted owl or snail darter.

4. We maintain the safety of our position by studying the changes in our environment. The gradual increase in spending, debt, government regulation justified by the environment or security have been going on the US for quite a while.

5. A failure to recognize dangerous conditions is often a failure of perspective. In politics, the winners seem to think they get into office based upon their own virtues rather than the mistakes of their opponents. First the Republican and then the Democrat Party misinterpreted the signs. The same frustration with government that cost the Republicans Congress and then the Presidency is now being ignored in the same way by the Democrats.

6. A change in climate can create new opponents. In politics, only a relatively few are more influenced by a political party than they are by the general political climate. Politicians, like sports teams, have "fair weather" supporters who quickly turn on them as conditions deteriorate.

7. There are standard processes by which threats emerge. The balancing of forces of politics can stay in the middle for a long time, but threats emerge as conditions work toward the extremes of complementary opposites.

9.1.1 Climate Rivals

Sun Tzu's six key methods for preparing against how changing conditions create opponents.

"Your rivals will multiply as your army collapses and they will begin against you."
Sun Tzu's The Art of War 2:1:20

"One man with 100 loyal friends is a lot stronger than one man with 1000 dead enemies, but only the former knows it, and only the latter cares."
Gregory Wallace Campbell

General Principle: Changes in climate can turn others into opponents.

Situation:

We normally think about changes in climate creating new opportunities, but such changes can also create new opposition as well. Strangely enough, both improving and worsening conditions can change former allies into opponents. Our vulnerability is to conditions in our environment, but rivals and opponents play a critical role in transforming those conditions into a fire storm against us. The danger is that we do not understand who our potential enemies are, trusting current allies for the wrong reasons. That danger is magnified as conditions get more challenging because we can too easily give them the time to use those conditions against us.

Opportunity:

Changes in climate creates new opponents but they also create the potential for new alliances. Current allies can become rivals and current rivals can become friends. Both opposition and alliances arise ultimately from our goals and values (1.6 Mission Values). According to Sun Tzu's competitive elements, Climate does not control mission, but its does change mission priorities (5.1 Mission Priorities). A downturn in the economy, for example, increases the importance of our financial concerns. This change of goals shifts who our friends and enemies may be.

Key Methods:

The following key methods explain how climate can create enemies.

1. Environmental changes can create enemies when new dangers arise. Changing conditions can force former allies to compete with one another. Tough times shift allies toward the broader, more basic concerns of physical preservation (1.4.1 Climate Shift).

2. Environmental changes can create enemies when dangers are removed. Diverging goals can change former allies into opponents. Good times shift allies toward the narrower, more personal issues of personal fulfillment and idealism (1.6.1 Shared Mission).

3. In tough times, we must create a common enemy, amplifying the danger to unite people. We must clarify the shared mission, specifically avoiding the dissipating situation. The challenge in dealing with tough times arising from fire storms is maintaining support (9.3.1 Mutual Danger).

4. During good times, we must expect ties to weaken and new rivalries to develop. We must protect our vulnerabilities from potential new opponents. This is one of the ways that good times create tough times (3.2.5 Dynamic Reversal).

5. Alliances are often more threatened by good times than bad. Good times create new rivalries. Old friends know our vulnerabilities better than most opponents. In exploiting our vulnerabilities, new rivals can create fire storms against us. These fire storms can lead to tough times (9.2.5 Organizational Risk)

6. Used correctly, we can use fire storms to bring people together. When conditions get more challenging, we can focus everyone on mutual defense. Since defense takes a priority over offense, we are drawn together by our mutual aversion to loss (9.3.1 Mutual Danger).

Illustration:

Let us look at a couple of simple examples of how enemies can be created in good times and bad.

1. Environmental changes can create enemies when new dangers arise. When a company announces that it is going to be downsizing, former business friends and partners are transformed into rivals and competitors, when they realized that they are competing directly with each other to maintain their position.

2. Environmental changes can create enemies when dangers are removed. In business, when a company is booming, partners who once struggled together against the common enemy of the marketplace can turn on each other. There is only room for one leader in an organization and as organizations grow, jealousies and contests for dominant positions naturally erupt.

3. In tough times, we must create a common enemy, amplifying the danger to unite people. When a sports team is losing, everyone starts looking for who to blame. The owner, coach, and star player who were once the best of friends are suddenly in a contest that requires them defending their positions against each other.

4. During good times, we must expect ties to weaken and new rivalries to develop. The history of Apple Computer offers a great example of this power struggle. First there was Jobs and Wozniak. When Jobs became dominant, he brought in Sculley from Pepsi. Sculley then pushed Jobs out. Job eventually made his way back. All of this, however, during one of the great business success stories.

5. Alliances are often more threatened by good times than bad. As the hi-tech market expands into new areas, Google, Microsoft, and Apple find themselves competing more seriously in more areas, even though they have all worked together in the past.

6. Used correctly, we can use fire storms to bring people together. The threat of government regulation, such as the regulation of the Internet by the FCC, often brings serious rivals such as Google, Microsoft, and Apple together.

9.1.2 Threat Development

Sun Tzu's seven key methods on how changing conditions create environmental threats.

"Use discipline to await the chaos of battle.
Keep relaxed to await a crisis."
Sun Tzu's The Art of War 2:1:20

"When did the future switch from being a promise to being a threat?"
Chuck Palahniuk

General Principle: Changes in climate can turn others into opponents.

Situation:

The vulnerabilities that undermine an established position seem to come from out of nowhere. We seem suddenly blind-sided by an unexpected crises. But is that really true? Our vulnerability to conditions in the environment come largely from our false expectations of stability. If something has remained the same for any period of time, we come to expect it to continue to remain the same indefinitely. Where there is change, we falsely expect it to continue in the same direction. This is simply not the way the real world works. The problem is that our expectations have been warped by our training in linear thinking.

Opportunity:

Our opportunity comes from recognizing that progress doesn't flow in a straight lines but changes directions, dictated by the forms of the environment not the wishes of men. The certainty of chaos is predictable. As Sun Tzu says, "Chaos gives birth to control." His strategy teaches the limits of knowledge and control. From those limits, we can predict that: 1) all attempts at controlling the environment will eventually fail (3.2.1 Environmental Dominance); 2) progress in one direction will be eventually balanced by natural opposing forces (3.2.3 Complementary Opposites); 3) any emptiness will be filled and every fullness will be emptied (3.2.4 Emptiness and Fullness); and 4) the longer a trend continues, the more dramatic the reversal can be (3.2.4 Emptiness and Fullness). Notice, these predictions are about what will happen not when it will happen.

Key Methods:

This knowledge allows us to foresee the environment changes that result in our vulnerabilities. This knowledge dictates a process cycle creating these vulnerabilities that we can recognize. The patterns follows clear stages:

1. Threat development starts with a period of stasis ending in a change. Conditions in the environment change in some way. A new law is passed. A new perspective or meme begins to spread. A new technology is introduced (1.1.1 Position Dynamics)

2. The change creating a threat evolves so slowly that we become complacent. When people first notice it, change may worry them, but after awhile it seems innocuous. Life continues as before.

Any predictions of threat from the change seem incorrect. People cry "wolf" and "the sky is falling" so often that real dangers in change are lost among false ones (7.5.2 The Spread of Innovation).

3. The threat goes through a long accumulation stage where the potential for crisis builds to a breaking point. Over time, change creates more and more resources for fueling the eventual fire storm. This fuel can take a variety of forms, from the building of negative opinions to the increase of bad tangible assets. Since a little of this fuel doesn't seem to be a problem, people, reasoning linearly, don't worry about its accumulation (1.2 Subobjective Positions).

4. As the fuel for a crisis accumulates, early warnings are easy to ignore. There are a few, sporadic events that indicate that a fire storm can result from the accumulation of fuel, but these events are minor and result from very uncommon events. They are easily written off because people see them as "non-typical." This is the point at which those trained in Sun Tzu's Playbook should recognize that fuel is accumulating in the environment and start erecting defenses (2.4.2 Climate Perspective).

5. The fuel in the environment builds to a flash point where crisis is unavoidable. The accumulation of fuel reaches the point where fire storms are easily sparked. The situation goes through a *phase transition* where any common, typical event can have a very different result than the past. Opponents begin to see that they can use these conditions against each other (1.3.1 Competitive Comparison.

6. A defense against the crisis must be mounted. After the flash point, the dangers become clear. People are forced, often against their will, to react to the situation. They erect defense against the dangers of the fuel that has accumulated in the environment (3.2.1 Environmental Dominance.

7. The danger wanes and the environmental threat diminishes. The situation rebalances itself in one of two ways. If defenses work, protection becomes universal. If defenses do not work, but the number of fire storms eventually depletes the accumulated resources necessary to bring a situation to the flash point (3.2.3 Complementary Opposites).

Illustration:

Let us look at this pattern to examine the latest financial crisis. I personally used this pattern recognition to get all of my assets out of the financial markets by August of 2008, protecting them from the fire storm.

1. Threat development starts with a period of stasis ending in a change. The changes from in the Community Redevelopment Act (CRA) promoting "affordable mortgages (1993-1998), the Sarbanes Oxley bill (2002) making IPOs more difficult for investment banks, and the bundling of "affordable mortgages" as investment instruments first by Fanny and Freddy (2005) and then by investment banks seeking new products to replace IPOs.

2. The change creating a threat evolves so slowly that we become complacent. During the growing economies of the 90s and early 21st century, the relatively small numbers of loan defaults made the new sub-prime mortgage investments seem safe. AIG begins to insure these instruments against loss.

3. The threat goes through a long accumulation stage where the potential for crisis builds to a breaking point. The number of bad assets mount in the system. Government policy gradually increases the required percentage of "affordable mortgage" loans made by banks. Soon these loans account for hundreds of billions and then trillions of dollars of assets. The accumulation was 4.7 trillion by 2007.

4. As the fuel for a crisis accumulates, early warnings are easy to ignore. In 2007, Lehman Brothers was liquidated, Bear Stearns and Merrill Lynch were sold at fire-sale prices, and Goldman Sachs and Morgan Stanley became commercial banks. General public is unaware of the problem.

5. The fuel in the environment builds to a flash point where crisis is unavoidable. During September 2008, the crisis hits its most critical stage triggering a run on the markets. Lending in all forms slows dramatically. Nearly one-third of the U.S. lending mechanism was frozen and continued to be frozen into June 2009.

6. *A defense against the crisis must be mounted.* Banks increase credit requirements for loans. People pull their money out of markets, increasingly distrusting government assurances.

7. *The danger wanes and the environmental threat diminishes.* Not yet. While standards have been tightened, the fuel of the bad loans, including many questionable commercial loans, is still in the environment.

9.2.0 Points of Vulnerability

Sun Tzu's five key methods on our points of vulnerability during an environmental crisis.

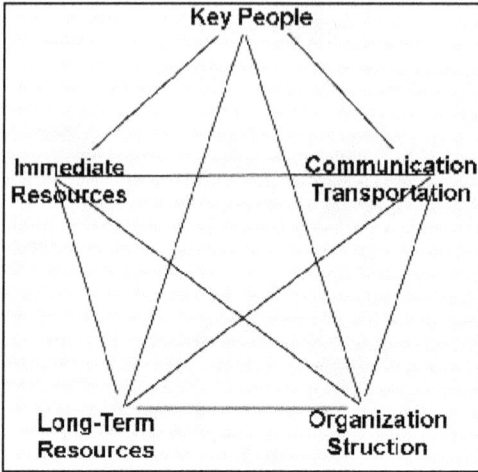

> *"There are five ways of attacking with fire."*
> Sun Tzu's The Art of War 12:1:1

> *"Upon the creatures we have made, we are, ourselves, at last, dependent."*
> Johann Wolfgang von Goethe

General Principle: There are five key points of vulnerability in every position.

Situation:

Once we have successfully claimed a valuable position, we must protect it against environmental threats. Environmental fuel can be sparked by chance, accident, or intentionally into fire storms that can undermine our position. To defend our position, we must defend all the points at which we are vulnerable to these threats. Enmity and vulnerability arise from changes of conditions in the environment (9.1 Climate Vulnerability). Vulnerability doesn't threaten a position as much as it threatens the resources on which a position depends. The danger is that many of us don't identify the resources on which we are dependent. If we don't consciously know our dependencies, we will almost certainly fail to see the dangers that threaten them before they arise.

Opportunity:

If we understand the resources on which our position depends, we can see threats to those resources before they mature, and actively work to secure those resources against those threats. If we understand the resources on which our allies and opponents depend, we can use that knowledge to secure our alliance and endanger our enemies. Though destruction is always easier than creation, it is much less costly to defend existing resources than it is to recreate them (1.8 Progress Cycle).

Key Methods:

Our position depends on five of types of resources. These five key sets of resources are listed in their order of importance. The five points of vulnerability are also are five key points of defense. They are:

1. The primary targets for threats are the key individuals whose decisions maintain our position. This group includes ourselves, but its also includes others such as our spouse, key employees, and bosses whose play a key role. If these people are threatened by a environmental crisis, our position is also threatened (9.2.1 Personnel Risk).

2. The second most critical targets to protect are the immediate resources we need to be productive. These include the assets, the raw materials, and equipment that we need immediate access to on a day-to-day basis. If we lose these assets, we cannot be productive until we replenish them. these are the same resources we need in excess to explore new opportunities (9.2.2 Immediate Resource Risk).

3. The third most important targets to protect are our communication and transportation network. Communication and transportation provide the flow of resources, including decisions, to where they are needed (9.2.3 Transportation/Communication Risk).

4. The fourth most important targets to protect are our fixed, longer term assets. These include our storage of excess resources and any resources that can be converted or transported to be used as immediate resources (9.2.4 Asset Risk).

5. The fifth most important target to protect is our organizational structure. The organization structure consists of the arrangement of activity, responsibility, and authority. Systems of organization divide responsibilities to increase the effectiveness of organization. (9.2.5 Organizational Risk).

Illustration:

Let us look at these five categories of targets from the perspective of business, personal life, and military conflict.

1. The primary targets for threats are the key individuals whose decisions maintain our position. In business, these are our key employees, suppliers, and customers. In our personal life, these are our spouse, family, and friends. In the military, these are our troops and supporters in the field.

2. The second most critical targets to protect are the immediate resources we need to be productive. In business, these are our cash on hand and cash flow. In our personal life, these are our cash, food, water, etc. on hand., In the military, these are food, ammunition, and other supplies in the field.

3. The third most important targets to protect are our communication and transportation network. In business, these are our transportation, communication, and information systems. In our personal life, these are our car, phones, computers, highways, etc. In the military, these are communication, transportation, and logistic systems.

4. The fourth most important targets to protect are our fixed, longer term assets. In business, these are the fixed assets used for production and storage. In our personal life, these are our house, savings, and so on. In the military, these are our stockpiles of supplies and national production systems.

5. The fifth most important target to protect is our organizational structure. In business, these are our business organization extending to suppliers and marketplaces. In our personal life, these are our neighborhood, community, and other local resources. In the military, these are our military bases and alliances.

9.2.1 Personnel Risk

Sun Tzu's five key methods on the vulnerability of key individuals.

"The only correct move is to preserve your troops."
Sun Tzu's The Art of War 10:3:19

*"Once a Marine, always a Marine. The challenge
and the camaraderie with players and coaches,
no one experiences anything like that but in team
sports, especially football. It's almost like a chemical
dependency. Whereas losses used to destroy them, now
they have the wisdom to be able to move on easier."*
Bill Walsh

General Principle: Our position requires us to protect the individuals on which it depends.

Situation:

If we don't understand exactly how Sun Tzu's concept of our strategic position depends on others, we cannot understand how to defend our position during a crisis. We depend on both the generic roles of groups and the unique roles of key individuals. Individuals are more susceptible to attacks than groups. As individuals, people can be isolated and attacked personally on many different levels: physically, mentally, emotionally, and spiritually. Groups can be attacked from outside only on the physical level: on their financial or physical base of support. If the individuals on which we depend are vulnerable, then we are vulnerable. We are especially vulnerable if we depend on the support of only a few, key people.

Opportunity:

In the end, half of our strength comes from sharing the goals of others (1.7.1 Team Unity). Without the support of others, even our victories can seem hollow, meaningless. When we share the journey with others, even setbacks can increase our strength (6.8.2 Strength in Adversity). It is safer to depend on groups for the physical resources and on key individuals for our intellectual, emotional, and spiritual support. While our support from groups can depend on the support of key individuals within that group, most individuals in groups can come and go because group interactions are often based on standard methods not individual character (1.5.2. Group Methods). The difference between an anonymous group and an organization to which we belong is the presence of a key individual who acts as the leader (1.5.1 Command Leadership).

Key Methods:

To defend our position, we must defend both our relationship with groups and our relationships with key people. We must also know when our relationship with the group depends on specific key people with their organizations. To defend the people on who we depend, we must:

1. Know the key relationships on which we depend. We cannot defend everywhere. We must focus on defensive resources on where they matter most (5.5 Focused Power).

2. Keep our key relationships secret. Attacks are more effective focused on individuals. We want to deny others a focus for their attacks (2.7 Information Secrecy).

3. Understand the motivations of these key individuals. We must understand their priority to understand where they are vulnerable (1.6.3 Shifting Priorities).

4. Recognize the individual weaknesses of key individuals. These weaknesses can provide the inspiration and the basis for personal attacks (4.7.1 Command Weaknesses).

5. Keep close enough to key individuals to know when they are the most susceptible to the attacks. Attacks are only damaging to people when they are launched when they are in a personally vulnerable position (1.4.1 Climate Shift).

Illustration:

What does it mean to depend upon a group instead of individual? As a business, it means to depend upon an anonymous group of customers instead of one, specific large customer. As an employee, it means depending upon a group of coworkers who may change as individuals. A key individual's role is different. For example, a business relationships with an entire group of buyers can depend on the good opinion of one key buyer to who the others look for guidance. As an employee, though we depend upon a changing group of coworkers to do our job, we may also depend upon the good opinion of our boss as the key individual to keep our job.

Examples of defending or failing to defend key individuals:

1. Know the key relationships on which we depend. Investors in Apple computer or BerkshireHathaway have to think about what happens to the value of their stock if Steve Jobs or Warren Buffet comes under attack from, for example, a disease.

2. *Keep our key relationships secret.* President Obama's personal relationships with those like Professor Gates or his former past, Jeremiah Wright change the nature of the discussion when they are public.

3. *Understand the motivations of these key individuals.* When a high-profile attorney like Mark Geragos is hired by a defendant like Scott Peterson, the defendant needs to understand that the attorney's primary interest is in self-promotion and winning the case is secondary to that goal.

4. *Recognize the individual weaknesses of key individuals.* Political leaders such as Bill Clinton, Newt Gingrich and John Edwards hurt their entire cohort because of their personal flaws regarding marital fidelity.

5. *Keep close enough to key individuals to know when they are the most susceptible to the attacks.* In Bill Clinton's case, the warning signs were there for years, but those close to him ignored those signs until the situation became a crisis.

9.2.2 Immediate Resource Risk

Sun Tzu's five key methods on the resources required for immediate use.

"Without supplies and food, your army will die."
Sun Tzu's The Art of War 7:2:19

"Time is more valuable than money. You can get more money, but you cannot get more time."
Jim Rohn

General Principle: We must protect the resources we need to maintain our current activities.

Situation:

All positions require resources to maintain them. If we do not have the resources our position requires, we cannot defend it. In terms of our vulnerability, our most common resource limitation is time. All positions require time to maintain them. Some positions require other immediate resources as well to keep them productive, such as energy, money, or raw materials. If these required resources run out, the position quickly begins to fail. How quickly they fail depends how quickly a position consumes resources for production. When these resources are consumed or destroyed by an environmental crisis, our position immediately becomes vulnerable. While these resources are used within an organization, the realm of planning , they come in from outside the organizations, the realm of strategy. While we have some control over our supplier relationships, our control is limited.

Opportunity:

An environment crisis can not endanger our immediate resources as long as we recognize the danger and respond appropriately. Positions normally consume immediate resources at a predictable rate. If we are concerned about our vulnerabilities, we pay attention to what we need rather than take immediate resources for granted. We line up alternative sources for resources. This is true even for time. Our personal time is limited, but there are almost seven billion people in the world, many of whom can exchange their time for other resources that they need. Though none of us get more than 24 hours in a day, we can increase the time we have by getting help from other people. We defend our immediate resources by assuring their continued flow during a crisis.

Key Methods:

To defend the immediate resources on which our positions depend, we must:

1. To protect the vulnerabilities of our immediate resources, we must identify those resources. Each position depends on different types of resources. We must know the types of resources on which our position depends (3.1.1 Resource Limitations).

2. To protect our immediate resource, we must know their rate of consumption. All resources are limited. We can only defend a position when we know what its maintenance requires (8.7.1 Evaluating Erosion).

3. To protect our immediate resource, we must keep our needs and their sources a secret. This is simply a matter of controlling information on a need to know basis (2.7 Information Secrecy).

4. To protect our immediate resource, we must always have alternative sources for them. We must never base our position on a single source of support. We must also know when a transition from one source to another will create its own vulnerability. A key part of developing positions is resource discovery ([nodecontent/761-resource-discovery link]).

5. To protect our immediate resource, we must know what excess resources can be exchanged for them. Good strategy requires us to accumulate excess resources for expansion but they are also used to eliminate vulnerabilities (3.3 Opportunity Resources).

6. To protect our immediate resource, we must keep a close watch on needed resources when climate changes. These changes are the precursor of all environmental attacks. The first sign of the dangers of an environmental attack can be the dwindling of resources (1.4.1 Climate Shift).

Illustration:

The most obvious example of this rule is a business position.

1. To protect the vulnerabilities of our immediate resources, we must identify those resources. A factory requires a flow of raw materials. A restaurant requires a flow of food. Businesses require a flow of money to pay their recurring expenses. Salespeople require a flow of new prospects, products, and promotions. Relationships require a flow of contact, communication, and moments. Our health requires a flow of exercise, nutrition, and rest. Sometime, the key resources are not obvious. For example, it is obvious that an army needs ammunition, but food and water is even more important because it is needed more often. As Napoleon observed, an army travels on its stomach.

2. To protect our immediate resource, we must know their rate of consumption. We must know the rate at which a given position consumes these liquid resources. What value of raw materials are needed to keep the factory running at current capacity? What volume of food does the restaurant need? What volume of case does the businesses require? How many new prospects, products, and promotions does a salesperson need? How much time does a relationship take?

3. To protect our immediate resource, we must keep our needs and their sources a secret. A business competitor can target a key supplier.

4. To protect our immediate resource, we must always have alternative sources for them. When a business, army, or individual depends upon a single supplier, its vulnerability increases. Of course, the one resource always affected by an environmental attack is time. Defending ourselves from a law suit, an IRS audit, bad publicity and so one always consumed time. Since time is limited, an attack in our position in one area can rob time and focus from another: a challenge at work can hurt our relationships at home and, reversing the view, problems in our relationship can rob time at work.

5. To protect our immediate resource, we must know what excess resources can be exchanged for them. While businesses usually assume that money can be exchanged, when supplies run short, prices goes up. We must consider other forms of exchange, such as exchanging time, getting needed resources today in exchange for a long-term contract, for example.

6. *To protect our immediate resource, we must keep a close watch on needed resources when climate changes*. When a key part of the environment changes, such as the recent change in healthcare laws, businesses and other organizations much pay closer attention to that area because it can be the source of new environmental attacks.

9.2.3 Logistics Risk

Sun Tzu's four key methods on how firestorms choke normal channels of movement and communication.

"If you make your army travel without good supply lines, your army will die."

Sun Tzu's The Art of War 7:2:18

"Logistics and transportation are among the many critical functions that rely on our converged communications network."

Doug Gardner

General Principle: We must protect our channels of communication and transportation from a change crisis.

Situation:

All positions depend on the flow of resources and information that we call logistics. These paths are potential choke points. A break anywhere in the path destroys its utility. Our vulnerability in transportation and communication only becomes visible during environmental "fire storms". This vulnerability is especially visible during the rare firestorms that panic the public. During such a panic, communication lines and transportation systems are jammed and unusable. Smaller scale firestorms, such as a denial of service attacks on a internet server, are much more common but much less visible forms of the same concept.

Opportunity:

The systems through which resources and information flows are networks which means that alternative paths are available(2.4 Contact Networks). Between any two points, there are any number of potential lines. Certain transportation and communication paths may work better but there are also other paths which can be used. Firestorms serve a purpose in highlighting the weaknesses in these systems. Communication and transportation systems are in our areas of "control" (1.9.2 Span of Control). We only recognize their unpredictability when their capacities are tested in a flare-up of competition (1.9.1 Production Comparisons).

Key Methods:

To defend our position, we must protect our need for a continuous flow of information and resources, but we also must understand that during a climatic firestorm, special methods apply to using those channels.

1. To defend communication/transportation vulnerabilities, we must not get panicked into using these channels unnecessarily. This is the first rule because it is our first reaction as part of the "flight or fight reflex". We conserve needed immediate resources by avoiding an expensive but unnecessary reaction (9.2.2 Immediate Resource Risk).

2. To defend communication/transportation vulnerabilities, we must use alternative channels during a crisis. It is best to address this challenge before a crisis arises. We must find the openings rather than following the crowd. (3.1.4 Openings).

3. To defend communication/transportation vulnerabilities, we must move or communicate based on our needs. We must not move or communicate simply because a crisis arises. Firestorms do not last so it is a mistake to change our position based on them. Our choice of action and nonaction must be dictated by the needs of our position not merely by what is happening at the moment (5.1.1 Event Pressure).

4. To defend communication/transportation vulnerabilities, we can choose less rather than more. The choice of actions or non-action is always central to good strategy. In facing the specific challenges presented by environmental firestorms, both being panicked into action or frightened into silence are both very common mistakes (4.2 Choosing Non-Action).

Illustration:

Let us look at the common mistakes that are made in communication and transportation during firestorms. The mainstream media provides us with a stream of "panics" that illustrate these principles. Indeed, we might say that the media itself has too often become choked with panics, preventing it from providing real new.

For our illustration, let us use a panic from last summer as our example, so we have a little strategic perspective on it, the "crisis" of high gas prices.

1. To defend communication/transportation vulnerabilities, we must not get panicked into using these channels unnecessarily. Instead of conserving gas by traveling less, people wait in lines at cheaper stations, buying gas before the price goes up whether they need it or not at the time.

2. To defend communication/transportation vulnerabilities, we must use alternative channels during a crisis. During a gas shortage or price panic, people waste gas in rush hour traffic instead of going into work earlier and avoiding the crowds.

3. To defend communication/transportation vulnerabilities, we must move or communicate based on our needs. The biggest mistakes of the gas shortage were made by the companies that decided to base their advertising campaigns on it. Those commercials about high gas prices were still running during the next firestorm, the financial meltdown, making those companies look silly and out of touch.

4. To defend communication/transportation vulnerabilities, we can choose less rather than more. When fuel prices go up, we should travel less and communicate more. It is always cheaper to move information than material.

9.2.4 Asset Risk

Sun Tzu's four key methods regarding the threats to our fixed assets.

"If you don't save the harvest, your army will die."
Sun Tzu's The Art of War 7:2:20

"You are your greatest asset. Put your time, effort and money into training, grooming, and encouraging your greatest asset."

Tom Hopkins

General Principle: We must protect our long-term, fixed assets during a crisis.

Situation:

Time may be our most valuable resource, but it doesn't last. If we cannot transform our time into longerterm resources, we will always be poor. The beauty of youth is a great example of a resource that cannot last. However, our reputation never gets old. A firestorm highlights the vulnerability of our long-term assets since they are usually not portable or quickly converted into other assets. What we build up over a lifetime, we can lose in a short-term change of climate.

Opportunity:

Long-term assets are the most easily defended aspects of our position (1.1.2 Defending Positions). Their stability give them a permanence that we can use to our advantage. Owning a long-term assets is a commitment. We cannot easily walk away from it. When it is endangered by a climatic threat, our mission to protect it should be crystal clear.

Key Methods:

The first rule of protecting long-term assets is that we must accept the job as our personal responsibility. Though it may be the formal responsibility of a set of professionals to protect us, it is always a mistake to abdicate our responsibility to them. No one cares as much about our assets as we do.

1. We work in advance to remove any potential fuel for threats to longer-term assets. For our assets to be hurt by a climate change, the threat must be based on an issue with ownership or legality. We must identify and remove these threats to assets long before a problem arises (9.1.2 Threat Development).

2. When a threat arises, we must expend immediate resources to protect long-term assets. During danger periods all excess resources must be converted into a form we can use for defense. (9.2.2 Immediate Resource Risk).

3. When a threat arises, we must mobilize others who have similar assets at risk. A group is always more powerful than an individual alone. A threat to similar long-term assets creates a powerful shared mission. We can use our shared mission to work together to protect our assets during a crisis (1.6.1 Shared Mission).

4. If the resource as a whole cannot be saved from a threat, we must rescue any parts that we can. Sometimes the nature of the calamity is such that it cannot be stopped. In that case, we must save what we can even if we cannot save everything (5.0 Minimizing Mistakes).

Illustration:

As an example, let us think about a home being threatened by a wildfire (9.1 Climate Vulnerability).

If our house is threatened by a wide-spread wildfire, we shouldn't expect firefighters to save it. During a wildfire, firefighters have bigger priorities that saving our house. We do not.

1. We work in advance to remove any potential fuel for threats to longer-term assets. If we live in a fire zone, we should keep the brush away from our house, put on a roof that is fire proof, and perhaps even make sure we have additional water supplies on hand.

2. When a threat arises, we must expend immediate resources to protect long-term assets. If we can borrow a water tanker, we should make the investment.

3. When a threat arises, we must mobilize others who have similar assets at risk. Sometimes, it is easier to protect our house by protecting the neighborhood. If the house next door is burning, we have a real problem. One person cannot create a fire break on their own, but a group of neighbors can.

4. If the resource as a whole cannot be saved from a threat, we must rescue any parts that we can. If the fire is going to claim the house, we can still save the dog.

9.2.5 Organizational Risk

Sun Tzu's five key methods on the targeting the roles and responsibilities within an organization.

"An organized force is braver than lone individuals. This is the art of organization."
Sun Tzu's The Art of War 11:4:18-19

"Responsibility is the price of greatness."
Winston Churchill

General Principle: Crises threaten organizations by undermining confidence in management ability.

Situation:

By definition, dealing with climatic threats fall outside the normal channels of organizational responsibility. During a firestorm, the chaotic, confusing external competitive environment intrudes directly into the normally orderly world of planning and organization. The normal result in organizations is fear. While organizations are less vulnerable than individuals to an environment attack, such attacks create a crisis of confidence. A dramatic, threatening change in climate arises, people's faith in the organization is often shattered. The threat of the firestorm is then amplified by the organizational chaos.

Opportunity:

When a firestorm descends on an organization, there is an opportunity to demonstrate our strategic vision in a way everyone can appreciate. If we want to move up in the organization, it is an opportunity to demonstrate our strategic skills. Trained in organization, design, and planning for controlled environments, most managers tend to panic during breakdowns of control, when an adaptive response is required. A unplanned threat provides a perfect showcase for those who can work confidently outside of the span of control (1.9.2 Span of Control). People at every level of the organization above us and below us will tend to follow our lead if we have been trained in what an environment challenge requires.

Key Methods:

To protect confidence in the organization during an climatic firestorm, we must step up to exercise or assume command guided by the following key methods.

1. We protect the organization's vulnerabilities by remaining calm and exhibiting decisiveness during a crisis. This is the single most important important role of a leader during a crisis. Even the choice of doing nothing if that is what is required must be made decisively (9.5.2 Avoiding Emotion).

2. We protect the organization's vulnerabilities by mobilizing resources to protect assets at risk. We identify the five areas of vulnerability that need safeguarding and know the steps necessary for defending them (9.2 Points of Vulnerability).

3. We protect the organization's vulnerabilities by winning people's support during a crisis. During danger periods all excess resources must be converted into a form we can use for defense (9.3 Crisis Leadership).

4. We protect the organization's vulnerabilities by responding correctly to the five methods of using firestorms. This is simply a matter of knowing the specific defensive key methods for each situation (9.4 Crisis Defense).

5. When the threat of crisis passes, we must switch from defense to offense. We must quickly rebuild or recapture any parts of the organization's position that were lost or damaged (5.6 Defensive Advances).

Illustration:

We have many recent political examples of poor jobs of handling a firestorms, usually by politicians--from which we have gotten the phrase, it's not the crime its the cover-up, but let us look at a positive example. One of the best jobs of defending the credibility of an organization during a firestorm was the work of Johnson & Johnson during the Tylenol scare of October, 1982. This firestorm arose from the news that someone had poisoned Tylenol capsules in the first major case of product tampering. When the crisis struck, no one knew how, where, or how many the pills had been poisoned.

If our house is threatened by a wide-spread wildfire, we shouldn't expect firefighters to save it. During a wildfire, firefighters have bigger priorities that saving our house. We do not.

1. We protect the organization's vulnerabilities by remaining calm and exhibiting decisiveness during a crisis. Management responded immediately and decisively, without a hint of defensiveness, showing none of the "flight or fight" behavior that less capable leaders usually demonstrate.

2. We protect the organization's vulnerabilities by mobilizing resources to protect assets at risk. Management immediately recognized that their most important asset was their reputation, especially the reputation of the leading product in its category. They immediately spent $100 million dollars recalling and destroying their entire stock of product everywhere.

3. We protect the organization's vulnerabilities by winning people's support during a crisis. J & J management treated their customers like members of their own family, exactly what is required during a crisis,

4. We protect the organization's vulnerabilities by responding correctly to the five methods of using firestorms. They did what was required and, despite the size of the crisis, they left their opponents no opening for attack.

5. When the threat of crisis passes, we must switch from defense to offense. The product was relaunched with a new triple-sealed package, a huge discounting program, and 2,250 sales people sent out to reassure medical people. In the end, the Tylenol product won market share through its good PR instead of losing it.

9.3.0 Crisis Leadership

Sun Tzu's nine key methods for maintaining the support of our supporters during attacks.

"Winning a battle is always a matter of people."
Sun Tzu's The Art of War 4:5:1

"The crisis of today is the joke of tomorrow."
H. G. Wells

General Principle: Win people's support during periods of vulnerability by understanding competitive psychology.

Situation:

Periods of crisis have a huge impact on our relationships. Even when our supporters are not the target of these threats, a crisis threatens our relationships with others. Even when those relationships have nothing to do with our authority within an organizational structure, fire storms pose a real risk to the trust and confidence that others place in us. Climatic change and a sudden threat from the environment creates fear and uncertainty. This surge of emotion often results in psychological desire to find someone to blame. One danger is that our rivals can use these periods of vulnerability to steal away our supporters, but these crises threaten relationships on a more basic level. Relationships have inertia. People stay in their current relationships unless they are given a reason to leave. If we don't manage our relationships correctly, a crisis can be the catalyst that destroys our relationships.

Opportunity:

Crises are always an opportunity to bring people closer together. They provide dramatic, memorable moment that, when handled correctly, can be a solid foundation of shared experience that can last lifetime. To navigate the immediate crisis, we must leverage relationships with others correctly, but our relationships are more important than the crisis. The crisis won't last, so we must see our relationship from a perspective that goes beyond the immediate danger. If we care about the people who are key to our position, people will want to stay with us. These situations have the potential to generate conflicts (9.1.1 Climate Rivals), but they can also generate a shared mission of survival.

Key Methods:

We cannot take people's support for granted. We must win their support every day.

1. We should let others depend on us in a crisis. People need a leader and we should always be ready to assume the role. When people depend on a leader, they lose their fear of the situation. If people depend on us, they will then defend us instead of abandoning us when challenges get difficult (1.5.1 Command Leadership).

2. In a crisis, we must communicate clearly, frequently, and send the same message to everyone. We can stop less people from worry and second-guessing us by making our messages clear. The more frequently that we make contact, the closer our relationships become. We must control what our supporters see and hear so we know what they are thinking (9.3.2 Message Control).

3. In a crisis, w e must emphasize the common threat to solidify the group. The challenge is to increase our sense of shared mission when others might try to destroy it. If rivals want to use our problems to steal our supporters, we should make our supporters feel that competitors are threatening them personally (9.3.1 Mutual Danger).

4. In a crisis, w e want to create a sense of belonging and family. We must make people see our groups as unique and special. Our people must see that we are committed to them and we must demand commitment back. People often judge how we will treat them by how they see us treat others (1.6.1 Shared Mission).

5. In a crisis, w e must give others a mission and a role to play. When people are busy, the lose their fear. When they have a role, they feel valuable. When we give people challenging work to do, they will pay attention and be part of the solution instead of the problem. If they can advance there position working with us, they will stay with us (1.6.2 Types of Motivations).

6. In a crisis, w e must emphasize how we depend on each individual in the group. No one should see themselves as baggage. Without being told, everyone should be asked to contribute for their mutual benefit. Without being asked, everyone must see what is needed. Without being monitored, our supporters will prove that they can be trusted (1.7.2 Goal Focus).

7. In a crisis, people should be partnered with others to minimize their weaknesses. More experienced people should be made responsible for less experienced people. By combining our efforts, we are all stronger (1.7.1 Team Unity).

8. In a crisis, w e must channel our emotions and avoid partiality. Leadership requires our confidence and detachment. We must care about our people, but we cannot let ourselves get wrapped up in their emotional issues (8.5 Leveraging Emotions)..

9. *After the crisis, we must share our success with others.* People want to be rewarded for being part of the team. The more transparent we can make our organizations rewards, the happier people are. If people are in the dark about rewards, they will imagine that they are being left out (8.0 Winning Rewards).

Illustration:

What should a business person do when his or her industry is threatened with an evironmental attack, for example, from a special interest group pressing for more destructive government regulation?

*1. **We should let others depend on us in a crisis**.* If you want to be seen as a leader, you should immediately contact everyone else in the industry to offer a clear vision for dealing with the situation.

*2. **In a crisis, we must communicate clearly, frequently, and send the same message to everyone.*** The leader should be clear about the problems of government and specific about how they can be mitigated and minimized by group response.

*3. **In a crisis, w must emphasize the common threat to solidify the group.*** The leader should create a way for his or her different competitors and those related to get together and work together through their common problem.

*4. **In a crisis, w e want to create a sense of belonging and family.*** When the business leader gets others within the industry together, he or she should give their association a name that promotes the positive benefits their industry offers to their customers, an identify to set them apart from the rest of the market that is affected by the crisis.

*5. **In a crisis, w e must give others a mission and a role to play**.* The business people starting the organization should identify the specific actions each member can take roles to help mitigate the problems of the crisis identifying specific people that can communicate a shared point of view with 1) their employees and customers in their marketplace to make it clear that they have a stake in the situation, 2) the industry media, local media, and general media, and 3) the government or other controlling organizations.

6. In a crisis, w e must emphasize how we depend on each individual in the group. The association should identify the best role for each member, giving the most important roles to the most important and visible members of their industry.

7. In a crisis, people should be partnered with others to minimize their weaknesses. The association cannot let its larger, more visible members to be targeted and isolated from the group. Large members have more resources, but smaller members have the advantage of numbers and distribution. Both types of members are valuable.

8. In a crisis, w e must channel our emotions and avoid partiality. The association must not panic so that one group sells out another. When it comes to government regulation, larger members usually sell out smaller because the larger organizations can bear the costs of regulation more than smaller. However, smaller members can sell out larger organizations, letting them draw direct attacks.

9. After the crisis, we must share our success with others. When the crisis passes, the industry will go back to competition, but it is best that they set up a permanent self-policing and lobbying organization to prevent future crises that draw government attention.

9.3.1 Mutual Danger

Sun Tzu's six key methods describing how we use mutual danger to create mutual strength.

"To command and get the most out of proud people, you must study adversity."

Sun Tzu's The Art of War 11:4:12

"The Chinese use two brush strokes to write the word 'crisis.' One brush stroke stands for danger; the other for opportunity. In a crisis, be aware of the danger - but recognize the opportunity."

Richard M. Nixon

General Principle: Leaders focus attention on the common enemy to create team unity and focus.

Situation:

While we use Sun Tzu's methods to do our best to avoid danger-ous situations, we cannot avoid crisis. Crisis creates mutual danger. Mutual danger threatens the survival of both organizations and, in the worst cases, individual lives. The two biggest dangers during a crisis is panic and division. Panic results in bad decisions, but division creates new forms of conflict that worsen the danger. If we want to avoid division, we must understand how to use a crisis.

Opportunity:

When the crisis eventually comes, we must use it as as an oppor-tunity to generate the sense of unity and focus that creates strength. A loving God created a world full of danger, pain, and trouble so that we would need one another. Sun Tzu used the analogy of men in a boat in a during a storm to capture the character of our mutual danger. In the face of mutual danger, people find a way to work together easily and naturally because of their shared mission (1.6.1 Shared Mission). Used correctly, the danger of crisis maximizes our strength. Sun Tzu teaches the strength of any group (1.7 Competi-tive Power) comes from the unity of its members (1.7.1 Team Unity) and their focus on a single, clear mission (1.7.2 Goal Focus). Shared danger is the opportunity to create a powerful shared mission of survival (1.6.1 Shared Mission).

Key Methods:

Under the methods for dealing with a crisis, the third rule is, "In a crisis, we must emphasize the common threat to solidify the group." (9.3 Crisis Leadership). There are six key methods for accomplishing this correctly.

1. The methods for highlighting mutual crisis must be used only in times of real danger. Like the boy who cried wolf, if we inflate every minor issue into a crisis, we will find that these power-ful methods work less and less well over time, and, when we need them, they will be unavailable (6.0 Situation Response).

2. During a crisis we must focus attention on the objective and concrete aspects of shared danger. We want to generate energy, not fear. People are afraid of the unknown, but the more tangible the enemy is, the more it concentrates the mind. (1.2.0 Subobjective Positions).

3. During a crisis we must make it clear that flight is not an option. We want people to face the crisis, not turn their backs on it. If people cannot run away, the only remaining instinctive mindset is to fight (2.3.3 Likely Reactions).

4. During a crisis we must accentuate that everyone is united against the danger. When people see themselves as part of a group, they also feel greater safety. There should be a sense that the greater danger is in leaving the group rather than staying together (6.8.2 Strength in Adversity).

5. During a crisis we must use the danger as an incentive to action. Whether we want people to hold our current position or move that position, seeking safety during a time of danger must be the highest priority (1.6.3 Shifting Priorities).

6. During a crisis we must emphasize the risks, costs, and the certainty of success. The danger isn't really a danger if there are nothing at risk. The costs are reasonable because of the risks. The certainty of success must arise from the unity and focus of the group (1.5.2 Group Methods).

Illustration:

In our recent times,.no one has used these ideas better than Churchill during World War II. We study his famous speeches during the period, and we see each of these principles being used clearly and concisely.

1. The methods for highlighting mutual crisis must be used only in times of real danger. Politicians and the media today have so consistently violated this rule and we are seeing the inevitable result. When everything is a crisis, from global warming to corporate profits, nothing is a crisis. Churchill, of course, had tried to get people to pay attention the real danger of Germany before WWII, with no affect.

2. During a crisis we must focus attention on the objective and concrete aspects of shared danger. Churchill did such a good job of making the enemy concrete that Hitler and the Nazis are still synonymous with evil.

3. During a crisis we must make it clear that flight is not an option. Churchill: "Never give in. Never give in. Never, never, never, never--in nothing, great or small, large or petty--never give in, except to convictions of honor and good sense. Never yield to force. Never yield to the apparently overwhelming might of the enemy."

4. During a crisis we must accentuate that everyone is united against the danger. Churchill ended his first speech as prime minister in 1940: "But I take up my task with buoyancy and hope. I feel sure that our cause will not be suffered to fail among men. At this time I feel entitled to claim the aid of all, and I say, 'Come then, let us go forward together with our united strength.'"

5. During a crisis we must use the danger as an incentive to action. Churchill in his "their finest hour" speech after the fall of France and the evacuation at Dunkirk: "During the first four years of the last war the Allies experienced nothing but disaster and disappointment. That was our constant fear: one blow after another, terrible losses, frightful dangers. Everything miscarried. And yet at the end of those four years the morale of the Allies was higher than that of the Germans, who had moved from one aggressive triumph to another, and who stood everywhere triumphant invaders of the lands into which they had broken. During that war we repeatedly asked ourselves the question: 'How are we going to win?' And no one was able ever to answer it with much precision, until at the end, quite suddenly, quite unexpectedly, our terrible foe collapsed before us, and we were so glutted with victory that in our folly we threw it away.

6. During a crisis we must emphasize the risks, costs, and the certainty of success. Churchill: "Do not let us speak of darker days:

let us speak rather of sterner days. These are not dark days; these are great days--the greatest days our country has ever lived; and we must all thank God that we have been allowed, each of us according to our stations, to play a part in making these days memorable in the history of our race."

9.3.2 Message Control

Sun Tzu's five key methods on communication methods to use during a crisis.

"*You must position your people to control what they see and hear.*"

Sun Tzu's The Art of War 7:4:14

"*Good communication does not mean that you have to speak in perfectly formed sentences and paragraphs. It isn't about slickness. Simple and clear go a long way.*"

John Kotter

General Principle: Leaders focus attention on the common enemy to create team unity and focus.

Situation:

The real danger during a crisis is always in our response. Nothing in that response is more critical than the messages that we send. During a crisis, people are overloaded with too much conflicting information. The chaotic conditions of the external environment disrupts the orderly flow of productive communication. Because of the high noise to message ratio, individuals can easily receive very different messages regarding the situation. When people have very different perspectives on a situation, they are likely to choose different responses. As people go in different directions, unity breaks down, diluting the effectiveness of every action.

Opportunity:

A single, clear voice can rise above the cacophony of the situation. A simply message can create a rallying point. The right message sent in the right way creates the unity (1.7.1 Team Unity) and focus (1.7.2 Goal Focus)required to generate the excess strength necessary to get through a crisis (1.7 Competitive Power). When we handle a crisis well, it always improves our position afterward. This is especially true about the subjective impressions that others have about our position. Those subjective impressions can be translated into objective rewards.

Key Methods:

Under the key methods for dealing with a crisis (9.3 Crisis Leadership), the second rule is, "In a crisis, we must communicate clearly, frequently, and send the same message to everyone." The following five key methods describe the process.

1. Crisis communication must keep messages about response short and simple. During a crisis, time is short and there is already too much information. Bandwidth is limited. We must use our limited resources wisely (3.1.1 Resource Limitations).

2. Crisis communication must repeat a consistent message over and over. Unless we repeat the message, most people will miss it because of competing distractions. On each repetition, we reach more people (7.4.1 Timing Methods).

3. Crisis communication must amplify and dramatize the message. Amplification is not only a matter of volume, but of using a variety of methods, pictures as well as sounds. (1.5.2. Group Methods).

4. Crisis communication must use a perspective that reaches everyone equally. When creating our message, we have to find a common denominator. We have to ask what everyone's different experiences have in common (2.0 Developing Perspective).

5. Crisis communication must make it easy for people to signal their position. Communication is not just a one-way street. We must have ways of knowing if people received the message and can respond. The easier we make it to respond, the easier it will be to keep everyone on the same page (5.4 Minimizing Action).

Illustration:

For concrete examples, let us look to our political class for examples of what happens when these principles for message management are violated. Though the defining health care situation as a crisis violates the first rule of using danger, since the Obama administration defined it that way, we can use this standard for evaluating their message. Since passage of the health care law, the sinking popularity of Obama, Democrats, and government leading to the loss of the House in 2010 demonstrates the danger of ignoring these principles.

1. Crisis communication must keep messages about response short and simple. A 2,000+ page health care bill is a long and complicated response that violates this rule.

2. Crisis communication must repeat a consistent message over and over. Not only was there one such bill, but about five competing versions so no one even knew what the response was. Even the repeated mantra "health care crisis" morphed into "health insurance crisis" and finally into "we will know what is in it when it passes."

3. Crisis communication must amplify and dramatize the message. The message was amplified using the bully pulpit of the White House, but its opposition was what was dramatized on the streets and town hall meetings.

4. Crisis communication must use a perspective that reaches everyone equally. The chosen message only made sense to those who thought that a government solution was an obvious solution and that spending more public funds is never a problem. This message missed middle America who does consider spending a problem and that government is as often the problem as the solution.

5. Crisis communication must make it easy for people to signal their position. Rather than understand where people were to develop a common perspective, the administration was much more interested in cutting off discussion.

9.4.0 Crisis Defense

Sun Tzu's five key methods on how vulnerabilities are exploited and defended during a crisis.

"Every army must know how to adjust to the five possible attacks by fire."

Sun Tzu's The Art of War 12:2:17

"Any fool can have bad luck; the art consists in knowing how to exploit it."

Frank Wedekind

General Principle: We must recognize the five ways our adversaries can use a crisis against us.

Situation:

Our type of vulnerability to an environment crisis depends on the methods used against us. When opponents work to spark a crisis, we can only defend by responding with the right counter measures. A crisis can weaken us temporarily, but inappropriate responses can destroy us completely. Opponents can try to spark a crisis in five different ways. Each of these different methods works to create a different type of mistake. These methods seek to either 1) create division; 2) cause panic; 3) use an opening; 4) damage alliances, or 5) tip a balance.

Opportunity:

If we are trained in crisis response, we know that there are only five different ways our vulnerabilities can be exploited during these situations. We can prepare against these five different forms of competitive challenges in the same way that we defined the five targets for these attacks: targeting our vulnerabilities (9.2 Points of Vulnerability). If we respond appropriately to these five different forms of sparking and using a crisis, these situations offer little danger (6.0 Situation Response). Situation response, as always, requires two components 1) identifying the situation, and 2) reflexively reacting appropriately. As with all of strategy, we must know how to adapt to them to continuously defend any valuable position.

Key Methods:

There are five key methods for recognizing and responding to opponents' efforts during an environmental crisis.

1. When opponents seek to create division during a crisis, we defend our periphery. When environmental conditions threaten our uniting mission, they will actively work to pick off our weakest and most distant supporters by targeting those furthest from us, geographically or philosophically (9.4.1 Division Defense).

2. When opponents seek to exploit panic during a crisis, we avoid overreactions. Opponents rely upon our overreactions to environmental challenges. If we remain calm in the face of an environment challenge, they will not challenge us. If we panic, they will jump into the fray, using our negative momentum against us in any way that they can (9.4.2 Panic Defense).

3. When opponents want to use an opening created by the crisis, we must fill it first. It takes time for crisis damage to create an opening, so opponents must wait to use it. They patiently watch as our problems with the external environment reach their peak and then they use the opening that the damage creates (9.4.3 Defending Openings).

4. When opponents hope to win our allies during a crisis, we must protect our key relationships. During a fire storm, allies can attempt to distance themselves from us for fear of "guilt by association." We must actively work to protect our allies from any spillover during the crisis. Otherwise, our opponents will use the crisis as evidence of our indifference and try to win our allies and other key relationships away from us. (9.4.4 Defending Alliances).

5. When our competition is evenly balanced, adversaries will use a crisis to tip the balance in their favor. When a temporary trend arises in a competitive arena, either side of an evenly matched contest can take advantage of it. The side that recognizes the opportunity first can use it as a tipping point shifting the basis of competition 9.4.5 Defensive Balance).

Illustration:

Below we offer different examples from business and politics for each of these five methods.

1. When opponents seek to create division during a crisis, we defend our periphery. For example, when Apple saw the Microsoft's Vista release was getting attacked in the media, they directly attacked the Vista operating system and tried directly to divide off those customers who were the least devoted to Windows.

2. When opponents seek to exploit panic during a crisis, we avoid overreactions. Consider the problems that companies can have with a product recall. If a company panics, such as the ***Peanut Corporation of America*** did in <u>trying to initially cover up their salmonella problem</u> in 2008 and 2009, they are finished. When a company doesn't panic and acts decisively, as Johnson & Johnson did during the cyanide scare of the eighties, they maintain their position easily (<u>9.2.5 Organizational Risk</u>).

3. When opponents want to use an opening created by the crisis, we must fill it first. We saw a good example of this technique during the last election as the Democrats leveraged unhappiness with the war in Iraq when it was at its height. They started working when this opening was created, before the surge. Though the surge can only be considered a success, the opening created by unpopularity with the war gave the Democrats control of congress and eventually the presidency.

4. When opponents hope to win our allies during a crisis, we must protect our key relationships. In sports, for example, coaches will often support an unpopular or under-performing player for the sake of the team as a whole. When this happens, the coach's opponents can undermine his or her position by keeping the focus and pressure on these weaker players.

5. When our competition is evenly balanced, adversaries will use a crisis to tip the balance in their favor. There was a great example of this technique in the Obama/McCain campaign. In the week before the vote, the financial crisis arose. McCain, after his initial panic (see number 2 above) suspending his campaign could have used the crisis to win the election by opposing the bailout, which was unpopular in both parties. Instead, Obama laid blame for the crisis at the Republicans door and McCain by failing to blame the Democratic Congress and, most importantly, by siding with Obama in supporting the bailout, gave up any chance of tipping the balance in his favor and lost the election.

9.4.1 Division Defense

Sun Tzu's five key methods for preventing organizational division during a crisis.

"You start a fire inside the enemy's camp. Then attack the enemy's periphery."

Sun Tzu's The Art of War 12:2:3-4

"Leaders must be close enough to relate to others, but far enough ahead to motivate them."

John Maxwell

General Principle: To avoid division, leaders must rally to their people.

Situation:

People seek the safety of organizations during times of crisis. Opponents can actively work to split people off from an organization. They do this by putting the group, its leaders, or its mission at the core of the crisis. Done correctly, this transforms the organization from a haven to a threat for its members. This use of a crisis is possible because one of the key vulnerabilities of groups is the distance separating the people. This distance can be either physical or psychological. Opponents can pick off the weakest and most distant by targeting those furthest away, either geographically or philosophically.

Opportunity:

A crisis gives leaders an opportunity to prove the value of their organization. During a crisis, leader prevents division by understanding strategic distance (4.4 Strategic Distance). This is especially important in large organizations where division is a natural consequence of size (3.4.1 Unity Breakdown). The mutual danger created by the crisis is a powerful tool for leaders (9.3.1 Mutual Danger) The sense of shared danger among the members of the organization is an opportunity to bring them all together into a shared point of view. The strength of an organization is its unity (1.7.1 Team Unity).

Key Methods:

Sun Tzu offers these principles to avoid panic during a crisis.

1. During a crisis, we protect our mission defending our supporters. This means moving closer to those who are being engaged by our adversaries. Nothing says more about the shared power of the mission than our willingness to defend others. (1.6.1 Shared Mission).

2. During a crisis, we focus our message on the value of our shared effort. The crisis is temporary while our goals will go on. Our progress toward our goals is still part of our position. We must use all of the techniques of message control to communicate the value of our shared defense (9.3.2 Message Control).

3. During a crisis, we emphasis the safety in working together especially for the most distant. Since our opponents will start trying to divide us working at the periphery, we reach out to those at the periphery. We make sure to include them in our message of shared mission, danger, and safety in numbers (9.3.1 Mutual Danger)

4. During a crisis, we use organized activities to give people an outlet. People are united by actions. If we give people activities to perform, it provides a focus for the emotional energy generated by the crisis. They must feel responsible to the group to feel that the group is responsive to them (6.5.1 Dissipating Response).

5. During a crisis, we address the organizational damage quickly. The worst danger is ignoring people's concerns with the organization. The more quickly we can get the crisis under control and behind us, the more meaningless opposition attacks become (6.1.1 Conditioned Reflexes).

Illustration:

As an example, let us examine Microsoft's response to the problems created by its 2005 release of the Vista operating system. This situation created the fuel for a crisis of confidence, which Apple sparked by their "I am a Mac and I am a PC" advertisements. While the Microsoft's problems with Vista fall into the category of a crisis from self-inflicted wounds, their response to the attack by Apple was a demonstration of solid strategy. This quality of response has been less common for Microsoft in recent years.

1. During a crisis, we protect our mission defending our supporters. Microsoft's response was to defend its users, who Apple, in selling their own cool were clearly using the crisis climate. Some videos here.

2. During a crisis, we focus our message on the value of our shared effort. Microsoft's "Windows versus walls" emphasized Apple's love for proprietary control.

3. During a crisis, we emphasis the safety in working together especially for the most distant. Microsoft had both the advantages and disadvantages of size. While Mac emphasized their cool, Microsoft emphasized their affordability for the masses, which reached the broadest group of people.

4. During a crisis, we use organized activities to give people an outlet. Instead of pushing Vista, Microsoft chose to emphasize the Windows brand. They took a number of steps to make it easier for people and organizations to stay with XP. This was a good decision compared with their normal methods for encouraging the use of the new operating system by limiting backward compatibility.

5. During a crisis, we address the organizational damage quickly. Windows 7 came out in record time and a record low price. Windows 7 built on the Windows brand and fixed the many visible shortcomings of Vista making it much easier for people to move on with Microsoft rather than leave.

9.4.2 Panic Defense

Sun Tzu's four key methods to prevent the mistakes from panic during a crisis.

"You launch a fire attack, but the enemy remains calm. Wait and do not attack."
Sun Tzu's The Art of War 12:2:3-4

"Doubts and mistrust are the mere panic of timid imagination, which the steadfast heart will conquer, and the large mind transcend.
Helen Keller

General Principle: To avoid panic, leaders must stay calm and know how to calm others.

Situation:

The greatest danger from a crisis is emotional over-reaction. People can attack us more easily for our bad reactions than they can on the basis of a crisis alone. We are not responsible for the external conditions that provide fuel for the crisis or our opponents' actions that sparked those conditions into a crisis, but we are always responsible for our responses. A crisis, by definition, falls outside of normal, expected conditions. Since most of us are not trained to respond to unexpected conditions we panic, that is, overreact out of the fear of the unknown. When we panic, we create a great opening for our opponents to attack us, even when the crisis itself does not.

Opportunity:

Training in Sun Tzu's methods are the ultimate protection against panic. His entire science is dedicated to dealing with situations where we must make decisions quickly under uncertain conditions with limited information. A crisis gives us the opportunity to demonstrate how "chaos gives birth to control," as Sun Tzu teaches. When we demonstrate our strategic leadership in a chaotic situation and improve how others perceive us, which is the key to improving our position over all (1.2 Subobjective Positions).

Key Methods:

The following principles describe how we defend ourselves and our organizations against panic.

1. To prevent panic during a crisis, we must reach out to our contact network. People tend to panic more when they feel isolated. This contact discourages panic in both directions. It decreases our own fear and the fears of those we contact (2.4 Contact Networks).

2. To prevent panic during a crisis, we must see uncertainty as normal. While we expect good information within our span of control, we must accept that most of the world lies out our control. We cannot let what is unknown spark fear because almost all of the universe is unknown. In a crisis, events normally run ahead of information, and we should make it clear to others that this is expected. Limited information doesn't stop us from responding and adapting our response as we learn more (2.1.1 Information Limits).

3. To prevent panic during a crisis, we must take visible actions. In Sun Tzu's system, leveraging knowledge means knowing when secrecy is required and when communication is required. Since people are more afraid of what is hidden. Secrecy and cover-ups always compound problems and increase panic. Visible action gives us an outlet for emotions and decreases panic. It is better to get information out as quickly as possible to demonstrate our confidence and ability to act decisively (2.1 Information Value).

4. To prevent panic during a crisis, we must act quickly and decisively but in scale with the problem. We use speed and visibility to create a sense of decisiveness, but we must keep reactions in proportion to the immediate dangers. While we must act, we must not over-react. This is consistent with Sun Tzu's entire philosophy of minimizing mistakes. The tendency in emotionally charged situations, especially those where people want to see action, is to do too much and create mistakes. A crisis is one of the many situations where less done quickly is usually more (5.4 Minimizing Action).

5. To prevent panic during a crisis, we must return to the enduring values of mission. The crisis is temporary. The shared mission is what matters. If we act consistently with our higher and the enduring aspects of our mission, those actions will increase confidence rather than diminish it (1.6 Mission Values).

Illustration:

We can use this as an opportunity to contrast the responses of Peanut Corporation of America trying to cover up their 2008-2009 salmonella problem and Johnson & Johnson response during the Tylenol cyanide scare of the eighties (illustration used in 9.2.5 Organizational Risk). The first was a clear example of panic while the other was a clear example of calm.

1. To prevent panic during a crisis, we must reach out to our contact network. The peanut people seem to be hiding from the story while the J & J people got in front of it on day one.

2. To prevent panic during a crisis, we must see uncertainty as normal. While neither side knew the dimensions of the problem, J&J didn't let that stop them from taking action. The peanut people, on the other hand, used the lack of information as an excuse not to take action.

3. To prevent panic during a crisis, we must take visible actions. This is where the peanut people made their biggest mistakes. The cover-up of internal problems became the entire basis of their response. While J&J didn't know where the investigation would lead, they opened their doors to investigators, confident that they would deal with any problems.

4. To prevent panic during a crisis, we must act quickly but avoid over-reactions. In a situation of public health where lives are in immediate danger, speed is critical, as J&J realized in immediately taking all their products off the shelves. It is hard to over-react in saving lives except when our reactions endanger more lives.

5. To prevent panic during a crisis, we must return to the enduring values of mission. In the end, J&J turned the crisis into a PR victory that is still getting them good reviews not only in articles like this, but in business schools across the nation. The peanut people? Not so much.

9.4.3 Defending Openings

Sun Tzu's four key methods on how to defend openings created by a crisis.

"The fire reaches its height. Follow its path if you can. If you can't follow it, stay where you are."
            Sun Tzu's The Art of War 12:2:7-9

"Illusion is an anodyne, bred by the gap between wish and reality."
            Herman Wouk

General Principle:

Adversaries will use openings created by our missteps during a crisis if we let them.

Situation:

We created openings during a crisis by mistakes and mismanagement. In other words, we make the wrong choices. These errors are unavoidable. Sun Tzu's strategy defines an opportunity as an opening. A crisis fueled by environmental conditions our mistakes that can create openings through which our opponent can attack us. An additional problem is that we cannot predict exactly where these openings will occur. If we knew what mistakes we were making, we wouldn't make them. Not knowing where a mistake might do its damage makes it difficult for us to defend ourselves. Though we cannot predict where we will create an opening, we can predict when our opponents' will move against us. When the situation has done its maximum damage. Our opponents are hoping that we are too consumed in dealing with internal damage control to recognize our external vulnerability.

Opportunity:

In dealing with openings within our positions, we always have the advantage of proximity. Our opponents must wait to attack to see where the mistakes will occur. Since we are closer to our situation than they are, we are always better positioned recognize a mistakes and plug an opening before they can act (4.4 Strategic Distance). Our opportunity is in our readiness to surprise opponents with an instant response, recognizing our own errors (6.1.1 Conditioned Reflexes). Done correctly, we can turn the situation around so that the crisis damages them in their mode of open attack more than it hurts us in our defensive mode.

Key Methods:

To deal with the openings created by our own mistakes

1. As we shift resources to deal with a crisis, we must know what weak points we are creating. An opening is a gap in the resources that we need to maintain our position. The first way in which an opening arises during a crisis is through our own actions, as we move resources to deal with the crisis. Every strength creates a corresponding weakness. To protect against a crisis, we reinforce certain areas and thereby weaken others. Such gaps may be unavoidable, but the mistake is not being aware of it. We must do this consciously to prepare to opposition attacks (3.5 Strength and Weakness).

2. As the crisis progresses, we must know where resources are lost or damaged. This is the second way in which openings as a gap in resources are generated by a crisis. This mistake is taking the lot resources and capabilities for granted, assuming we still have them. We must be aware of the five points of vulnerability to know where we are being damaged by the crisis so that we can prepared to defend ourselves (9.2 Points of Vulnerability).

3. As the crisis progresses, we can use deception proactively to cover up our weak points. If opponents believe that we are prepared for them at the point of attack, they are less likely to attack. The mistake is letting our real internal problems appear externally as weaknesses. It is easier and less costly to prevent attack than to defend against it. We must find ways to communicate a state of readiness, especially when it doesn't exist, to discourage attacks (2.1.3 Strategic Deception).

4. As the crisis reaches its peak, we must ready a rapid defense team to move. The mistake here is not having reserves. Despite our best efforts, we may not see the opening until our opponents use it and we must have resources ready to respond (3.3 Opportunity Resources).

Illustration:

We saw a good example of this technique during the 2008 US election cycle as the Democrats leveraged public unhappiness with the war in Iraq when it was at its height. They started working when this opening was created, before the surge. Though the surge can only be considered a success, the opening created by unpopularity with the war gave the Democrats control of congress and eventually the presidency. Let us look at the weaknesses of Republican's strategy.

1. As we shift resources to deal with a crisis, we must know what weak points we are creating. While the surge tipped the balance in Iraq, the Republicans did not seem to even recognize the change in climate that made it into a handicap.

2. As the crisis progresses, we must know where resources are lost or damaged. The war in Iraq did the most damage to the Republican channels of communication (9.2.3 Transportation/Communication Risk) concerning the value of winning in Iraq. The administration was traumatized by their earlier non-response to "Mission Accomplished" attacks and never recovered.

3. As the crisis progresses, we can use deception proactively to cover up our weak points. Instead of a non-claim of non-victory, the Republican candidates should have laid the groundwork for a conservative anti-war plank. They could have discussed the surge in terms of larger endgame of disengagement. Ron Paul demonstrated how a conservative could be pro-defense but against the idea of a long-lasting war on fiscal grounds. Like Nixon's "secret plan to win" in Vietnam, this policy could have ended up maintaining the status quo while claiming to be a new approach. This is exactly what Obama's has done in Iraq and Afghanistan, continuing existing policies while claiming to do something new.

4. As the crisis reaches its peak, we must ready a rapid defense team to move. The Republicans and the Bush administration were extremely poor in responding in anything like a timely manner to Democratic attacks, whether those attack were warranted or not.

9.4.4 Defending Alliances

Sun Tzu's five key methods for dealing with weakness by association.

"Spreading fires on the outside of camp can kill.
You can't always get fire inside the enemy's camp.
Take your time in spreading it."
Sun Tzu's The Art of War 12:2:10-12

"What I don't appreciate - and what I'm confident the
voters will reject - is the attempt by some of the media
and others to engage in guilt by association."
Ralph Reed

General Principle:

Unless dealt with quickly, weakness-by-association undermines positions over time.

Situation:

A crisis can be used against our position even when the controversy isn't about us directly. We can be damaged by a fire storm of controversy through our alliances with others. This is an interesting threats because it can affect us even if we are completely innocent. Weakness or, as it is more commonly known, guilt by association can easily become a slow, bleeding wound. Initially, we can make the mistake of thinking of them as minor nuisances but they don't go away weakening our position over time. Any defense against "weakness by association" attacks must deal with incomplete information. As that information slowly comes out, the damage to our position mounts over time. We also cannot control what our associates do, which can hurt us despite our best attempts to defend them.

Opportunity:

The good news is that weakness by association attacks do not instantly get us in trouble. As always, everything depends upon our response. There is a certain unfairness about guilt by association that people initially resist. This means that these threats require time to develop into threats against us. Because of this perception of unfairness, these attacks can be turned around against our attackers. To do this successfully, we have to react quickly and discover the right defense, which depends on information about the crisis that we may not have. The attacks also give us a real opportunity to clarify our values. Our goals and values are the core of our position. We should welcome any opportunity to talk about those values. These firestorms are always about the past, past actions of past associates. What is important going forward is our values. The past cannot be changed, but we can always learn from it, especially about the importance of values.

Key Methods:

The best strategy here starts with avoiding the common mistakes in weakness-by-association attacks. The most common mistakes are:

1. When an ally faces a crisis, we must initially refuse to speculate and point out the danger in speculation. We must be clear about the dangers of false accusations and guilt by association. We must not instantly rush to defend or attack an ally when we don't know the facts. Defense of the guilty is a self-inflicted wound, transforming our ignorance into injury. Attack makes us look disloyal and foolish if the facts end up clearing our ally. It may also support the values of our opponents when they are not our values (2.1.1 Information Limits).

2. When an ally is in a crisis, we must instantly admit what we did and did not know. We cannot ignore the crisis of an ally for too long. This makes us look like we are hiding something. Since the damage seems minor, we can hope they will simply disappear, but over time our opponents can point to our reticence as evidence of guilt, and, as every bit of new information that comes out provides new fuel for the fire. If we should have recognized a problem, we can admit it and identify the signs we missed specifically, and sincerely apologize, but we can safely add the minor caveat that we always want to think best of our friends. (2.1.2 Leveraging Uncertainty).

3. When an ally has a crisis, we must keep all statements short but cover everything that must be covered. We must say what needs to be said and be willing to answer questions but avoid going on and on. Saying more than we need to say is as bad as saying nothing. We need to address the attack and quickly, but saying too much leads almost inevitably into one of the other errors (5.4 Minimizing Action).

4. When an ally is in a crisis, we must avoid dishonestly distancing ourselves from the relationship. This invites more exposures of those associations. This shift the issue from our allies misdeeds to our dishonesty (1.5.1 Command Leadership).

5. When an ally is in a crisis, we must make a clear distinction between our values and those of our opponents. This uses the crisis as an opportunity. A crisis is dangerous because it is used and often triggered by opponents, who by definition, have very different values. If our allies are accused of violating our values, we can defend those values strongly without attacking an ally who may or may not be guilty. If these attacks are really against our values, we must defend those values, strongly and clearly, against the attackers. While more people can agree with vague platitudes, values only have impact when connected to the specifics of a situation (1.6.3 Shifting Priorities).

Illustration:

During the 2008 election, candidate Obama dealt with questions about past associations. Unfortunately, he did so less than adequately and it could have cost him the election had McCain not given him the election by mishandling the financial crisis in the weeks before the vote. Questions about Obama's associations didn't cost him the election, but they set up the slow bleed that has weakened his position over time.

1. When an ally faces a crisis, we must initially refuse to speculate and point out the danger in speculation. If candidate Obama didn't know the facts, which is what he claimed at the time, he should have said nothing, reserving judgment. Instead, he defended Wright only having to repudiate him later.

2. When an ally is in a crisis, we must instantly admit what we did and did not know. Obama's unwillingness to discuss his relationships kept this story alive. This controversy built to such a degree that candidate Obama ended up making an entire speech about race to address it.

3. When an ally has a crisis, we must keep all statements short but cover everything that must be covered. While his speech about race was praised highly in the mainstream media, what does anyone remember about that speech today other than the "throwing his grandmother under the bus" moment. Obama said that he could not repudiate Wright, but then he did repudiate him only a few weeks later.

4. When an ally is in a crisis, we must avoid dishonestly distancing ourselves from the relationship. New connections between President Obama and various individuals and groups continues to be interesting because those associations are only discussed specifically by Obama's opponents.

5. When an ally is in a crisis, we must make a clear distinction between our values and those of our opponents. The biggest mistake then and now was not getting specific about what was learned from past associations and how his future associations are going to be different. During the campaign, he should have specifically addressed how Wright's ideas are wrong for the future. He should have contradicted Wright's specific statements and called them clearly racist and used that to emphasize his mission of moving on from partisan and racial divisions of the past.

9.4.5 Defensive Balance

Sun Tzu's four key methods for using short-term conditions to tip the competitive balance in a crisis.

"Set the fire when the wind is at your back.
Don't attack into the wind."
Sun Tzu's The Art of War 12:2:17-18

"Trends, like horses, are easier to ride in the direction
they are going."
John Naisbitt

General Principle:

During a crisis, we can flank opponents or be outflanked ourselves by utilizing the onrushing trends of change.

Situation:

Fuel for a crisis builds up slowly in our environment until a spark triggers it into a firestorm. The flames of the crisis, however, are fanned by the short-term trends in the environment. A crisis amplifies the dangers of positioning ourselves against even the slightest trends. Normally, we position ourselves considering the stronger and longer-lasting conditions of the ground: gravity (4.3.1 Tilted Forms) and long-term flow (4.3.2 Fluid Forms) when meeting opposition. During a crisis, however, we must also consider the less powerful and short-term trends of climate: the shifts of emotion and fad.

Opportunity:

These short-term trends can work just as easily for us as against us. As with using the advantages of the ground, using the shifts of climate are largely just a matter of knowing which way the wind is blowing. If we flank our opponents correctly, we can not only prevent opposition attacks from starting, but turn any attacks that they try back on them. These situations also create the opportunity for surprise, where we can feign a vulnerable position to invite and attack and then reveal our true position.

Key Methods:

The strategy here is easy to understand and, when the opportunity is there, simple to execute:

1. During a crisis, we must know which way the trend is going. Another way of saying this is know which way the wind is blowing. This usually requires more than sticking up a finger up in the air. Local conditions can be misleading, so we need to get a broader perspective from the sources that we have cultivated (2.4 Contact Networks).

2. During a crisis, we must make a judgment about how long the trend will last. By definition, these are all short-term trends, but they must persist long enough to make a move worthwhile. Generally, more visible trends involve more people. The more area a trend covers, the longer it will last. (3.1.6 Time Limitations).

3. During a crisis, we must know where opponents stand. It is our position relative to our adversaries that is important. We want the direction of the trend to support our position against our opponents Until they have taken a position, we cannot take a favorable stand (1.3.1 Competitive Comparison).

4. During a crisis, we must angle into a position that puts the trend behind us and against our opponents. This usually requires a minimum of movement, just getting the angles right (5.4 Minimizing Action).

Illustration:

There was a great example of this technique in the final days of Obama/McCain 2008 presidential context, again, as is usual with politics, a great illustration of the bad strategy rather than good. In the week before the election, the financial crisis arose generating the first bailout bill. McCain's first mistake was his initial panic suspending his campaign (9.4.2 Panic Defense). He could have easily defended himself against Obama's attacks based on the financial crisis had he used the trends in his favor and changed the momentum of the campaign. What would he have had to do?

1. During a crisis, we must know which way the trend is going. McCain failed to recognize that the public, Republican, independent, and Democrat, were all against the bailout. This was largely because he listened only to those inside of the beltway.

2. During a crisis, we must make a judgment about how long the trend will last. With the election so close, it should have been obvious that this was going to be the deciding issue of the campaign. Indeed, discussing any other issue during the crisis was a waste of air.

3. During a crisis, we must know where opponents stand. Obama took a clear stand in favor of the bailout. This stand was supported mostly by the Democrats in Congress, with the Republican legislators, despite President Bush's support, largely opposed.

4. During a crisis, we must angle into a position that puts the trend behind us and against our opponents. McCain should have taken a clear position against the bailouts, with the trend of public opinion. He should have used it to position himself against big government supporting big corporations with big spending. He should have also used it as a clear opportunity to break with President Bush's fiscal policy saving himself from the guilt-from-association charges of Obama (9.4.4 Defending Alliances). Would this have provided a tipping point in the election? Like Kerry's failure to use decent strategy against Bush in 2004, we will never know.

9.5.0 Crisis Exploitation

Sun Tzu's five key methods about how to successfully use an opponent's crisis.

"When you use fire to assist your attacks, you are clever."

Sun Tzu's The Art of War 12:3:1

"Rhythm is the basis of life, not steady forward progress. The forces of creation, destruction, and preservation have a whirling, dynamic interaction."

Kabbalah

General Principle:

We must use environment vulnerabilities against opponents only when it advances *our* position.

Situation:

While our primary concern is defending our position during a crisis, we cannot overlook opportunities to use a crisis against rivals, but sparking a crisis to attack an opponent is very dangerous. The firestorms that we spark are unpredictable and can easily blow back on us. One of the most common and easily avoidable mistakes in competitive strategy is to focus on hurting competitors rather than on advancing our own position. If these attacks weaken our position while destroying a competitor, it is just a matter of time until a new competitor arises to attack our weakened position. No matter how many competitors we destroy, we will always have new competitors arise to take their place (1.3.1 Competitive Comparison).

Opportunity:

Exploiting a crisis is most valuable in fixed sum competitions where we can only advance our position at our competitor's expense (7.6 Productive Competition). It works best when it is used productively, to create partnerships and alliances with former enemies. When either undermining opponents, sparking a crisis is like a loophole in the rule about conflict being too costly (3.1.3 Conflict Cost). The environment does the damage to our opponents, and we simply take advantage of it. The question is really whether or not sparking a crisis for competitors really helps us. This is not a question of altruism but of rational selfinterest.

Key Methods:

The five key methods for using a crisis simply reverse the methods for defense against a firestorm (3.2.5 Dynamic Reversal).

1. To spark a crisis against opponents, we wait for enough fuel in the environment. It takes time for fuel to build up. We cannot create this fuel. It must build up in the environment in sufficient quantities that we can use it to create a real crisis. We must simply recognize how it can be used against an opposing position (9.1 Climate Vulnerability).

2. To spark a crisis against opponents, we must know where our opponents are vulnerable to a crisis. This determines where we want to damage our opponent's resources: individual people, liquid resources, transportation and communication, long-term assets, or organizational reputation. (9.2 Points of Vulnerability).

3. To spark a crisis against opponents, we need a safe method to utilize the crisis. This is the most difficult step because each of the five methods for using crisis against an opponents can hurt us if we do not execute them correctly (9.4 Crisis Defense).

4. To spark a crisis against opponents, we need a clear, long-term benefit creating the crisis. This benefit can be an alliance as well as hurting the competitor. Because the risks are certain and the decision irrevocable, the benefit must even be more certain than our usual high standards for exploring opportunities (9.5.1 Adversarial Opportunities).

5. To spark a crisis against opponents, we must act on rational self-interest not on emotion. Emotions are temporary and we will almost certainly feel different in the future (9.5.2 Avoiding Emotion).

Illustration:

A negative example of how these principles were violated is provided by the Kerry campaign against Bush in the 2004 US presidential election. In that campaign, Kerry ran primarily on attacking Bush for going to war in Iraq.

1. To spark a crisis against opponents, we wait for enough fuel in the environment. In 2004, there wasn't enough war weariness among the general public and there wouldn't be until the 2006 Congressional elections when issues of corruption and government spending were added to the mix.

2. To spark a crisis against opponents, we must know where our opponents are vulnerable to a crisis. Kerry choose to make these attacks personal, portray Bush simultaneously as a fool for thinking there were WMDs in Iraq and an evil genius for convincing the world of it. This was a difficult target because people don't want to think of their president in a bad *personal* light, even when they may not want him to continue as president. A better target would have been the organization, the Republican Party.

3. To spark a crisis against opponents, we need a safe method to utilize the crisis. Because Kerry launched his attack too directly, one of the primary issues of the campaign became Kerry's flip-flops on the war. "He was for it before he was against it," is one of the more memorable lines from the campaign because of this miscalculation. A less overt method of using the situation was required.

4. To spark a crisis against opponents, we need a clear, long-term benefit creating the crisis. Because elections are a fixed-sum game, there is always a clear benefit. Here, the question is about a long-term one. Kerry left himself in no position to come back from a very close loss because of this miscalculation. He positioned himself solely an anti-Bush candidate and Bush wasn't running again.

5. To spark a crisis against opponents, we must act on rational self-interest not on emotion. Kerry could have won easily if he had based his campaign on retiring President Bush with honor because his time had passed rather than attacking him. Kerry could have made a strong argument that Bush's decisions on war, right or wrong, had changed the situation so that we needed a different type of leadership. However, the anger on the left against Bush required turning the election into an attack rather than a success.

9.5.1 Adversarial Opportunities

Sun Tzu's eight key methods on how our opponents' crises can create opportunities.

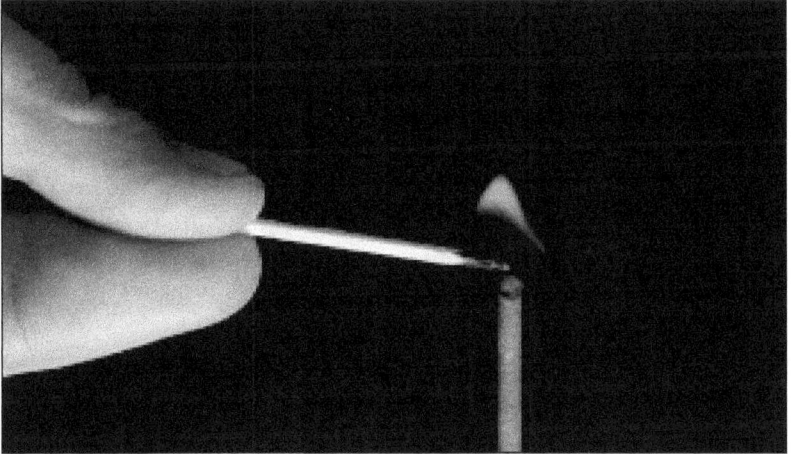

"Never waste an opportunity to defeat your enemy."
Sun Tzu's The Art of War 4:3:25

"An opponent is entitled to the same regard for his principles as we would expect others to have for ours. Non-violence demands that we should seek every opportunity to win over opponents."
Mohandas Gandhi

General Principle:

We must use a crisis against opponents when it strengthens our position.

Situation:

Our success depends on making the moves that improve our position. We must never undertake an action simply to create problems for competitors, but we must always make problems for our competition when it profits our position to do so. If there is no advantage using a crisis against our competitors, we cannot let the pressure of events seduce us into acting against them. If there is a advantage, however, we cannot ignore the opportunity out of some misplaced sense of benevolence. While we may actively work to spark a crisis, it comes from the environment. If we don't take advantage of the situation, another competitor is likely to. We can destroy our own position by fighting our opponents, but we can also destroy our position by not using every reasonable opportunity to advance it.

Opportunity:

Expanding into undefended areas is the usual basis for improving our position because it allows us to control resource while avoiding costly conflict (3.1.2 Strategic Profitability). Sun Tzu's method is to develop positions that others want to join rather than fight. A crisis can aid us in both directions: getting opponents to join us or opening opposing positions to attack. Getting resources from competitors weakens them while strengthening our position (3.5 Strength and Weakness). A victory over a once dominating competitor can dramatically change our momentum (7.0 Creating Momentum). Because most people judge competition in terms of winners and losers, a visible victory over a competitor changes people's opinions more than more subtle advances in position (1.2 Subobjective Positions).

Key Methods:

Using a crisis must meet a similar cost/benefits analysis that we use in choosing opportunities and actions. There are eight key methods we use.

1. We act only if using the crisis is likely to return more over the long term than it costs. The crisis decreases our costs, but it may also decrease our potential benefits (3.1 Strategic Economics.

2. We act only if we have the excess resources needed to trigger the crisis. Especially during a crisis, we cannot risk resources needed for production or defense (3.3 Opportunity Resources).

3. We act only if the nature of the crisis is likely to make us stronger and our opponents weaker. This means understanding the objective nature of the crisis and the nature of our relative strengths and weaknesses (3.5 Strength and Weakness).

4. We act only if the nature of the ground and the distance between us favors our move. If we don't understand the nature of the ground, we are always better passing the opportunity (4.3 Leveraging Form , 4.4 Strategic Distance , 4.5 Opportunity Surfaces).

5. We act only if the general climate supports our move. We cannot fight the general trends in the competitive arena even if we can ally or defeat a competitor (4.8 Climate Support).

6. We act only to serve our mission rather than acting under the pressure of events. This is especially a problem under the pressure of a crisis because it is so time sensitive (5.1 Mission Priorities , 5.1.1 Event Pressure).

7. We act only if we can complete our move before the crisis passes. Again, because of the temporary nature of a crisis, this window of opportunity is smaller than usual (5.3 Reaction Time).

8. We act only if we can use the crisis with a small, focused surgical strike. The whole purpose of using a crisis is to minimize our direct involvement. If we have to undertake a major program, this doesn't make sense (5.5 Focused Power5.4 Minimizing Action).

Illustration:

For our illustration, let us discuss Goldman Sachs's use of the financial crisis of 2008-2010 because it demonstrates both the value and dangers of an environmental crisis.

1. We act only if using the crisis is likely to return more over the long term than it costs. In 200607, Goldman was issuing subprime-mortgage securities (CDOs) to investors. At the same time, shorting the subprime-mortgage market through credit default swaps (CDS). This means that it made money selling the securities at the time, and, over the longer-term, it would make money if those investments turned bad. This gave them an incentive to expose the problems with subprime investments, at least secretly.

2. We act only if we have the excess resources needed to trigger the crisis. As always, the fuel was provided by the environment, We are not going to speculate on what resources, if any, Goldman use to spark the crisis. In February, 2007, The Federal Home Loan Mortgage Corporation (Freddie Mac) announced that it will no longer buy the most risky subprime mortgages and related securities. By June, Standard and Poor's and Moody's rating services downgraded over 100 subprime mortgages bonds. Goldman's biggest rival, Bear Stearns, had to liquidate two hedge funds of mortgage-backed securities.

3. We act only if the nature of the crisis is likely to make us stronger and our opponents weaker. When the market collapsed, Goldman made a huge trading profit - including about $13 billion provided by U.S. taxpayers as part of the AIG bailout. These profits became the basis for an SEC fraud lawsuit, but not until 2010.

4. We act only if the nature of the ground and the distance between us favors our move. The head of the Treasury determines how the government acts in addressing financial markets. Robert Rubin, Clinton's Treasury Secretary, spent 26 years at Goldman. Bush's Treasury Secretary Paulson was Goldman CEO for 25 years. Obama's Treasury Secretary is Tim Geithner, chose Mark Patterson, an ex-lobbyist from Goldman Sachs, to be his chief of staff. Among his chief advisors are several Goldman executives, including John Thain, Goldman's former co-president. Neel Kashkari, who heads the $700 billion TARP bailout, was vice president at Goldman. Paulson put Goldman vicechairman, Ed Liddy, as CEO of AIG.

5. We act only if the general climate supports our move. Goldman's network of industry and political connections shaped the way government has responded to the economic crisis. Merrill CEO John Thain's Goldman credibility caused Secretary Paulson and Geithner to help the quick sale of Merrill to Bank of America and, on the same weekend let Lehman Brothers, which did not have Goldman's strong connections in Washington, fail. Some claim that Paulson and Geithner permitted Lehman to fail in order to eliminate a significant Goldman competitor. Paulson and Geithner were kinder to AIG, who insured Goldman's investments through credit swaps. They gave AIG an $85 billion loan, later increased to $123 billion, to prevent the insurance giant from failing.

6. We act only to serve our mission rather than acting under the pressure of events. Getting more than $23 billion in direct and indirect federal aid, Goldman initially emerged intact from the crisis, limiting its subprime losses to $1.5 billion. By repaying $10 billion in direct federal bailouts, it escaped tough federal limits on 2009 executives' bonuses. Goldman announced record earnings in July, and surpassed $50 billion in revenue in 2009, paying its employees more than $20 billion in year-end bonuses.

7. We act only if we can complete our move before the crisis passes. At the beginning of 2007, there were five investment banks. Afterward, Lehman Brothers was in bankruptcy and two others, Merrill Lynch, and Bear Stearns were acquired by other companies with their stockholders as the big losers. Two companies survived, Morgan Stanley and Goldman Sachs. Both were allowed to change their stature from from an investment bank to bank holding company to eliminate much of their regulatory burdens.

8. We act only if we can use the crisis with a small, focused surgical strike. This is where Goldman Sachs ran into problems because the crisis and its fallout continues. The current SEC suit for fraud is serious, but not life-threatening. However, the SEC discovery process will enable government lawyers to search Goldman's records, quite potentially raising Goldman's liabilities. This lawsuit could end up breaking up Goldman Sachs.

9.5.2 Avoiding Emotion

Sun Tzu's six key methods on the danger of exploiting environmental vulnerabilities for purely emotion reasons.

"As leader, you cannot let your anger interfere with the success of your forces.
As commander, you cannot let yourself become enraged before you go to battle."

Sun Tzu's The Art of War 12:4:10-12

"To be angry about trifles is mean and childish; to rage and be furious is brutish; and to maintain perpetual wrath is akin to the practice and temper of devils; but

to prevent and suppress rising resentment is wise and glorious, is manly and divine."

Alan Watts

General Principle:

We must never trigger a crisis for opponents on the basis of emotions.

Situation:

Negative emotions such as anger and hatred are true enemies of strategic decision-making. Emotion is good for creating action but bad for making decisions. Such emotions transform opponents into villains. Villains must be stopped at any cost but Sun Tzu's strategy requires balancing costs and benefits, risks and rewards. During a crisis, over-reaction is the real danger, and strong emotions encourage overreaction. Emotions arise naturally from competitive situations because we care about our mission and our values. By definition, adversaries oppose those values. The problem is that seeking to hurt others takes us away from our goal of advancing our position. Wars of attrition are the opposite of developing positions that others want to join rather than oppose.

Opportunity:

Ignorance about the future creates fear, but we must accept our ignorance to see opportunities (2.3.2 Reaction Unpredictability). Seemingly unpleasant events can open paths that lead to great things. Sun Tzu's strategy is a method of adapting because what goes "wrong" can be a fertile source of opportunities (3.2.5 Dynamic Reversal). Our adversaries are rivals because they are like us. Someone with whom we are competing today can be our ally tomorrow. We may portray our enemies as absolute evil to unite and rally our supporters, but we cannot afford to make our decisions about opponents based on emotion (1.1.1 Position Dynamics).

Key Methods:

These key methods help us avoid emotional decisions that are all too common crisis.

1. We must reserve our emotions for caring about our mission and our people. Caring creates strength and unity. We work to serve our mission so we should not get upset because others work for their mission. The best solution is always finding a way to bring our missions together (1.6.1 Shared Mission).

2. We must focus on positions not personalities. Personalities can rub us the wrong way, but it is harder to get angry when we think conceptually about positions. When we automatically think in terms of positions, it takes personal conflict out of our analysis (3.2.5 Dynamic Reversal).

3. We must see opposing positions from an outside, not opposing, perspective. We develop broad contact networks so that we don't miss vital elements from our own point of view (2.0 Developing Perspective).

4. We must remember that we must make each move pay. Emotions of hostility tempt us into expensive conflicts and can create feuds which lead to more conflict in the future (3.1.3 Conflict Cost).

5. We must respond to the situation, not to the emotion it creates. Learning to recognize situations is a powerful prescription for controlling emotion since it channels our energy into instant reaction. The complex array of conditions should engage our mind to such a degree that we don't have time for emotions (5.1.1 Event Pressure , 6.0 Situation Response).

6. We must think in terms of the big picture and long-term rather than the local moment. Our positions last. Our emotions don't. Because of this, we cannot let our temporary emotions hurt our position (1.1 Position Paths).

Illustration:

Let's apply these principles to the strategic problem of deciding whether or not to get even with a co-worker. This is from an actual case from a Science of Strategy Institute member, let's call him John. After a meeting where a coworker, let us call her Jane, stabbed him in the back, John found himself consumed with plotting revenge. We must reserve our emotion for caring about our mission and our people. After thinking about it, John realized that Jane was a pure distractions from his goals within the organization and that hurting her couldn't get him any closer to those goals.

1. We must focus on positions not personalities. Though he found Jane a detestable person, her position on the organization really had no affect on his own, neither obstructing him or competing with him.

2. We must see opposing positions from an outside, not opposing, perspective. John realized that from the perspective of the people who matter, his bosses and customers, a vendetta against Jane could only make him look bad.

3. We must remember that we must make each move pay. John realized that in thinking about Jane, he was wasting valuable time he should be spending on his project.

4. We must respond to the situation, not to the emotion it creates. Though the problem during the meeting was personally insulting, no one realized it but him so there was no real problem that needed to be addressed.

5. We must think in terms of the big picture and long-term rather than the local moment. John decided to forget about Jane, to avoid dealing with her in the future if he could, but generally put the event behind him.

9.6.0 Constant Vigilance

Sun Tzu's five key methods describing where to focus our attention to preserve our positions.

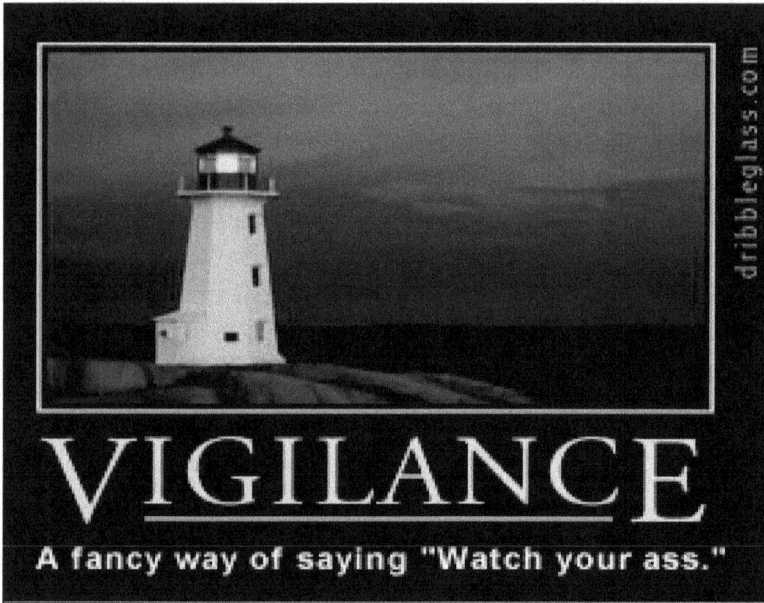

"You can watch and guard for years.
Then a single battle can determine victory in a day."
Sun Tzu's The Art of War 13:1:10-11

"Eternal vigilance is the price of liberty."
John Philpot Curran

General Principle:

We must use constant vigilance to defend our position.

Situation:

Constant vigilance sounds good, but it presents a real challenge. Though the world is constantly changing, we are often blind to change. We offer an exercise in our live training that demonstrates how difficult to see what has changed in a static picture much less a complex situation (3.0 Identifying Opportunities). Since we miss so many of the critical changes taking place around us, facing the dynamics of change requires courage. Since the unknown creates fear, we are often in denial about the changes taking place around us. This is especially important regarding our vulnerabilities. Positions naturally decay over time. As positions get older, they become more and more vulnerable.

Opportunity:

While we don't know what the future will bring, change creates opportunities as well as vulnerabilities. Much of the same vigilance that allows us to identify our vulnerabilities also allows us to see our opportunities (3.0 Identifying Opportunities). If we see our vulnerabilities before a crisis, our existing position is always easy to defend. Though positions are constantly changing, these changes are not random. Our positions follow a certain path anchored in the past while moving into the future. Both opportunities and vulnerabilities are difficult to see by their nature (3.2.2 Opportunity Invisibility). The direction of our position is much easier to see if we continually compare it to the past using the right yardsticks.

Key Methods:

Vigilance, like all of Sun Tzu's strategy, is an adaptive loop (1.8.2 The Adaptive Loop). The following five key methods define its most valuable components.

1. We must continually re-examine each of the five elements that define our position. We do this normally in comparing our position with alternative positions, but in the analysis we want to look at what has changed in our current positions (1.3 Elemental Analysis).

2. We must continually re-evaluate our changing balance of strengths and weaknesses. Even improvements in our position in any given area can generate weaknesses (3.5 Strength and Weakness).

3. We must continually gauge the accumulation of fuel for a crisis in the environment. Strangely enough, our success itself can create fuel in the environment that can be used to fuel a crisis (9.1 Climate Vulnerability).

4. We must continually check the susceptibility of our five points of vulnerability. Our changing strengths and the accumulation of fuel threatens some areas more than others (9.2 Points of Vulnerability).

5. We must continually adjust our allocation of resources to shore up any points of vulnerability. As a defense, these adjustments are usually much less significant than moves used to pursue opportunities (6.0 Situation Response).

Illustration:

The aging of our bodies is a great demonstration of this principle. As we get older, our defenses break down. We can maintain our health only by more and more constant vigilance. As someone who is now in his late fifties and has already survived a fairly scary bout with cancer, I find that I am becoming more vigilant about defending my health. Applying the principles above to a health strategy:

1. We must continually re-examine each of the five elements that define our position. This means having a health mission, recognizing what drives changes and our limited control over our body, taking responsibility for our decisions, and having good healthy methods.

2. We must continually re-evaluate our changing balance of strengths and weaknesses. These changes in our health are driven both by time, events beyond our control, and our decisions.

3. We must continually gauge the accumulation of fuel for a crisis in the environment. Fuel for a crisis ranges from body fat to unhealthy habits. Our success in other areas in life can lead directly to less exercise and a worse diet.

4. We must continually check the susceptibility of our five points of vulnerability. While we might think that the only target is physical body, but key people (our doctors), our immediate resources (health insurance), communication and transportation (local accessibility to health care providers), our long-term assets (physical strength, good habits), and organization (our network of regular health care providers) are also important. As we age, it is especially important to have developed a reliable network of health care providers that we can access quickly should a problem arise. We cannot afford to trust to luck.

5. We must continually adjust our allocation of resources to shore up any points of vulnerability. Getting more disciplined about exercise, cutting down on drinking, and so on.

Glossary of Key Concepts from Sun Tzu's *The Art of War*

This glossary is keyed to the most common English words used in the translation of *The Art of War*. Those terms only capture the strategic concepts generally. Though translated as English nouns, verbs, adverbs, or adjectives, the Chinese characters on which they are based are totally conceptual, not parts of speech. For example, the character for conflict is translated as the noun "conflict," as the verb "fight," and as the adjective "disputed." Ancient written Chinese was a conceptual language, not a spoken one. More like mathematical terms, these concepts are primarily defined by the strict structure of their relationships with other concepts. The Chinese names shown in parentheses with the characters are primarily based on Pinyin, but we occasionally use Cantonese terms to make each term unique.

Advance (*Jeun* 進): to move into new **ground**; to expand your **position**; to move forward in a campaign; the opposite of **flee**.

Advantage, *benefit* (*Li* 利): an opportunity arising from having a better **position** relative to an **enemy**; an opening left by an **enemy**; a **strength** that matches against an **enemy's weakness**; where fullness meets emptiness; a desirable characteristic of a strategic **position**.

Aim, *vision, foresee* (*Jian* 見): **focus** on a specific **advantage**, opening, or opportunity; predicting movements of an **enemy**; a skill of a **leader** in observing **climate**.

Analysis, *plan* (*Gai* 計): a comparison of relative **position**; the examination of the five factors that define a strategic **position**; a combination of **knowledge** and **vision**; the ability to see through **deception**.

Army: see **war.**

Attack, *invade* (*Gong* 攻): a movement to new **ground**; advancing a strategic **position**; action against an **enemy** in the sense of moving into his **ground**; opposite of **defend**; does not necessarily mean **conflict**.

Bad, *ruined* (*Pi* 圮): a condition of the **ground** that makes **advance** difficult; destroyed; terrain that is broken and difficult to traverse; one of the nine situations or types of terrain.

Barricaded: see **obstacles.**

Battle (*Zhan* 戰): to challenge; to engage an **enemy;** generically, to meet a challenge; to choose a confrontation with an **enemy** at a specific time and place; to focus all your resources on a task; to establish superiority in a **position**; to challenge an **enemy** to increase **chaos**; that which is **controlled** by **surprise**; one of the four forms of **attack;** the response to a **desperate situation;** character meaning was originally "big meeting," though later took on the meaning "big weapon"; not necessarily **conflict**.

Bravery, *courage* (<u>Yong</u> 勇): the ability to face difficult choices; the character quality that deals with the changes of **CLIMATE;** courage of conviction; willingness to act on vision; one of the six characteristics of a leader.

Break, *broken, divided* (<u>Po</u> 破): to **divide** what is **complete**; the absence of a **uniting philosophy**; the opposite of <u>unity</u>.

Calculate, *count* (<u>Shu</u> 數): mathematical comparison of quantities and qualities; a measurement of **distance** or troop size.

Change, *transform* (<u>Bian</u> 變): transition from one **condition** to another; the ability to adapt to different situations; a natural characteristic of **climate**.

Chaos, *disorder* (<u>Juan</u> 亂): **conditions** that cannot be **foreseen**; the natural state of confusion arising from **battle**; one of six weaknesses of an organization; the opposite of **control**.

Claim, *position, form* (<u>Xing</u> 形): to use the **ground**; a shape or specific condition of **ground**; the **ground** that you **control**; to use the benefits of the **ground**; the formations of troops; one of the four key skills in making progress.

Climate, *heaven* (<u>Tian</u> 天): the passage of time; the realm of uncontrollable **change**; divine providence; the weather; trends that **change** over time; generally, the future; what one must **aim** at in the future; one of five key factors in **analysis;** the opposite of **ground**.

Command (<u>Ling</u> 令): to order or the act of ordering subordinates; the decisions of a **leader**; the creation of **methods**.

Competition: see <u>war.</u>

Complete: see <u>unity.</u>

Condition: see **ground.**

Confined, *surround* (<u>Wei</u> 圍): to encircle; a **situation** or **stage** in which your options are limited; the proper tactic for dealing with an **enemy** that is ten times smaller; to seal off a smaller **enemy**; the characteristic of a **stage** in which a larger **force** can be attacked by a smaller one; one of nine **situations** or **stages**.

Conflict, *fight* (<u>Zheng</u> 爭): to contend; to dispute; direct confrontation of arms with an **enemy**; highly desirable **ground** that creates disputes; one of nine types of **ground,** terrain, or stages.

Constricted, *narrow* (<u>Ai</u> 狹): a confined space or niche; one of six field positions; the limited extreme of the dimension distance; the opposite of **spread-out**.

Control, *govern* (<u>Chi</u> 治): to manage situations; to overcome disorder; the opposite of **chaos**.

Dangerous: see **serious.**

Dangers, *adverse* (Ak 阨): a condition that makes it difficult to **advance**; one of three dimensions used to evaluate advantages; the dimension with the extreme field **positions** of **entangling** and **supporting**.

Death, *desperate* (<u>Si</u> 死): to end or the end of life or efforts; an extreme situation in which the only option is **battle**; one of nine **stages** or types of **terrain**; one of five types of **spies**; opposite of **survive**.

Deception, *bluffing, illusion* (<u>Gui</u> 詭): to control perceptions; to control information; to mislead an **enemy**; an attack on an opponent's **aim**; the characteristic of war that confuses perceptions.

Defend (<u>Shou</u> 守): to guard or to hold a **ground**; to remain in a **position**; the opposite of **attack**.

Detour (<u>Yu</u> 迂): the indirect or unsuspected path to a **position**; the more difficult path to **advantage**; the route that is not **direct**.

Direct, *straight* (<u>Jik</u> 直.): a straight or obvious path to a goal; opposite of **detour**.

Distance, *distant* (<u>Yuan</u> 遠): the space separating **ground**; to be remote from the current location; to occupy **positions** that are not close to one another; one of six field positions; one of the three dimensions for evaluating opportunities; the emptiness of space.

Divide, *separate* (<u>Fen</u> 分): to break apart a larger force; to separate from a larger group; the opposite of **join** and **focus**.

Double agent, *reverse* (<u>Fan</u> 反): to turn around in direction; to change a situation; to switch a person's allegiance; one of five types of spies.

Easy, *light* (<u>Qing</u> 輕): to require little effort; a **situation** that requires little effort; one of nine **stages** or types of terrain; opposite of **serious**.

Emotion, *feeling* (<u>Xin</u> 心): an unthinking reaction to **aim**, a necessary element to inspire **moves**; a component of esprit de corps; never a sufficient cause for **attack**.

Enemy, *competitor* (<u>Dik</u> 敵): one who makes the same **claim**; one with a similar **goal**; one with whom comparisons of capabilities are made.

Entangling, *hanging* (<u>Gua</u> 懸): a **position** that cannot be returned to; any **condition** that leaves no easy place to go; one of six field positions.

Evade, *avoid* (<u>Bi</u> 避): the tactic used by small competitors when facing large opponents.

Fall apart, *collapse* (<u>Beng</u> 崩): to fail to execute good decisions; to fail to use a **constricted position**; one of six weaknesses of an organization.

Fall down, *sink* (<u>Haam</u> 陷): to fail to make good decisions; to **move** from a **supporting position**; one of six weaknesses of organizations.

Feelings, *affection, love* (<u>Ching</u> 情): the bonds of relationship; the result of a shared **philosophy**; requires management.

Fight, *struggle* (Dou 鬥): to engage in **conflict**; to face difficulties.

Fire (*Huo* 火): an environmental weapon; a universal analogy for all weapons.

Flee, *retreat, northward* (*Bei* 北) :to abandon a **position**; to surrender **ground**; one of six weaknesses of an **army**; opposite of **advance**.

Focus, *concentrate* (*Zhuan* 專): to bring resources together at a given time; to **unite** forces for a purpose; an attribute of having a shared **philosophy**; the opposite of *divide*.

Force (*Lei* 力): power in the simplest sense; a **group** of people bound by **unity** and **focus**; the relative balance of **strength** in opposition to **weakness**.

Foresee: see **aim**.

Fullness: see **strength**.

General: see **leader**.

Goal: see **philosophy**.

Ground, *situation, stage* (*Di* 地): the earth; a specific place; a specific condition; the place one competes; the prize of competition; one of five key factors in competitive analysis; the opposite of **climate**.

Groups, *troops* (*Dui* 隊): a number of people united under a shared **philosophy**; human resources of an organization; one of the five targets of fire attacks.

Inside, *internal* (*Nei* 內): within a **territory** or organization; an insider; one of five types of spies; opposite of *Wai*, outside.

Intersecting, *highway* (*Qu* 衢): a **situation** or **ground** that allows you to **join**; one of nine types of terrain.

Join (*Hap* 合): to unite; to make allies; to create a larger **force**; opposite of **divide**.

Knowledge, *listening* (*Zhi*: 知): to have information; the result of listening; the first step in advancing a **position**; the basis of strategy.

Lax, *loosen* (*Shii* 弛): too easygoing; lacking discipline; one of six weaknesses of an army.

Leader, *general, commander* (*Jiang* 將): the decision-maker in a competitive unit; one who **listens** and **aims**; one who manages **troops**; superior of officers and men; one of the five key factors in analysis; the conceptual opposite of fa, the established methods, which do not require decisions.

Learn, *compare* (*Xiao* 效): to evaluate the relative qualities of **enemies**.

Listen, *obey* (*Ting* 聽): to gather **knowledge**; part of **analysis**.

Listening: see **knowledge**.

Local, *countryside* (*Xiang* 鄉): the nearby **ground**; to have **knowledge** of a specific **ground**; one of five types of **spies**.

Marsh (*Ze* 澤): **ground** where footing is unstable; one of the four types of **ground**; analogy for uncertain situations.

Method: see **system**.

Mission: see **philosophy**.

Momentum, *influence* (*Shi* 勢): the **force** created by **surprise** set up by **standards**; used with **timing**.

Mountains, *hill, peak* (*Shan* 山):uneven **ground**; one of four types of **ground**; an analogy for all unequal **situations**.

Move, *march, act* (*Hang* 行): action toward a position or goal; used as a near synonym for *dong*, act.

Nation (*Guo* 國): the state; the productive part of an organization; the seat of political power; the entity that controls an **army** or competitive part of the organization.

Obstacles, *barricaded* (*Xian* 險): to have barriers; one of the three characteristics of the **ground**; one of six field positions; as a field position, opposite of **unobstructed**.

Open, *meeting, crossing* (*Jiao* 來): to share the same **ground** without conflict; to come together; a **situation** that encourages a race; one of nine **terrains** or **stages**.

Opportunity: see *advantage.*

Outmaneuver (*Sou* 走): to go astray; to be **forced** into a **weak position**; one of six weaknesses of an army.

Outside, *external* (*Wai* 外): not within a **territory** or **army**; one who has a different perspective; one who offers an objective view; opposite of **internal**.

Philosophy, *mission, goals* (*Tao* 道): the shared **goals** that **unite** an **army**; a system of thought; a shared viewpoint; literally "the way"; a way to work together; one of the five key factors in **analysis**.

Plateau (*Liu* 陸): a type of **ground** without defects; an analogy for any equal, solid, and certain **situation**; the best place for competition; one of the four types of **ground**.

Resources, *provisions* (*Liang* 糧): necessary supplies, most commonly food; one of the five targets of fire attacks.

Restraint: see **timing.**

Reward, *treasure, money* (<u>*Bao*</u> 賞): profit; wealth; the necessary compensation for competition; a necessary ingredient for **victory**; **victory** must pay.

Scatter, *dissipating* (<u>*San*</u> 散): to disperse; to lose **unity**; the pursuit of separate **goals** as opposed to a central **mission**; a situation that causes a **force** to scatter; one of nine conditions or types of terrain.

Serious, *heavy* (<u>*Chong*</u> 重): any task requiring effort and skill; a **situation** where resources are running low when you are deeply committed to a campaign or heavily invested in a project; a situation where opposition within an organization mounts; one of nine **stages** or types of **terrain.**

Siege (<u>*Gong Cheng*</u> 攻城): to move against entrenched positions; any movement against an **enemy's strength**; literally "strike city"; one of the four forms of attack; the least desirable form of attack.

Situation: see **ground.**

Speed, *hurry* (Sai 馳): to **move** over **ground** quickly; the ability to **advance positions** in a minimum of time; needed to take advantage of a window of opportunity.

Spread-out, *wide* (<u>*Guang*</u> 廣): a surplus of **distance**; one of the six **ground positions**; opposite of **constricted.**

Spy, *conduit, go-between* (<u>*Gaan*</u> 間): a source of information; a channel of communication; literally, an "opening between."

Stage: see **ground.**

Standard, *proper, correct* (<u>*Jang*</u> 正): the expected behavior; the standard approach; proven methods; the opposite of <u>surprise</u>; together with **surprise** creates **momentum.**

Storehouse, *house* (<u>*Ku*</u> 庫): a place where resources are stockpiled; one of the five targets for fire attacks.

Stores, *accumulate, savings* (<u>*Ji*</u> 糧): resources that have been stored; any type of inventory; one of the five targets of fire attacks.

Strength, *fullness, satisfaction* (<u>*Sat*</u> 壹): wealth or abundance or resources; the state of being crowded; the opposite of <u>Xu</u>, empty.

Supply wagons, *transport* (<u>*Zi*</u> 輜): the movement of **resources** through **distance**; one of the five targets of fire attacks.

Support, *supporting* (<u>*Zhii*</u> 支): to prop up; to enhance; a **ground position** that you cannot leave without losing **strength**; one of six field positions; the opposite extreme of <u>gua</u>, entangling.

Surprise, *unusual, strange* (<u>*Qi*</u> 奇) : the unexpected; the innovative; the opposite of **standard**; together with **standards** creates **momentum**.

Surround: see **confined**.

Survive, *live, birth* (<u>Shaang</u> 生): the state of being created, started, or beginning; the state of living or surviving; a temporary condition of fullness; one of five types of spies; the opposite of **death**.

System, *method* (<u>Fa</u> 法): a set of procedures; a group of techniques; steps to accomplish a **goal**; one of the five key factors in analysis; the realm of groups who must follow procedures; the opposite of the **leader**.

Territory, *terrain*: see **ground**.

Timing, *restraint* (<u>Jie</u> 節): to withhold action until the proper time; to release tension; a companion concept to **momentum**.

Troops: see **group**.

Unity, *whole, oneness* (<u>Yi</u> 一): the characteristic of a **group** that shares a **philosophy**; the lowest number; a **group** that acts as a unit; the opposite of **divided**.

Unobstructed, *expert* (<u>Tong</u> 通): without obstacles or barriers; **ground** that allows easy movement; open to new ideas; one of six field positions; opposite of **obstructed**.

Victory, *win, winning* (<u>Sing</u> 勝): success in an endeavor; getting a reward; serving your mission; an event that produces more than it consumes; to make a profit.

War, *competition, army* (Bing 兵): a dynamic situation in which **positions** can be won or lost; a contest in which a **reward** can be won; the conditions under which the principles of strategy work.

Water, *river* (<u>Shui</u> 水): a fast-changing **ground**; fluid **conditions**; one of four types of **ground**; an analogy for change.

Weakness, *emptiness, need* (<u>Xu</u> 虛): the absence of people or resources; devoid of **force**; the point of **attack** for an **advantage**; a characteristic of **ground** that enables **speed**; poor; the opposite of <u>strength</u>.

Win, *winning*: see **victory**.

Wind, *fashion, custom* (<u>Feng</u> 風): the pressure of environmental forces.

The *Art of War Playbook* Series

There are over two-hundred and thirty articles on Sun Tzu's competitive principles in the nine volumes of the *Art of War Playbook*. Each volume covers a specific area of Sun Tzu strategy.

VOLUME ONE: - POSITIONS

VOLUME TWO: -PERSPECTIVE

VOLUME THREE: - OPPORTUNITIES

VOLUME FOUR: - PROBABILITY

VOLUME FIVE: - MISTAKES

VOLUME SIX: - SITUATIONS

VOLUME SEVEN: - MOMENTUM

VOLUME EIGHT: - REWARDS

VOLUME NINE: - VULNERABILITIES.

About the Translator and Author

Gary Gagliardi is recognized as America's leading expert on Sun Tzu's *The Art of War*. An award-winning author and business strategist, his many books on Sun Tzu's strategy have been translated around the world. He has appeared on hundreds of talk shows nationwide, providing strategic insight on the breaking news. He has trained decision makers from some of the world's most successful organizations in competitive thinking. His workshops convert Sun Tzu's many principles into a series of practical tools for handling common competitive challenges.

Gary began using Sun Tzu's competitive principles in a successful corporate career and when he started his own software company. In 1990, he wrote his first *Art of War* adaptation for his company's salespeople. By 1992, his company was on *Inc. Magazine's* list of the 500 fastest-growing privately held companies in America. He personally won the U.S. Chamber of Commerce Blue Chip Quality Award and was an Ernst and Young Entrepreneur of the Year finalist. His customers—AT&T, GE, and Motorola, among others— began inviting him to speak at their conferences. After becoming a multimillionaire when he sold his software company in 1997, he continued teaching *The Art of War* around the world.

Gary has authored several breakthrough works on *The Art of War*. Ten of his books on strategy have won book award recognition in nine different non-fiction categories.

If you enjoyed this work, contact the author at Garyg@SunTzuS.com and let him know. He enjoys communicating with interested readers.

Art of War Books by Gary Gagliardi

Gary Gagliardi's Books are Available at:

SunTzus.com
Amazon.com
BarnesAndNoble.com
Itunes.apple.com

www.ingramcontent.com/pod-product-compliance
Lightning Source LLC
Chambersburg PA
CBHW060830220326
41599CB00017B/2297